PSYCHO BUSTERS

2

**Story by
Yuya Aoki**

**Manga by
Akinari Nao**

Translated and adapted by
Stephen Paul

Lettered by
North Market Street Graphics

Ballantine Books ∗ New York

A Del Rey Manga/Kodansha Trade Paperback Original

Psycho Busters volume 2 copyright © 2006 by Yuya Aoki and Akinari Nao
English translation copyright © 2008 by Yuya Aoki and Akinari Nao

Published in the United States by Del Rey Books, an imprint of The Random House Publishing Group, a division of Random House, Inc., New York.

DEY REY is a registered trademark and the Del Rey colophon is a trademark of Random House, Inc.

Publication rights arranged through Kodansha Ltd.

First published in Japan in 2006 by Kodansha Ltd., Tokyo.

ISBN 978-0-345-50172-1

Printed in the United States of America

www.delreymanga.com

9 8 7 6 5 4 3 2 1

Translator/adapter: Stephen Paul
Lettering: North Market Street Graphics

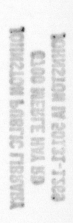

Contents

Honorifics Explained

Throughout the Del Rey Manga books, you will find Japanese honorifics left intact in the translations. For those not familiar with how the Japanese use honorifics and, more important, how they differ from American honorifics, we present this brief overview.

Politeness has always been a critical facet of Japanese culture. Ever since the feudal era, when Japan was a highly stratified society, use of honorifics—which can be defined as polite speech that indicates relationship or status—has played an essential role in the Japanese language. When addressing someone in Japanese, an honorific usually takes the form of a suffix attached to one's name (example: "Asuna-san"), is used as a title at the end of one's name, or appears in place of the name itself (example: "Negi-sensei," or simply "Sensei!").

Honorifics can be expressions of respect or endearment. In the context of manga and anime, honorifics give insight into the nature of the relationship between characters. Many English translations leave out these important honorifics and therefore distort the feel of the original Japanese. Because Japanese honorifics contain nuances that English honorifics lack, it is our policy at Del Rey not to translate them. Here, instead, is a guide to some of the honorifics you may encounter in Del Rey Manga.

-*san*: This is the most common honorific and is equivalent to Mr., Miss, Ms., or Mrs. It is the all-purpose honorific and can be used in any situation where politeness is required.

-*sama*: This is one level higher than "-san" and is used to confer great respect.

-*dono*: This comes from the word "tono," which means "lord." It is an even higher level than "-sama" and confers utmost respect.

-*kun*: This suffix is used at the end of boys' names to express familiarity or endearment. It is also sometimes used by men among friends, or when addressing someone younger or of a lower station.

-chan: This is used to express endearment, mostly toward girls. It is also used for little boys, pets, and even among lovers. It gives a sense of childish cuteness.

Bozu: This is an informal way to refer to a boy, similar to the English terms "kid" and "squirt."

Sempai/
Senpai: This title suggests that the addressee is one's senior in a group or organization. It is most often used in a school setting, where underclassmen refer to their upperclassmen as "sempai." It can also be used in the workplace, such as when a newer employee addresses an employee who has seniority in the company.

Kohai: This is the opposite of "sempai" and is used toward underclassmen in school or newcomers in the workplace. It connotes that the addressee is of a lower station.

Sensei: Literally meaning "one who has come before," this title is used for teachers, doctors, or masters of any profession or art.

[blank]:   This is usually forgotten in these lists, but it is perhaps the most significant difference between Japanese and English. The lack of honorific means that the speaker has permission to address the person in a very intimate way. Usually, only family, spouses, or very close friends have this kind of permission. Known as *yobisute*, it can be gratifying when someone who has earned the intimacy starts to call one by one's name without an honorific. But when that intimacy hasn't been earned, it can be very insulting.

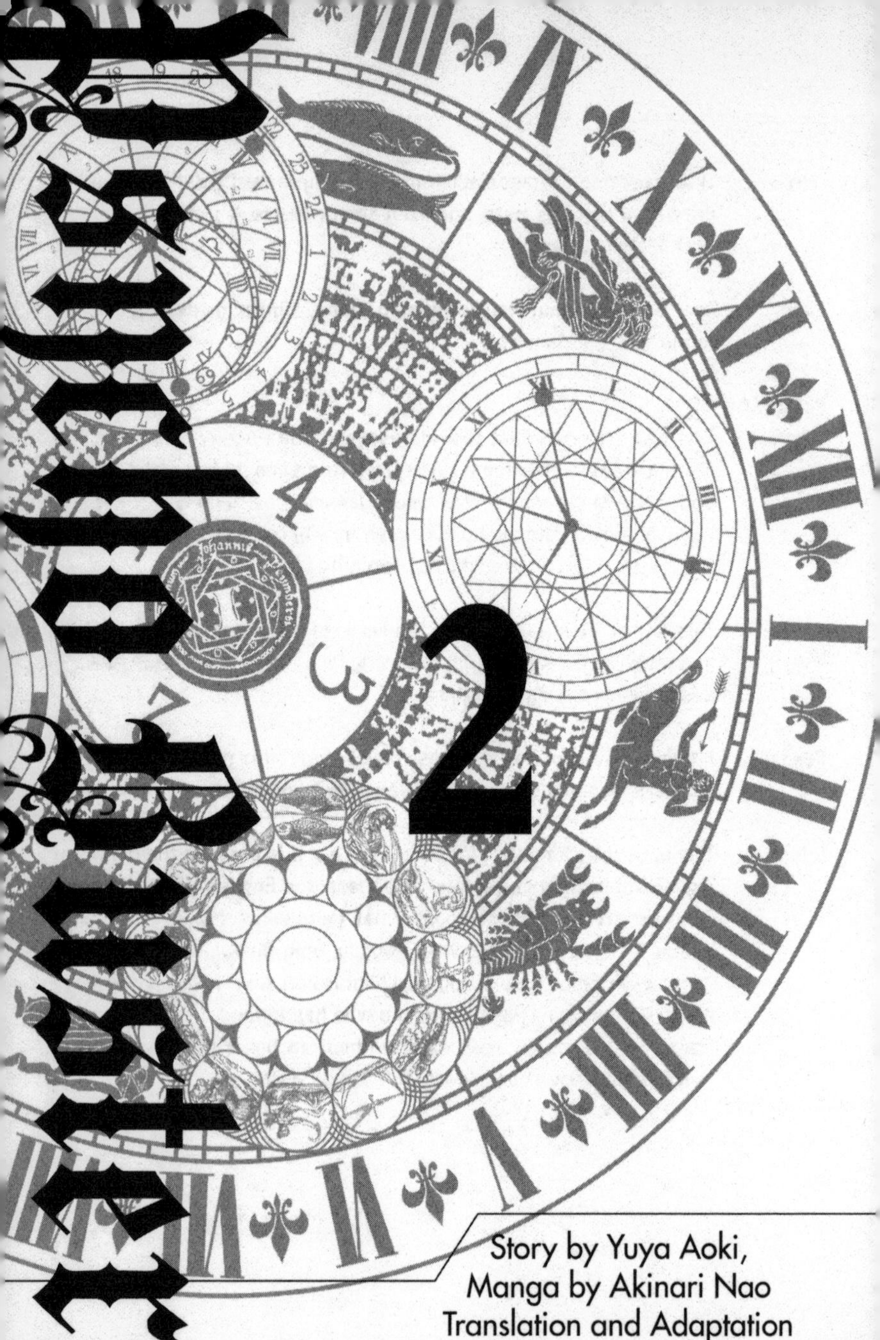

Psycho Busters

2

Story by Yuya Aoki,
Manga by Akinari Nao
Translation and Adaptation
by Stephen Paul

Contents

CASE 5 – Jôi

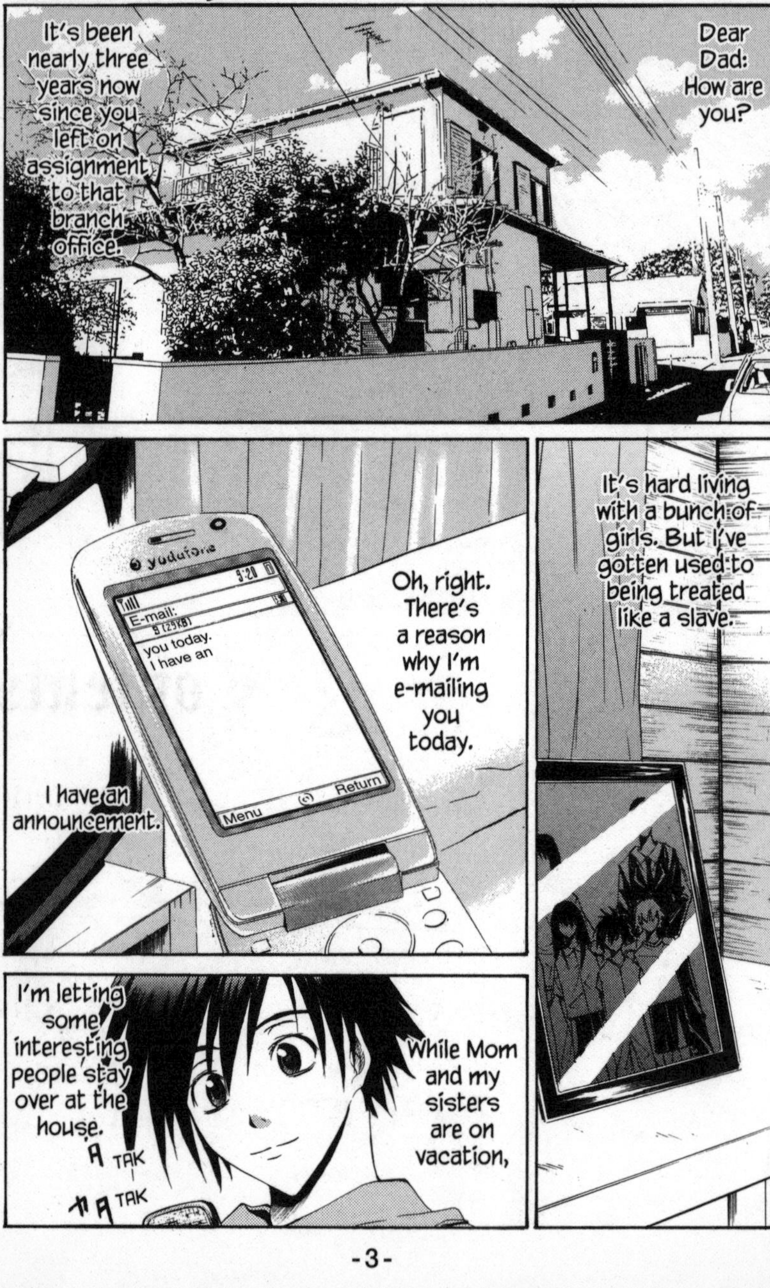
Dear Dad: How are you?
It's been nearly three years now since you left on assignment to that branch office.
It's hard living with a bunch of girls. But I've gotten used to being treated like a slave.
Oh, right. There's a reason why I'm e-mailing you today.
E-mail:
you today.
I have an
Menu
Return
I have an announcement.
While Mom and my sisters are on vacation,
I'm letting some interesting people stay over at the house.
TAK
TAK

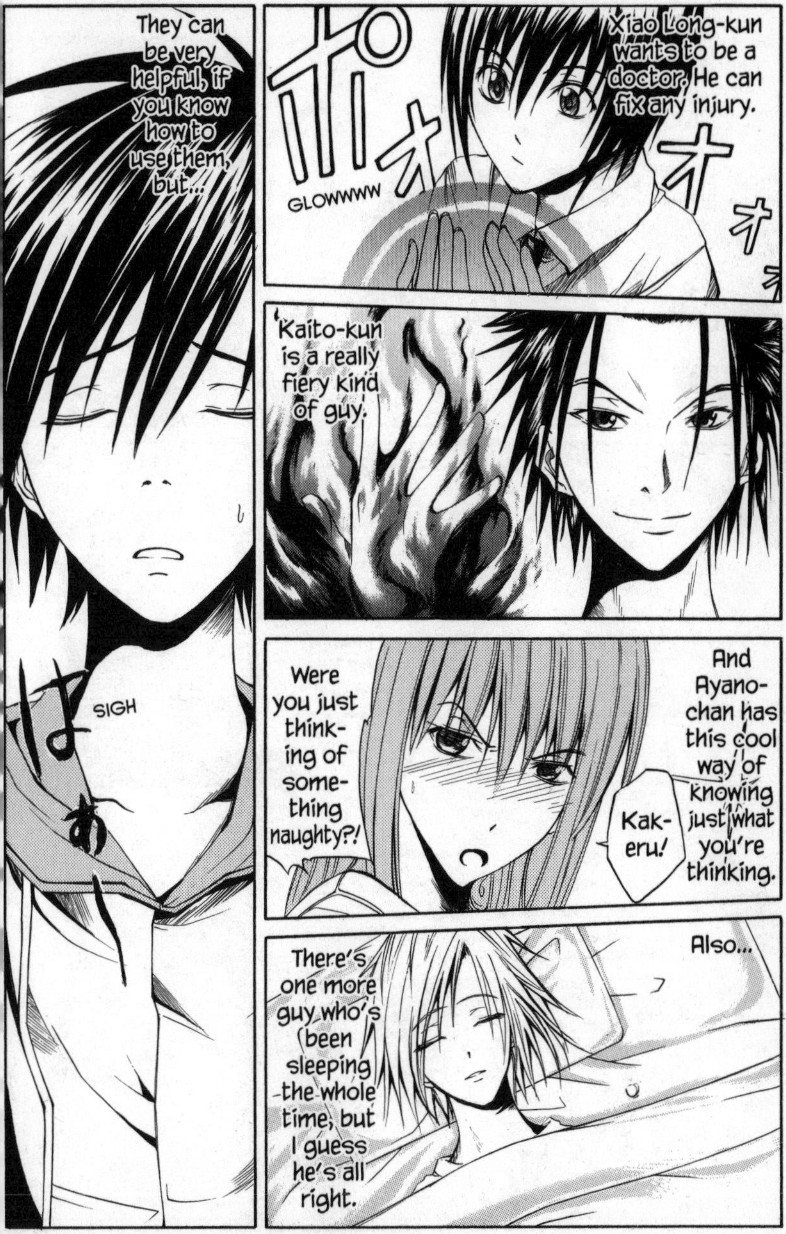
Xiao Long-kun wants to be a doctor. He can fix any injury.
GLOWWWW
Kaito-kun is a really fiery kind of guy.
And Ayano-chan has this cool way of knowing just what you're thinking.
Kak-eru!
Were you just think-ing of some-thing naughty?!
Also...
There's one more guy who's been sleeping the whole time, but I guess he's all right.
They can be very helpful, if you know how to use them, but...
SIGH

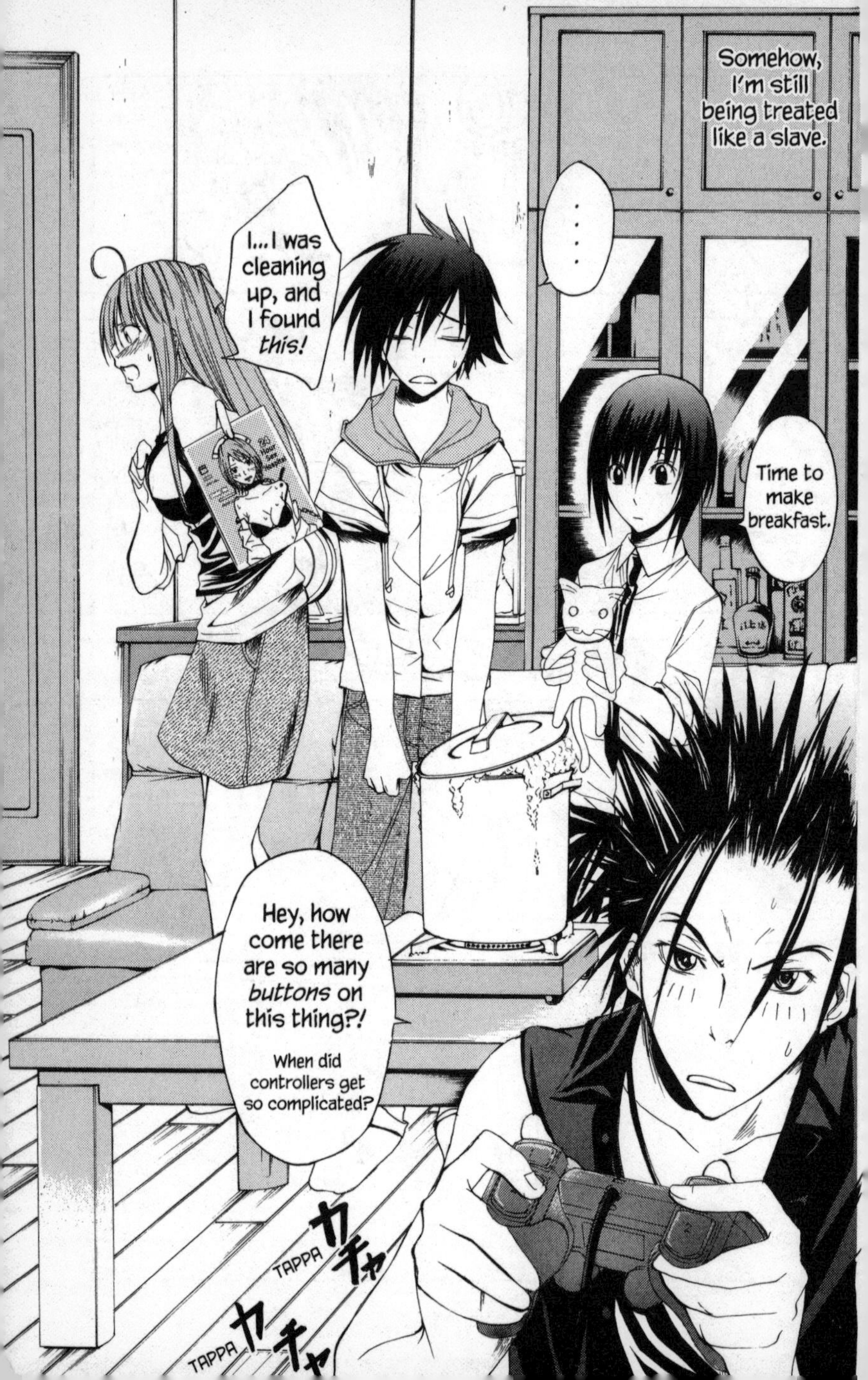
Somehow, I'm still being treated like a slave.
...
I...I was cleaning up, and I found *this!*
Time to make breakfast.
Hey, how come there are so many *buttons* on this thing?!
When did controllers get so complicated?
TAPPA
TAPPA

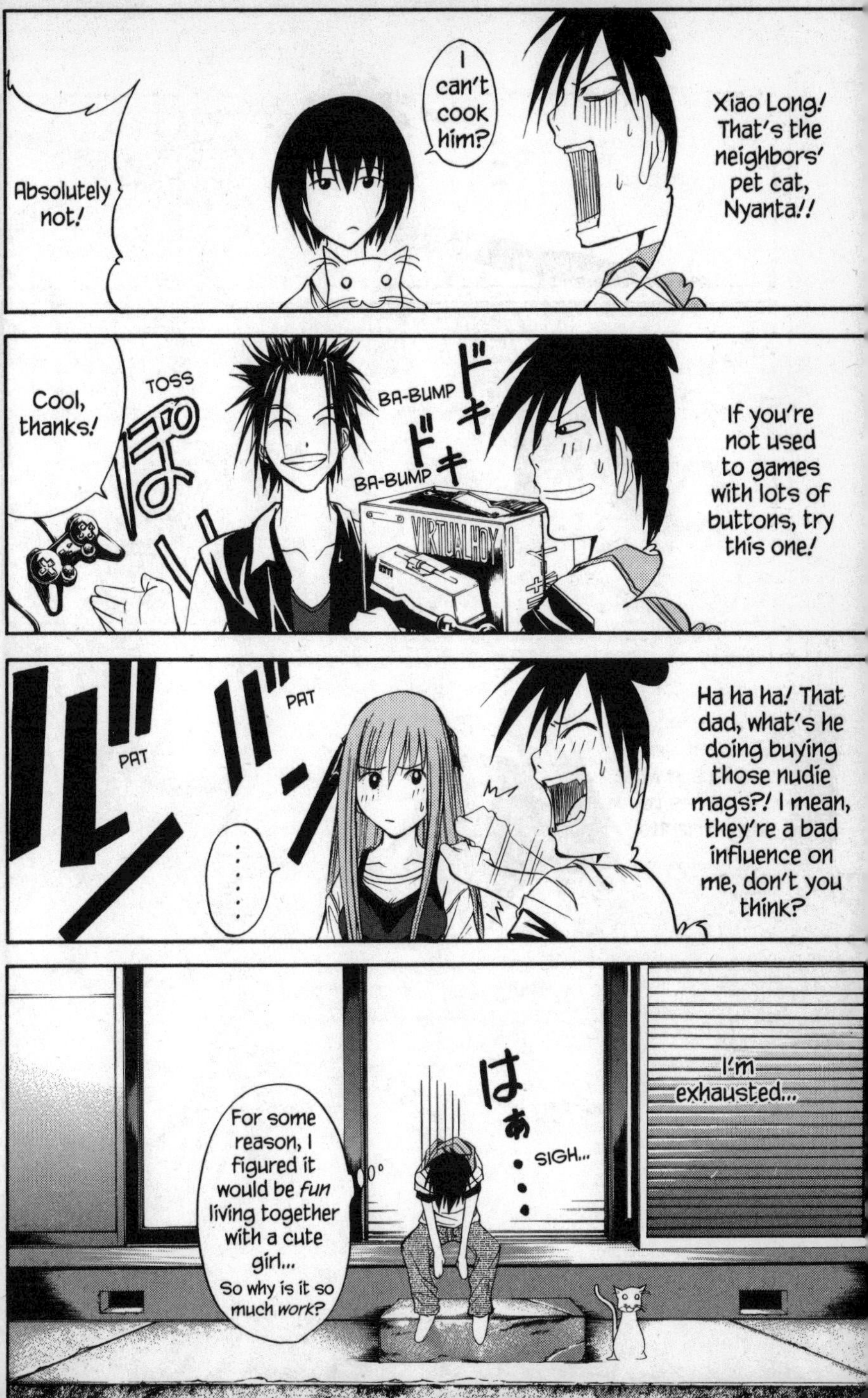

Xiao Long! That's the neighbors' pet cat, Nyanta!!
I can't cook him?
Absolutely not!
If you're not used to games with lots of buttons, try this one!
BA-BUMP
BA-BUMP
VIRTUALHOY
TOSS
Cool, thanks!
Ha ha ha! That dad, what's he doing buying those nudie mags?! I mean, they're a bad influence on me, don't you think?
PAT
PAT
......
I'm exhausted...
SIGH...
For some reason, I figured it would be *fun* living together with a cute girl...
So why is it so much *work*?

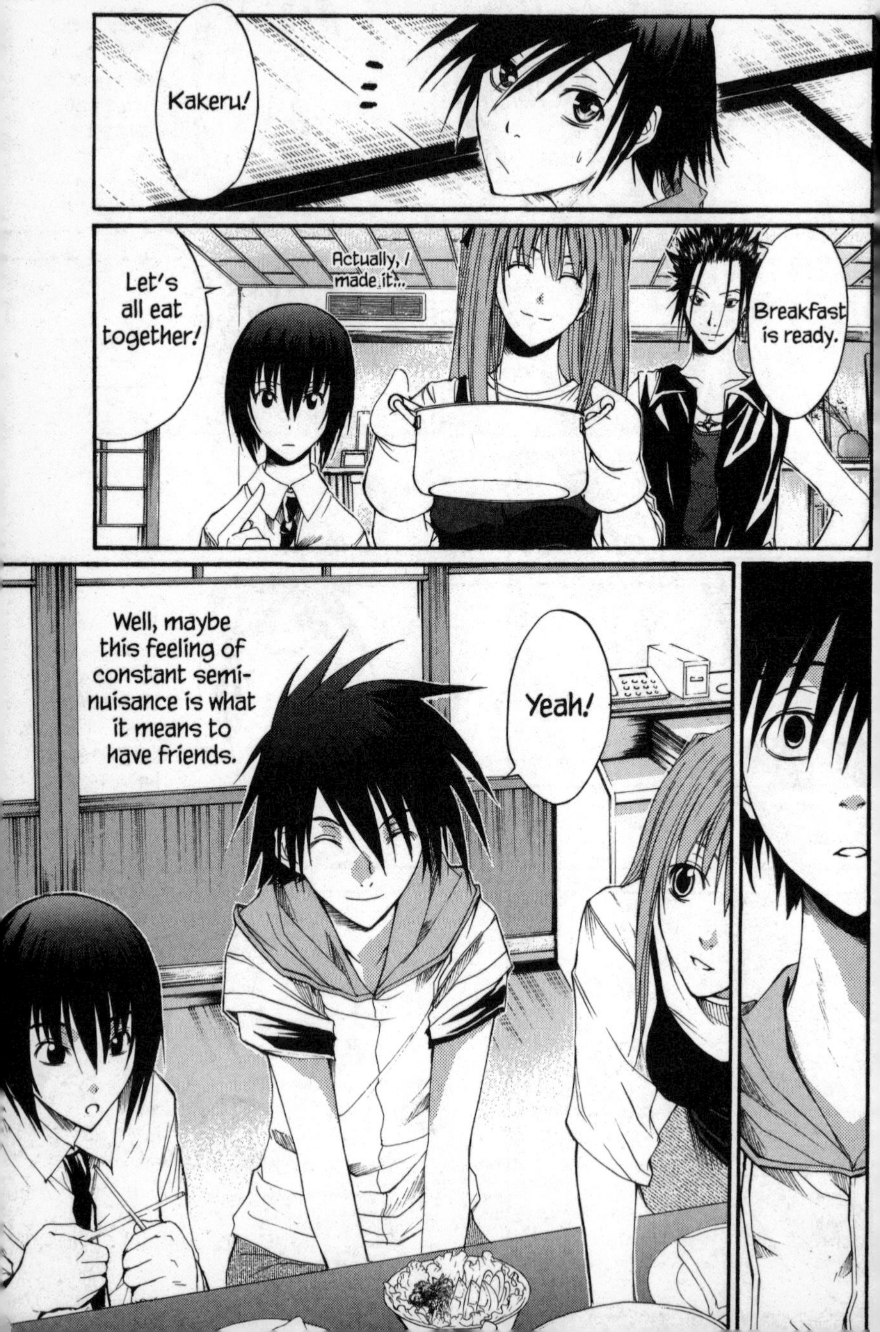
Kakeru!
Breakfast is ready.
Actually, I made it...
Let's all eat together!
Yeah!
Well, maybe this feeling of constant semi-nuisance is what it means to have friends.

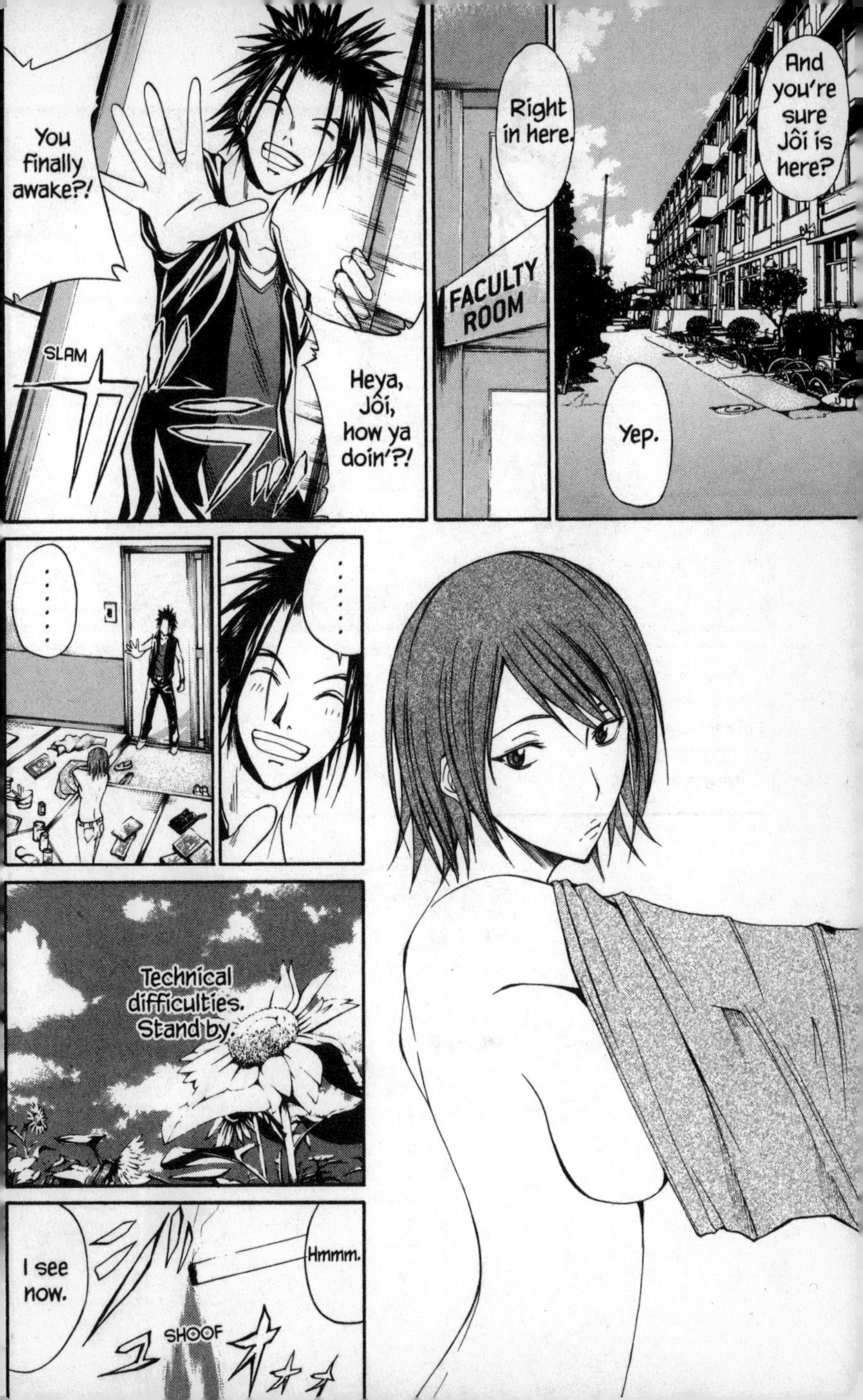

And you're sure Jôi is here?
Yep.
Right in here.
FACULTY ROOM
Heya, Jôi, how ya doin'?!
You finally awake?!
SLAM
......
......
Technical difficulties. Stand by.
Hmmm.
I see now.
SHOOF

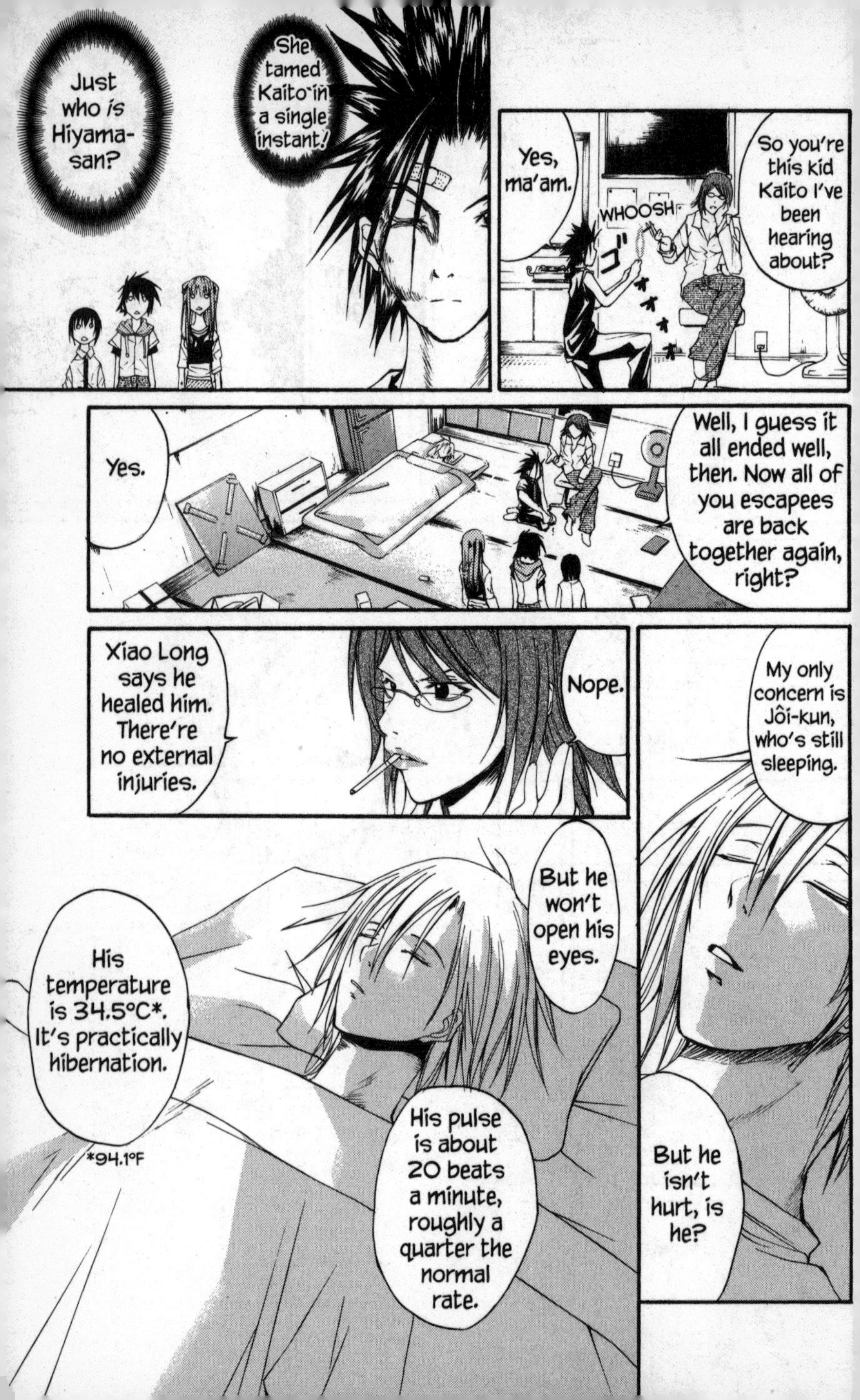
So you're this kid Kaito I've been hearing about?
WHOOSH
Yes, ma'am.
She tamed Kaito in a single instant!
Just who *is* Hiyama-san?
Well, I guess it all ended well, then. Now all of you escapees are back together again, right?
Yes.
My only concern is Jôi-kun, who's still sleeping.
But he isn't hurt, is he?
Nope.
Xiao Long says he healed him. There're no external injuries.
But he won't open his eyes.
His temperature is 34.5°C*. It's practically hibernation.
His pulse is about 20 beats a minute, roughly a quarter the normal rate.
*94.1°F

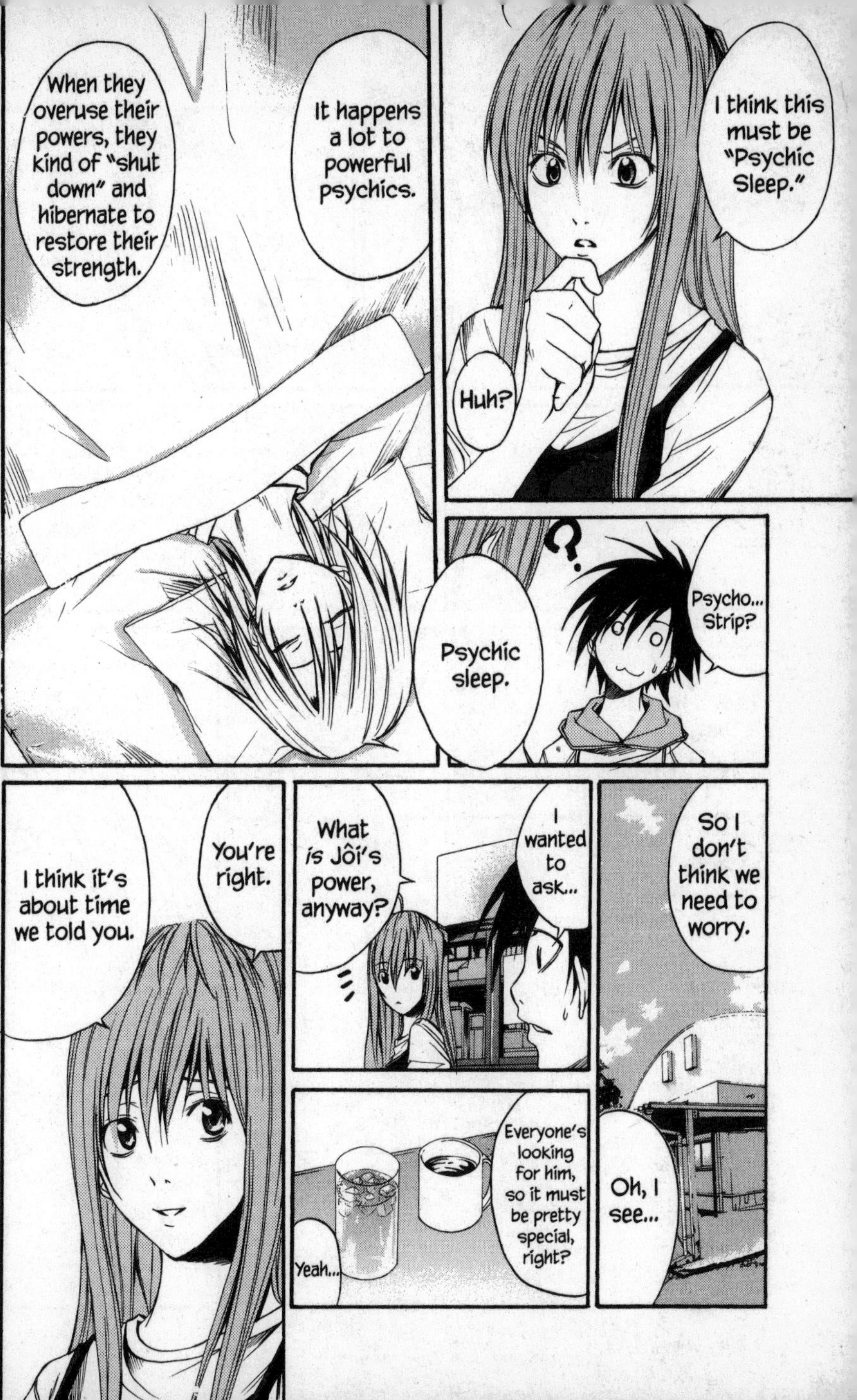
I think this must be "Psychic Sleep."
Huh?
Psycho... Strip?
Psychic sleep.
It happens a lot to powerful psychics.
When they overuse their powers, they kind of "shut down" and hibernate to restore their strength.
So I don't think we need to worry.
Oh, I see...
I wanted to ask...
What is Jôi's power, anyway?
Everyone's looking for him, so it must be pretty special, right?
Yeah...
You're right.
I think it's about time we told you.

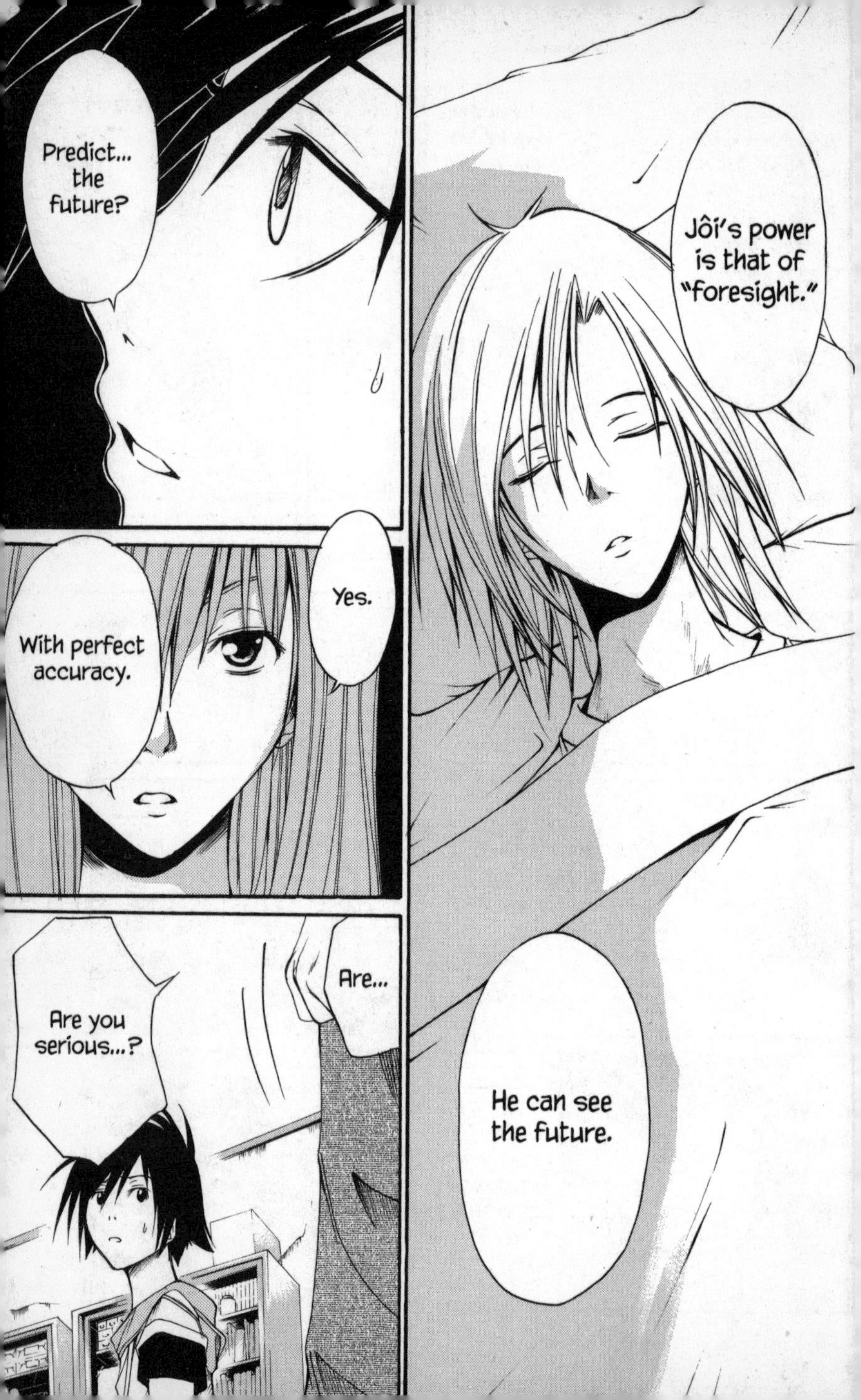
Jôi's power is that of "foresight."
He can see the future.
Predict... the future?
Yes.
With perfect accuracy.
Are...
Are you serious...?

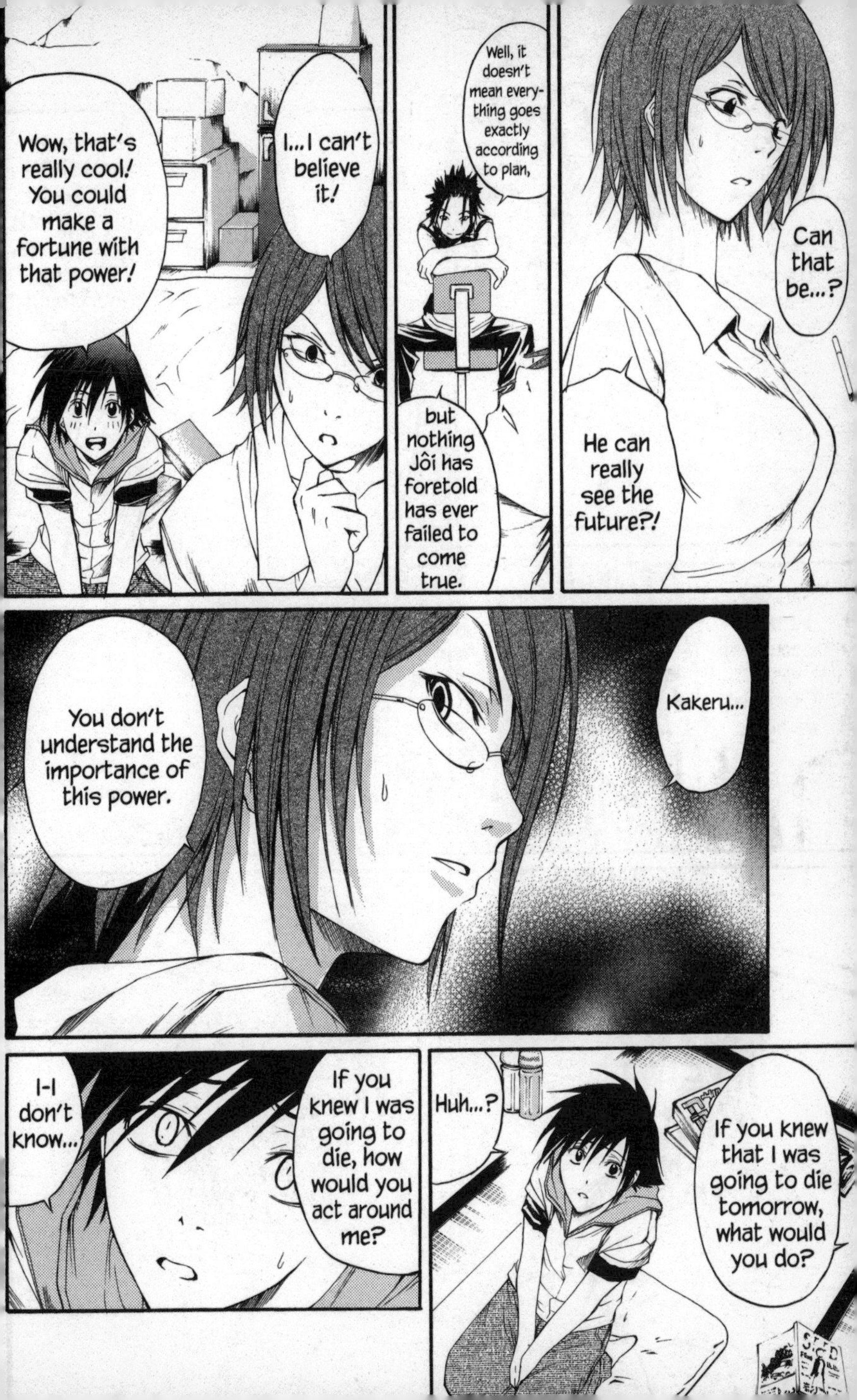
Can that be...?
He can really see the future?!
Well, it doesn't mean everything goes exactly according to plan,
but nothing Jôi has foretold has ever failed to come true.
I...I can't believe it!
Wow, that's really cool! You could make a fortune with that power!
Kakeru...
You don't understand the importance of this power.
If you knew that I was going to die tomorrow, what would you do?
Huh...?
If you knew I was going to die, how would you act around me?
I-I don't know...

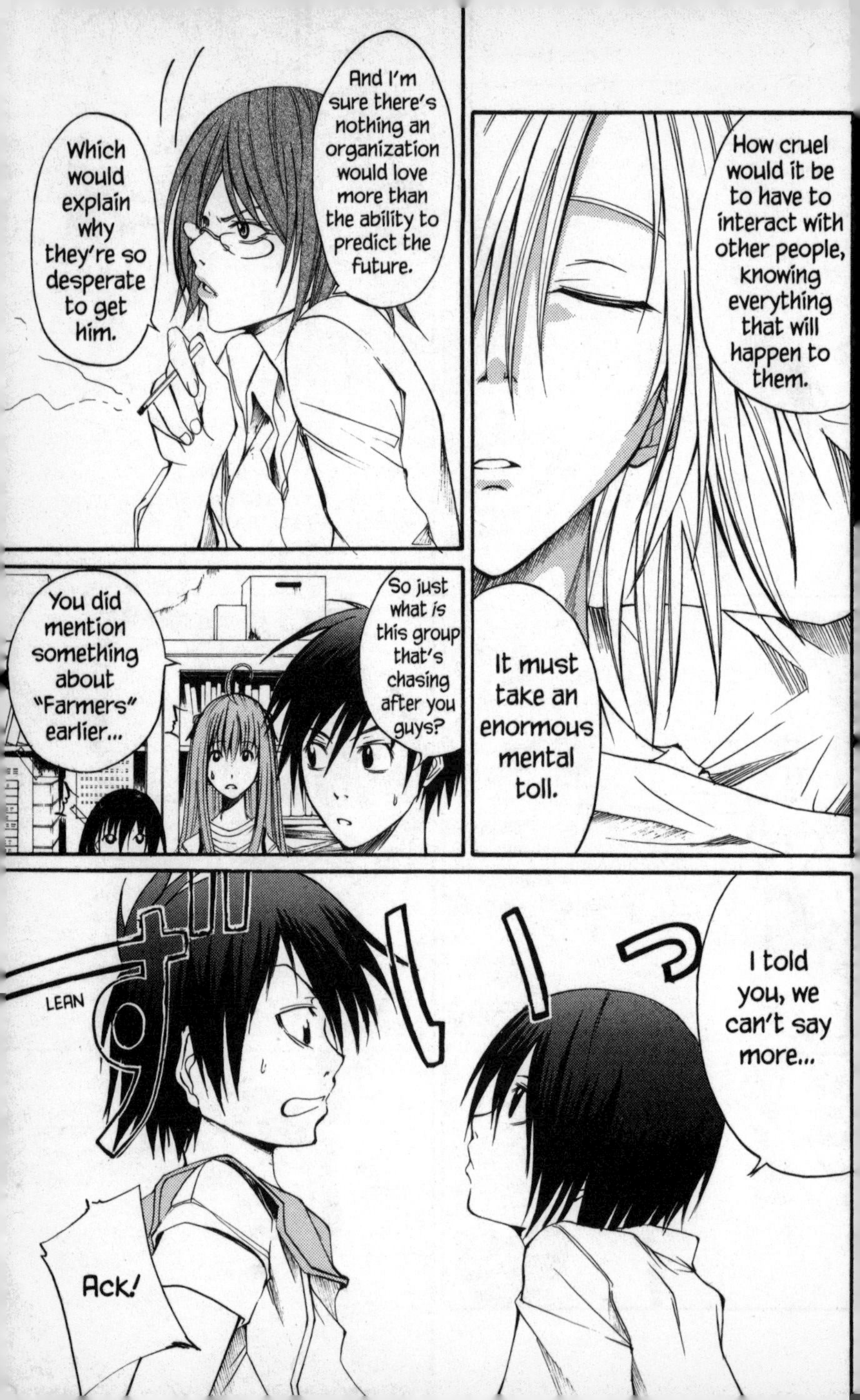
How cruel would it be to have to interact with other people, knowing everything that will happen to them.
It must take an enormous mental toll.
And I'm sure there's nothing an organization would love more than the ability to predict the future.
Which would explain why they're so desperate to get him.
So just what *is* this group that's chasing after you guys?
You did mention something about "Farmers" earlier...
I told you, we can't say more...
LEAN
Ack!

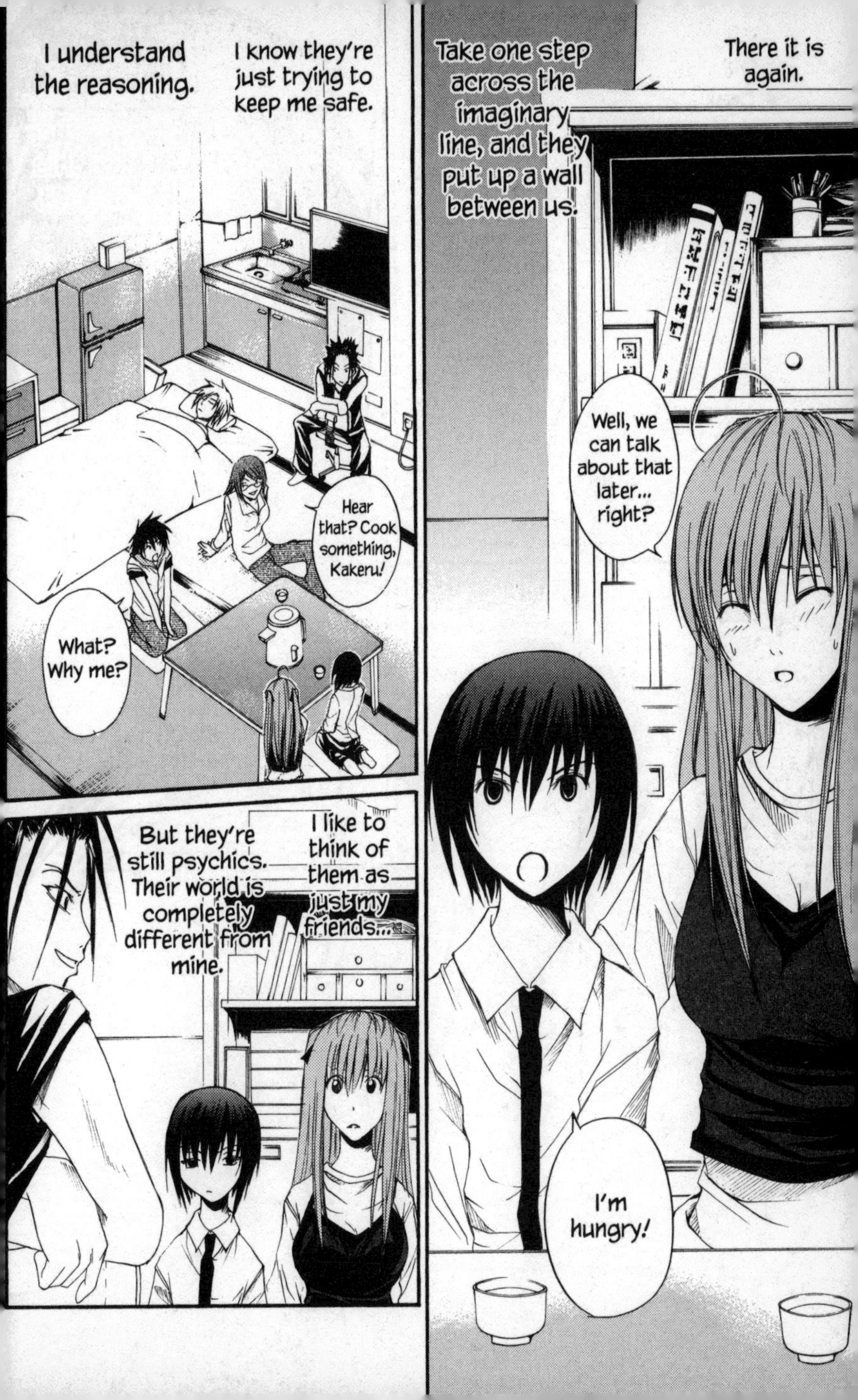
There it is again.
Take one step across the imaginary line, and they put up a wall between us.
Well, we can talk about that later... right?
I'm hungry!
I know they're just trying to keep me safe.
I understand the reasoning.
Hear that? Cook something, Kakeru!
What? Why me?
I like to think of them as just my friends...
But they're still psychics. Their world is completely different from mine.

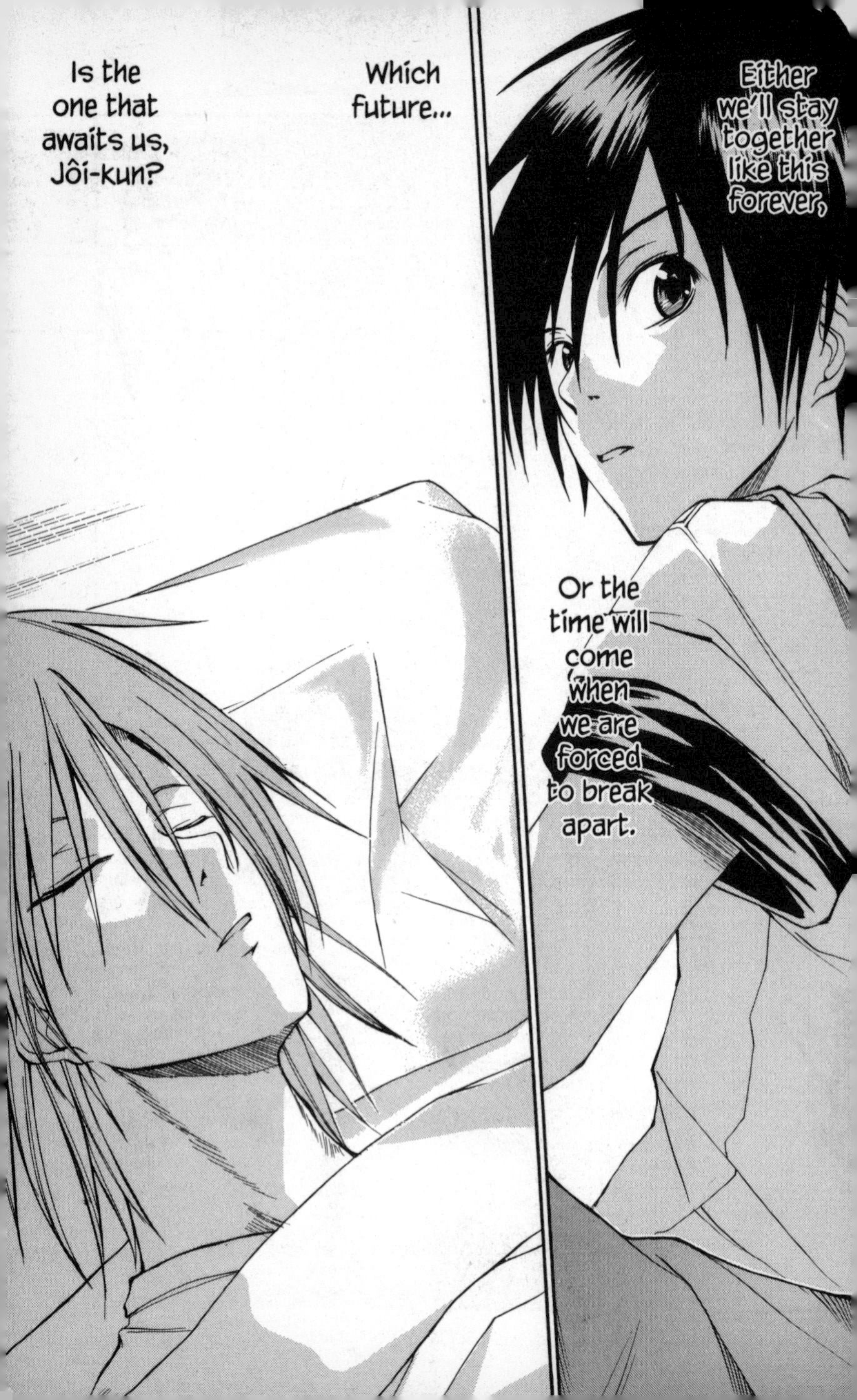
Either we'll stay together like this forever,
Or the time will come when we are forced to break apart.
Which future...
Is the one that awaits us, Jôi-kun?

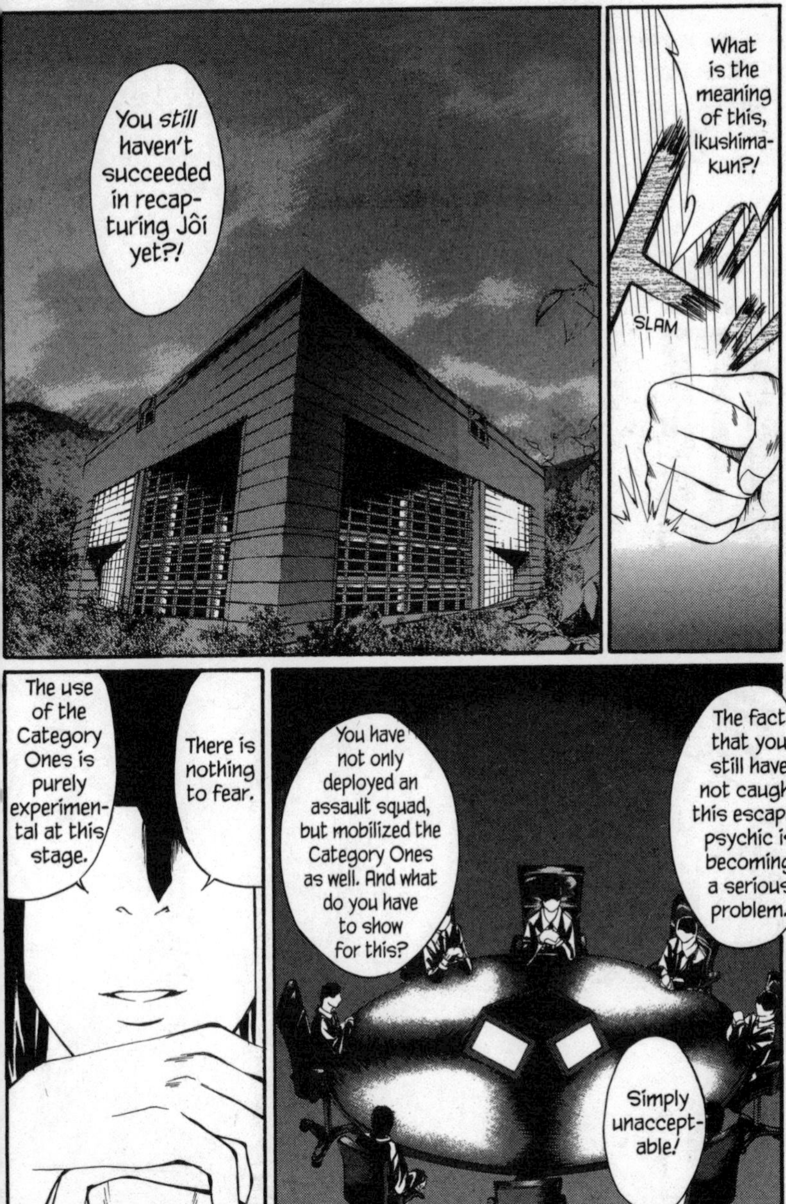
What is the meaning of this, Ikushima-kun?!
SLAM
You *still* haven't succeeded in recapturing Jôi yet?!
The fact that you still have not caught this escaped psychic is becoming a serious problem.
You have not only deployed an assault squad, but mobilized the Category Ones as well. And what do you have to show for this?
Simply unacceptable!
There is nothing to fear.
The use of the Category Ones is purely experimental at this stage.

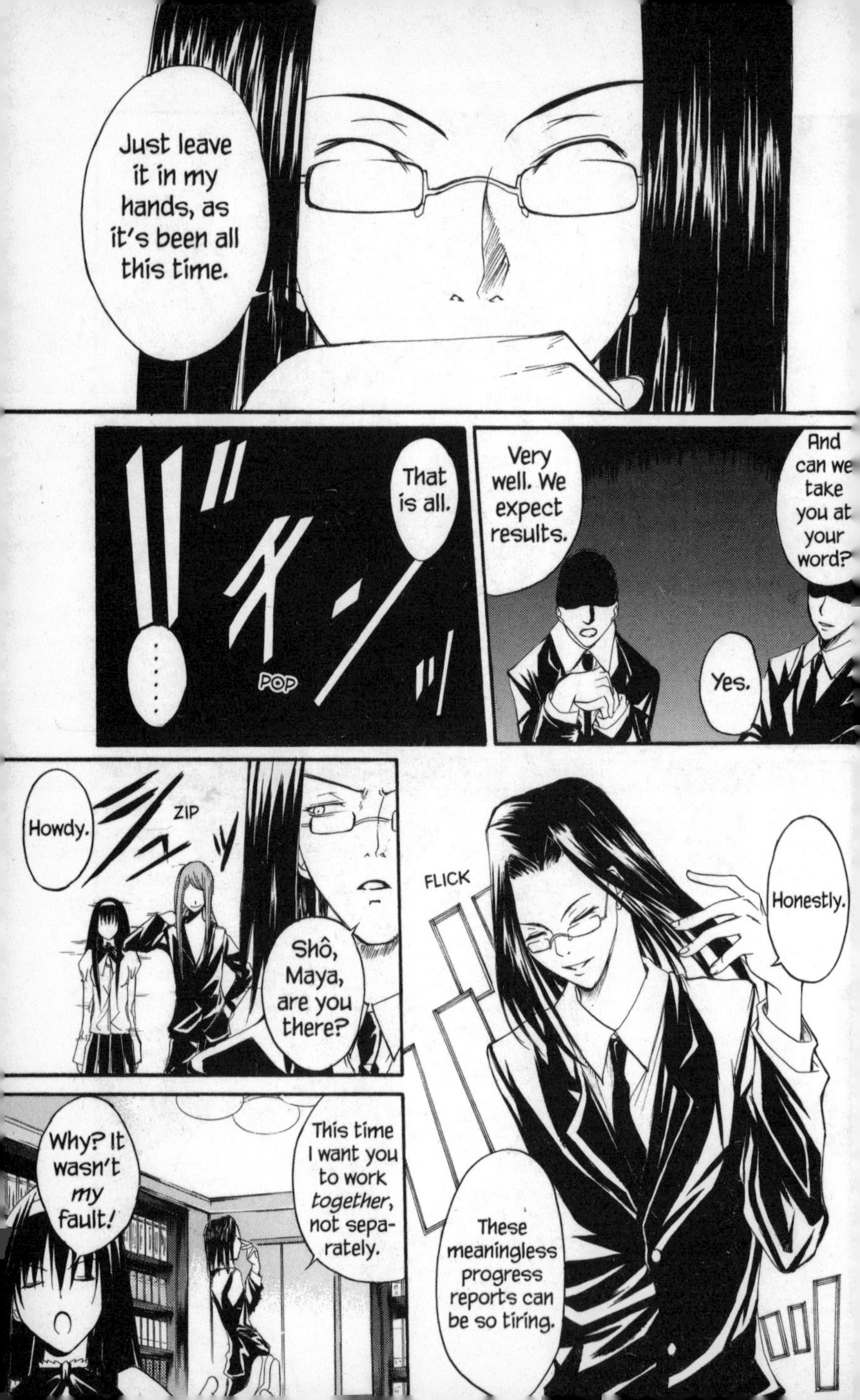
Just leave it in my hands, as it's been all this time.
And can we take you at your word?
Very well. We expect results.
Yes.
That is all.
POP
......
Honestly.
FLICK
These meaningless progress reports can be so tiring.
Shô, Maya, are you there?
ZIP
Howdy.
This time I want you to work *together*, not separately.
Why? It wasn't *my* fault!

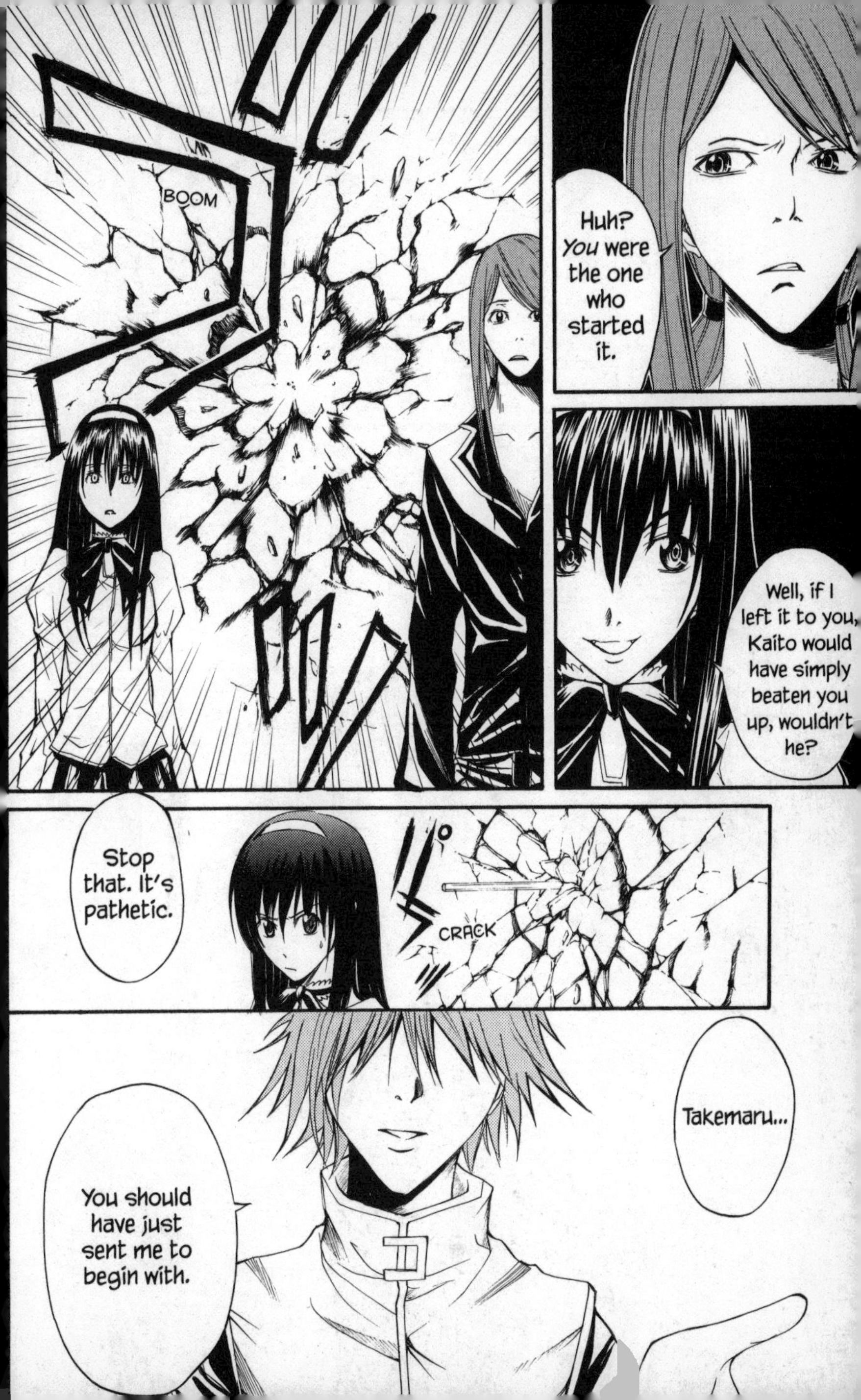
Huh? *You* were the one who started it.
Well, if I left it to you, Kaito would have simply beaten you up, wouldn't he?
BOOM
CRACK
Stop that. It's pathetic.
Takemaru...
You should have just sent me to begin with.

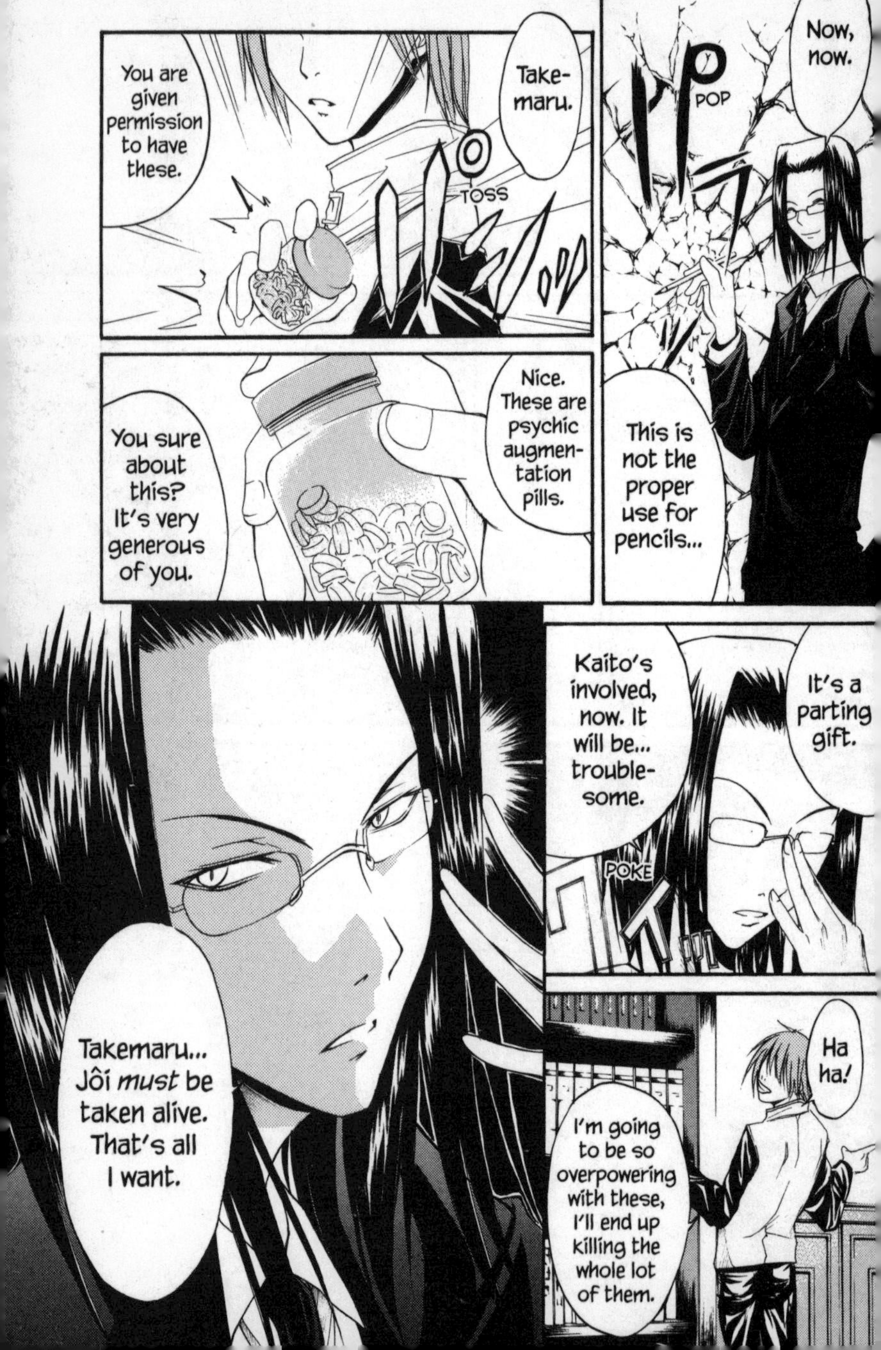
Now, now.
POP
This is not the proper use for pencils...
Take-maru.
TOSS
You are given permission to have these.
Nice. These are psychic augmentation pills.
You sure about this? It's very generous of you.
It's a parting gift.
Kaito's involved, now. It will be... trouble-some.
POKE
Ha ha!
I'm going to be so overpowering with these, I'll end up killing the whole lot of them.
Takemaru... Jôi *must* be taken alive. That's all I want.

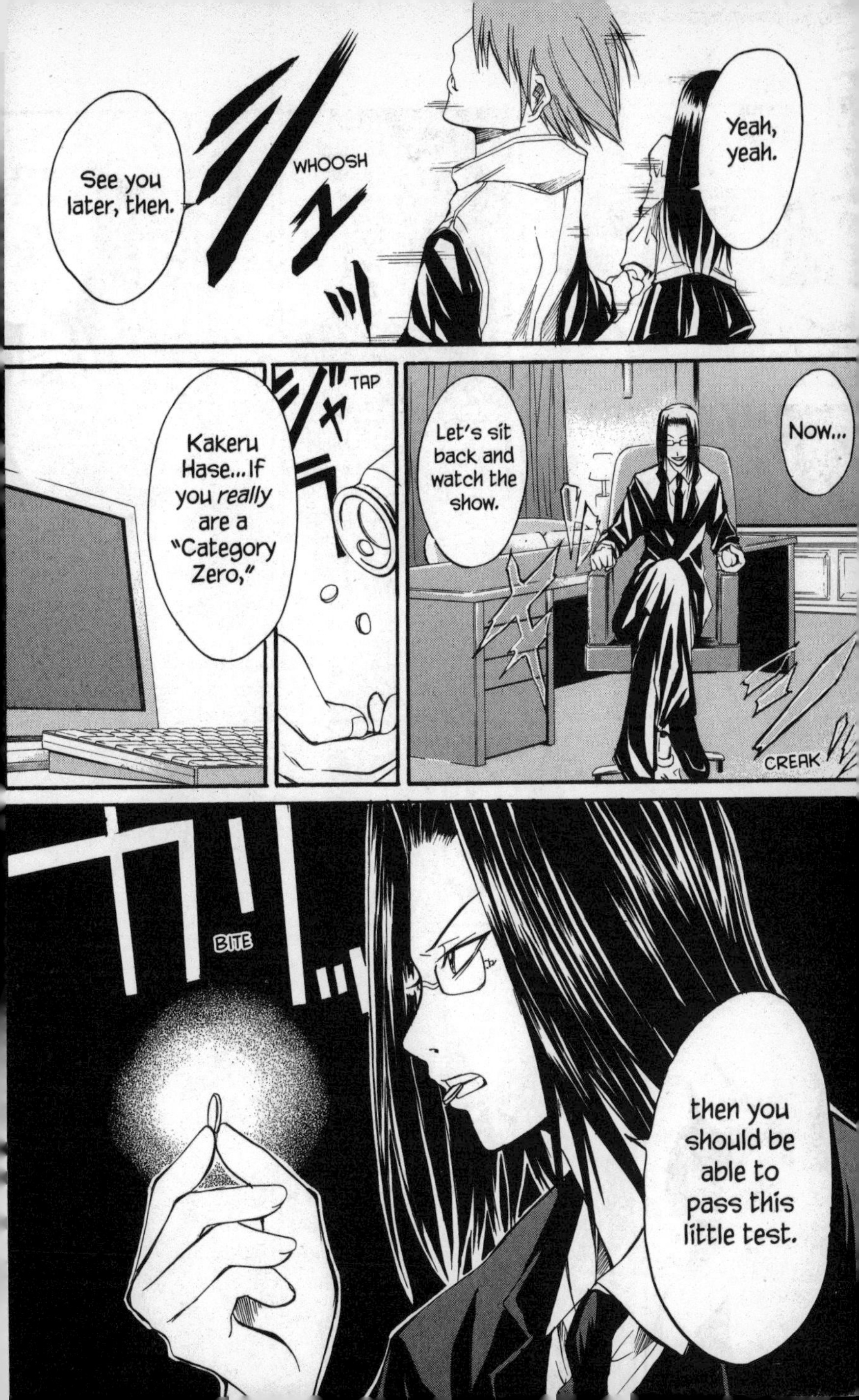
Yeah, yeah.
WHOOSH
See you later, then.
Now...
Let's sit back and watch the show.
CREAK
TAP
Kakeru Hase...If you *really* are a "Category Zero,"
BITE
then you should be able to pass this little test.

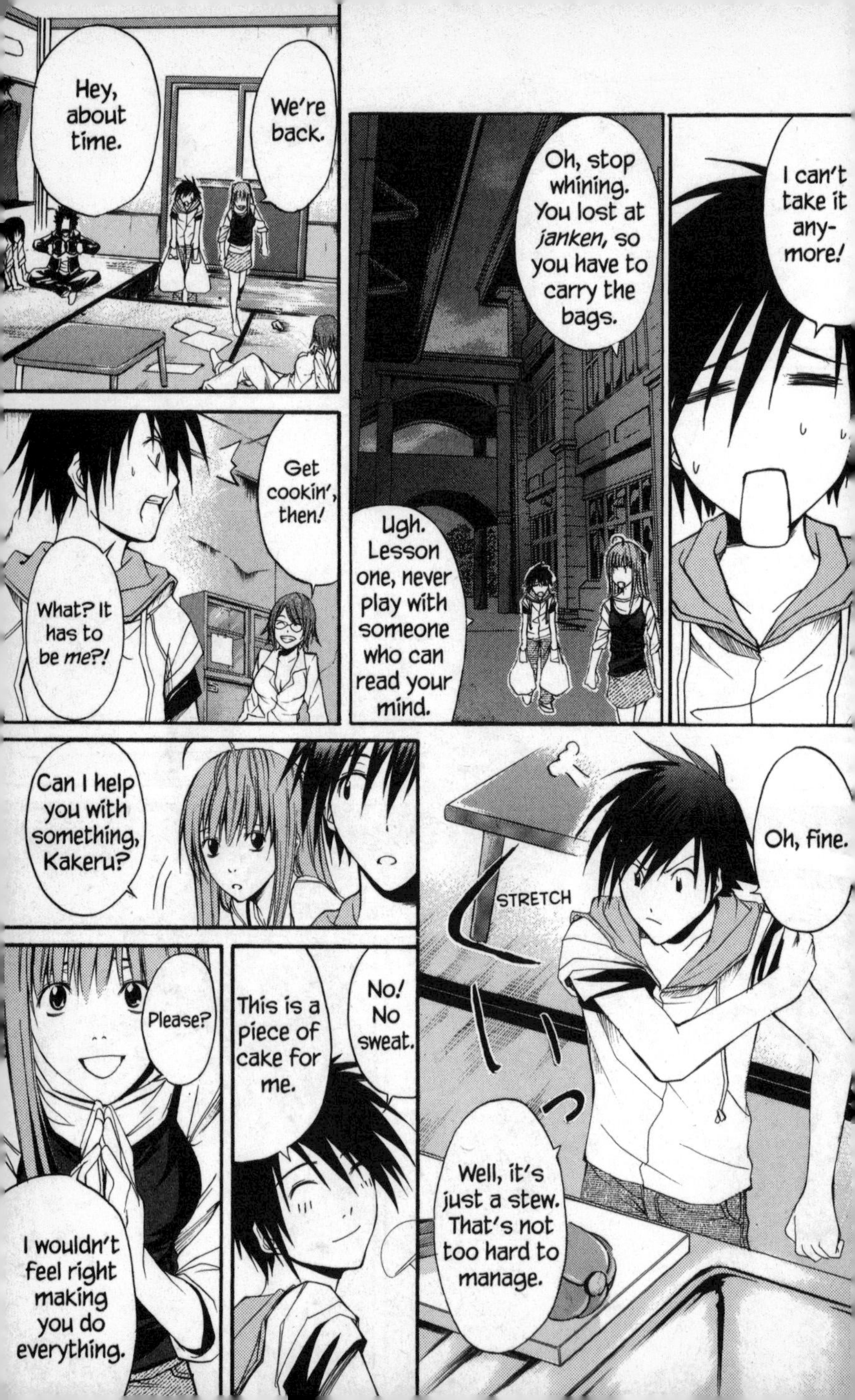
I can't take it any-more!
Oh, stop whining. You lost at *janken*, so you have to carry the bags.
Ugh. Lesson one, never play with someone who can read your mind.
We're back.
Hey, about time.
Get cookin', then!
What? It has to be *me*?!
Oh, fine.
STRETCH
Well, it's just a stew. That's not too hard to manage.
Can I help you with something, Kakeru?
No! No sweat.
This is a piece of cake for me.
Please?
I wouldn't feel right making you do everything.

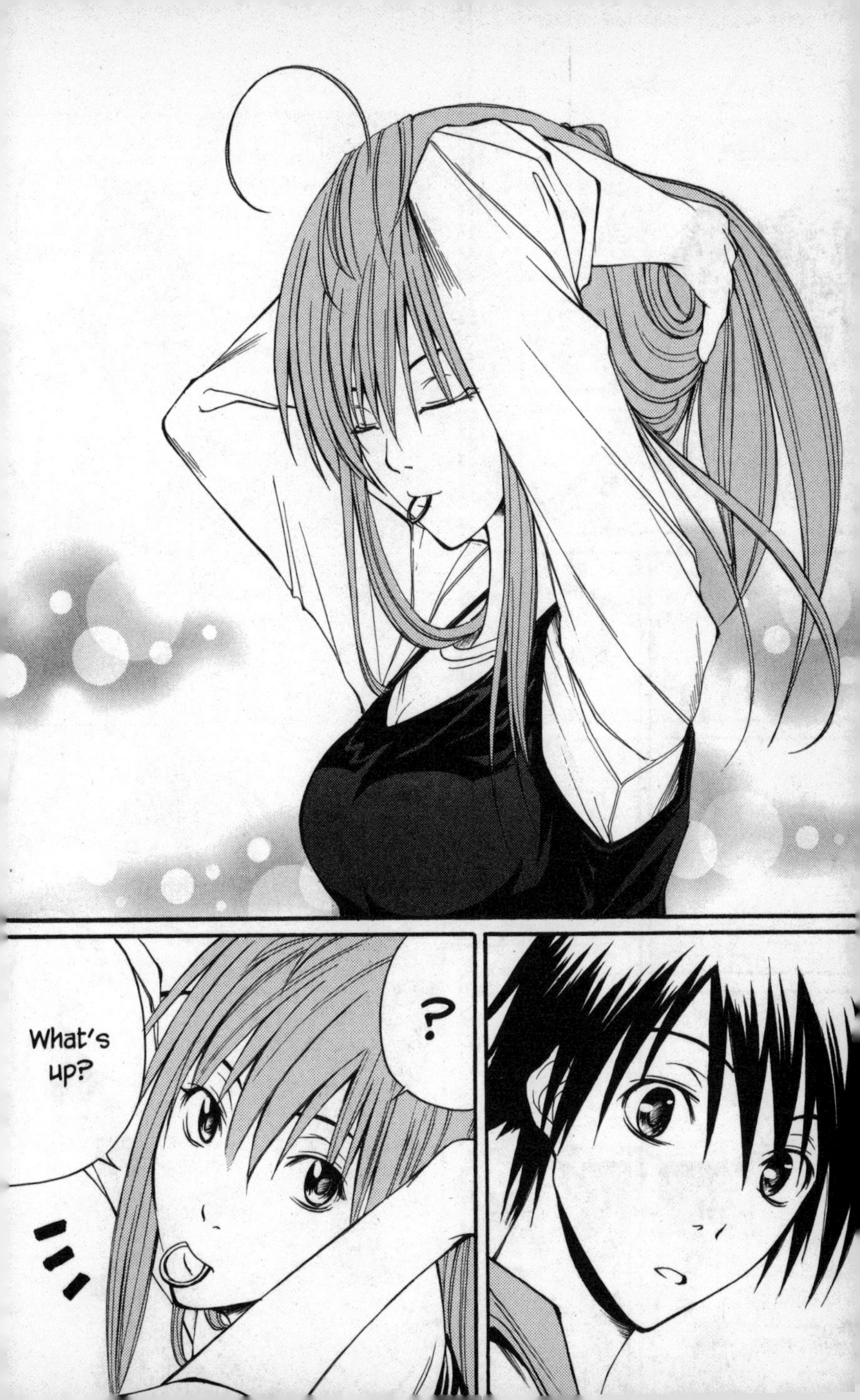
?
What's up?

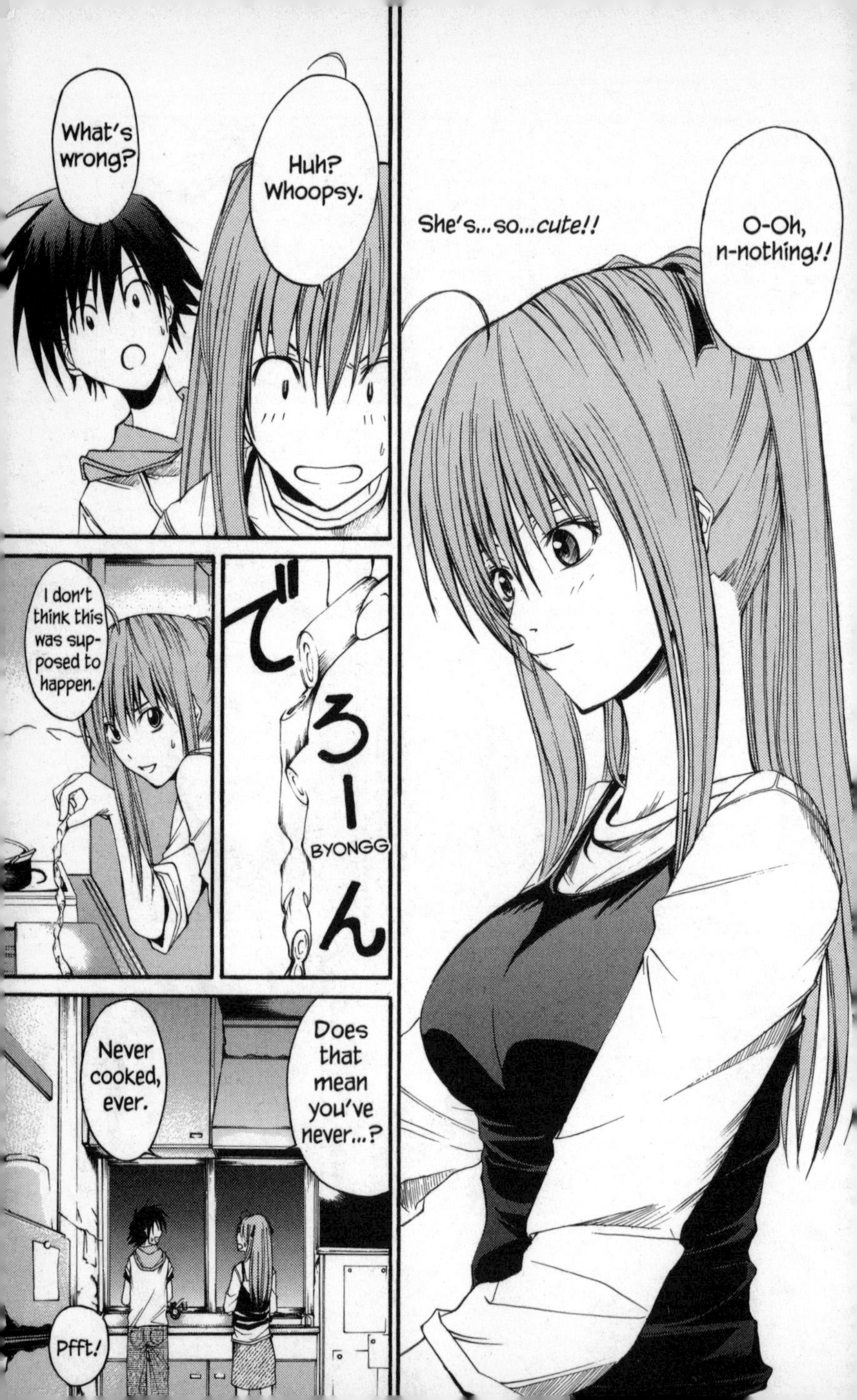

O-Oh, n-nothing!!
She's...so...cute!!
Huh? Whoopsy.
What's wrong?
でろーん
BYONGG
I don't think this was sup-posed to happen.
Does that mean you've never...?
Never cooked, ever.
Pfft!

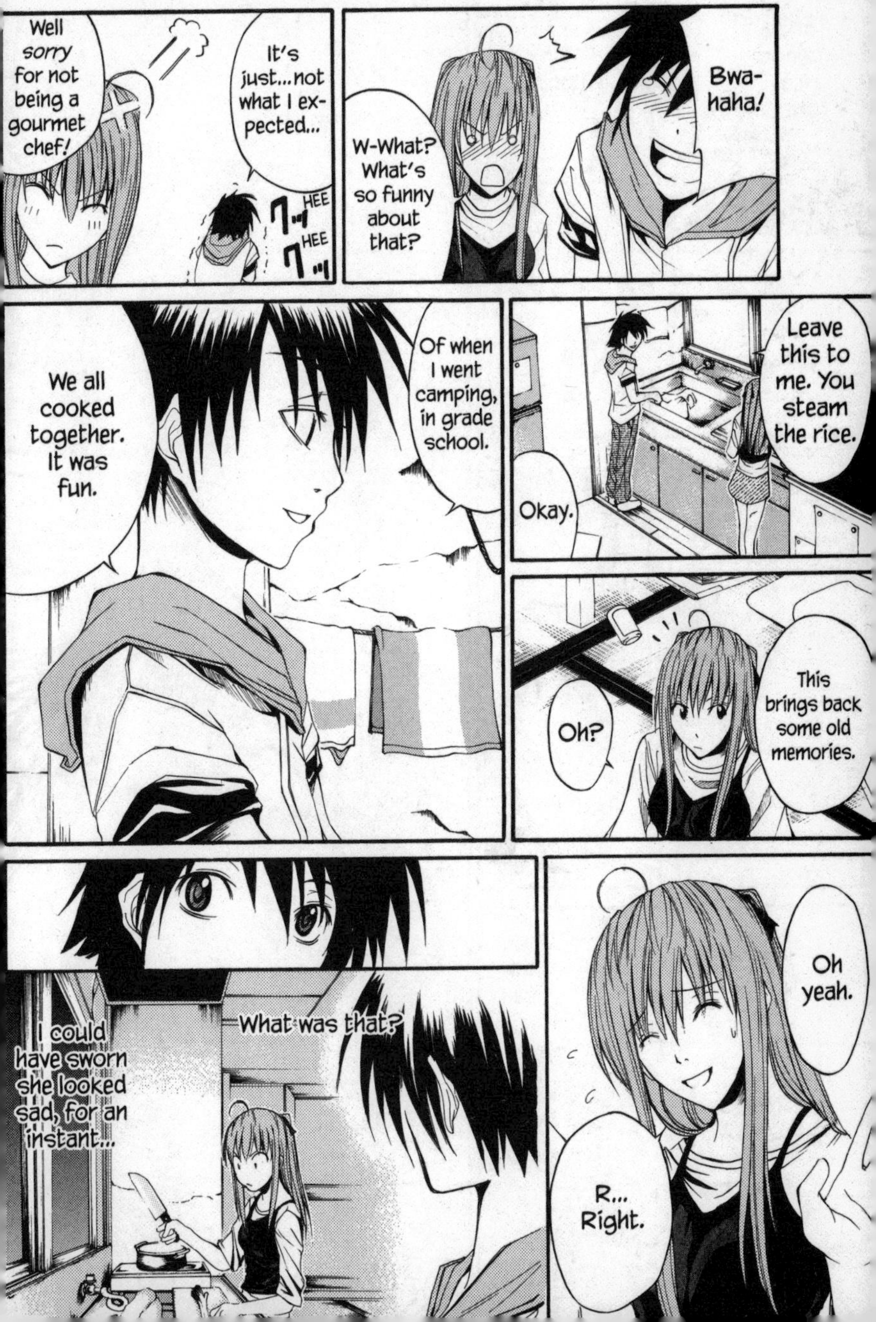
Bwa-haha!
W-What? What's so funny about that?
It's just...not what I expected...
HEE HEE
Well sorry for not being a gourmet chef!
Leave this to me. You steam the rice.
Okay.
This brings back some old memories.
Oh?
Of when I went camping, in grade school.
We all cooked together. It was fun.
Oh yeah.
R... Right.
What was that?
I could have sworn she looked sad, for an instant...

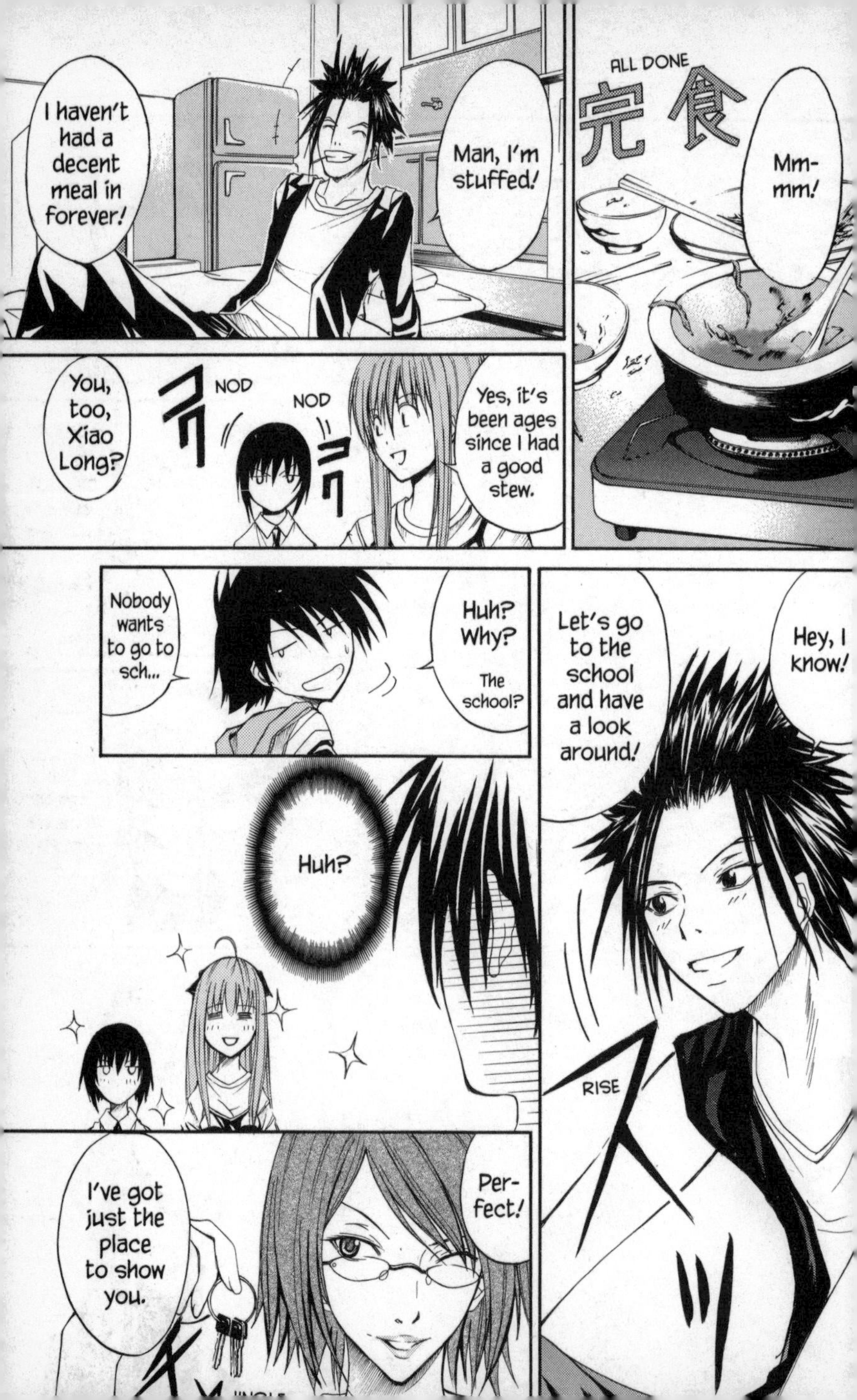
ALL DONE
完食
Mm-mm!
Man, I'm stuffed!
I haven't had a decent meal in forever!
Yes, it's been ages since I had a good stew.
NOD
NOD
You, too, Xiao Long?
Hey, I know!
Let's go to the school and have a look around!
RISE
Huh? Why?
The school?
Nobody wants to go to sch...
Huh?
Per-fect!
I've got just the place to show you.

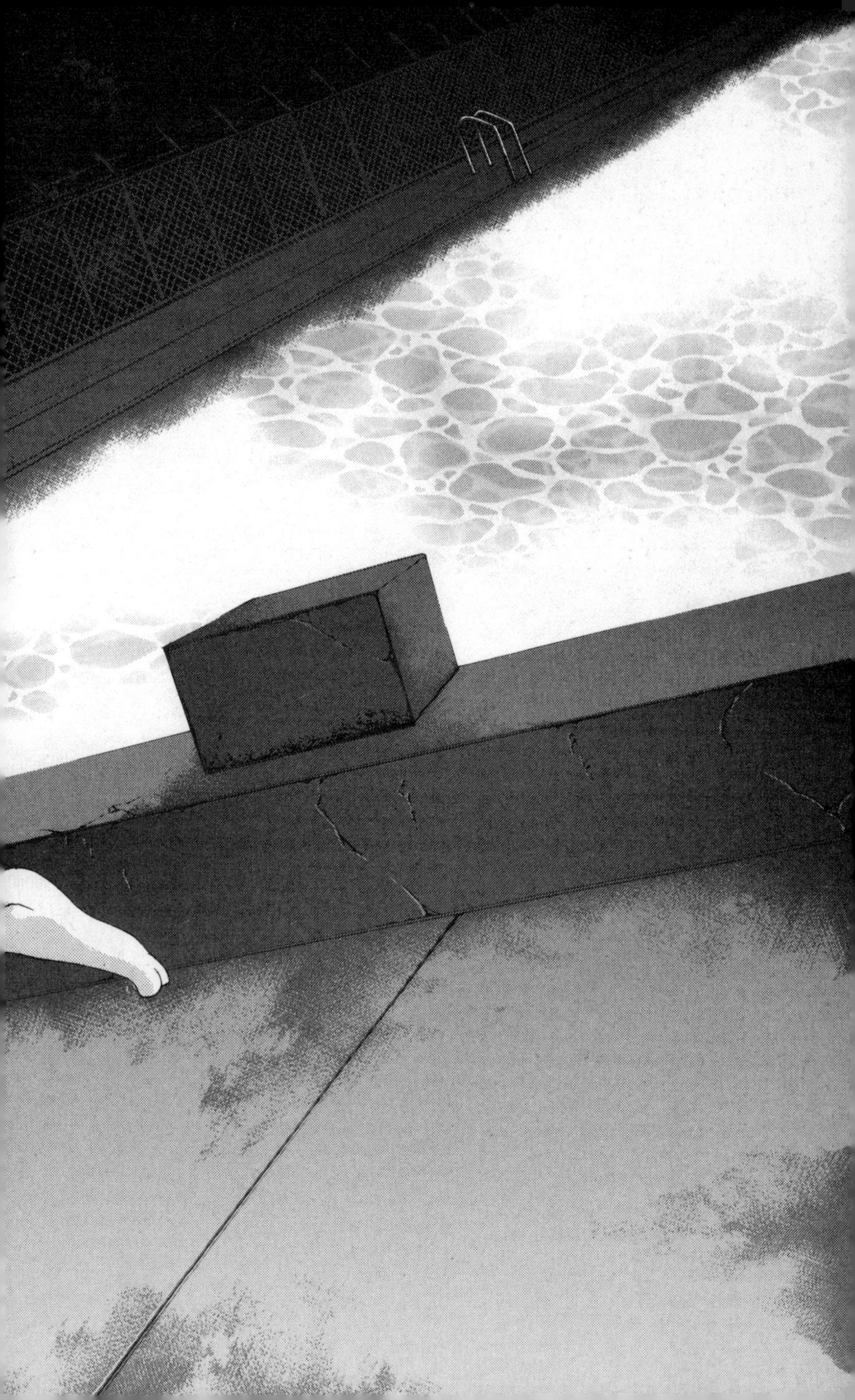

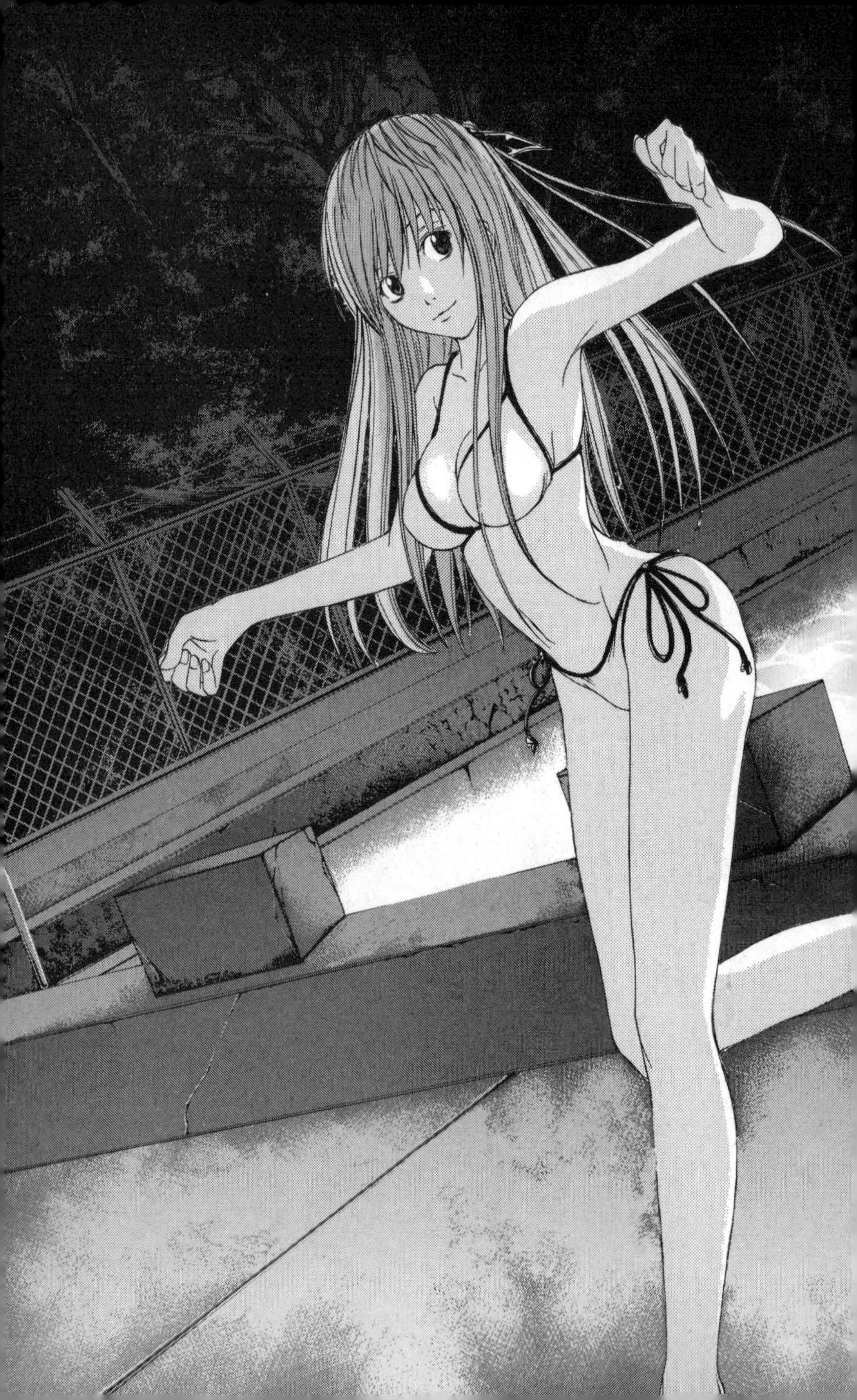

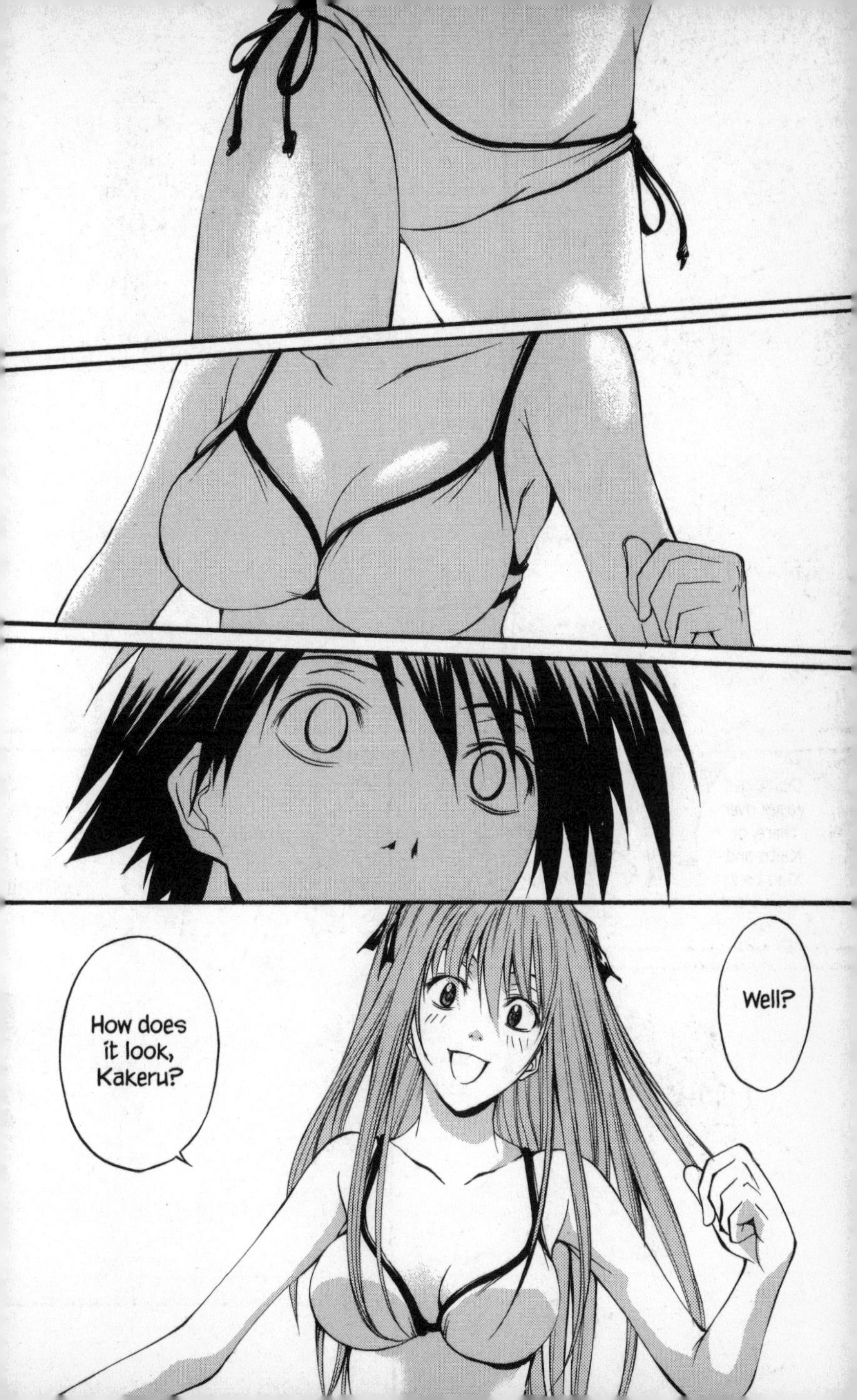
Well?
How does it look, Kakeru?

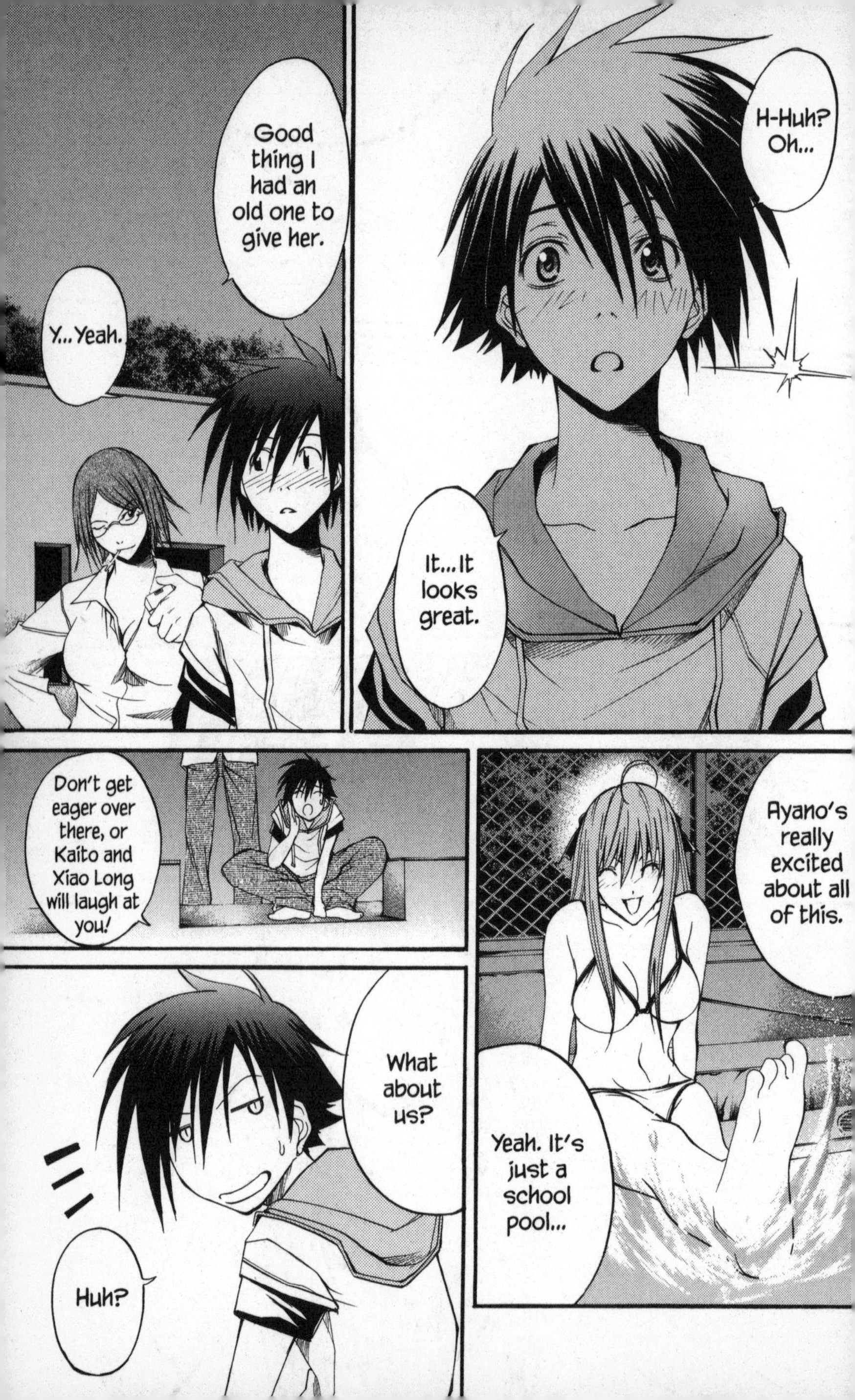
H-Huh? Oh...
It...It looks great.
Good thing I had an old one to give her.
Y...Yeah.
Ayano's really excited about all of this.
Yeah. It's just a school pool...
Don't get eager over there, or Kaito and Xiao Long will laugh at you!
What about us?
Huh?

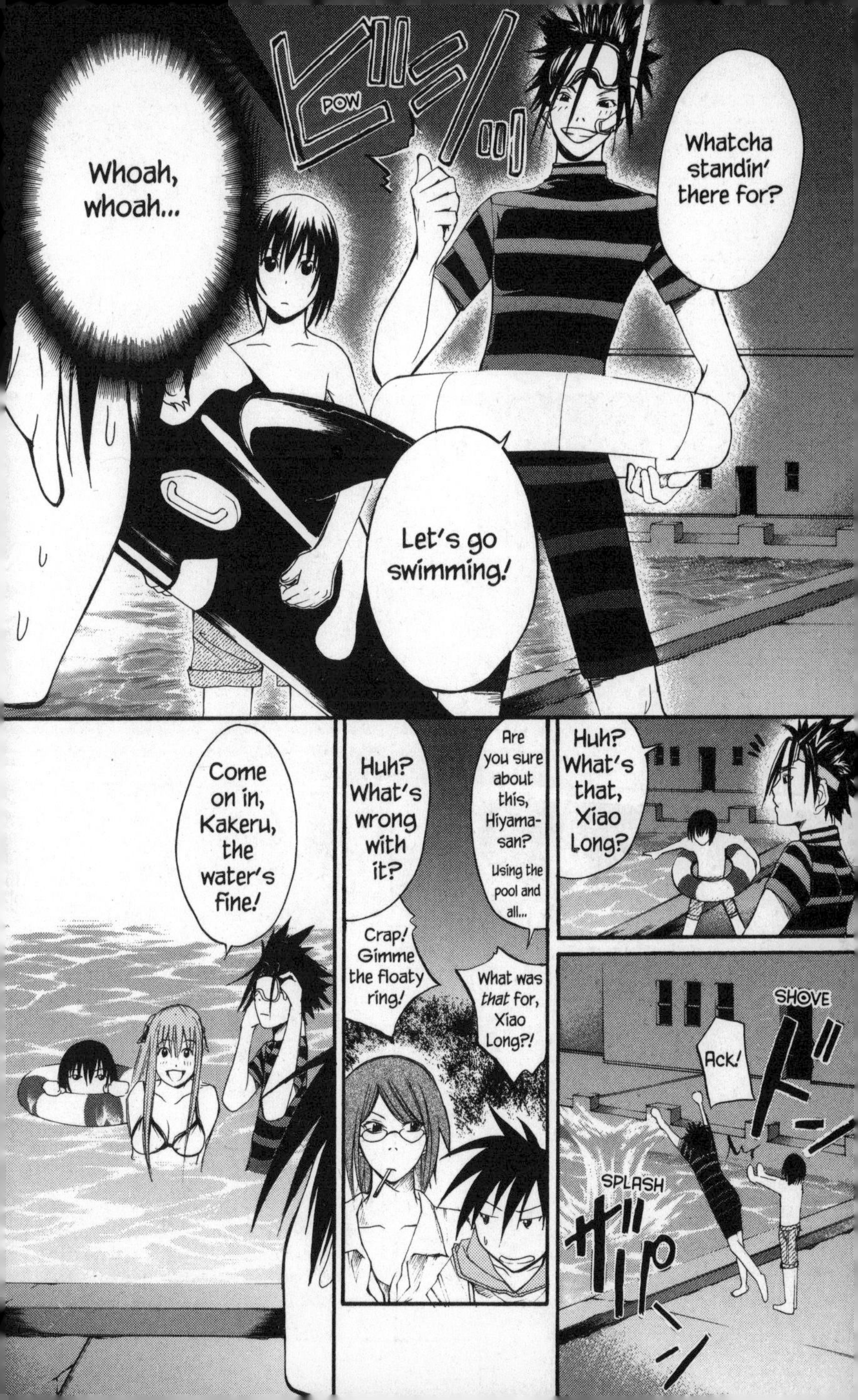
POW
Whatcha standin' there for?
Let's go swimming!
Whoah, whoah...
Huh? What's that, Xiao Long?
Ack!
SHOVE
SPLASH
Are you sure about this, Hiyama-san? Using the pool and all...
Huh? What's wrong with it?
What was *that* for, Xiao Long?!
Crap! Gimme the floaty ring!
Come on in, Kakeru, the water's fine!

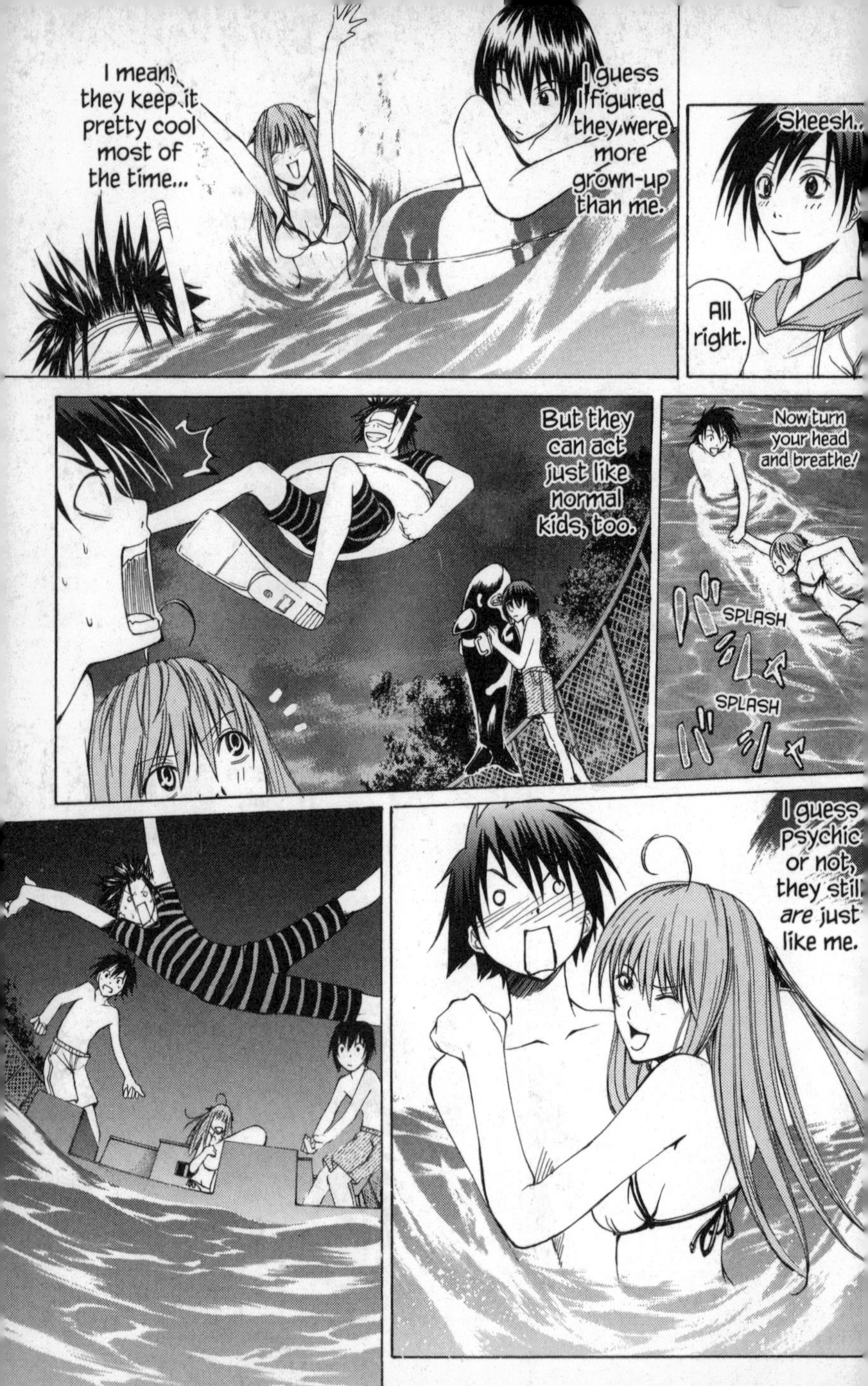
Sheesh..
All right.
I guess I figured they were more grown-up than me.
I mean, they keep it pretty cool most of the time...
Now turn your head and breathe!
SPLASH
SPLASH
But they can act just like normal kids, too.
I guess psychic or not, they still *are* just like me.

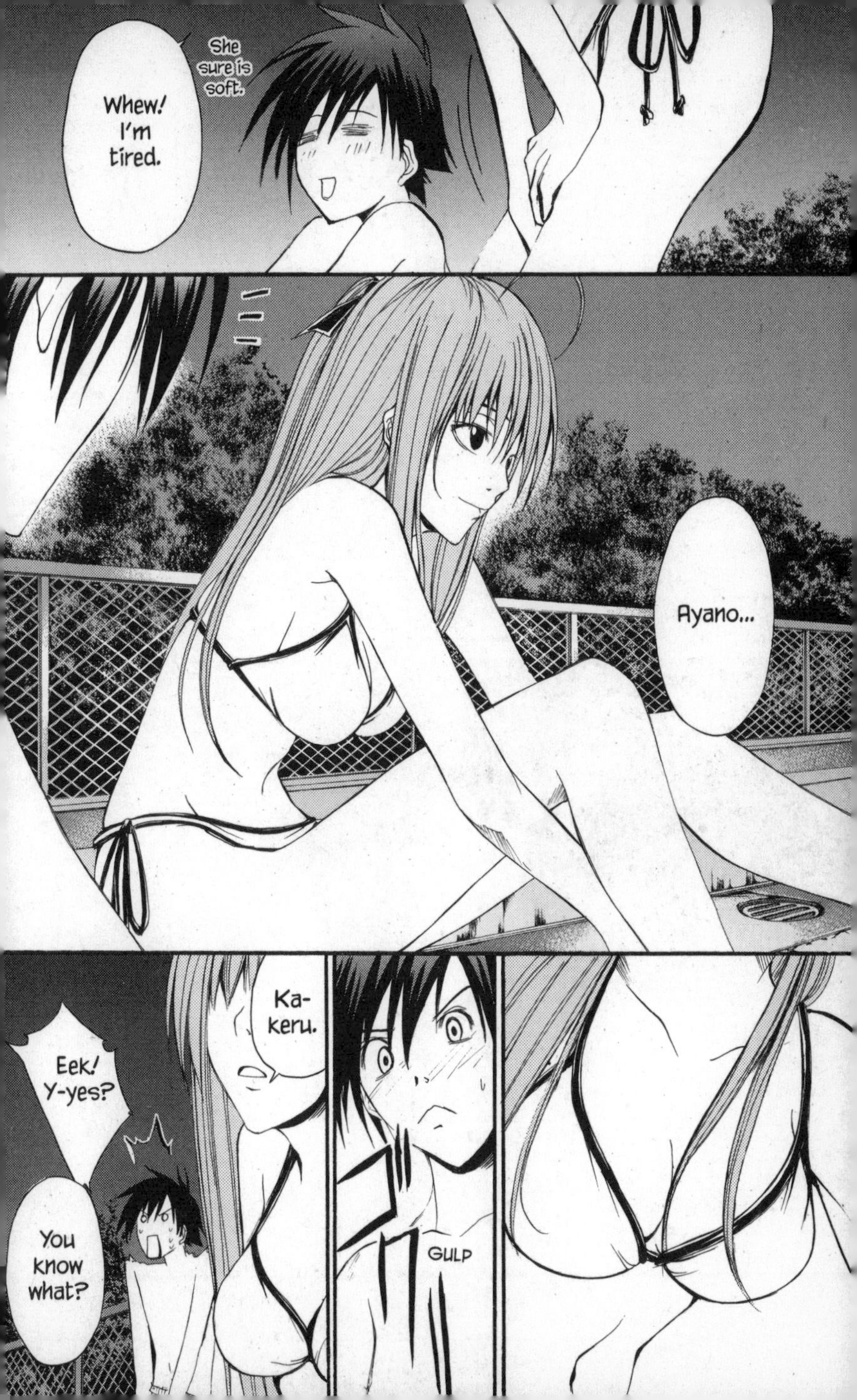
She sure is soft.
Whew! I'm tired.
Ayano...
GULP
Ka-keru.
Eek! Y-yes?
You know what?

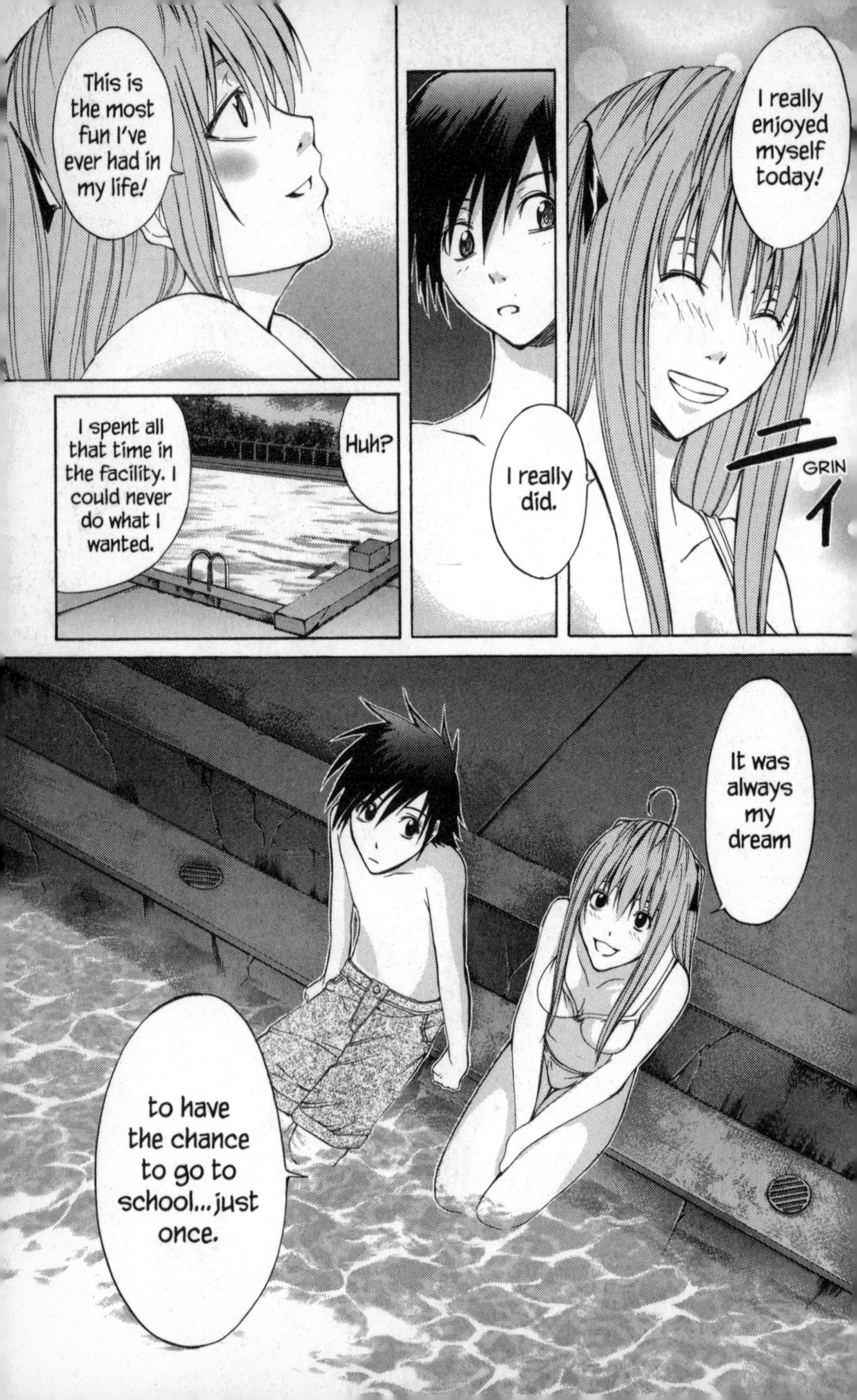
I really enjoyed myself today!
GRIN
I really did.
This is the most fun I've ever had in my life!
Huh?
I spent all that time in the facility. I could never do what I wanted.
It was always my dream
to have the chance to go to school...just once.

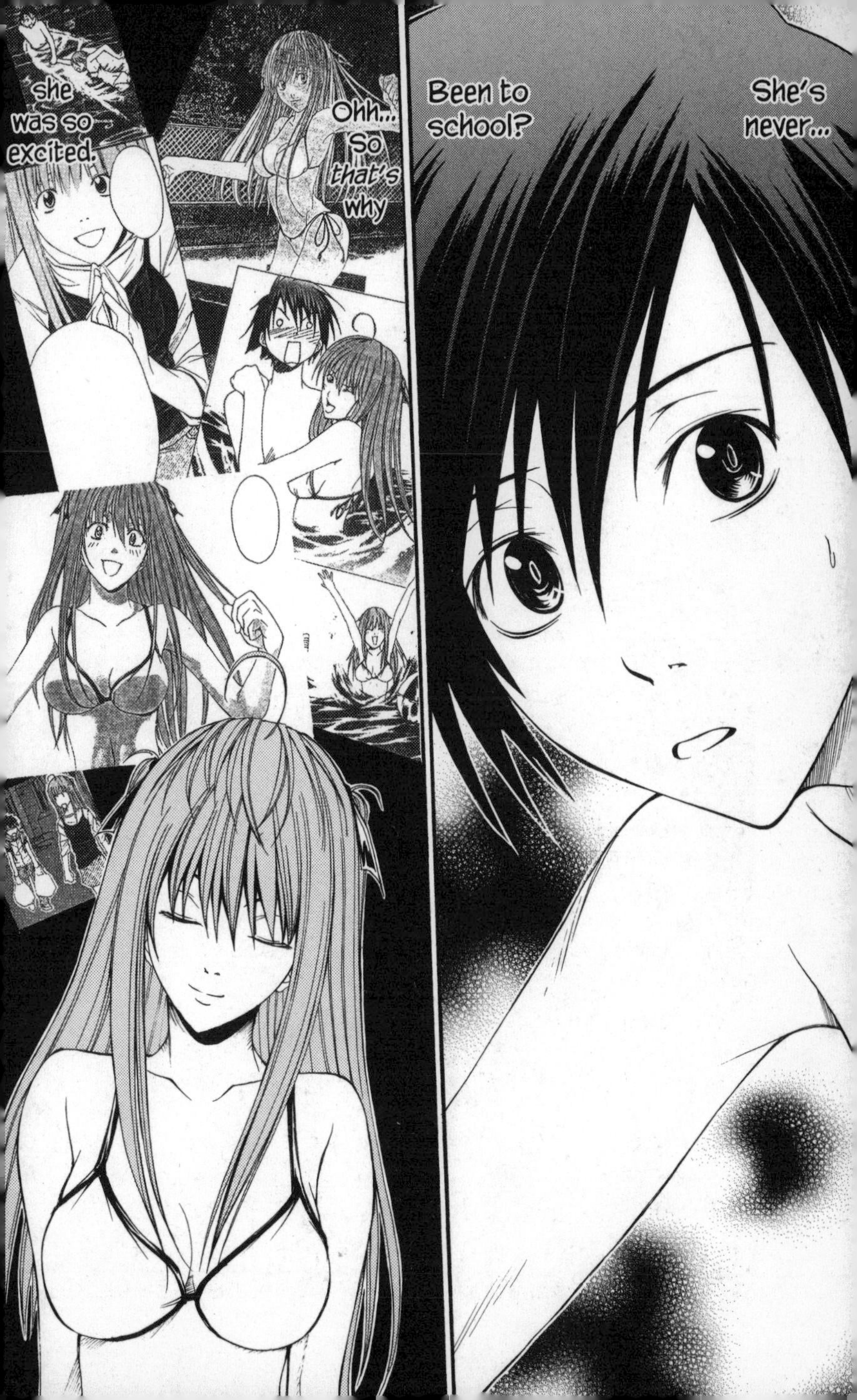
She's never...
Been to school?
Ohh... So that's why
she was so excited.

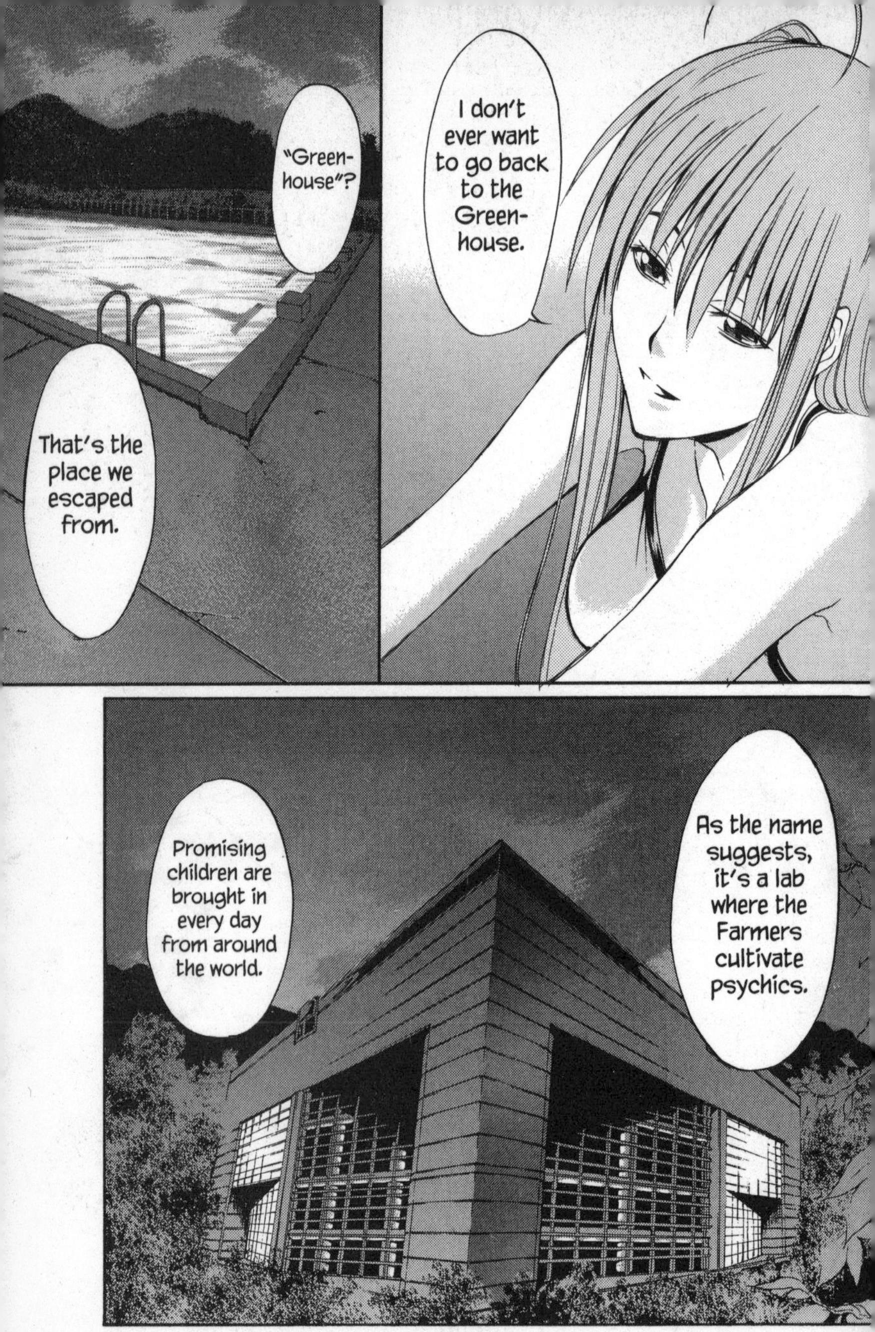
I don't ever want to go back to the Green-house.
"Green-house"?
That's the place we escaped from.
As the name suggests, it's a lab where the Farmers cultivate psychics.
Promising children are brought in every day from around the world.

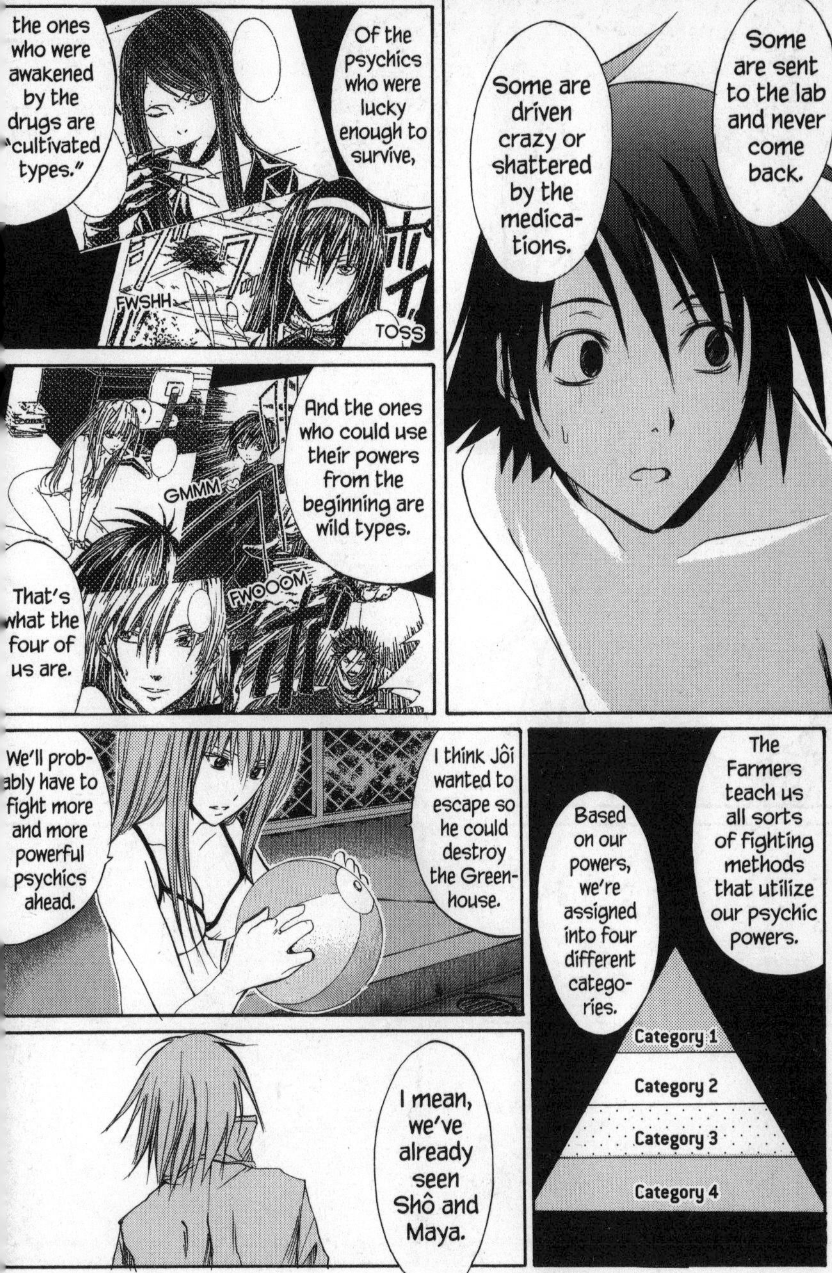

Some are sent to the lab and never come back.
Some are driven crazy or shattered by the medica-tions.
Of the psychics who were lucky enough to survive,
the ones who were awakened by the drugs are "cultivated types."
TOSS
FWSHH
And the ones who could use their powers from the beginning are wild types.
GMMM
FWOOOM
That's what the four of us are.
The Farmers teach us all sorts of fighting methods that utilize our psychic powers.
Based on our powers, we're assigned into four different catego-ries.
Category 1
Category 2
Category 3
Category 4
I think Jôi wanted to escape so he could destroy the Green-house.
We'll prob-ably have to fight more and more powerful psychics ahead.
I mean, we've already seen Shô and Maya.

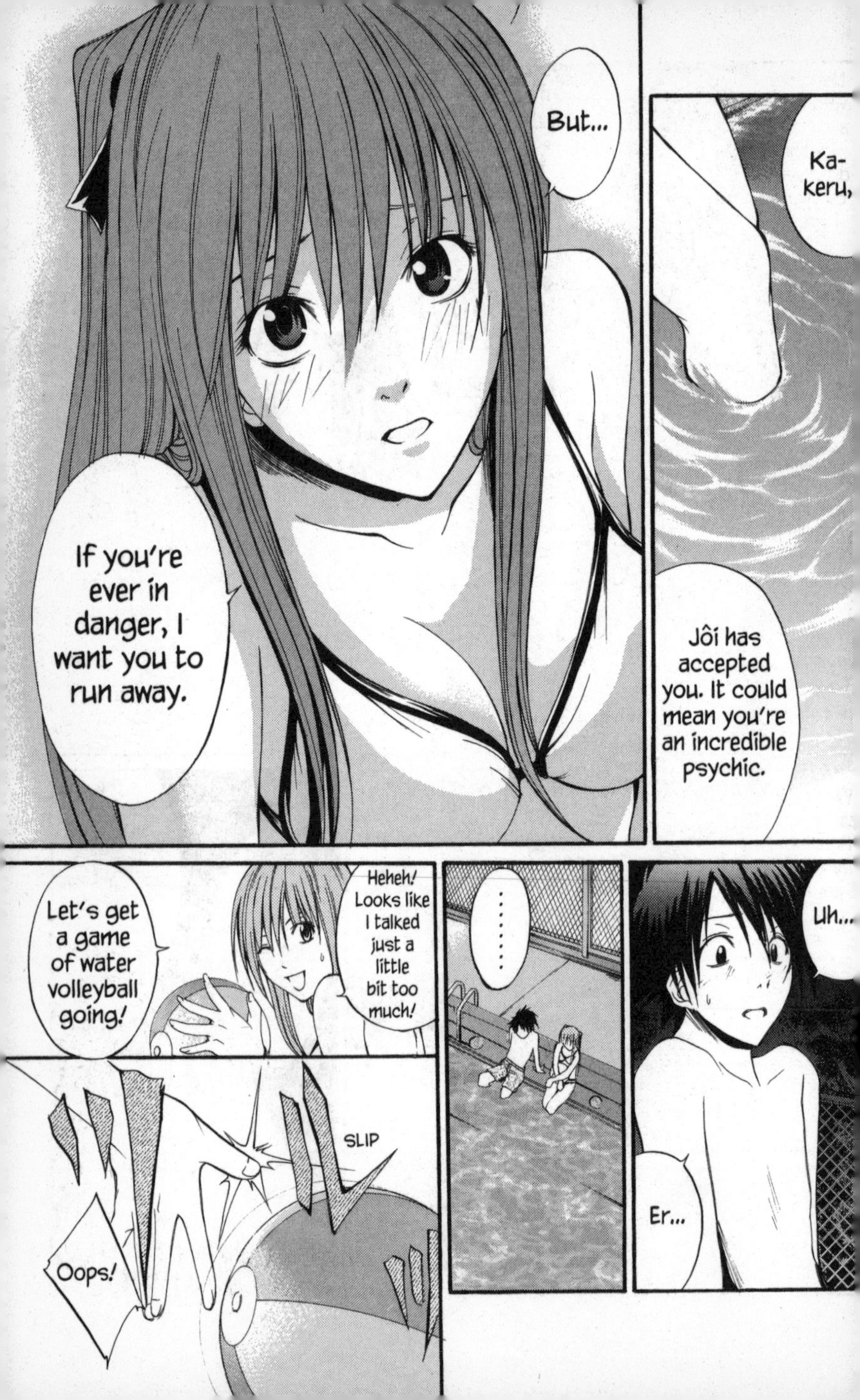
Kakeru,
Jôi has accepted you. It could mean you're an incredible psychic.
But...
If you're ever in danger, I want you to run away.
Uh...
Er...
......
Heheh! Looks like I talked just a little bit too much!
Let's get a game of water volleyball going!
SLIP
Oops!

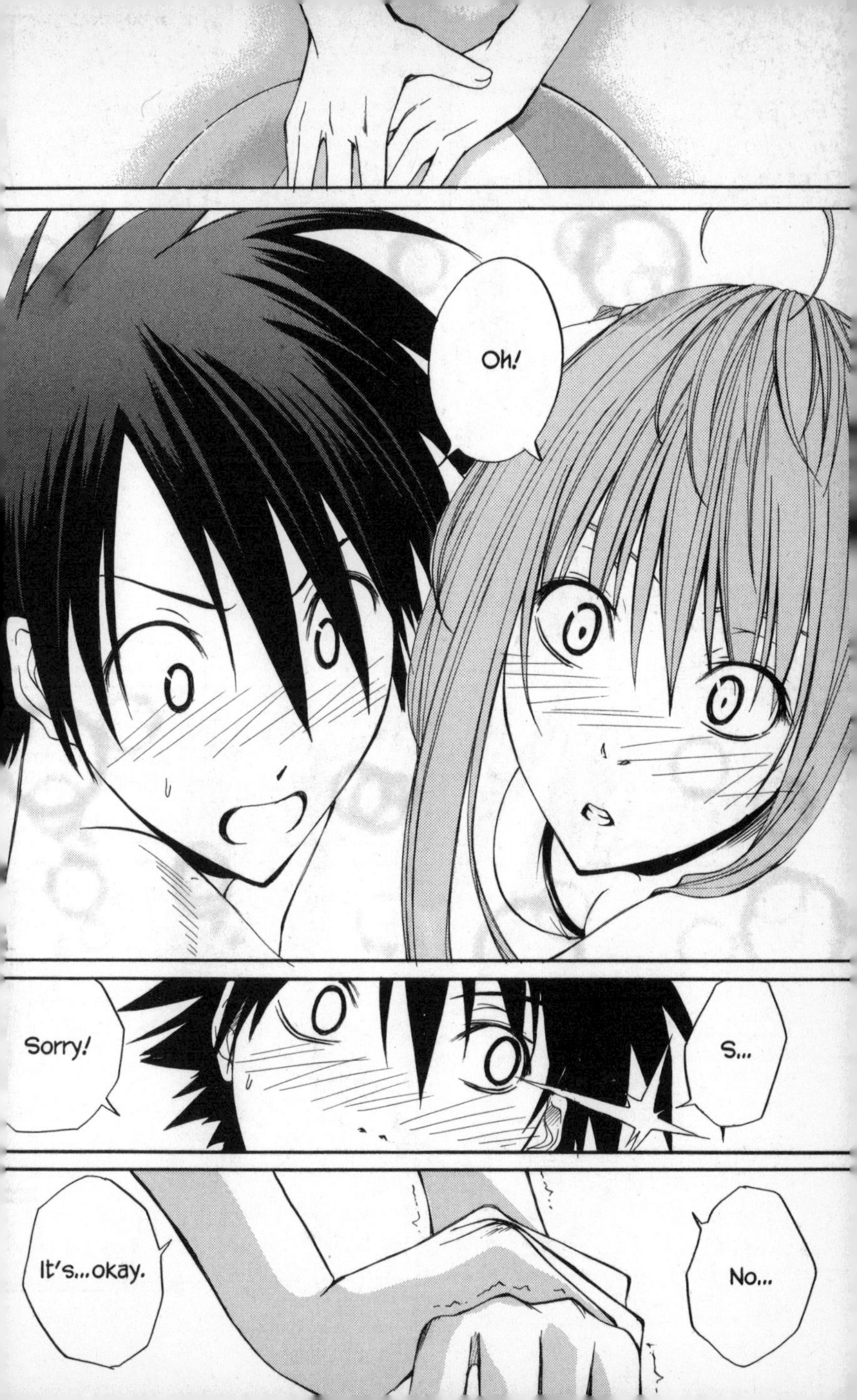

Oh!
S...
Sorry!
No...
It's...okay.

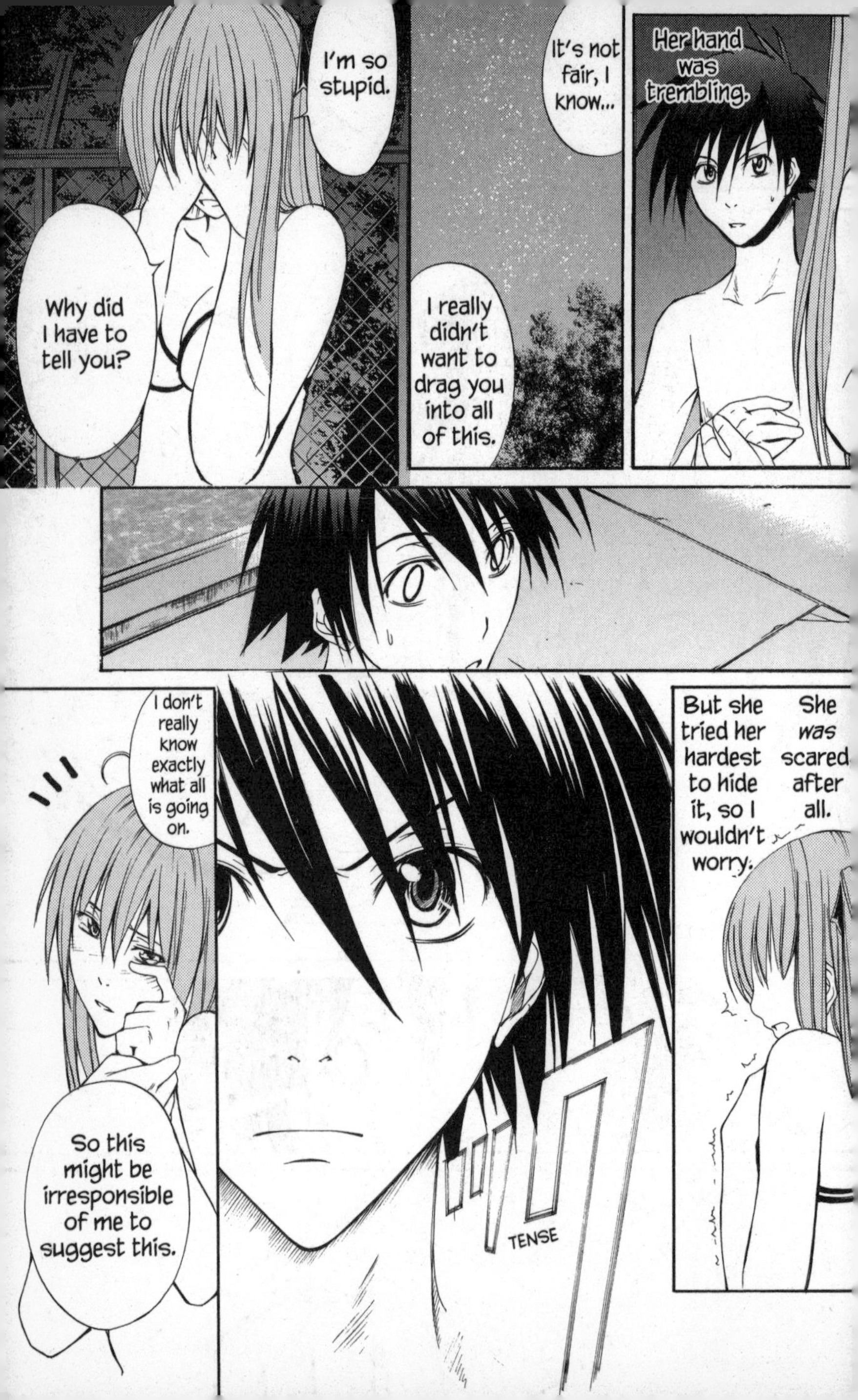
Her hand was trembling.
It's not fair, I know...
I really didn't want to drag you into all of this.
I'm so stupid.
Why did I have to tell you?
She was scared after all.
But she tried her hardest to hide it, so I wouldn't worry.
I don't really know exactly what all is going on.
TENSE
So this might be irresponsible of me to suggest this.

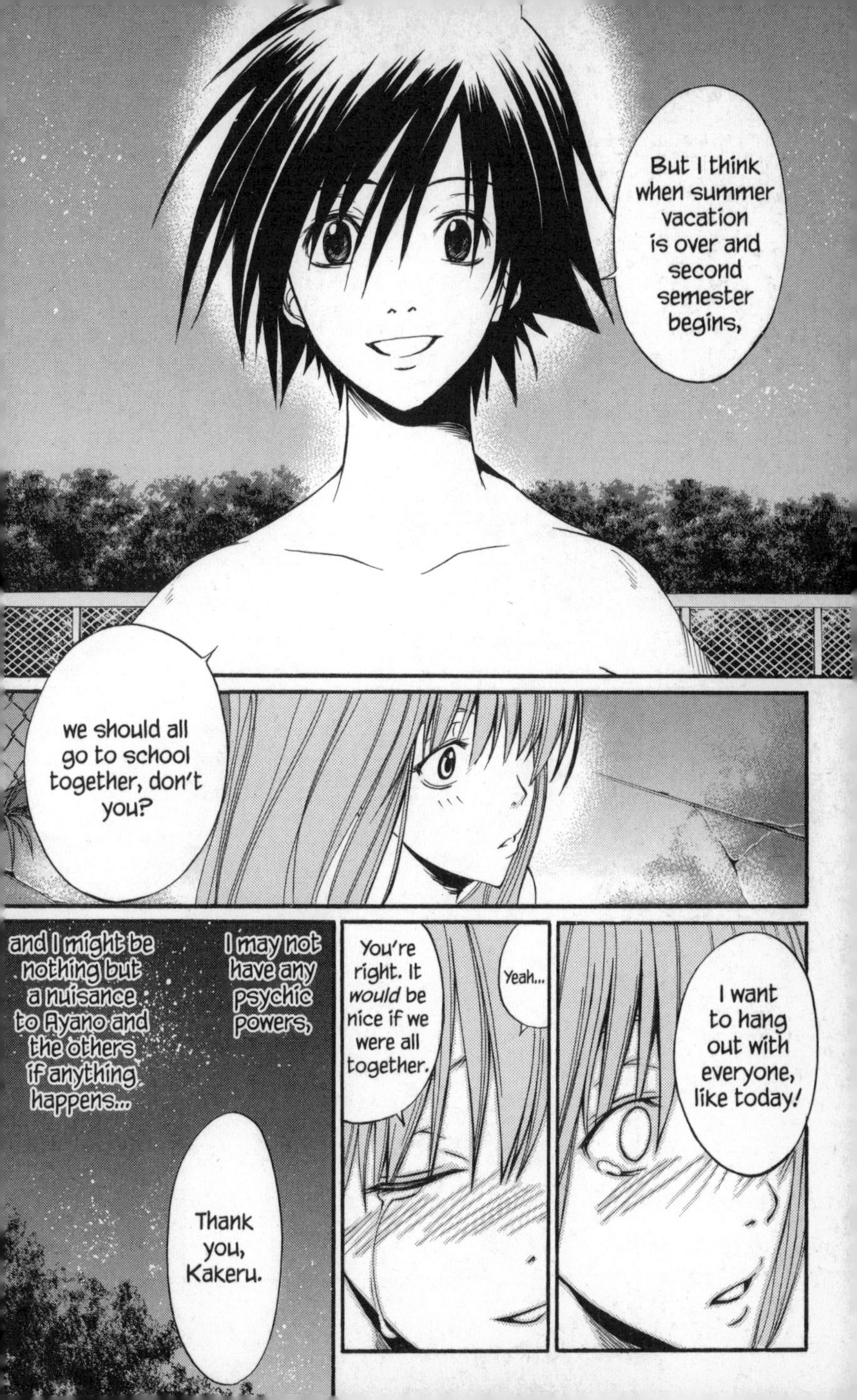
But I think when summer vacation is over and second semester begins,
we should all go to school together, don't you?
I want to hang out with everyone, like today!
Yeah...
You're right. It *would* be nice if we were all together.
I may not have any psychic powers,
and I might be nothing but a nuisance to Ayano and the others if anything happens...
Thank you, Kakeru.

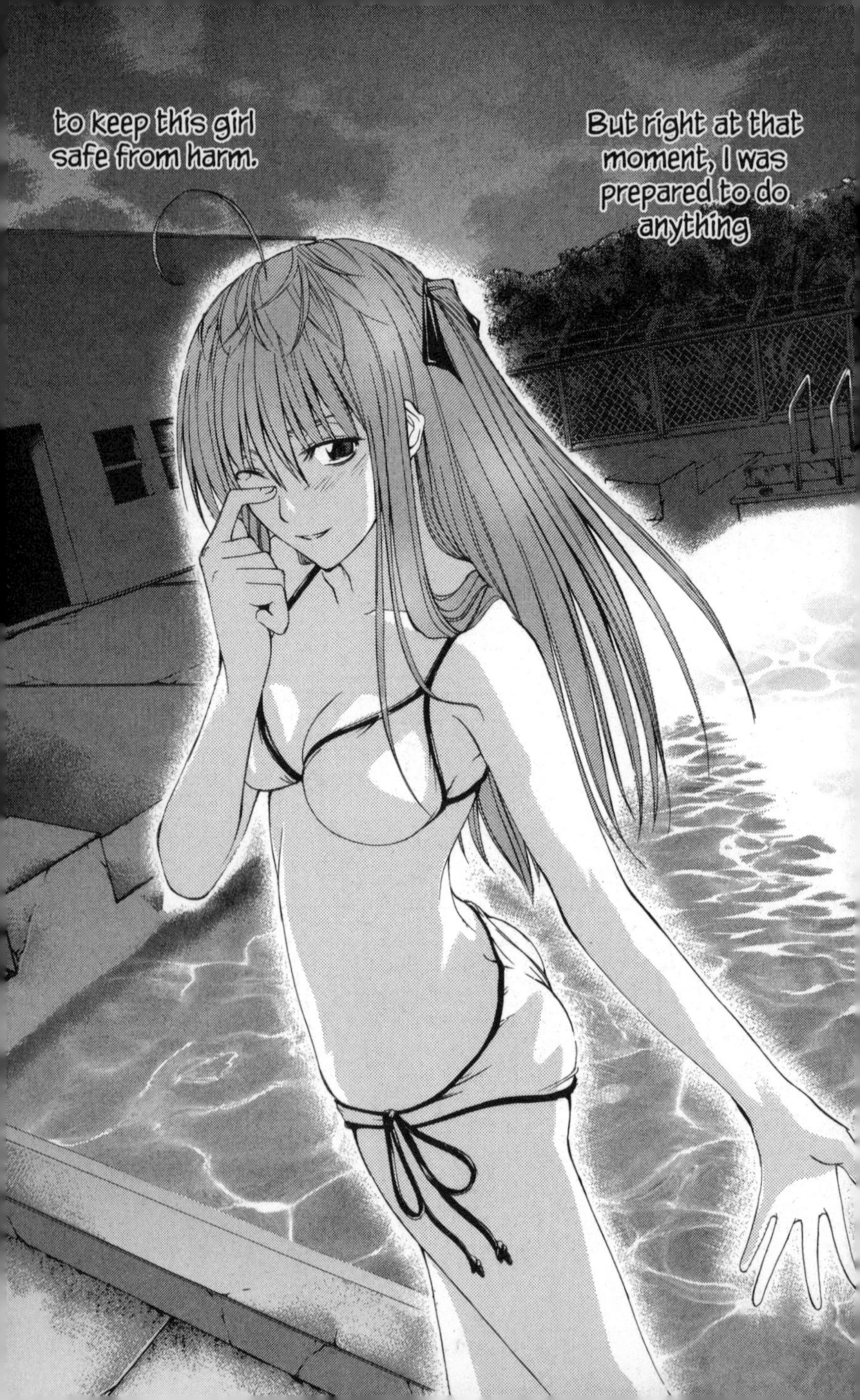
But right at that moment, I was prepared to do anything
to keep this girl safe from harm.

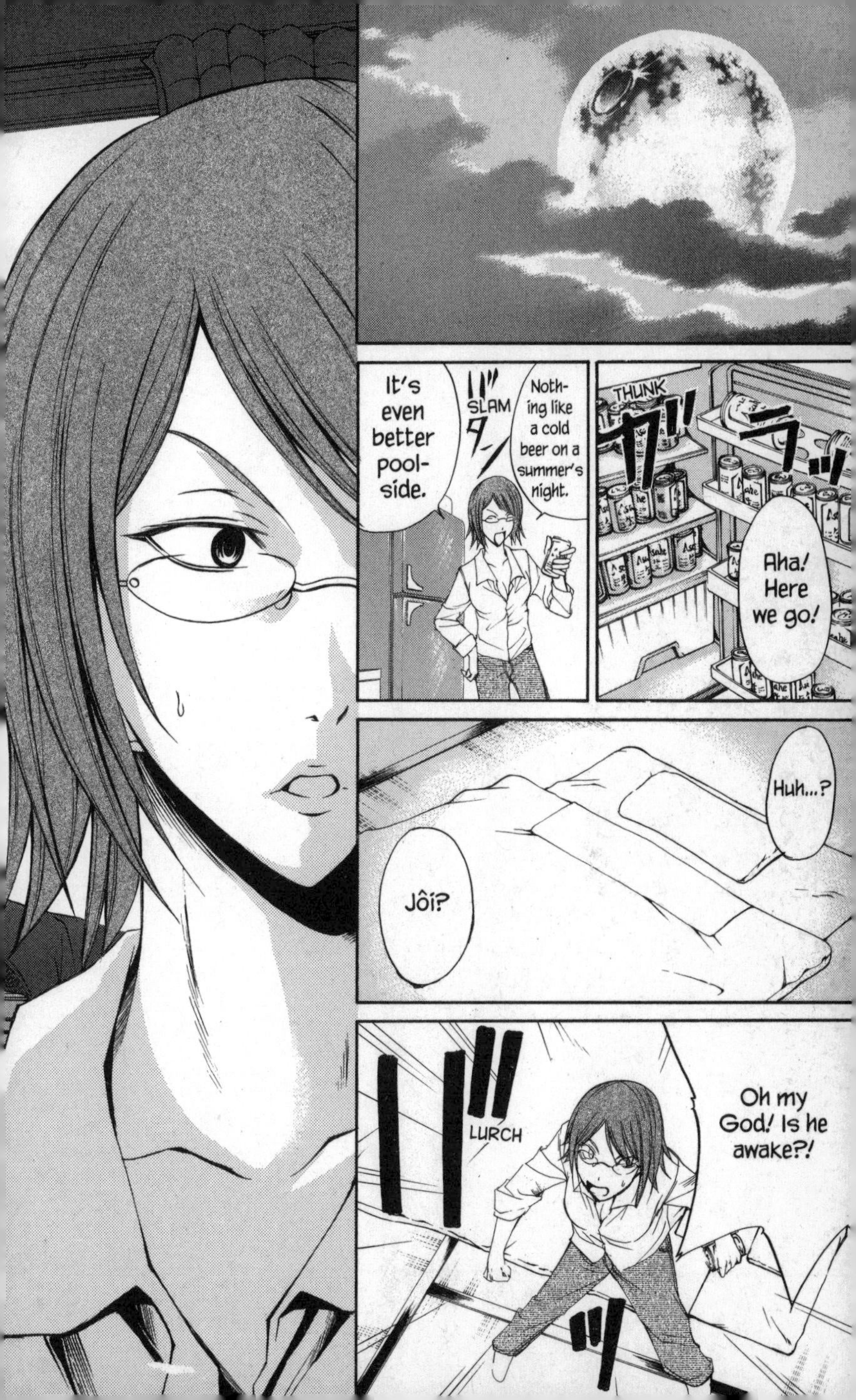
THUNK
Aha! Here we go!
Nothing like a cold beer on a summer's night.
SLAM
It's even better poolside.
Huh...?
Jôi?
Oh my God! Is he awake?!
LURCH

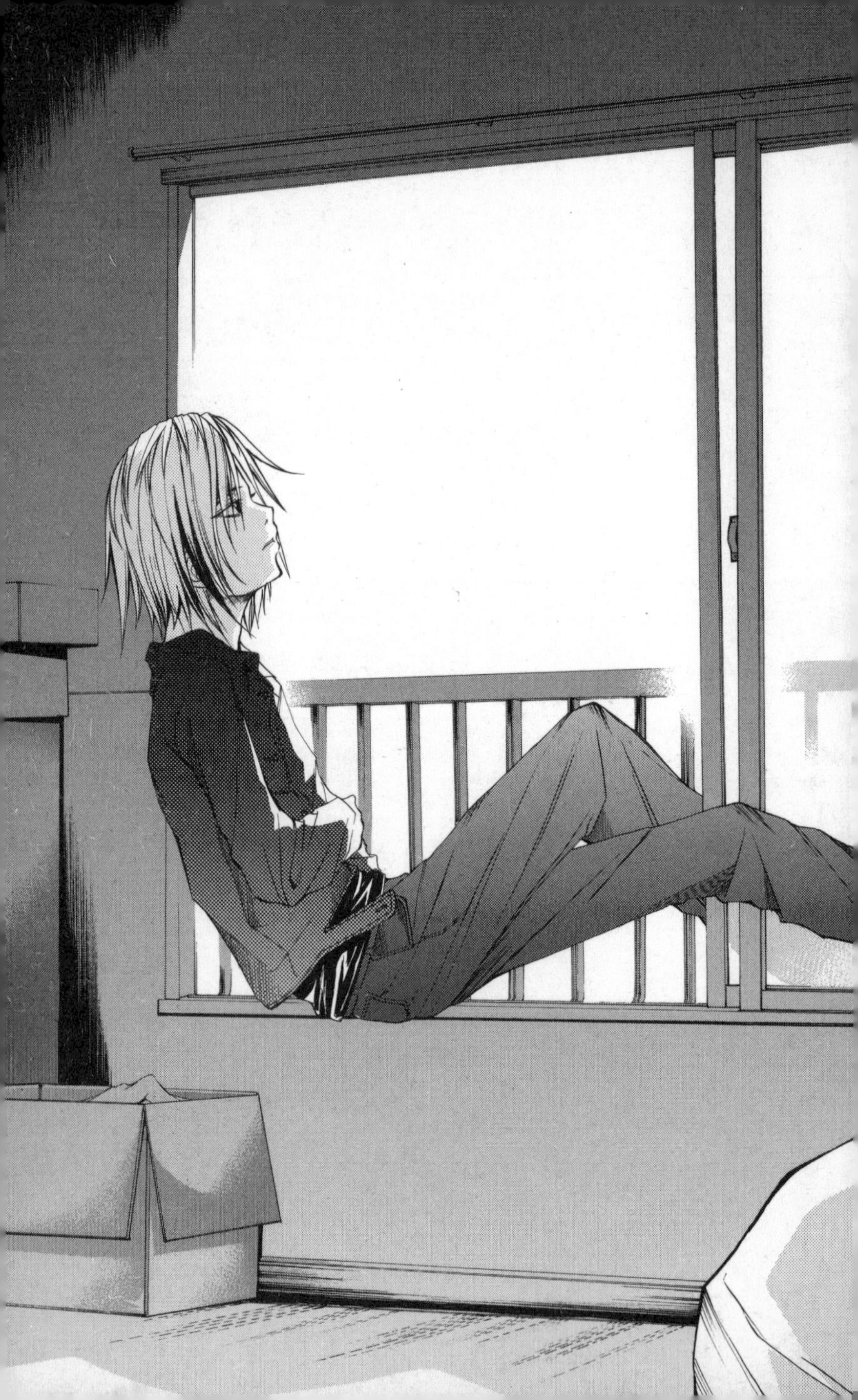

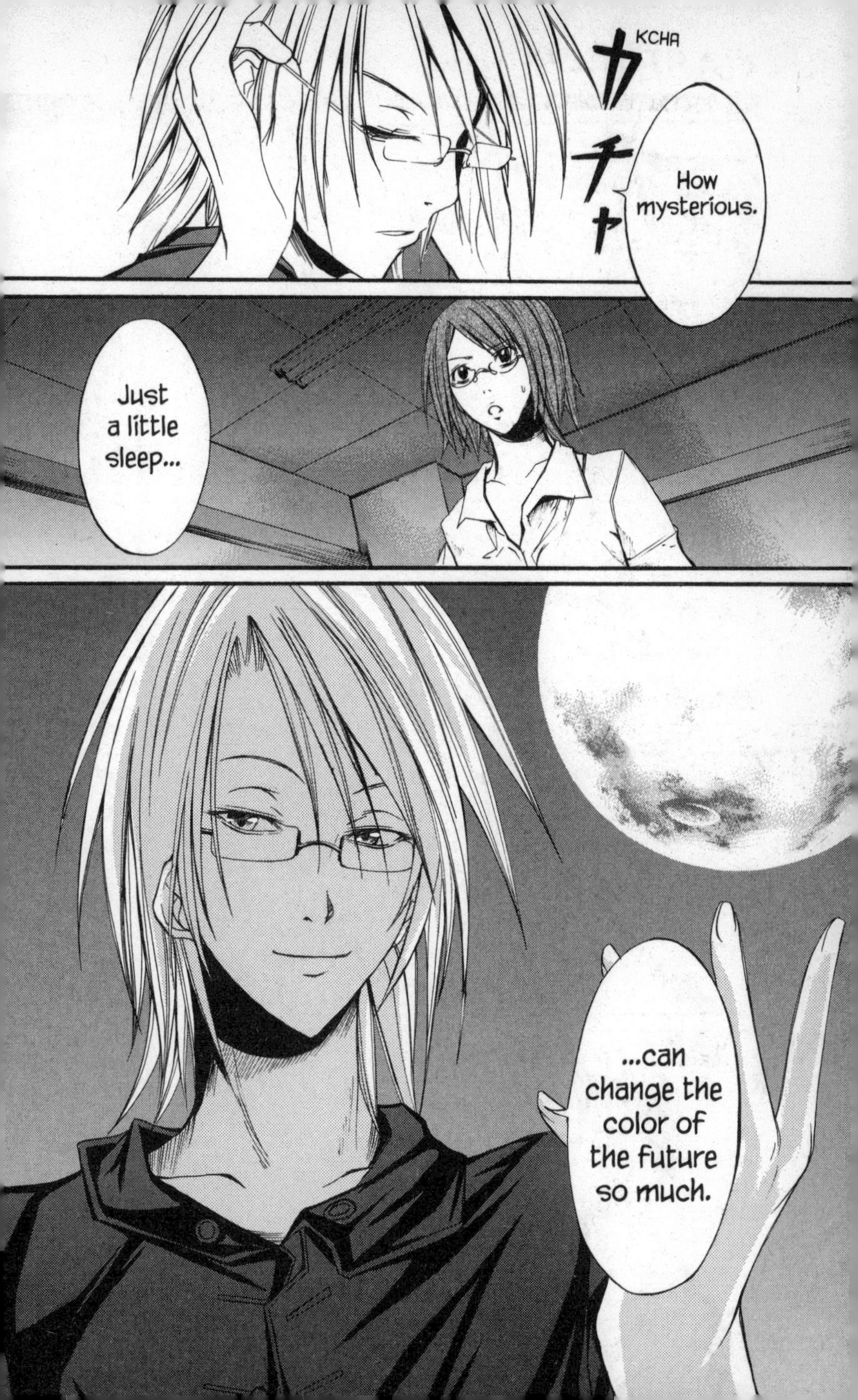

カチャ KCHA
How mysterious.
Just a little sleep...
...can change the color of the future so much.

CASE 6 – Future

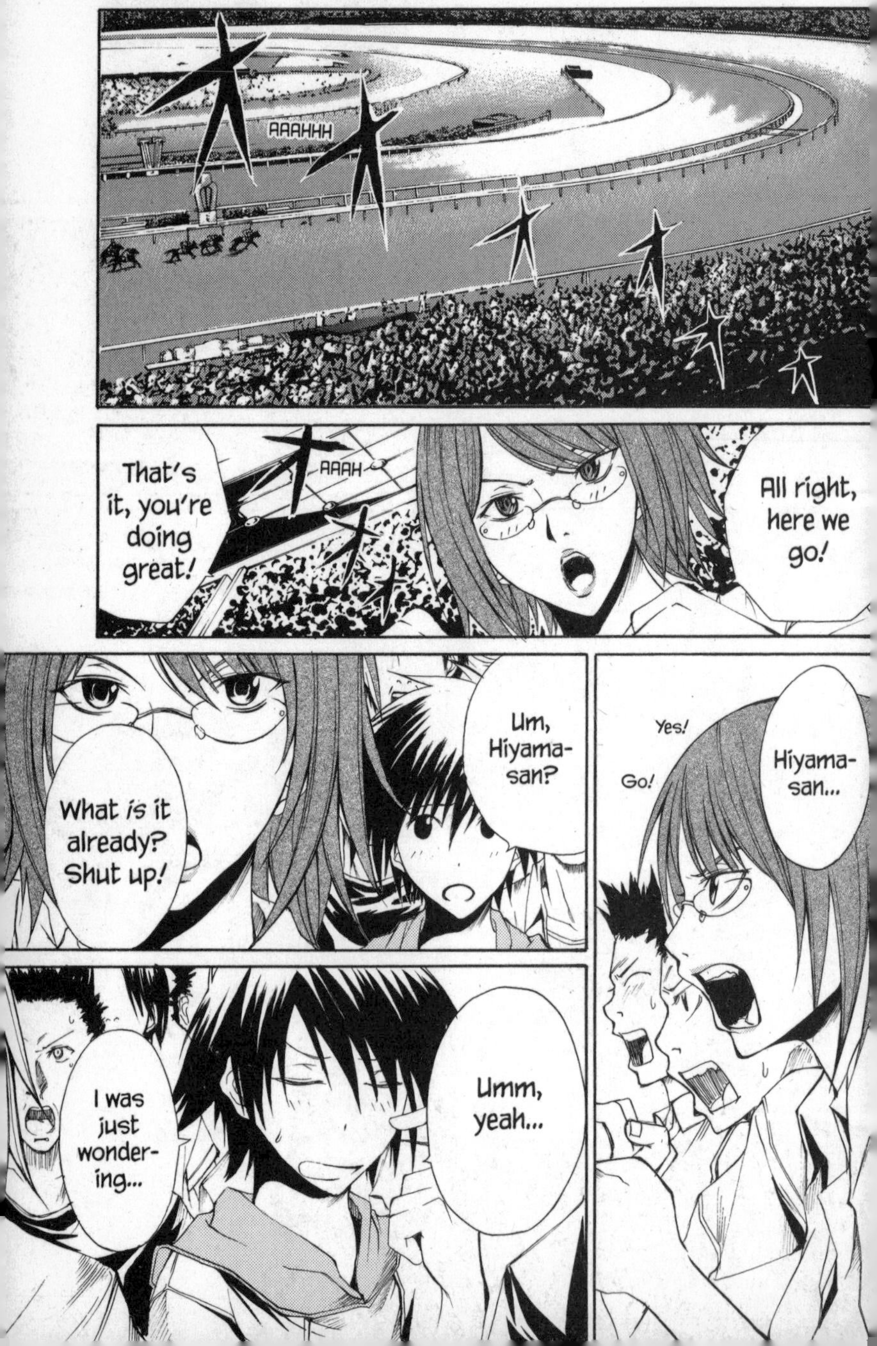
AAAHHH
All right, here we go!
AAAH
That's it, you're doing great!
Hiyama-san...
Yes!
Go!
Um, Hiyama-san?
What *is* it already? Shut up!
Umm, yeah...
I was just wonder-ing...

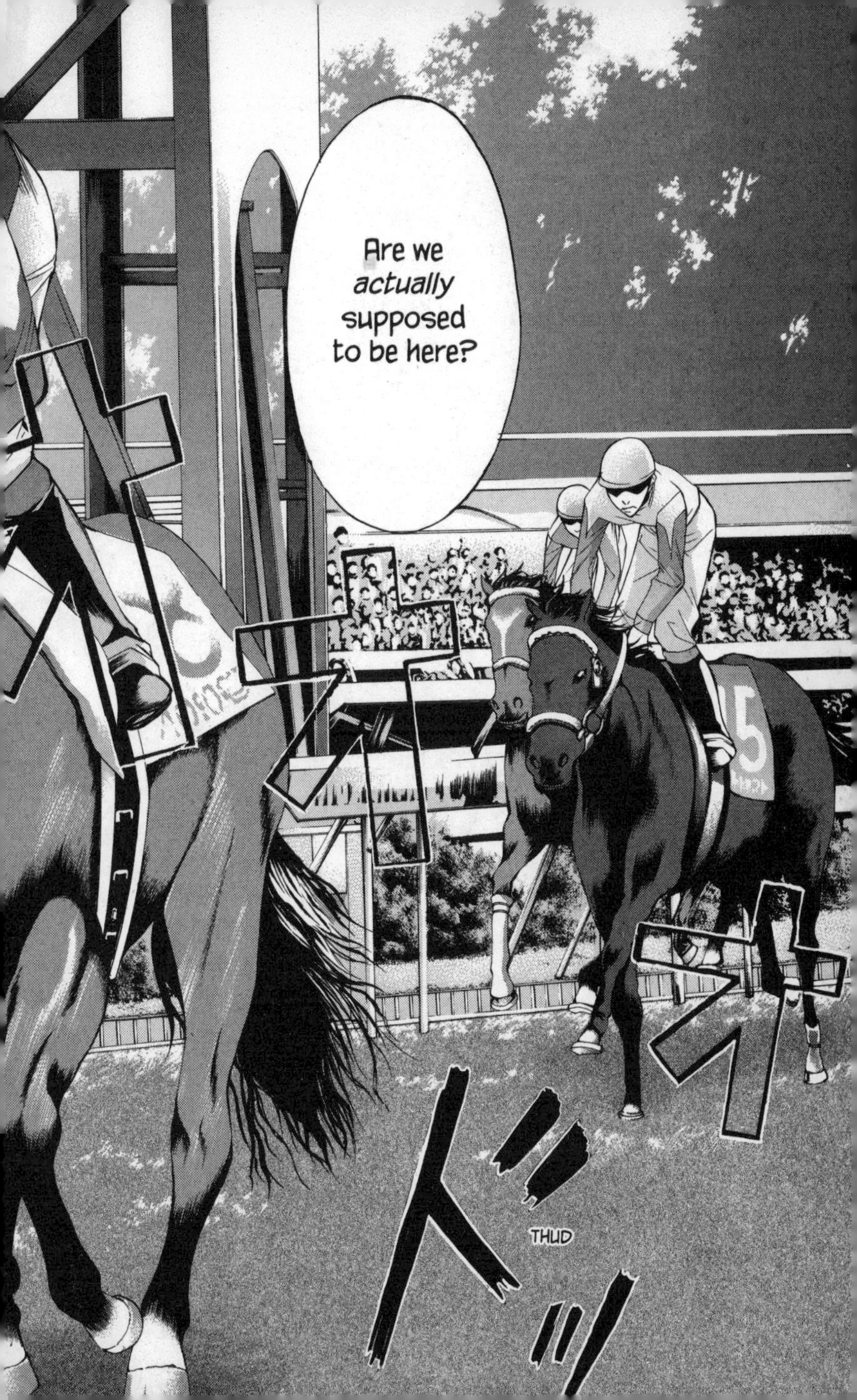
Are we *actually* supposed to be here?
THUD

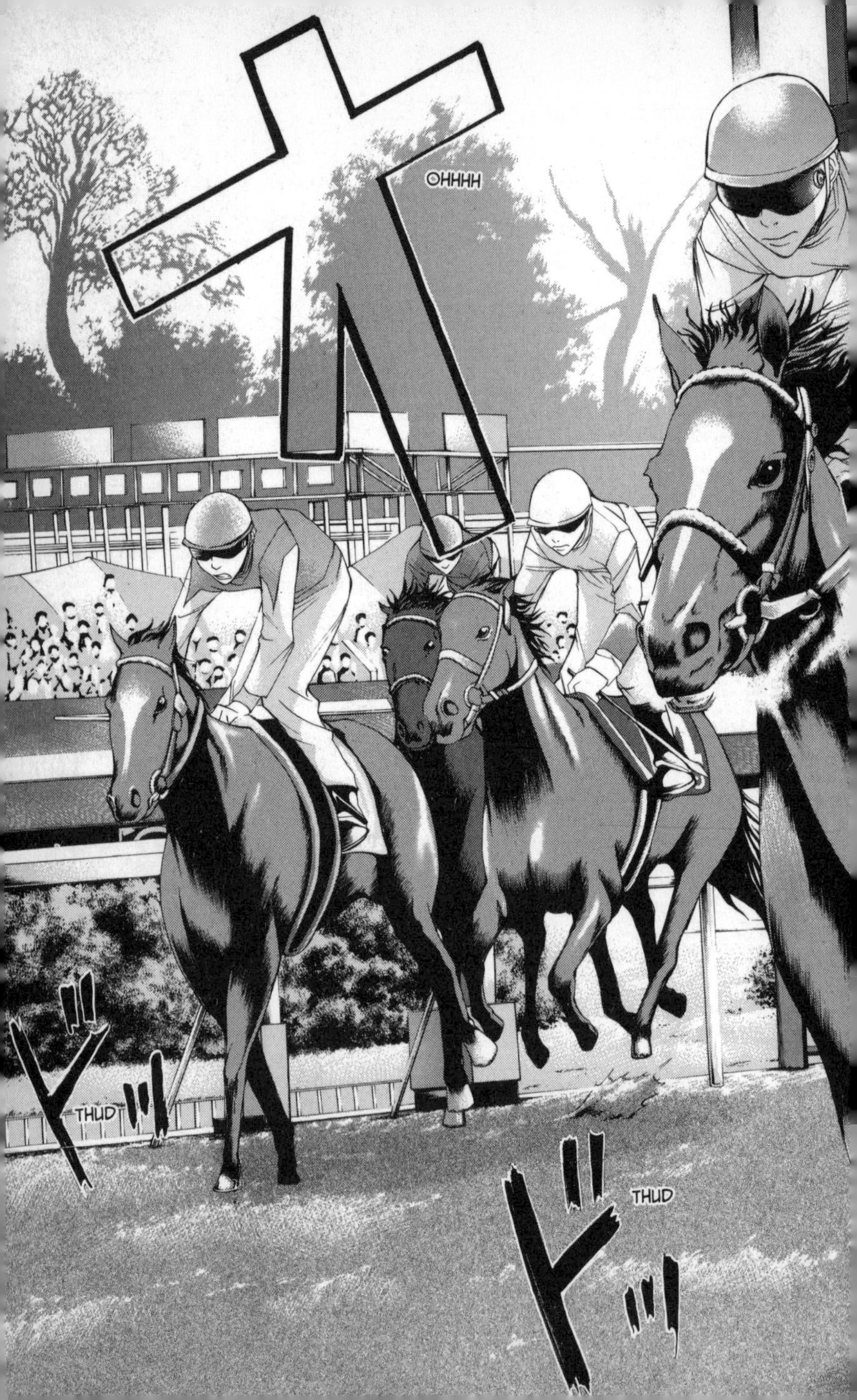
OHHHH
THUD
THUD

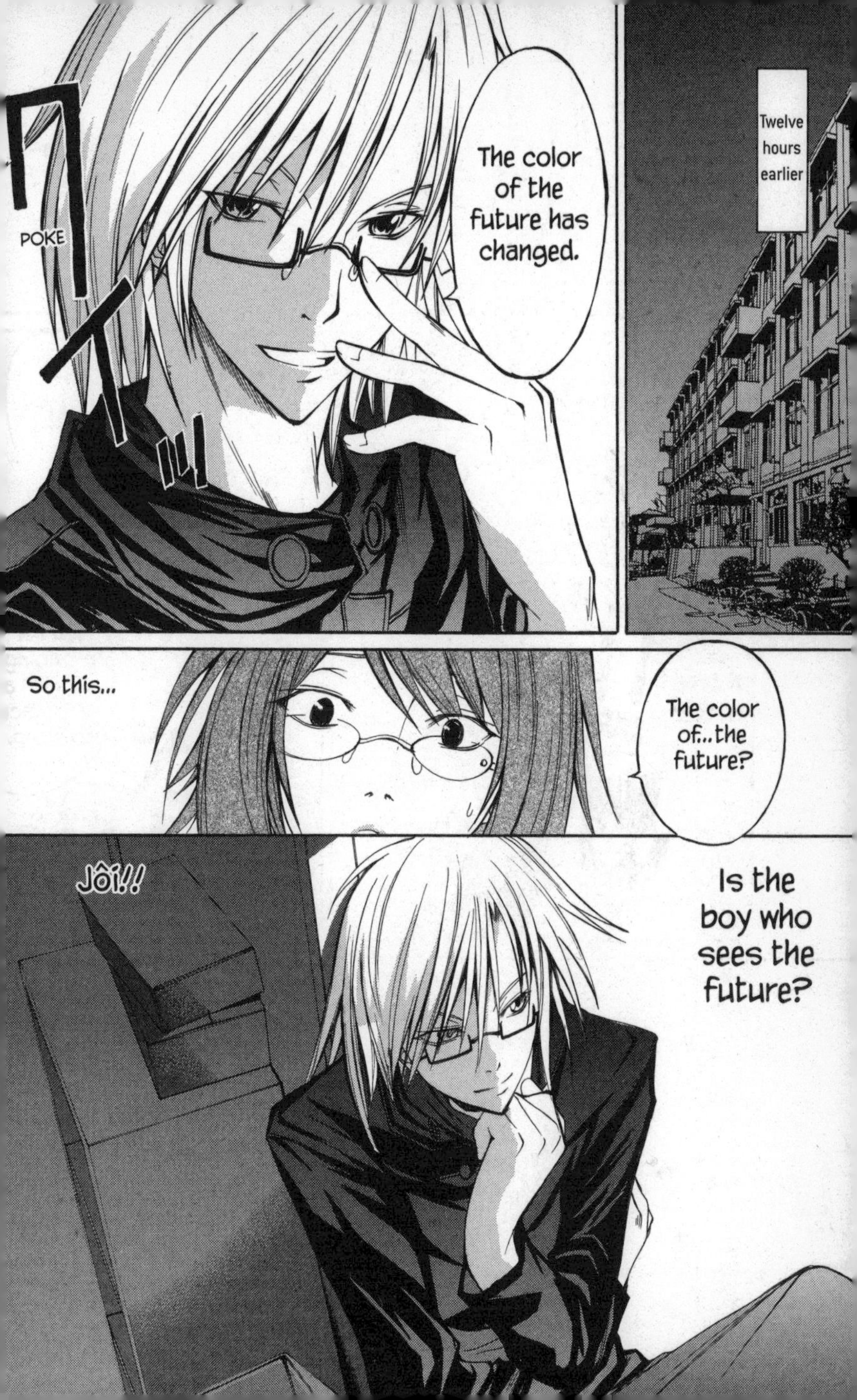

Twelve hours earlier
The color of the future has changed.
POKE
The color of...the future?
So this...
Is the boy who sees the future?
Jôi!!

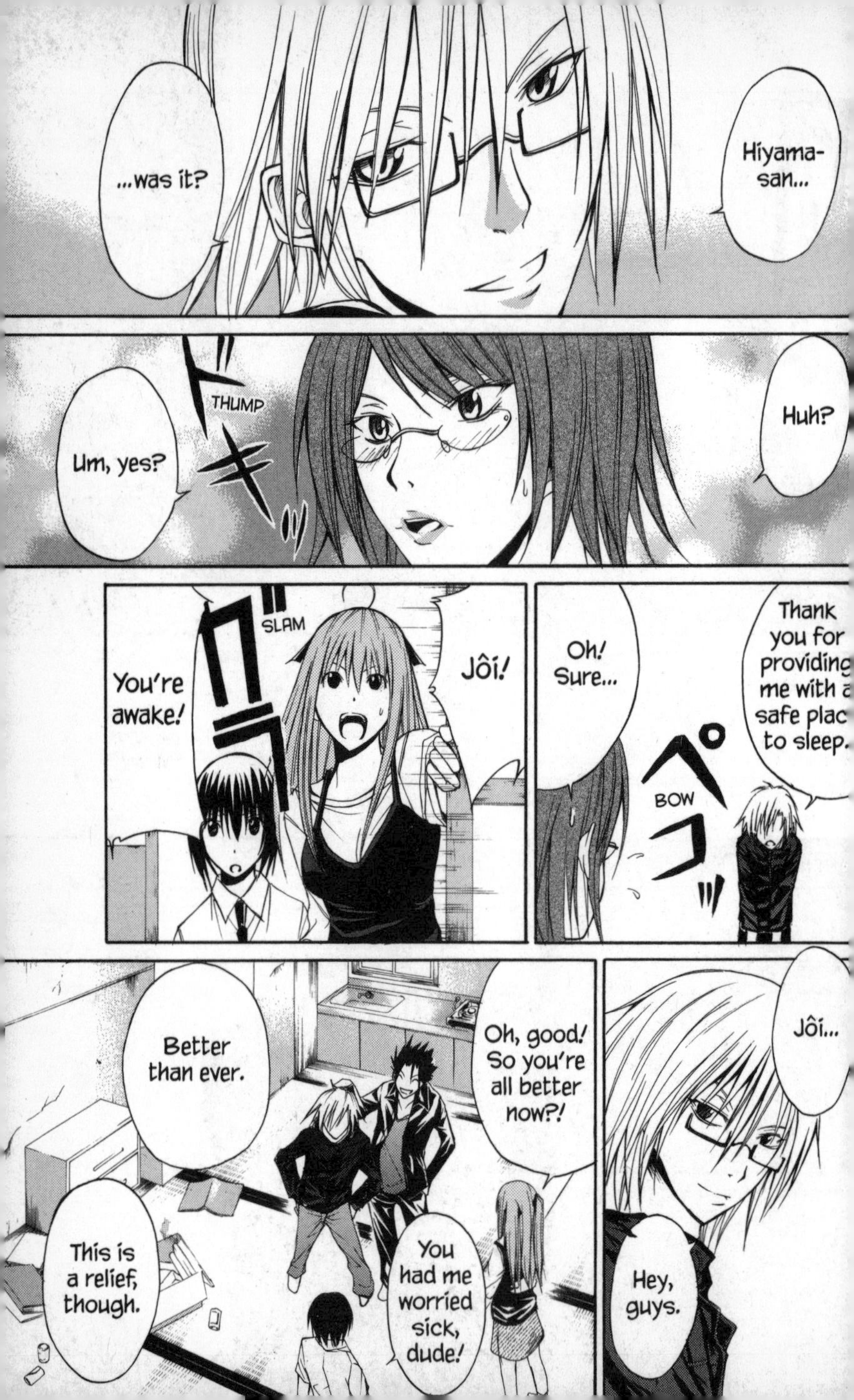
Hiyama-san...
...was it?
Huh?
THUMP
Um, yes?
Thank you for providing me with a safe plac to sleep.
BOW
Oh! Sure...
Jôi!
SLAM
You're awake!
Jôi...
Hey, guys.
Oh, good! So you're all better now?!
Better than ever.
You had me worried sick, dude!
This is a relief, though.

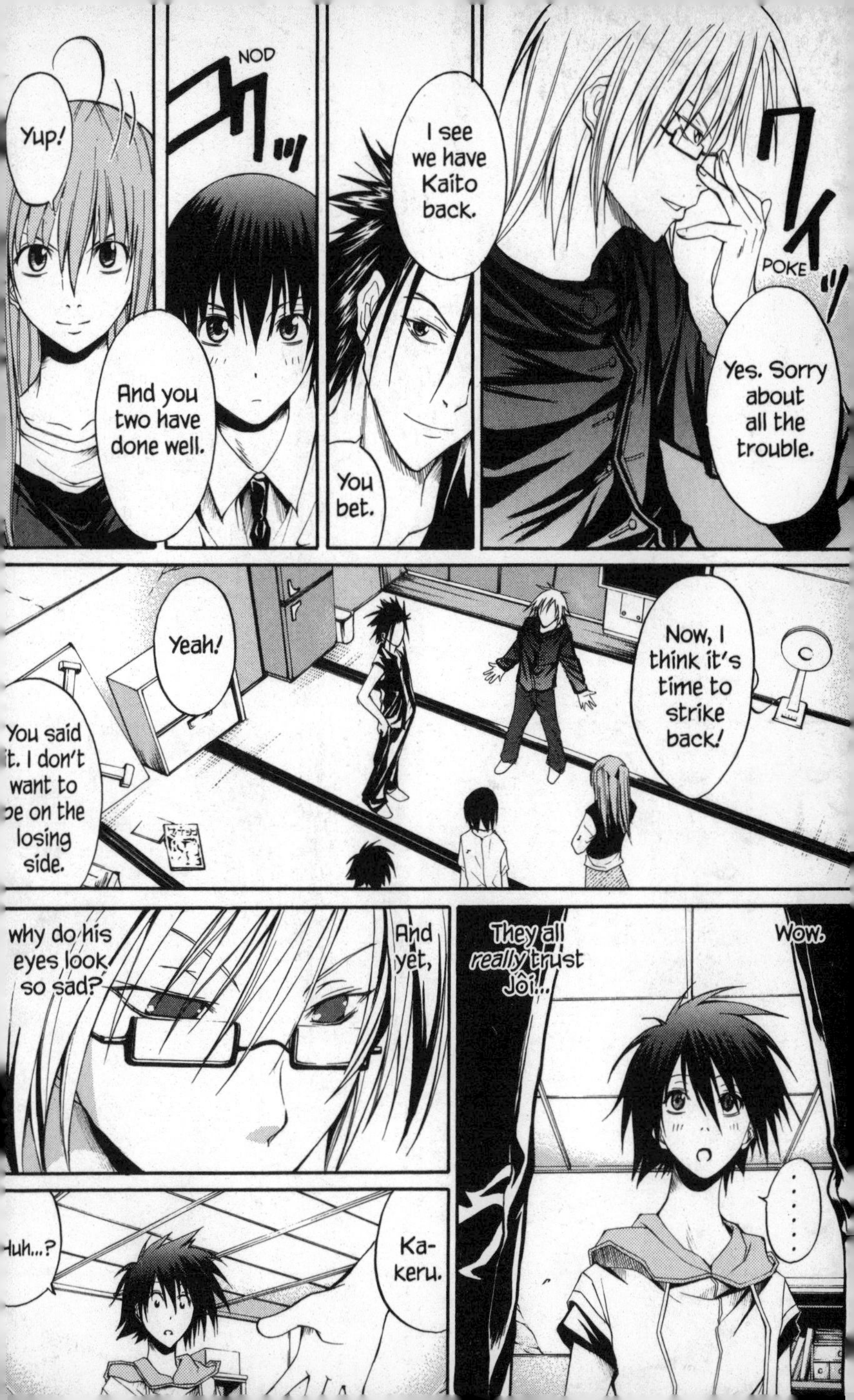
POKE
Yes. Sorry about all the trouble.
I see we have Kaito back.
You bet.
NOD
And you two have done well.
Yup!
Now, I think it's time to strike back!
Yeah!
You said it. I don't want to be on the losing side.
Wow.
They all *really* trust Jôi...
......
And yet,
why do his eyes look so sad?
Ka-keru.
Huh...?

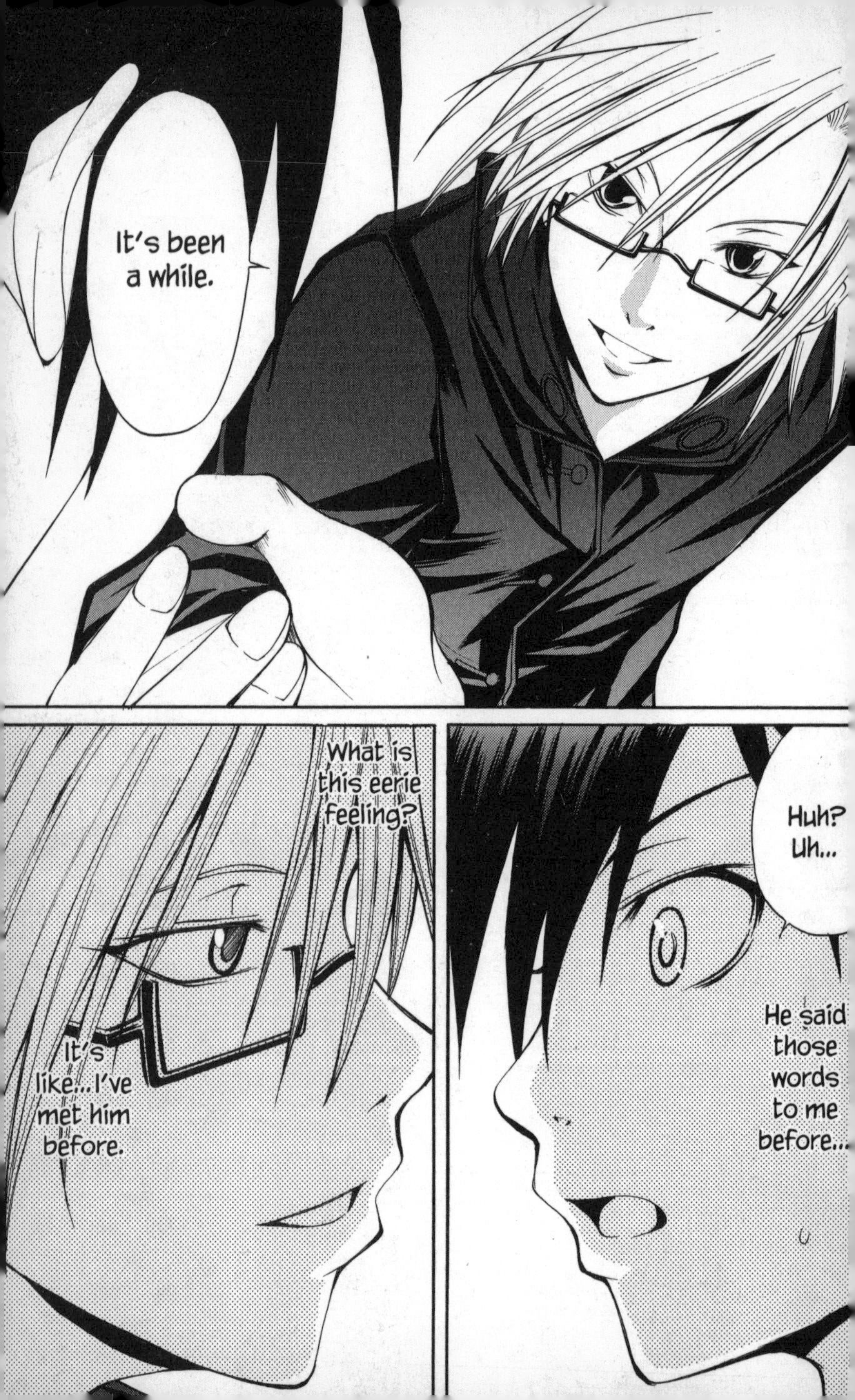
It's been a while.
Huh? Uh...
He said those words to me before...
What is this eerie feeling?
It's like...I've met him before.

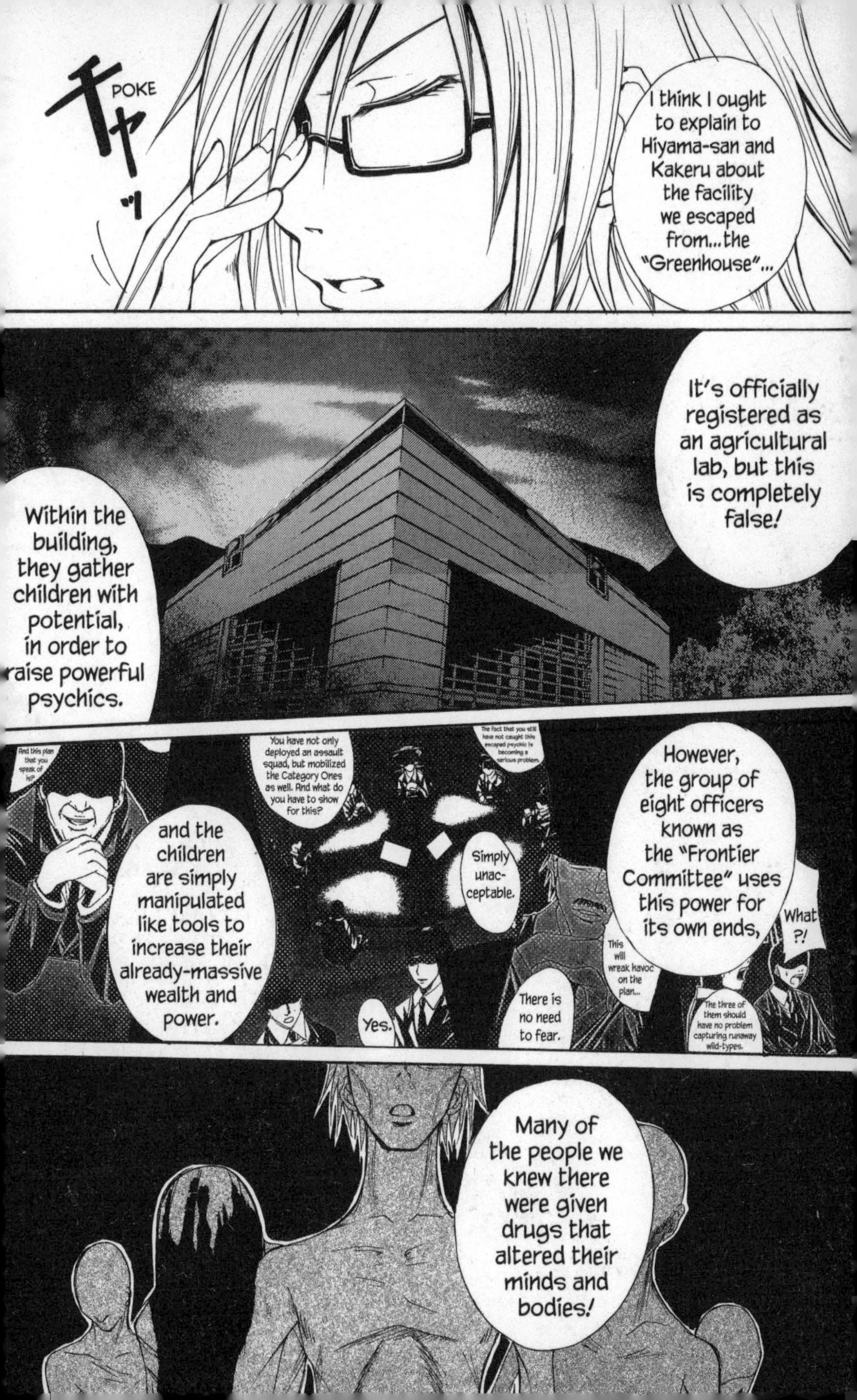
I think I ought to explain to Hiyama-san and Kakeru about the facility we escaped from...the "Greenhouse"...
POKE
It's officially registered as an agricultural lab, but this is completely false!
Within the building, they gather children with potential, in order to raise powerful psychics.
However, the group of eight officers known as the "Frontier Committee" uses this power for its own ends,
What ?!
The three of them should have no problem capturing runaway wild-types.
This will wreak havoc on the plan...
There is no need to fear.
The fact that you still have not caught this escaped psychic is becoming a serious problem.
Simply unac-ceptable.
You have not only deployed an assault squad, but mobilized the Category Ones as well. And what do you have to show for this?
Yes.
and the children are simply manipulated like tools to increase their already-massive wealth and power.
And this plan that you speak of is?
Many of the people we knew there were given drugs that altered their minds and bodies!

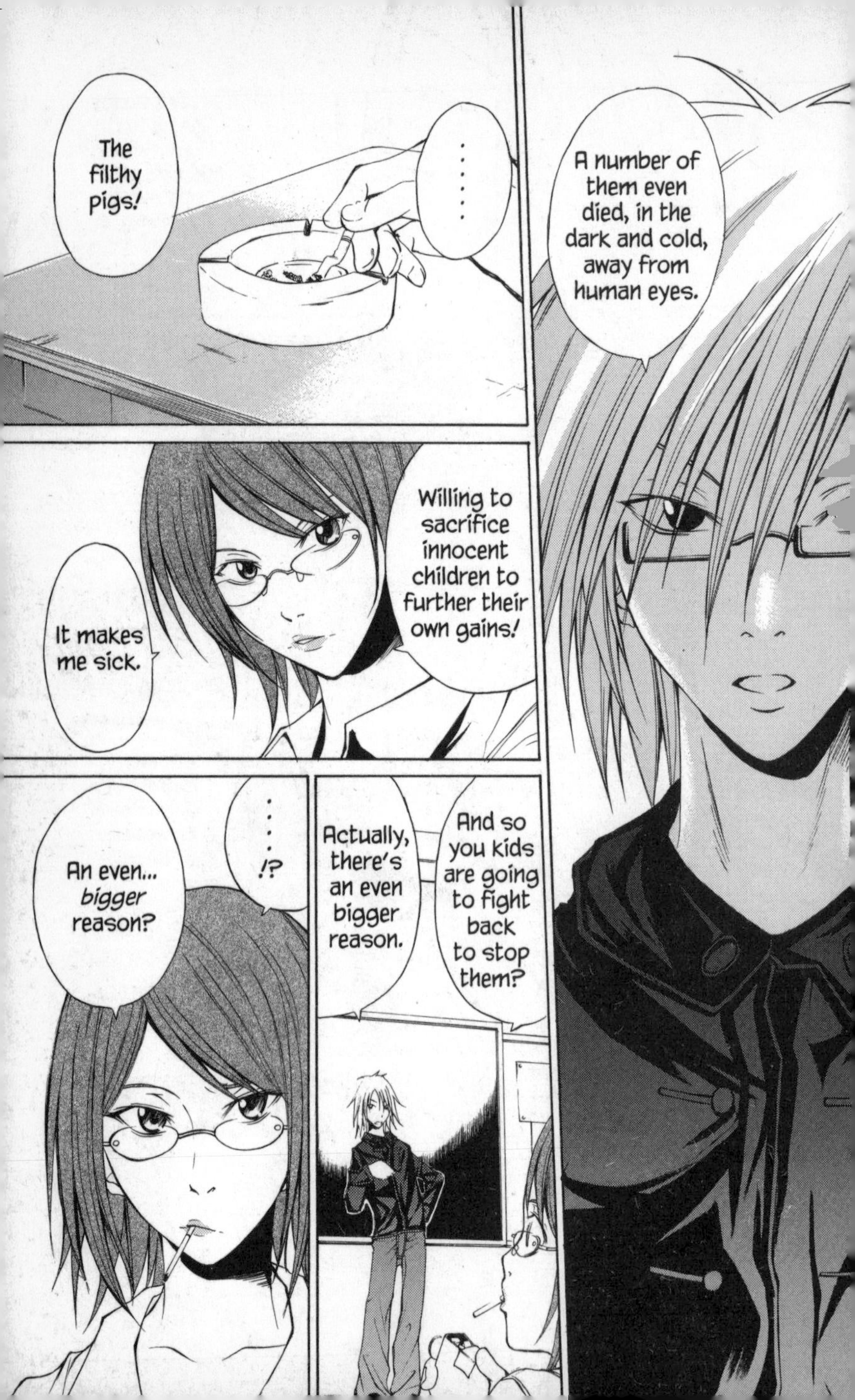

A number of them even died, in the dark and cold, away from human eyes.
......
The filthy pigs!
Willing to sacrifice innocent children to further their own gains!
It makes me sick.
And so you kids are going to fight back to stop them?
Actually, there's an even bigger reason.
......!?
An even... *bigger* reason?

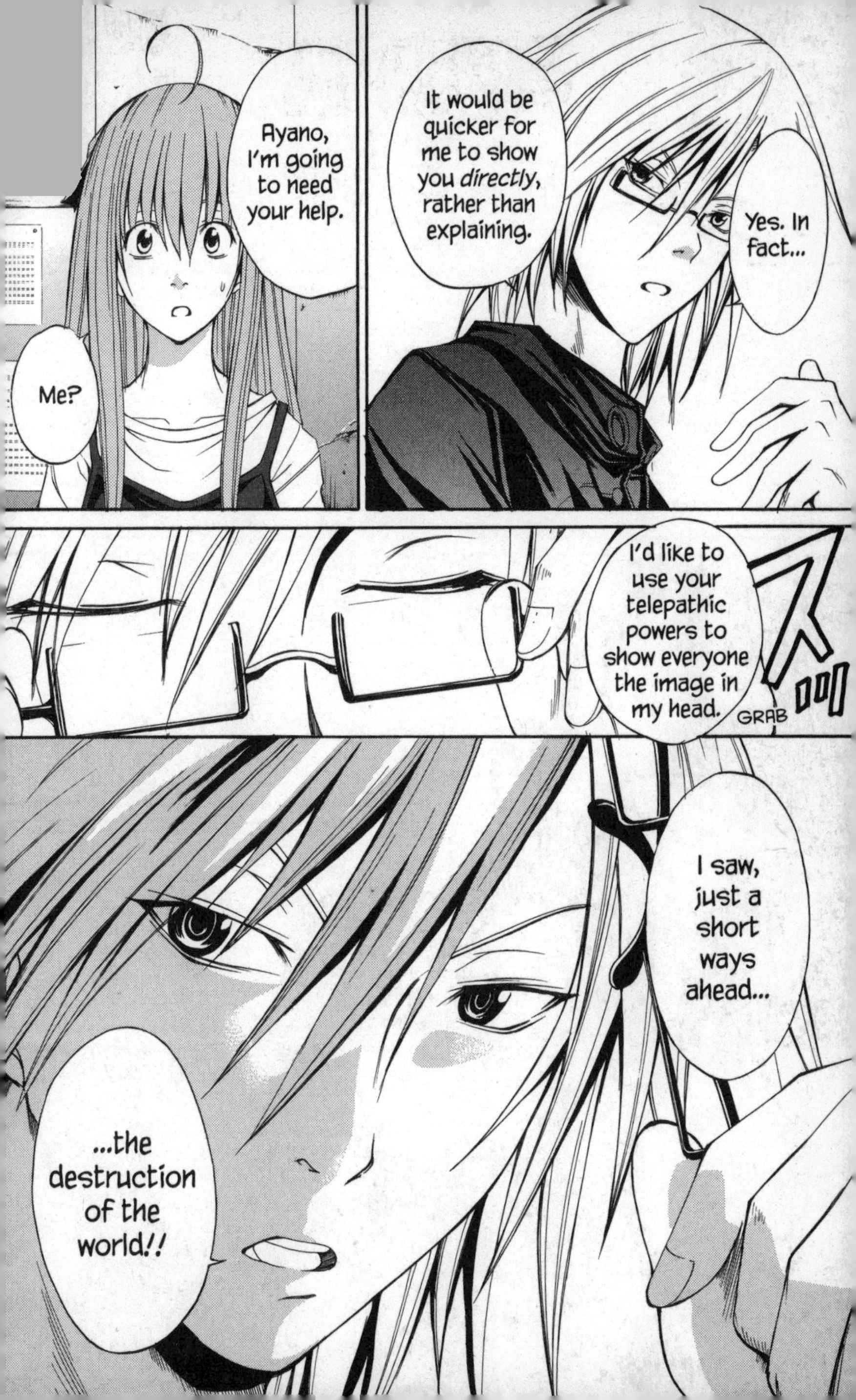
It would be quicker for me to show you *directly*, rather than explaining.
Ayano, I'm going to need your help.
Me?
Yes. In fact...
I'd like to use your telepathic powers to show everyone the image in my head.
GRAB
I saw, just a short ways ahead...
...the destruction of the world!!

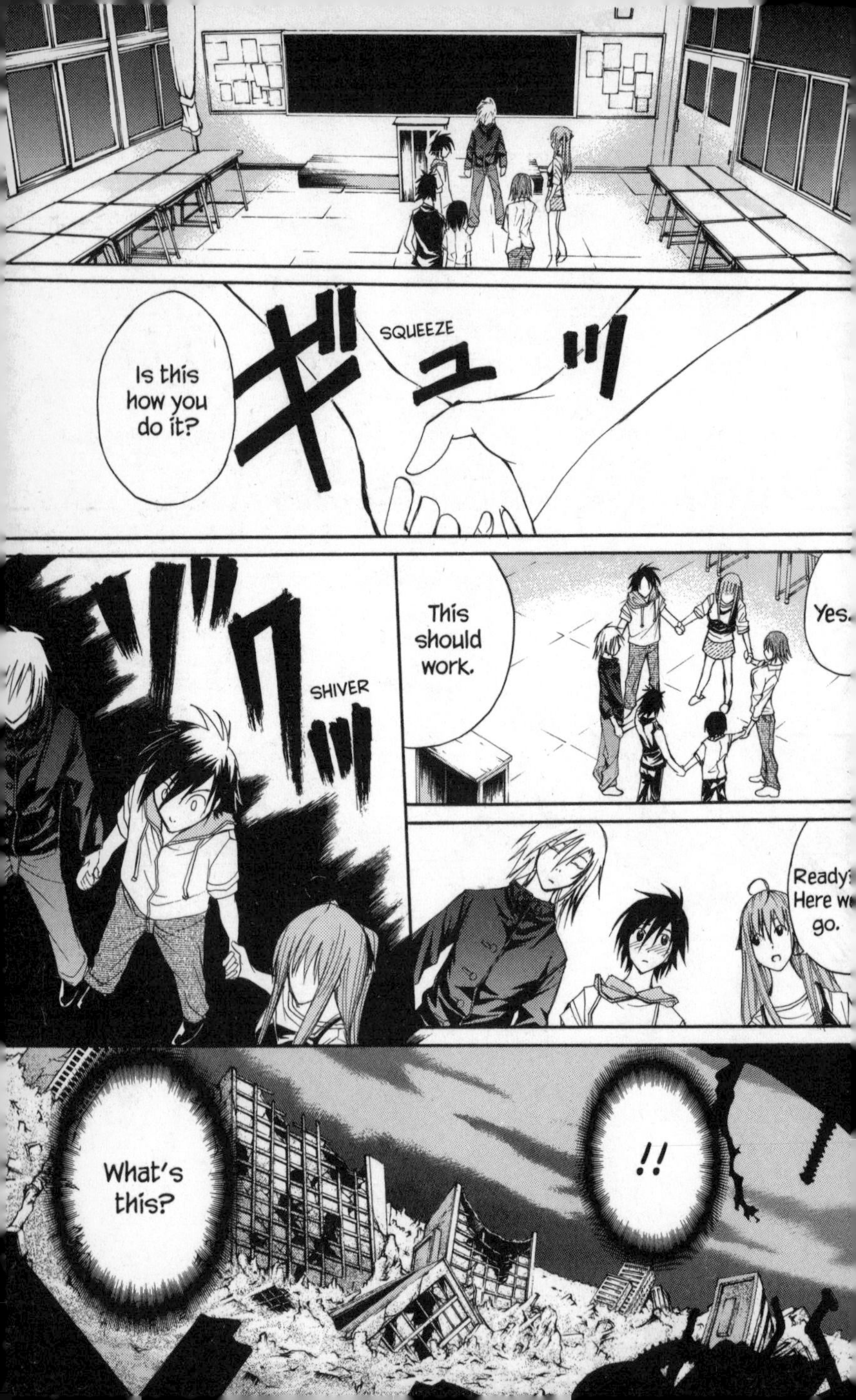
SQUEEZE
Is this how you do it?
Yes.
This should work.
Ready? Here we go.
SHIVER
!!
What's this?

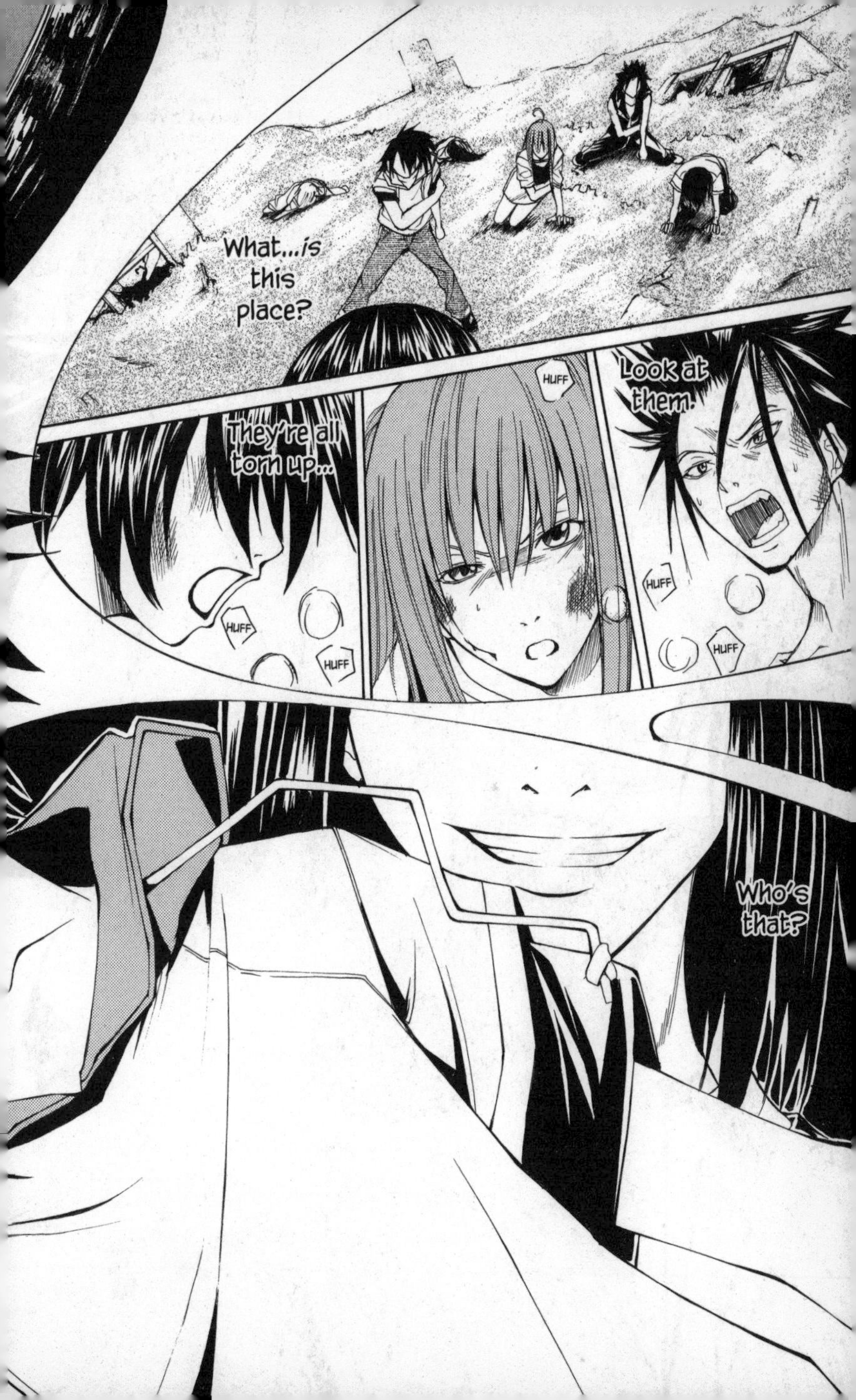
What...is this place?
Look at them.
HUFF
HUFF
HUFF
They're all torn up...
HUFF
HUFF
Who's that?

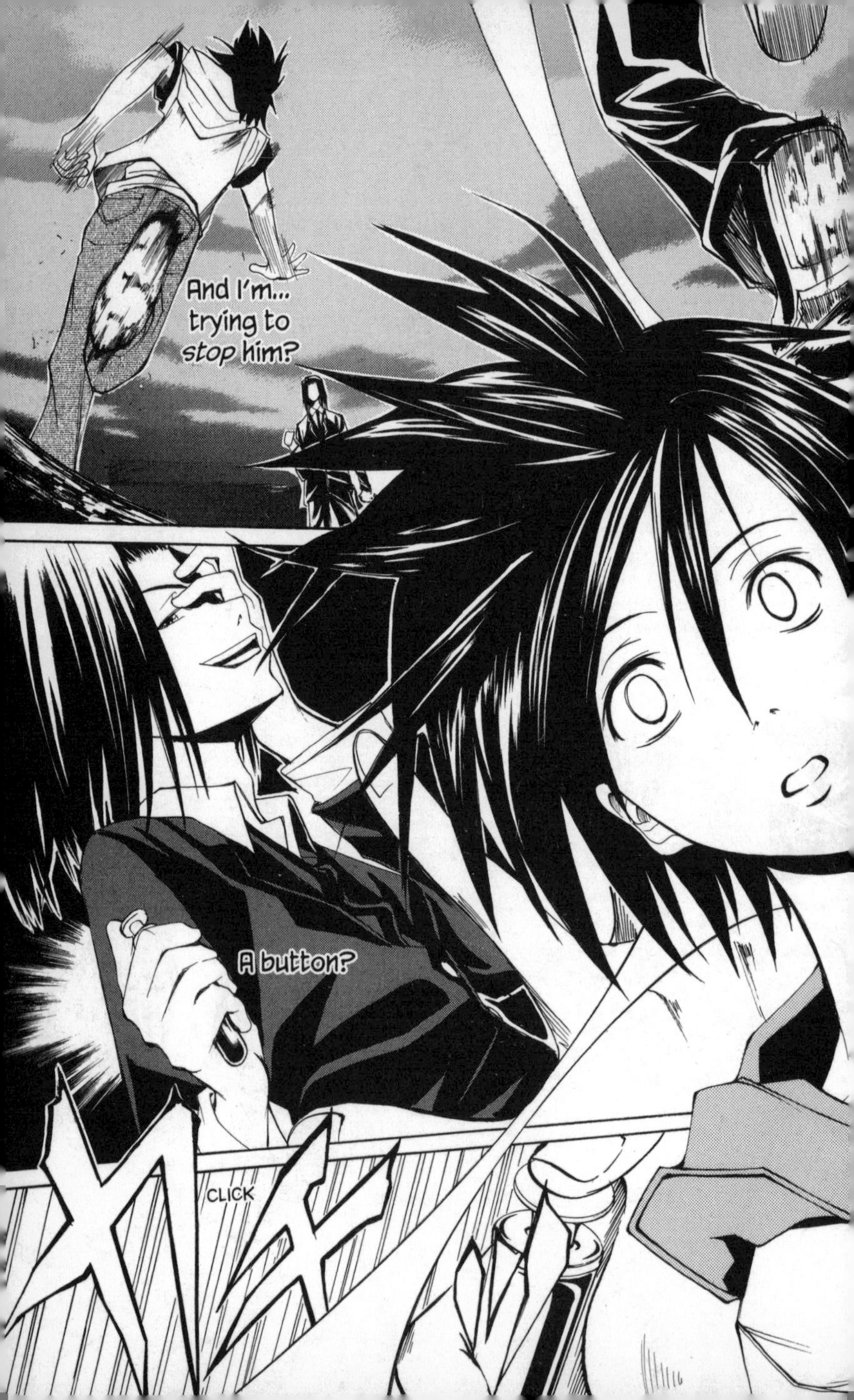
And I'm... trying to stop him?
A button?
CLICK

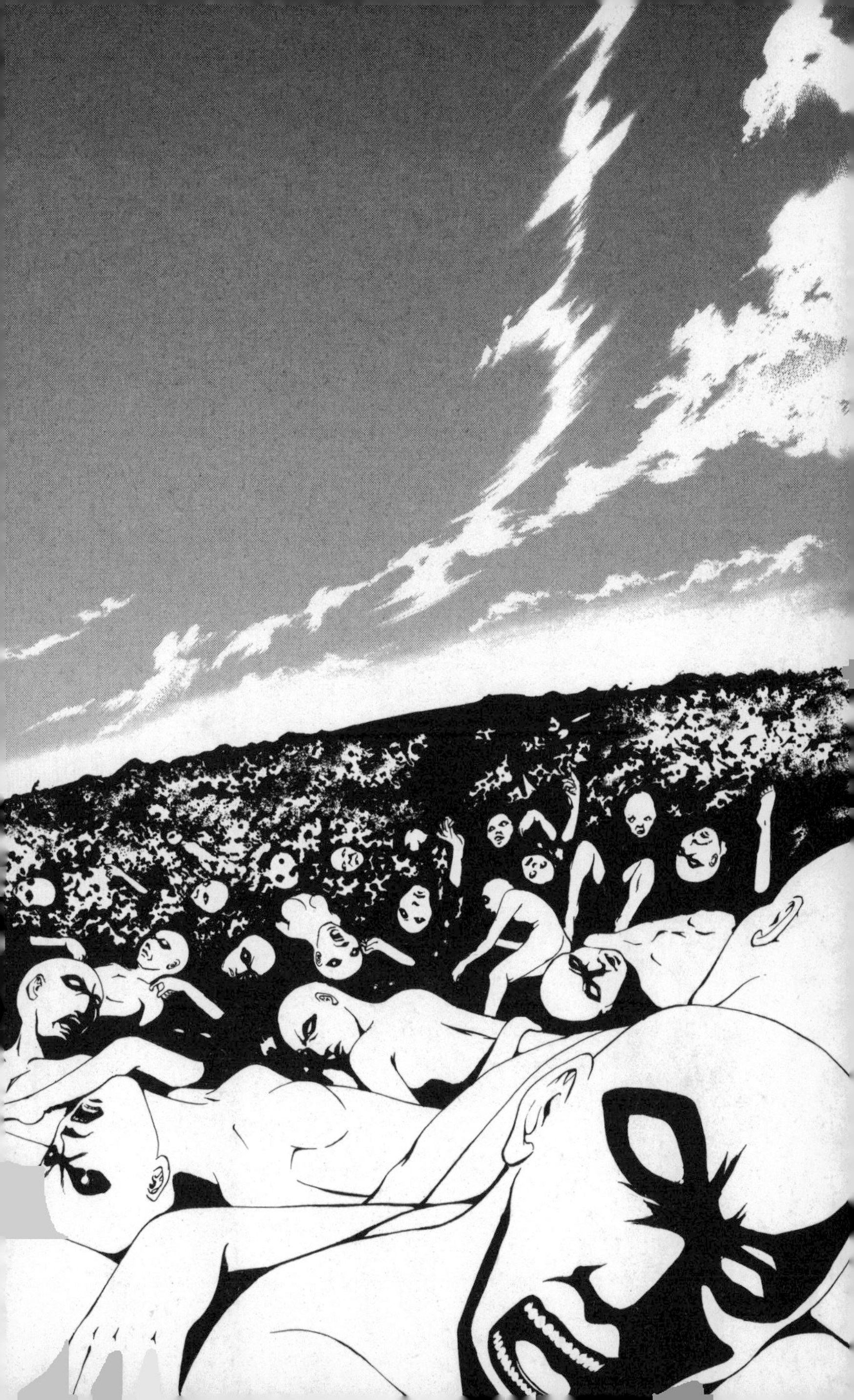

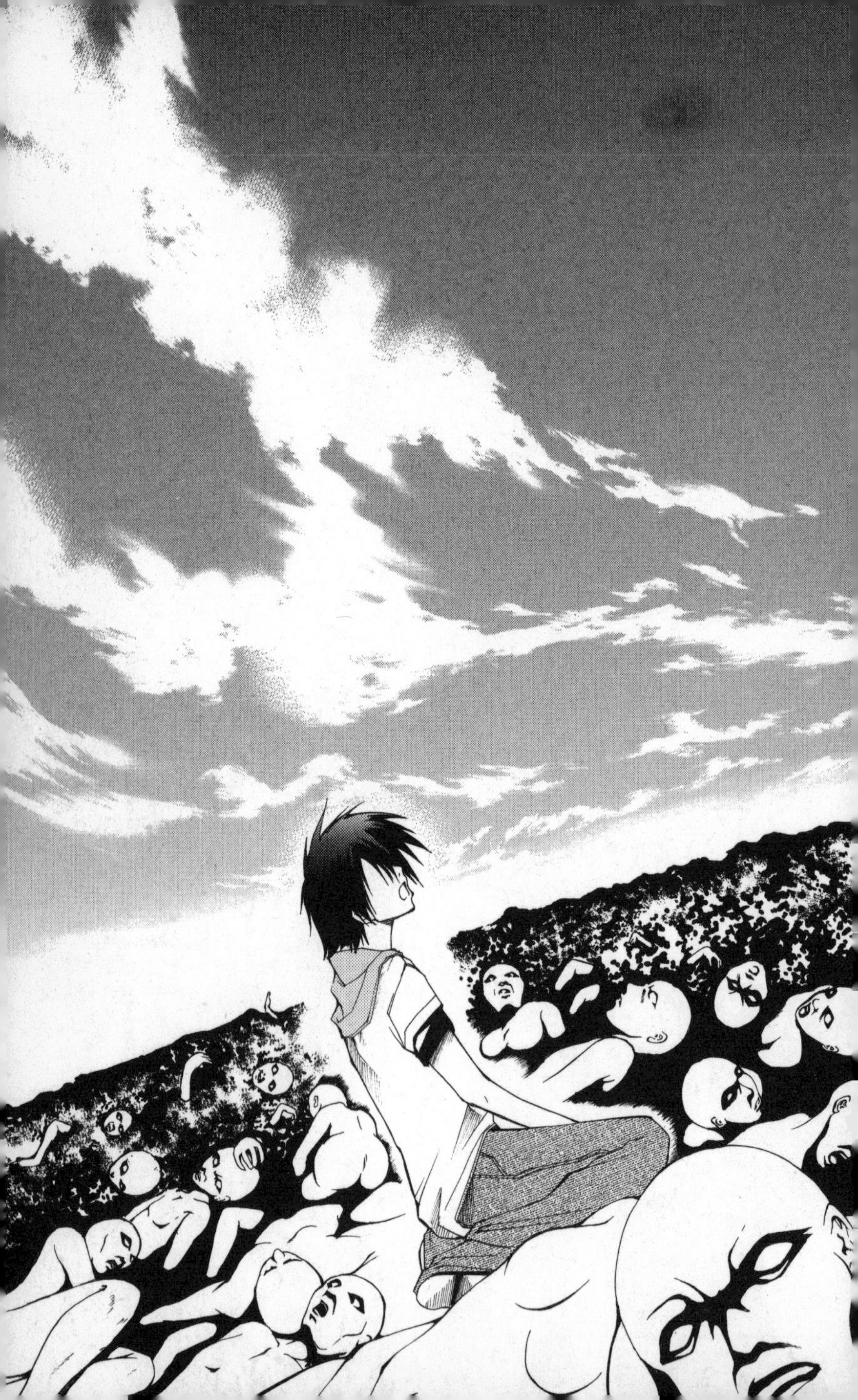

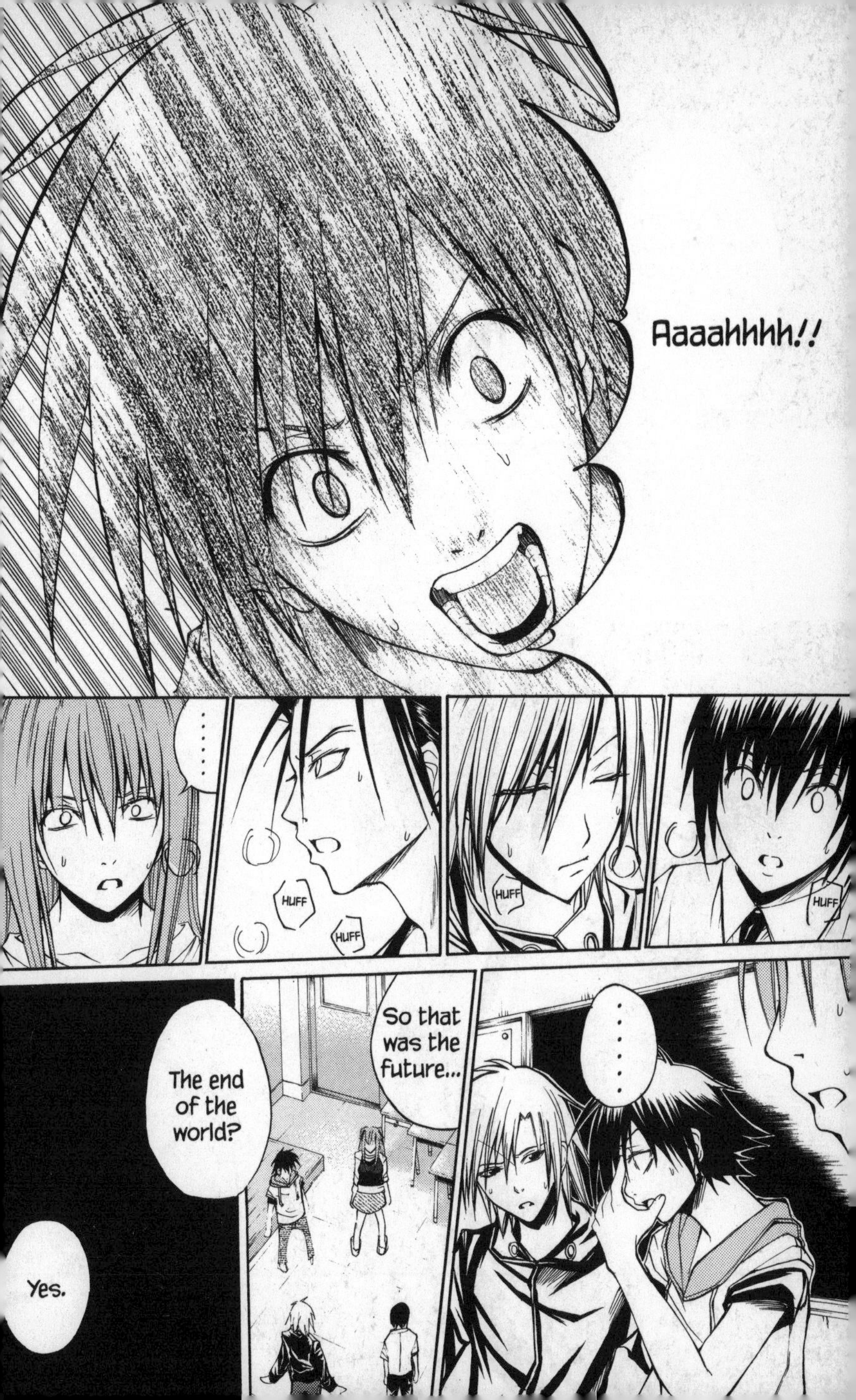
Aaaahhhh!!
HUFF
HUFF
HUFF
HUFF
......
......
So that was the future...
The end of the world?
Yes.

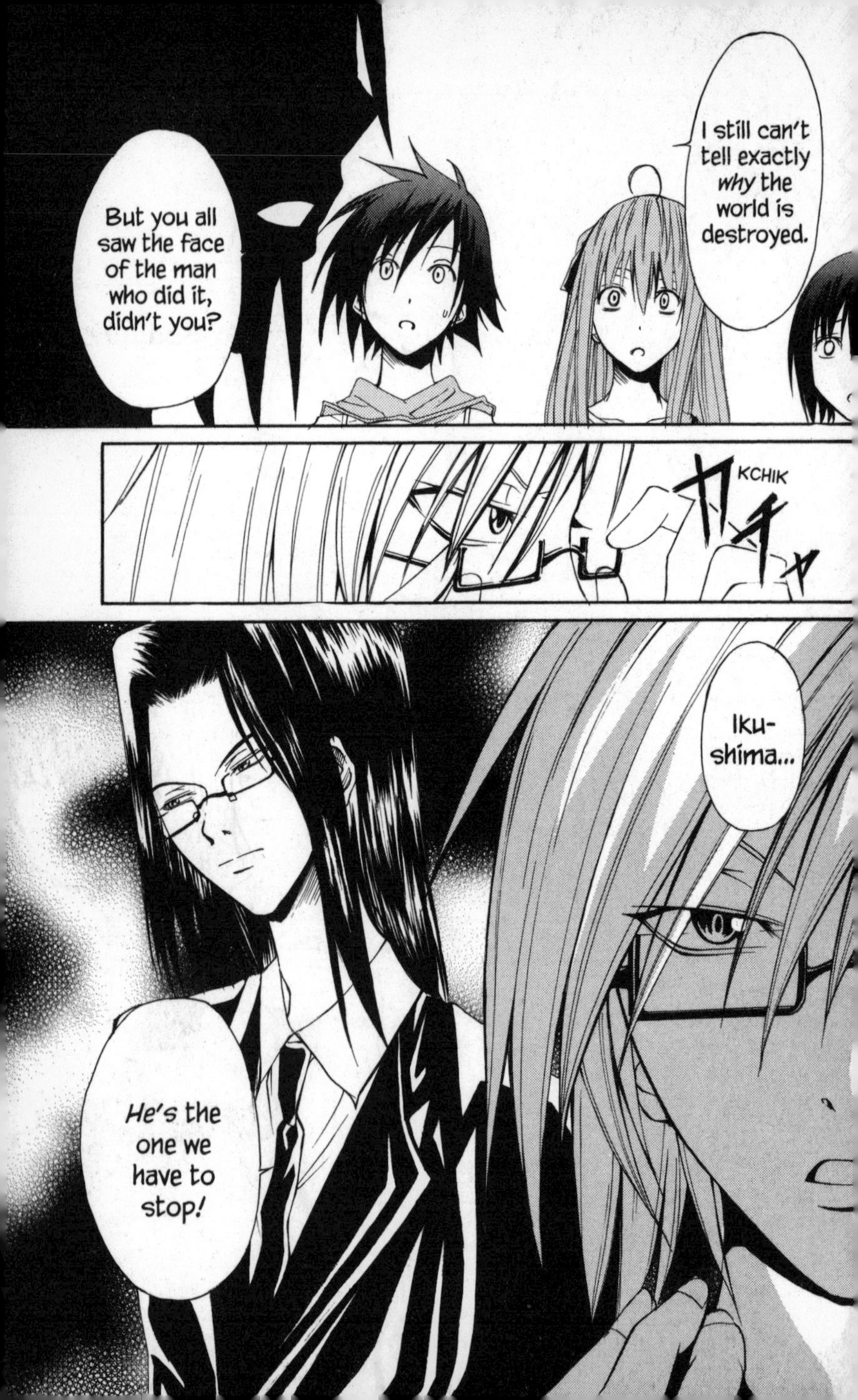
I still can't tell exactly *why* the world is destroyed.
But you all saw the face of the man who did it, didn't you?
カチャ
KCHIK
Iku-shima...
He's the one we have to stop!

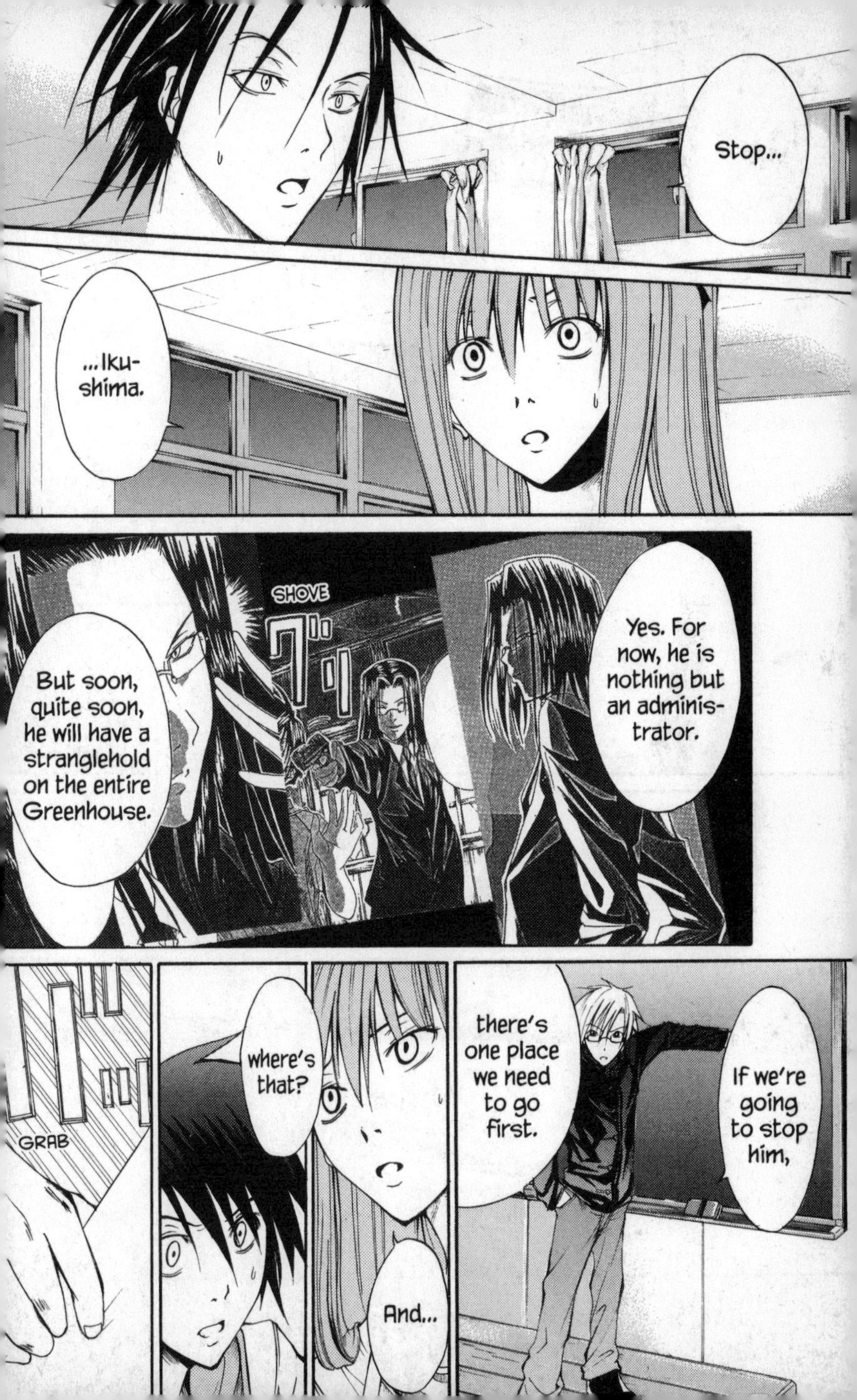
Stop...
...Iku-shima.
Yes. For now, he is nothing but an adminis-trator.
SHOVE
But soon, quite soon, he will have a stranglehold on the entire Greenhouse.
If we're going to stop him,
there's one place we need to go first.
And...
where's that?
GRAB

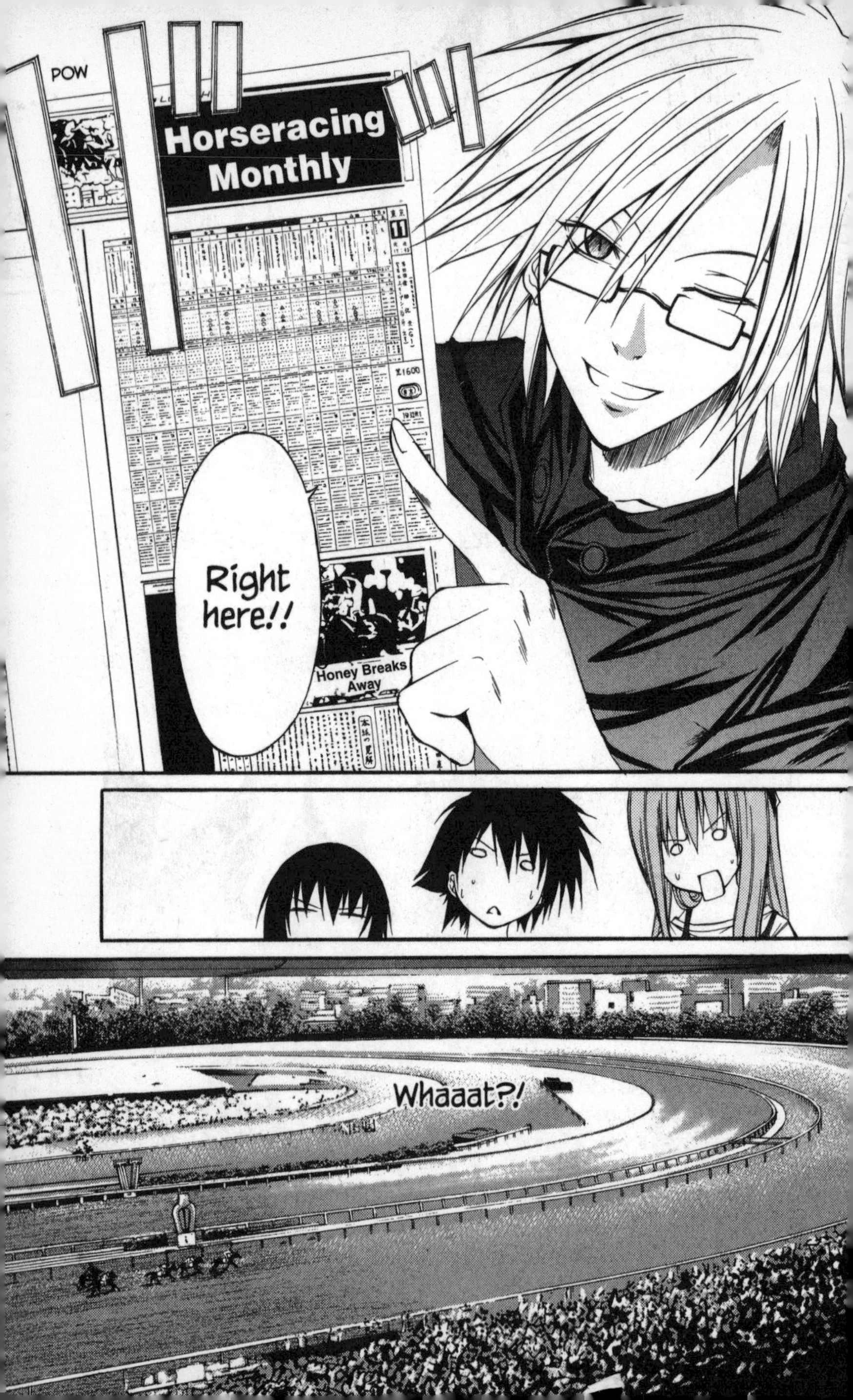
Horseracing Monthly
POW
Right here!!
Honey Breaks Away
Whaaat?!

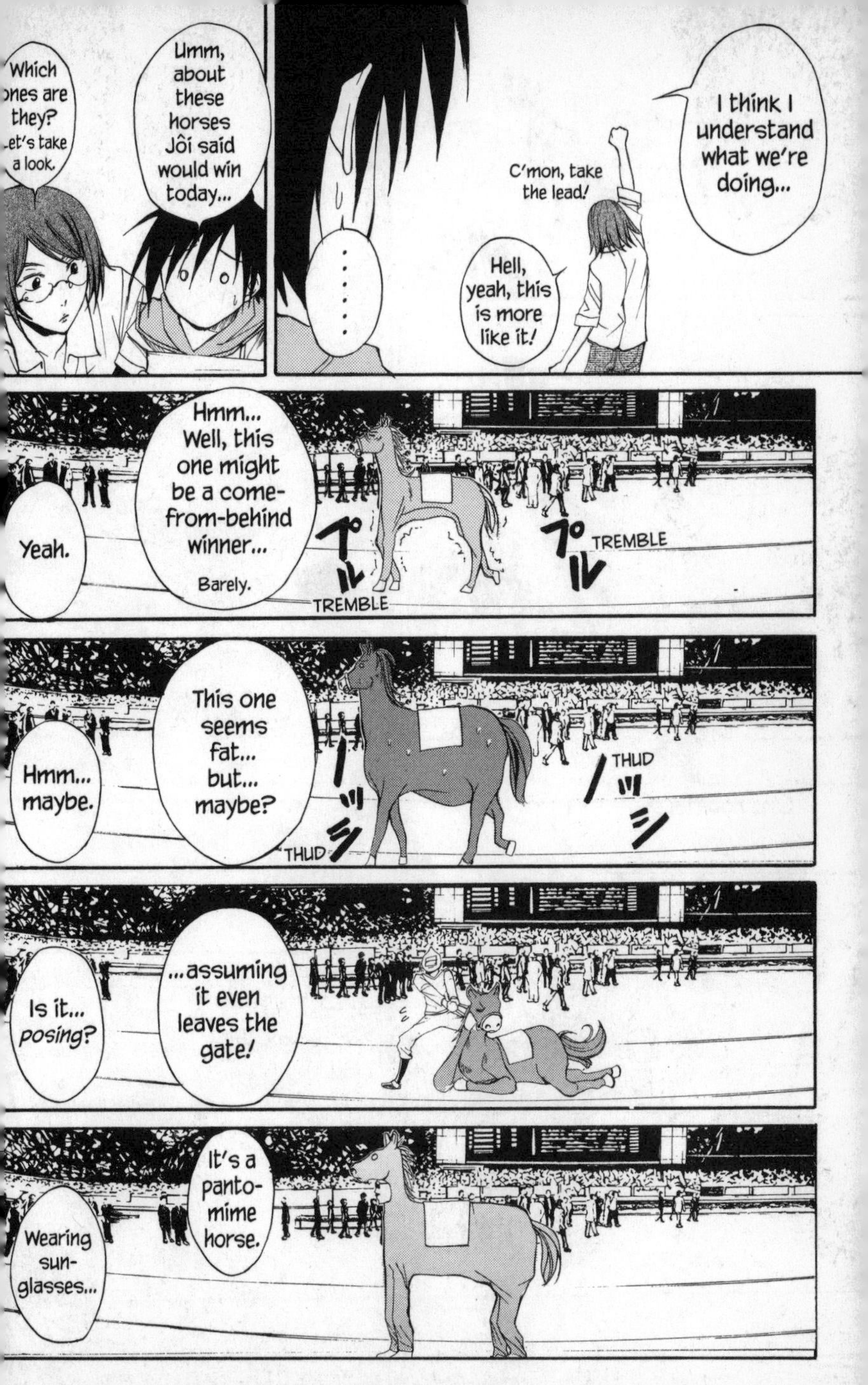
I think I understand what we're doing...
C'mon, take the lead!
Hell, yeah, this is more like it!
......
Umm, about these horses Jôi said would win today...
Which ones are they? Let's take a look.
プル TREMBLE
Hmm... Well, this one might be a come-from-behind winner...
Barely.
プル TREMBLE
Yeah.
ノッシ THUD
This one seems fat... but... maybe?
ノッシ THUD
Hmm... maybe.
...assuming it even leaves the gate!
Is it... posing?
It's a panto-mime horse.
Wearing sun-glasses...

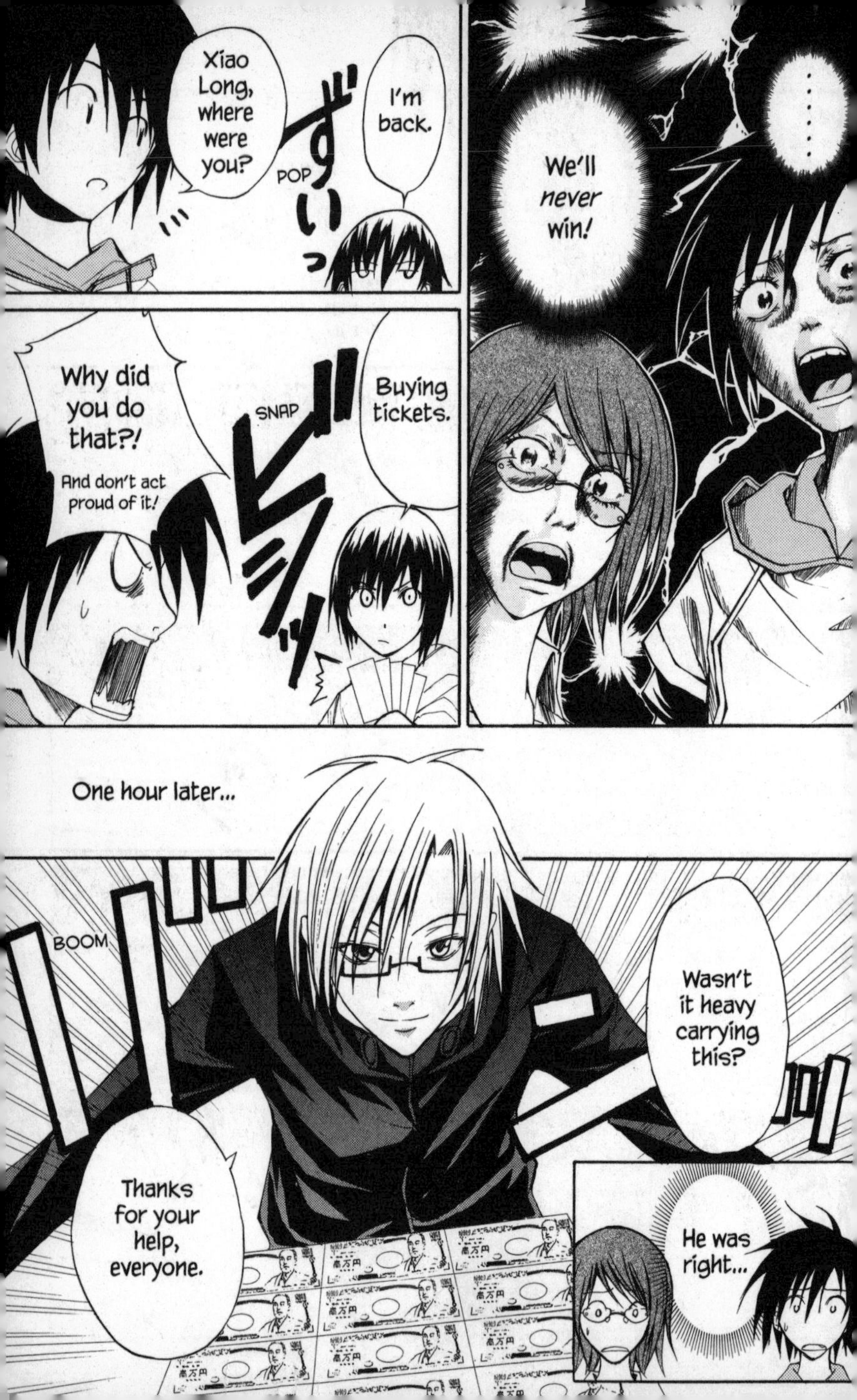

...
We'll never win!
I'm back.
POP
Xiao Long, where were you?
Buying tickets.
SNAP
Why did you do that?!
And don't act proud of it!
One hour later...
Wasn't it heavy carrying this?
BOOM
He was right...
Thanks for your help, everyone.

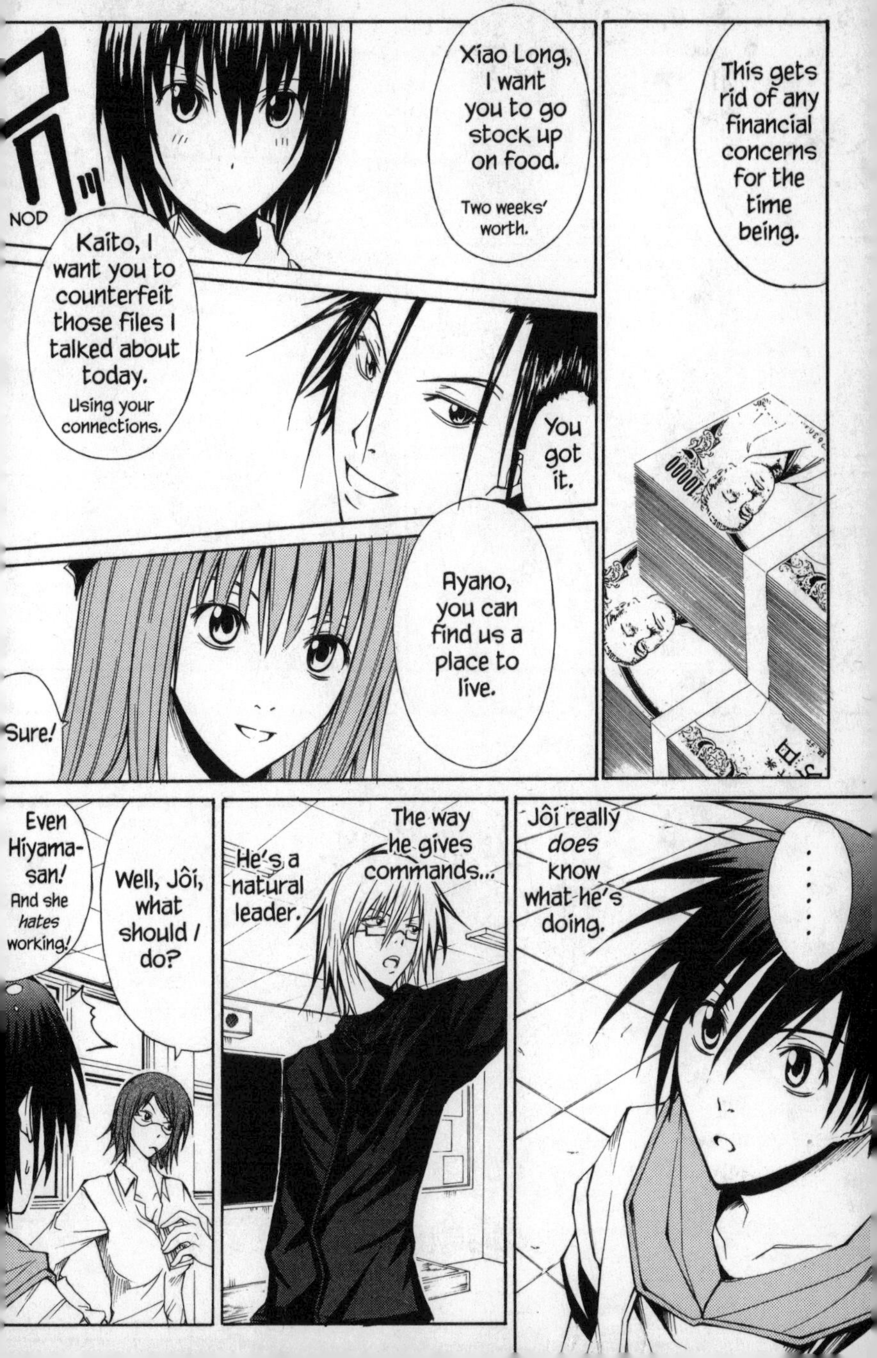
This gets rid of any financial concerns for the time being.
Xiao Long, I want you to go stock up on food.
Two weeks' worth.
NOD
Kaito, I want you to counterfeit those files I talked about today.
Using your connections.
You got it.
Ayano, you can find us a place to live.
Sure!
......
Jôi really *does* know what he's doing.
The way he gives commands...
He's a natural leader.
Well, Jôi, what should I do?
Even Hiyama-san!
And she *hates* working!

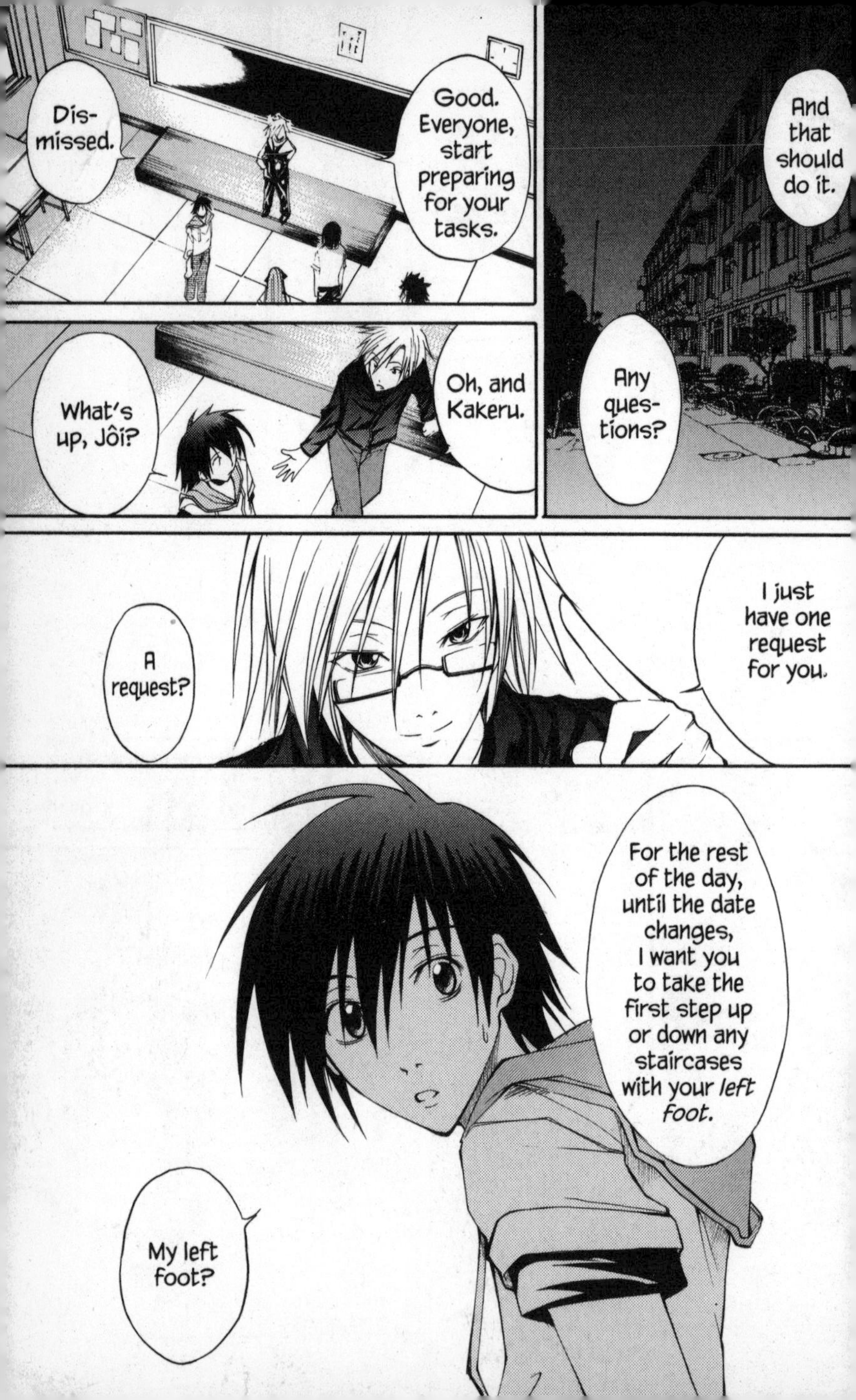
And that should do it.
Any questions?
Good. Everyone, start preparing for your tasks.
Dis-missed.
Oh, and Kakeru.
What's up, Jôi?
I just have one request for you.
A request?
For the rest of the day, until the date changes, I want you to take the first step up or down any staircases with your *left foot*.
My left foot?

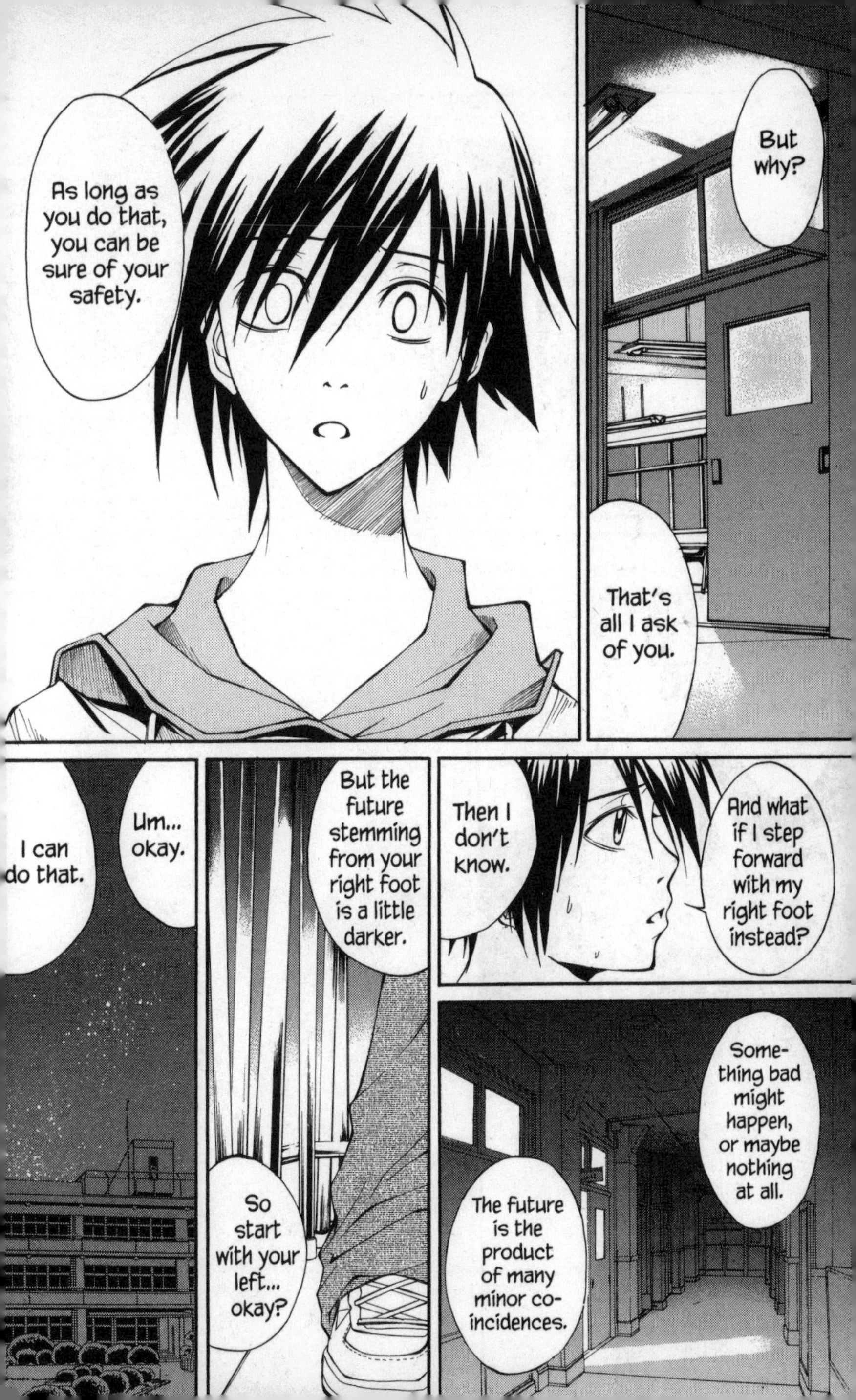
But why?
That's all I ask of you.
As long as you do that, you can be sure of your safety.
And what if I step forward with my right foot instead?
Then I don't know.
Some-thing bad might happen, or maybe nothing at all.
The future is the product of many minor co-incidences.
But the future stemming from your right foot is a little darker.
So start with your left... okay?
Um... okay.
I can do that.

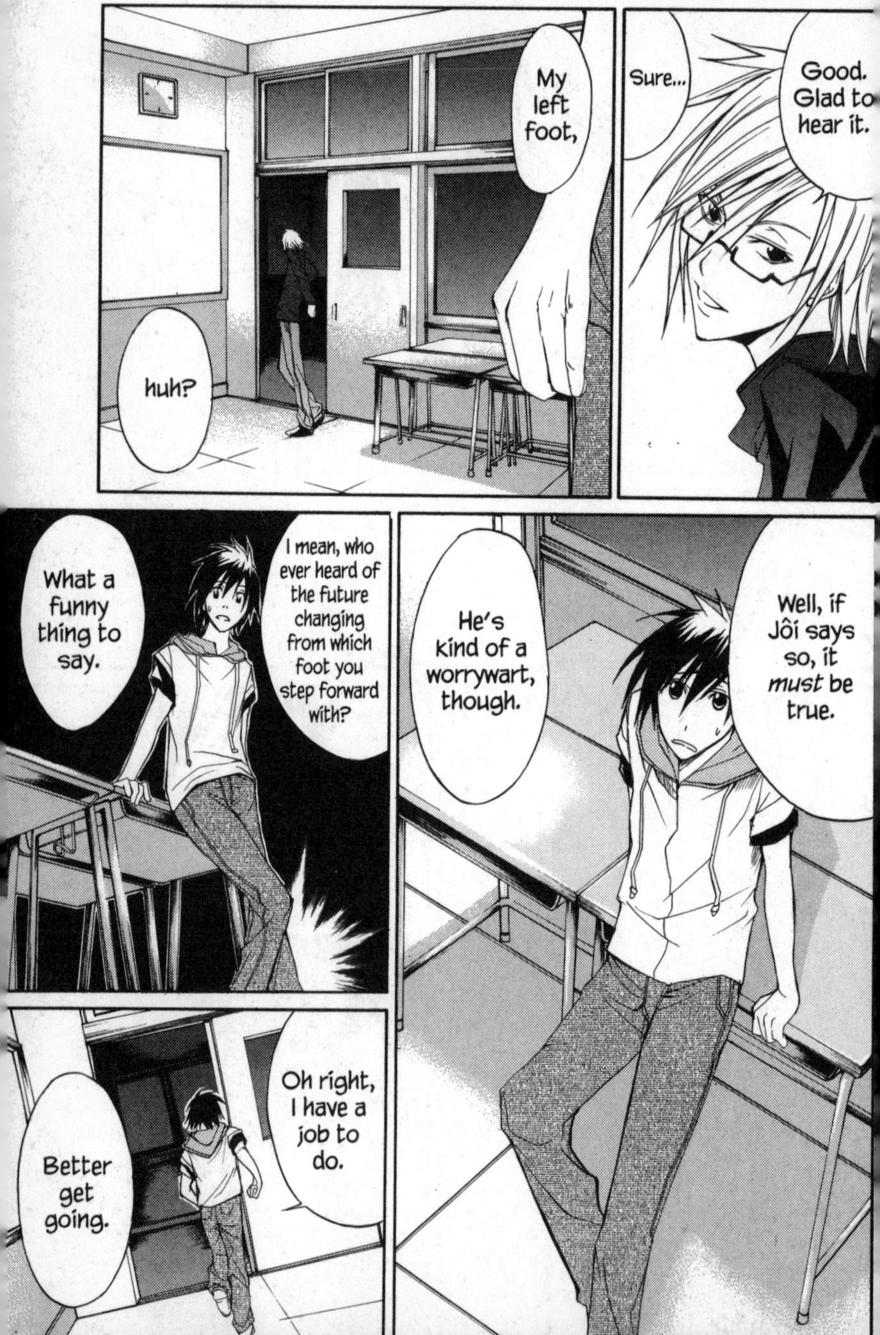
Good. Glad to hear it.
Sure...
My left foot,
huh?
Well, if Jôi says so, it *must* be true.
He's kind of a worrywart, though.
I mean, who ever heard of the future changing from which foot you step forward with?
What a funny thing to say.
Oh right, I have a job to do.
Better get going.

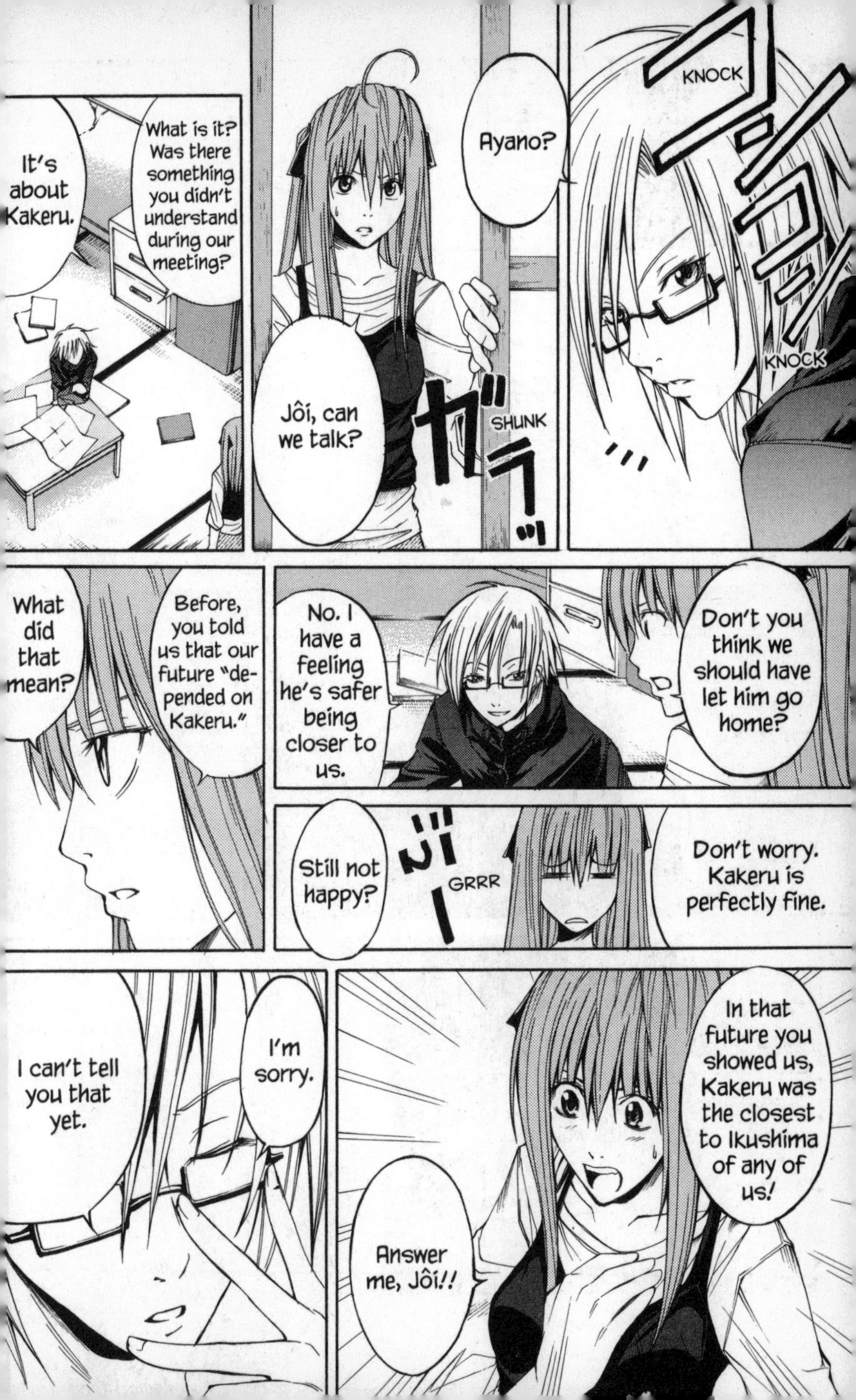
KNOCK
KNOCK
...
Ayano?
SHUNK
Jôi, can we talk?
What is it? Was there something you didn't understand during our meeting?
It's about Kakeru.
Don't you think we should have let him go home?
No. I have a feeling he's safer being closer to us.
Don't worry. Kakeru is perfectly fine.
GRRR
Still not happy?
Before, you told us that our future "depended on Kakeru."
What did that mean?
In that future you showed us, Kakeru was the closest to Ikushima of any of us!
Answer me, Jôi!!
I'm sorry.
I can't tell you that yet.

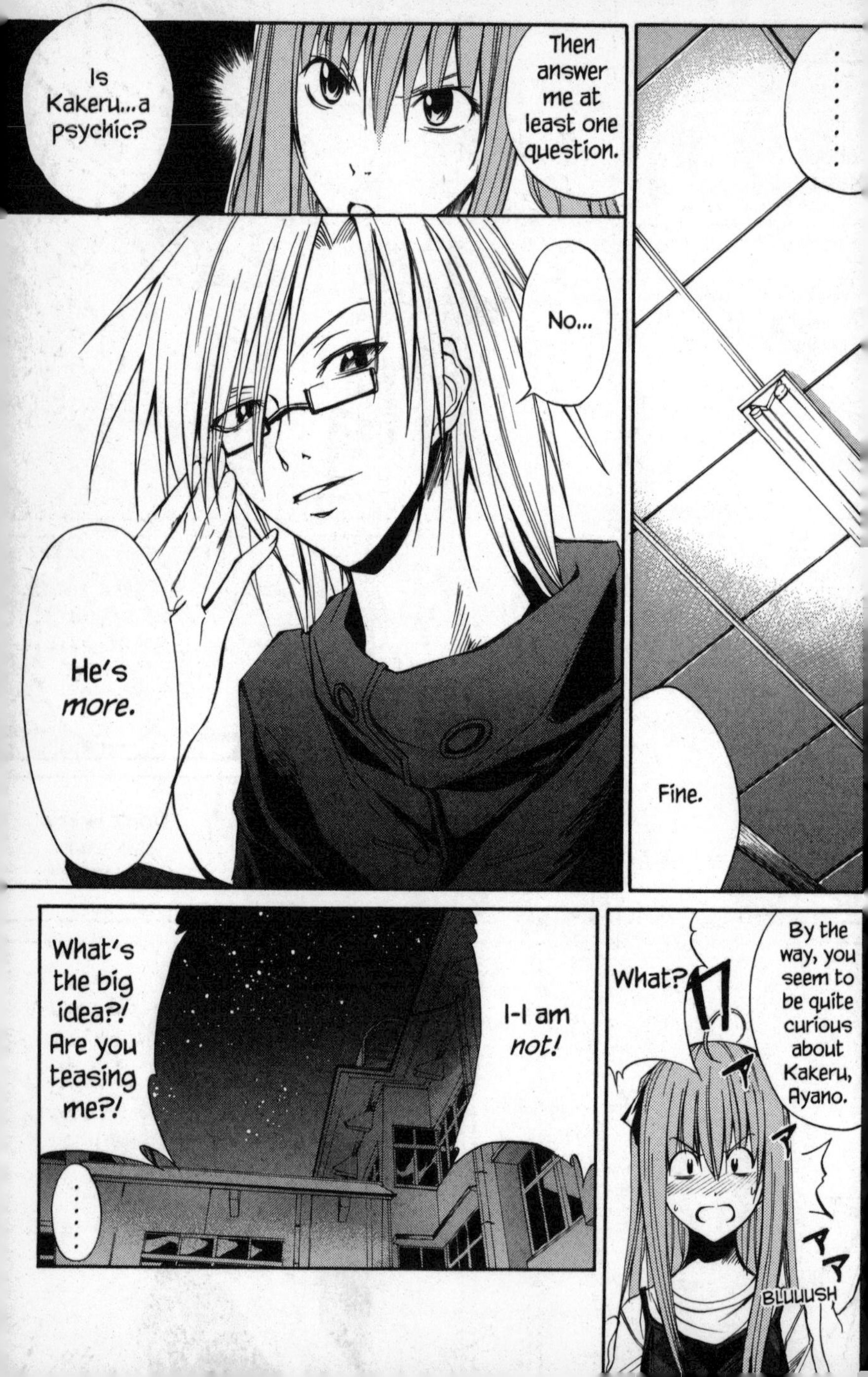
......
Fine.
Then answer me at least one question.
Is Kakeru...a psychic?
No...
He's *more.*
By the way, you seem to be quite curious about Kakeru, Ayano.
What?
BLUUUSH
I-I am *not!*
What's the big idea?! Are you teasing me?!
......

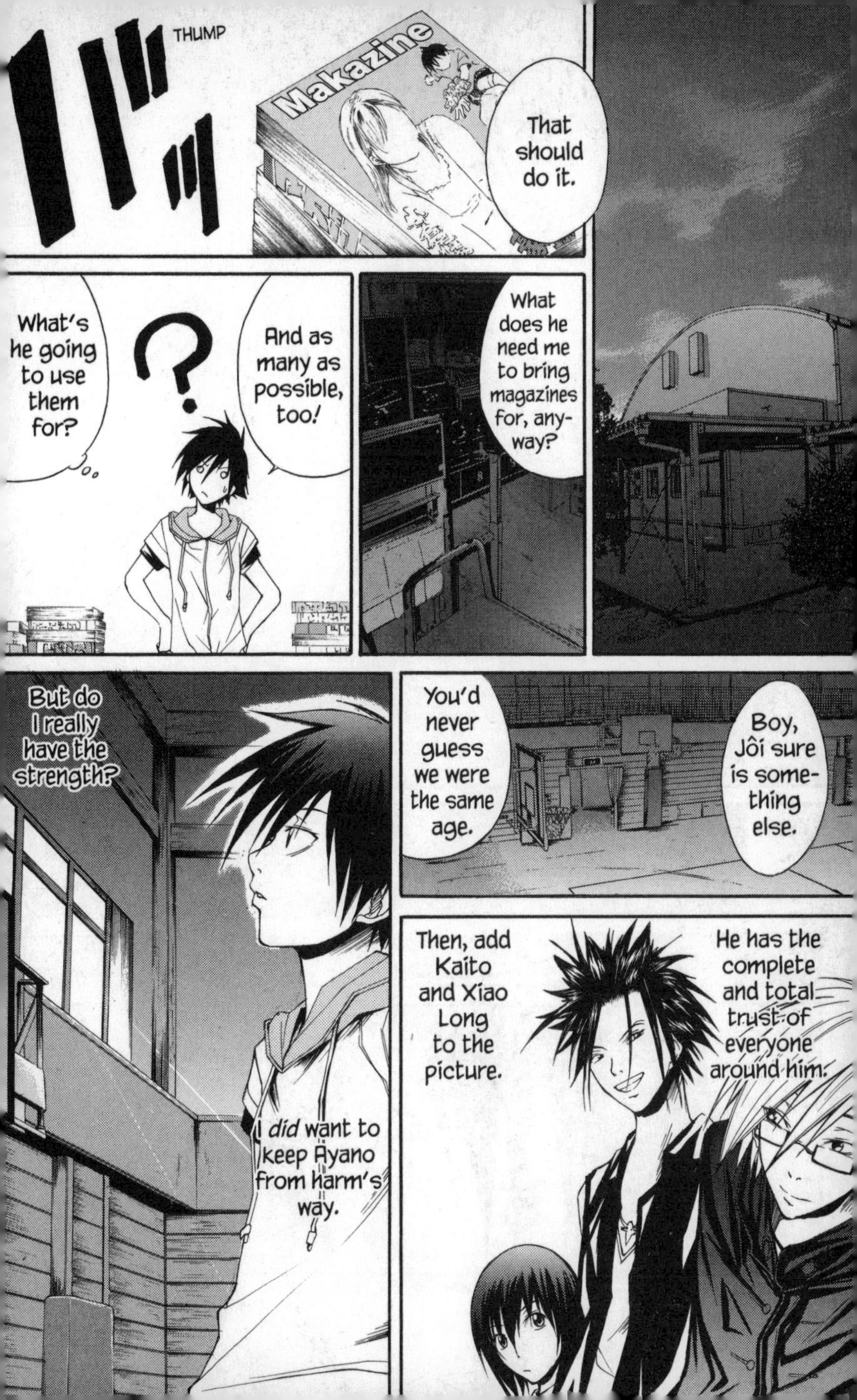
THUMP
That should do it.
What does he need me to bring magazines for, anyway?
And as many as possible, too!
?
What's he going to use them for?
Boy, Jôi sure is some-thing else.
You'd never guess we were the same age.
He has the complete and total trust of everyone around him.
Then, add Kaito and Xiao Long to the picture.
But do I really have the strength?
I *did* want to keep Ayano from harm's way.

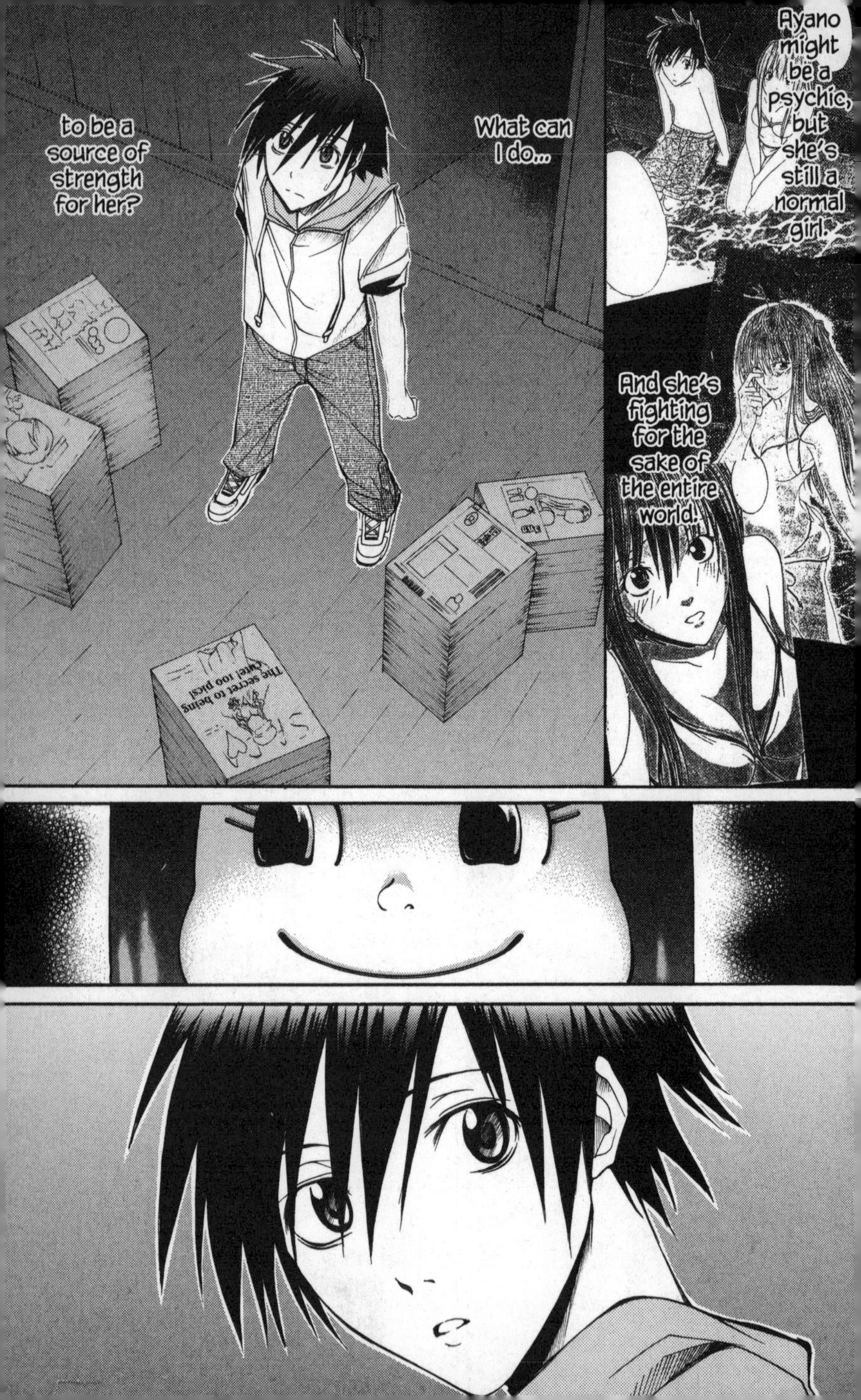
Ayano might be a psychic, but she's still a normal girl.
And she's fighting for the sake of the entire world.
What can I do...
to be a source of strength for her?
The secret to being cute! 100 pics!

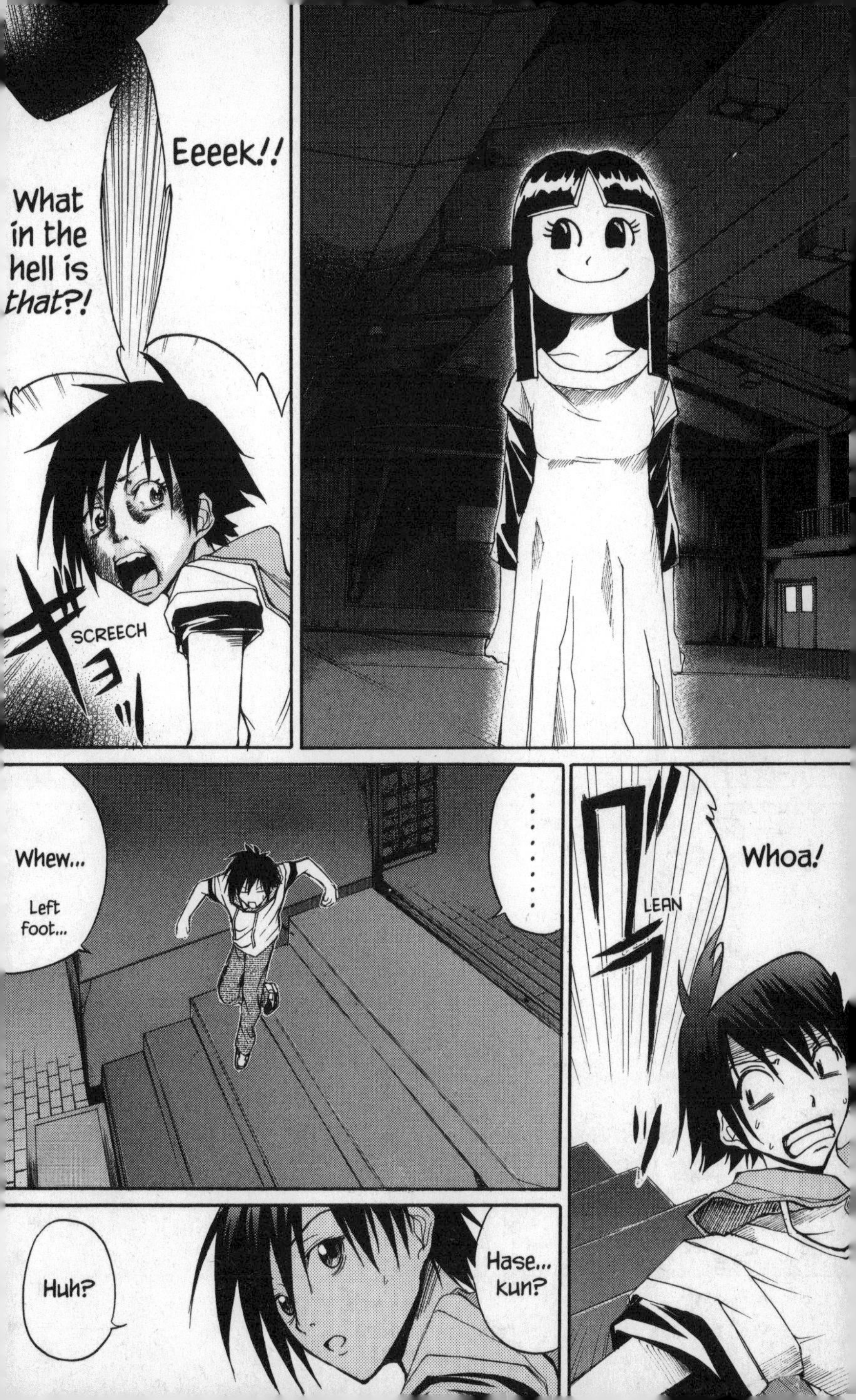
Eeeek!!
What in the hell is that?!
SCREECH
Whoa!
LEAN
......
Whew...
Left foot...
Hase... kun?
Huh?

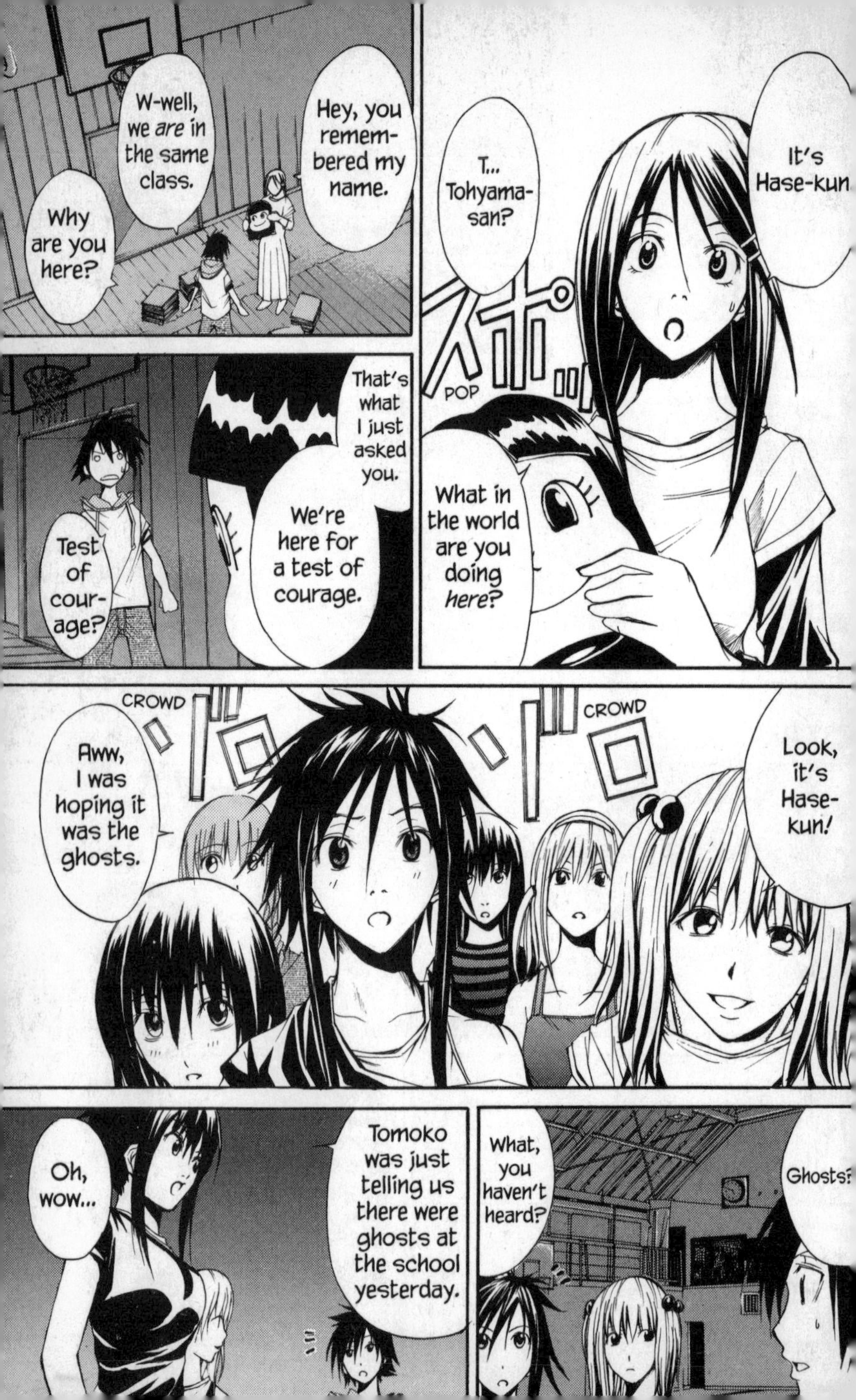
It's Hase-kun
T... Tohyama-san?
POP
What in the world are you doing *here*?
Hey, you remembered my name.
W-well, we *are* in the same class.
Why are you here?
That's what I just asked you.
We're here for a test of courage.
Test of courage?
CROWD
Look, it's Hase-kun!
CROWD
Aww, I was hoping it was the ghosts.
Ghosts?
What, you haven't heard?
Tomoko was just telling us there were ghosts at the school yesterday.
Oh, wow...

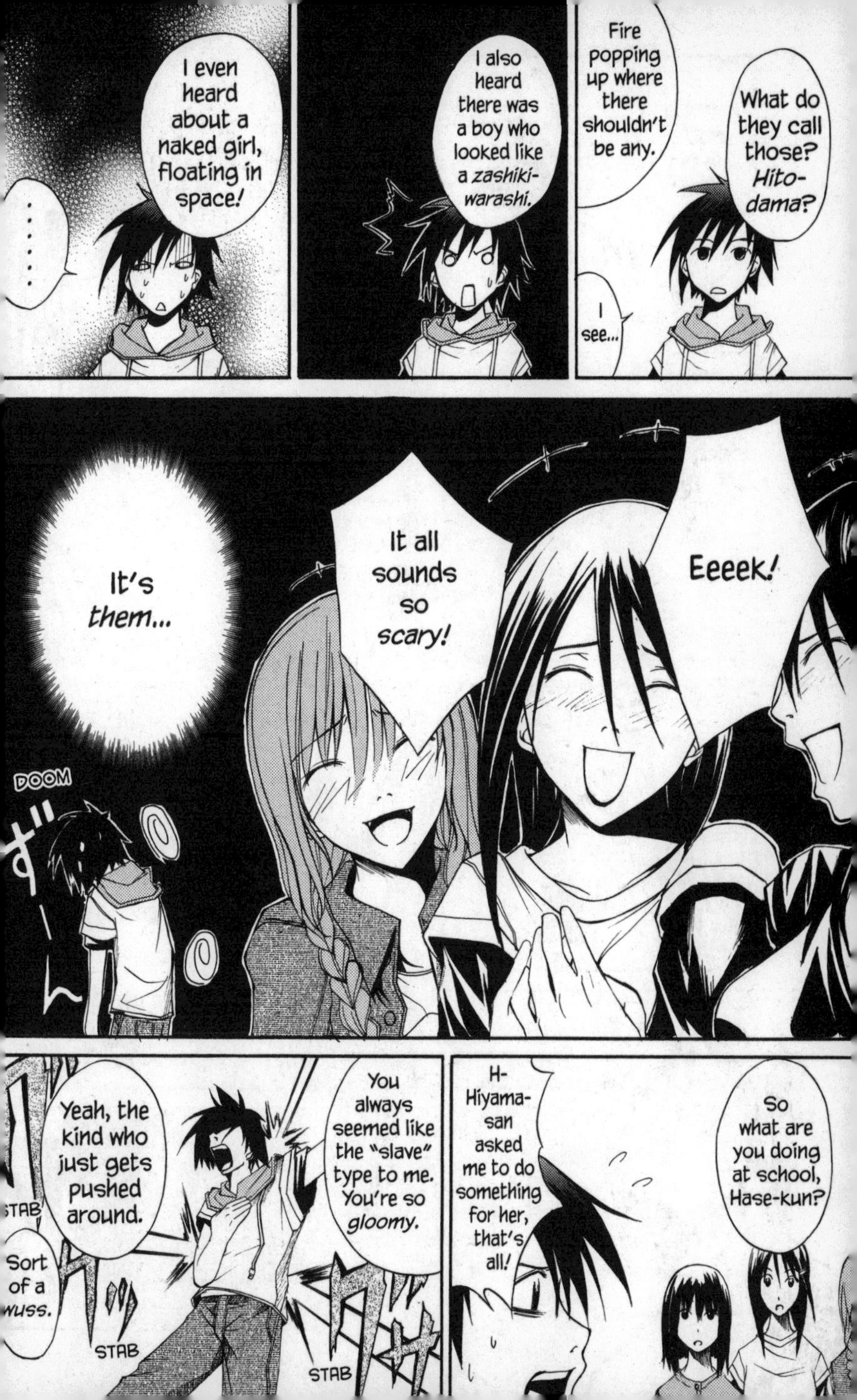
Fire popping up where there shouldn't be any.
What do they call those? *Hito-dama?*
I see...
I also heard there was a boy who looked like a *zashiki-warashi.*
I even heard about a naked girl, floating in space!
......
Eeeek!
It all sounds so *scary!*
It's *them...*
DOOM
ずーん
So what are you doing at school, Hase-kun?
H-Hiyama-san asked me to do something for her, that's all!
You always seemed like the "slave" type to me. You're so *gloomy.*
Yeah, the kind who just gets pushed around.
STAB
Sort of a wuss.
STAB
STAB

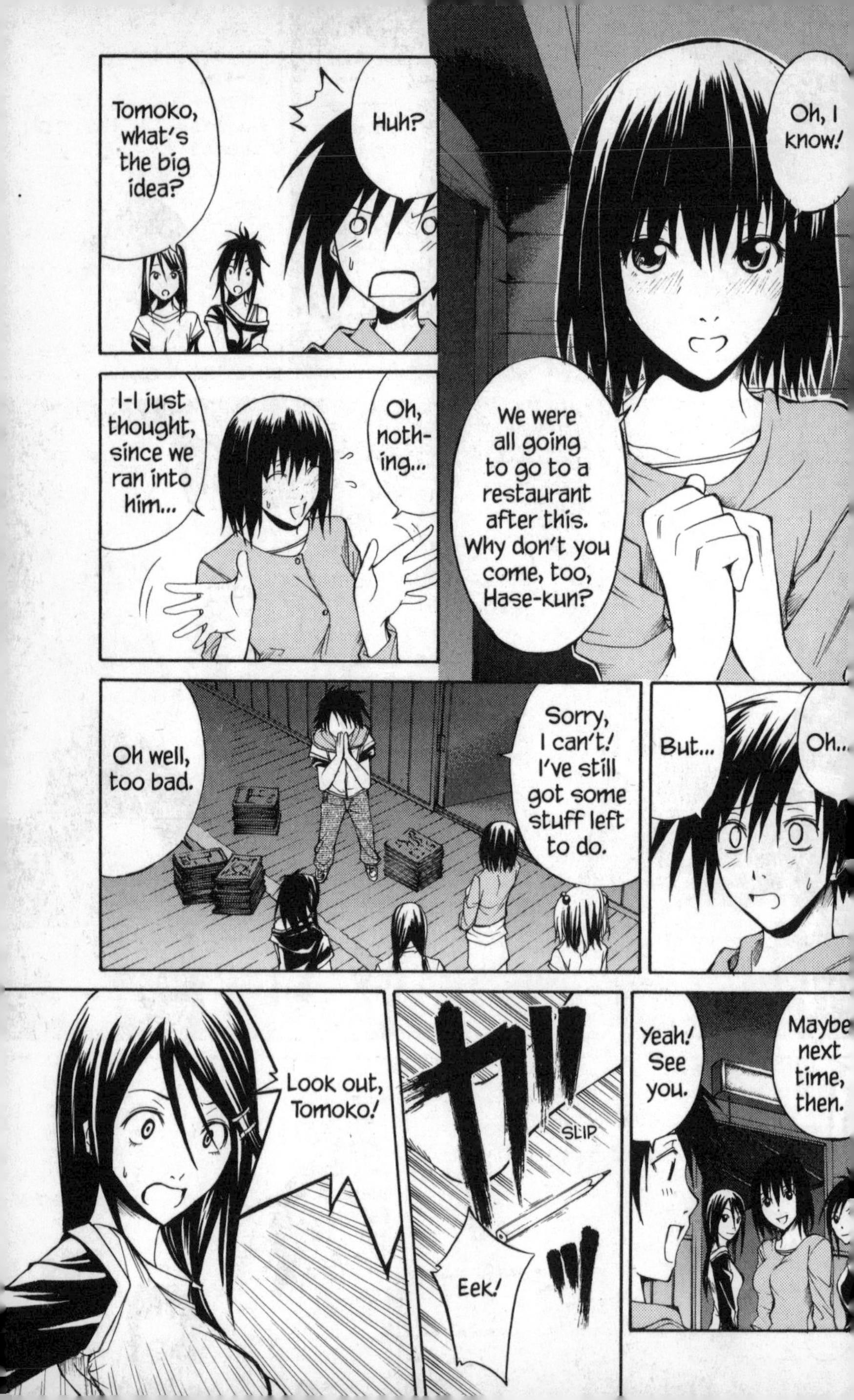
Oh, I know!
We were all going to go to a restaurant after this. Why don't you come, too, Hase-kun?
Huh?
Tomoko, what's the big idea?
Oh, nothing...
I-I just thought, since we ran into him...
Oh...
But...
Sorry, I can't! I've still got some stuff left to do.
Oh well, too bad.
Maybe next time, then.
Yeah! See you.
SLIP
Eek!
Look out, Tomoko!

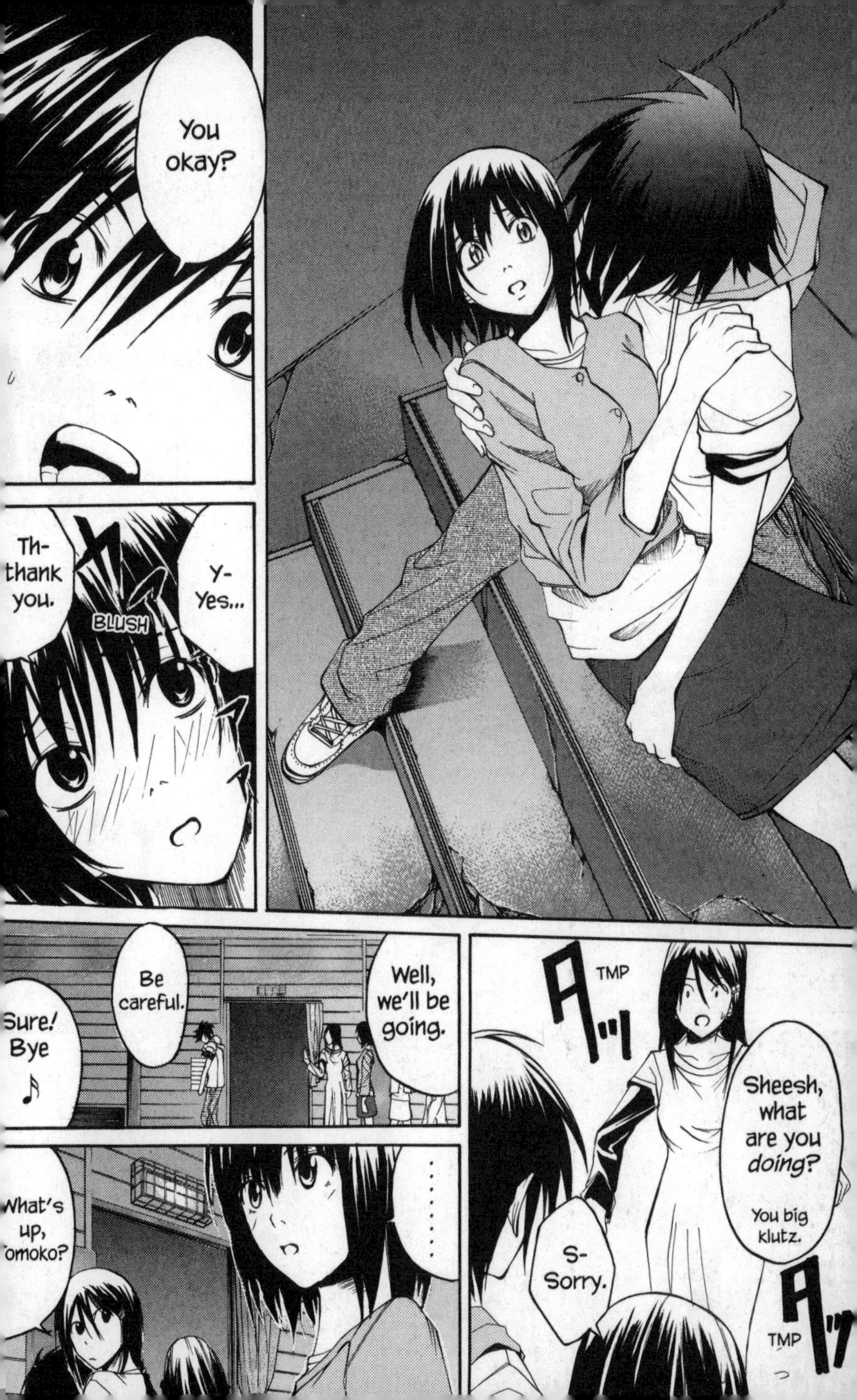

You okay?
Y- Yes...
BLUSH
Th- thank you.
TMP
Sheesh, what are you *doing*?
You big klutz.
S- Sorry.
TMP
Well, we'll be going.
Be careful.
Sure! Bye ♪
......
What's up, omoko?

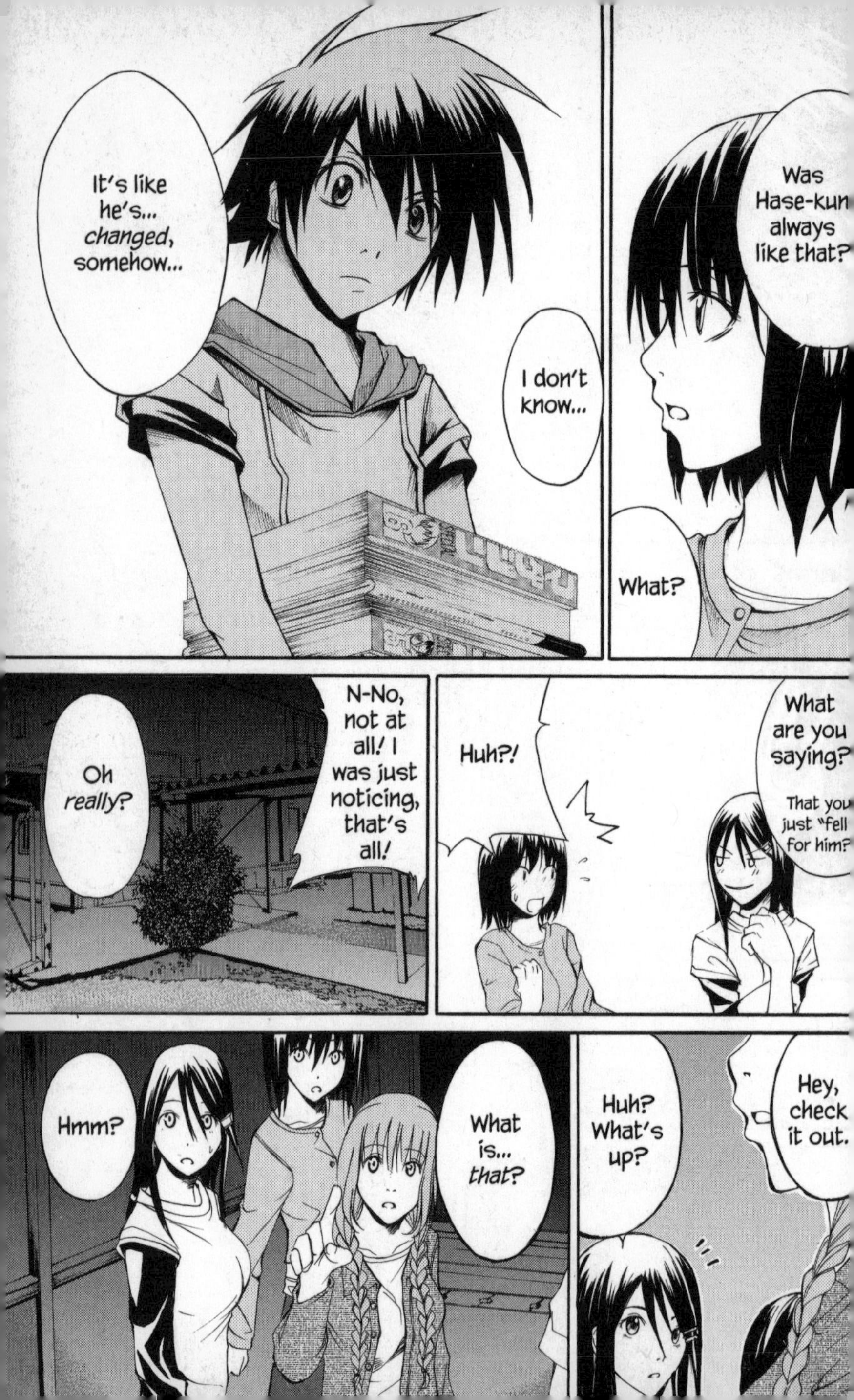
Was Hase-kun always like that?
What?
I don't know...
It's like he's... *changed*, somehow...
What are you saying?
That you just "fell for him?
Huh?!
N-No, not at all! I was just noticing, that's all!
Oh *really*?
Hey, check it out.
Huh? What's up?
What is... *that*?
Hmm?

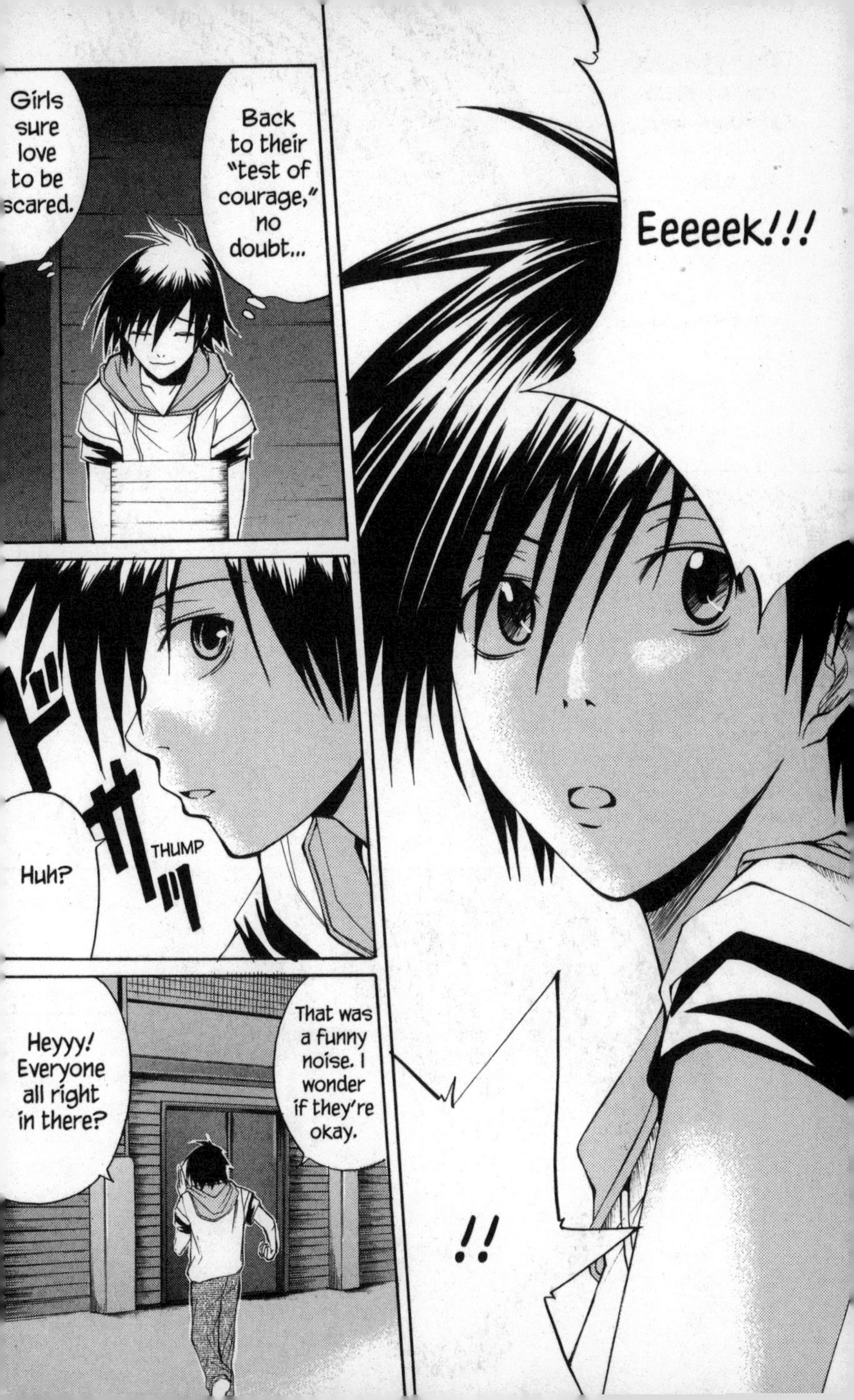
Eeeeek!!!
!!
Back to their "test of courage," no doubt...
Girls sure love to be scared.
THUMP
Huh?
That was a funny noise. I wonder if they're okay.
Heyyy! Everyone all right in there?

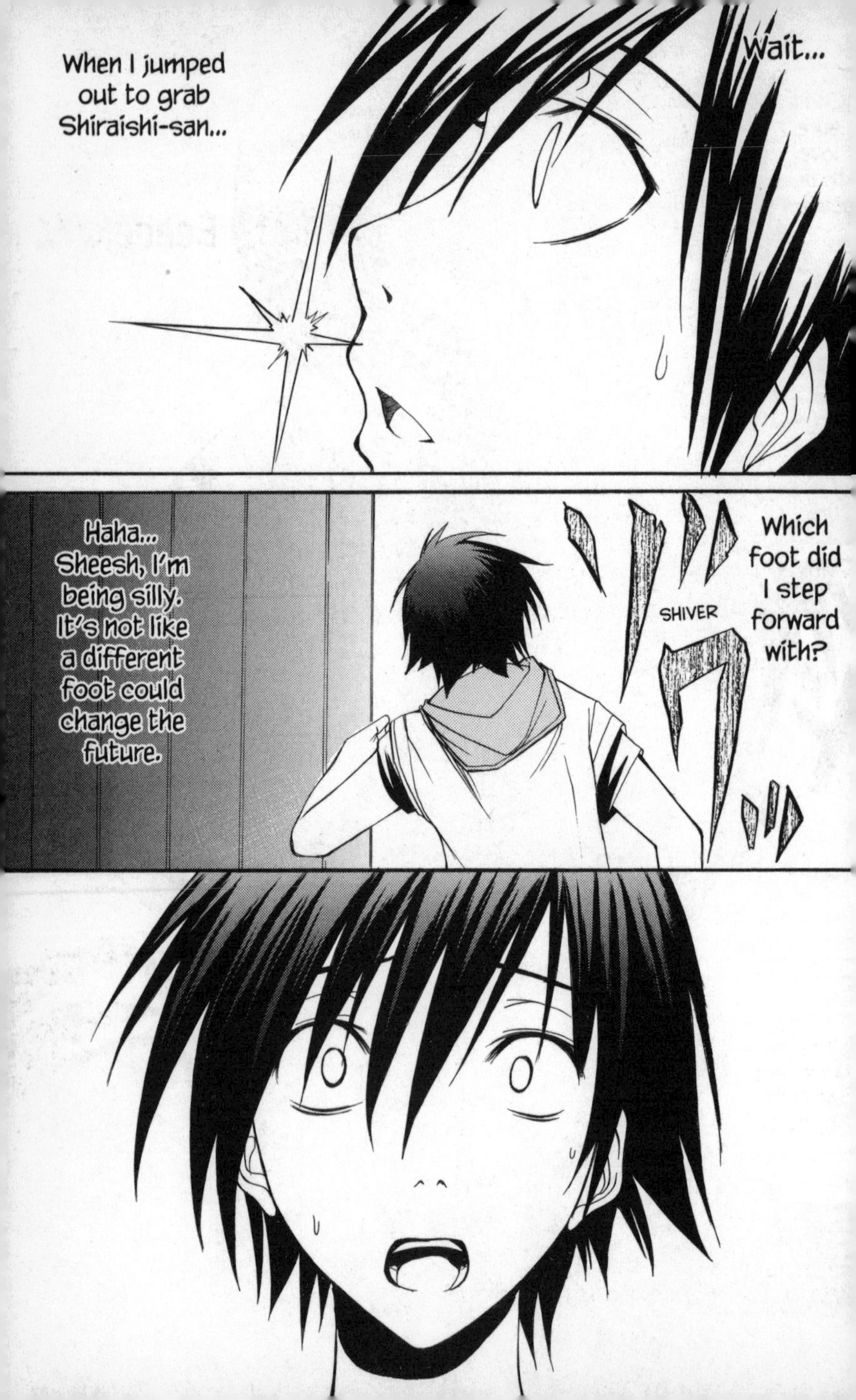
Wait...
When I jumped out to grab Shiraishi-san...
Which foot did I step forward with?
SHIVER
Haha... Sheesh, I'm being silly. It's not like a different foot could change the future.

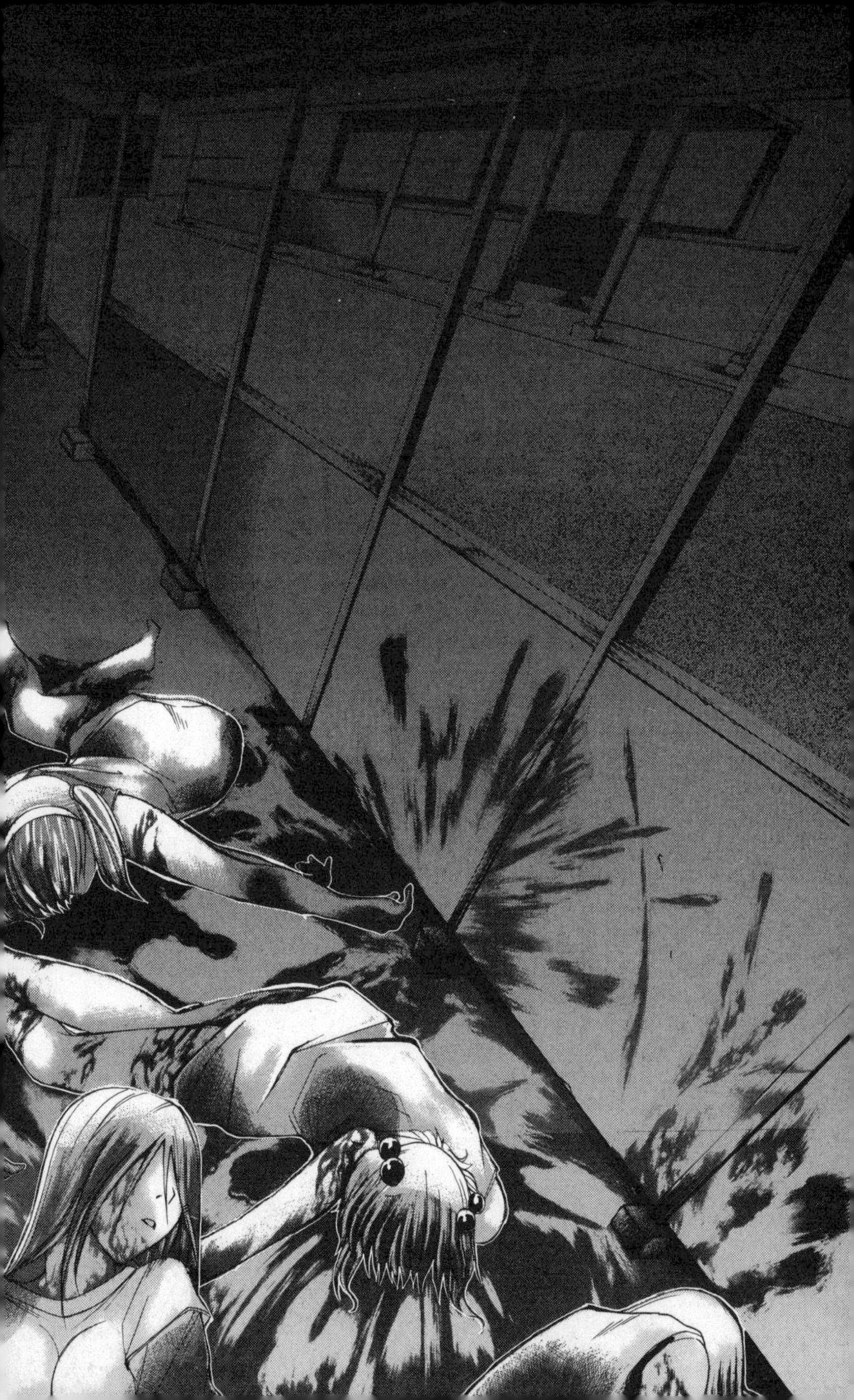

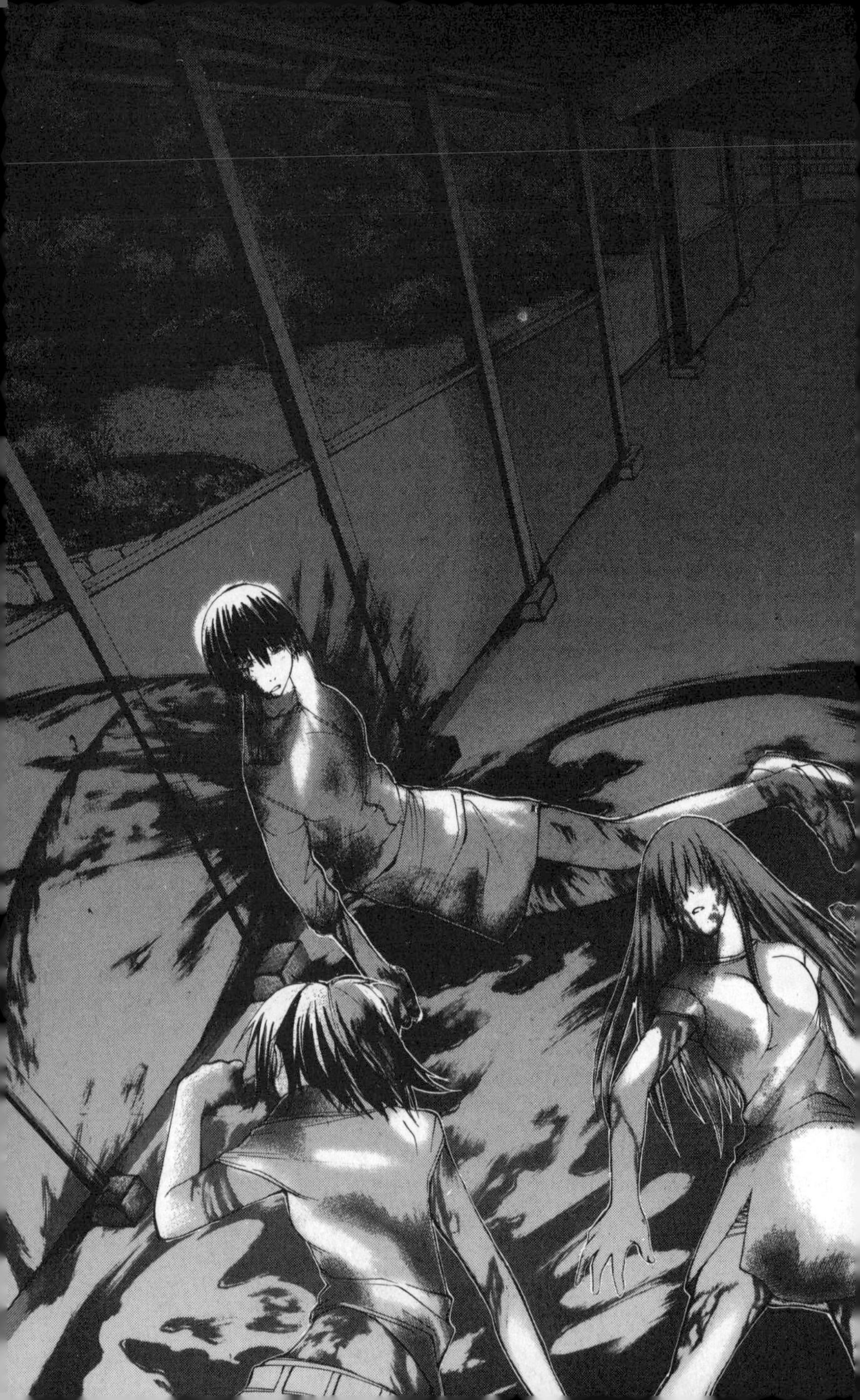

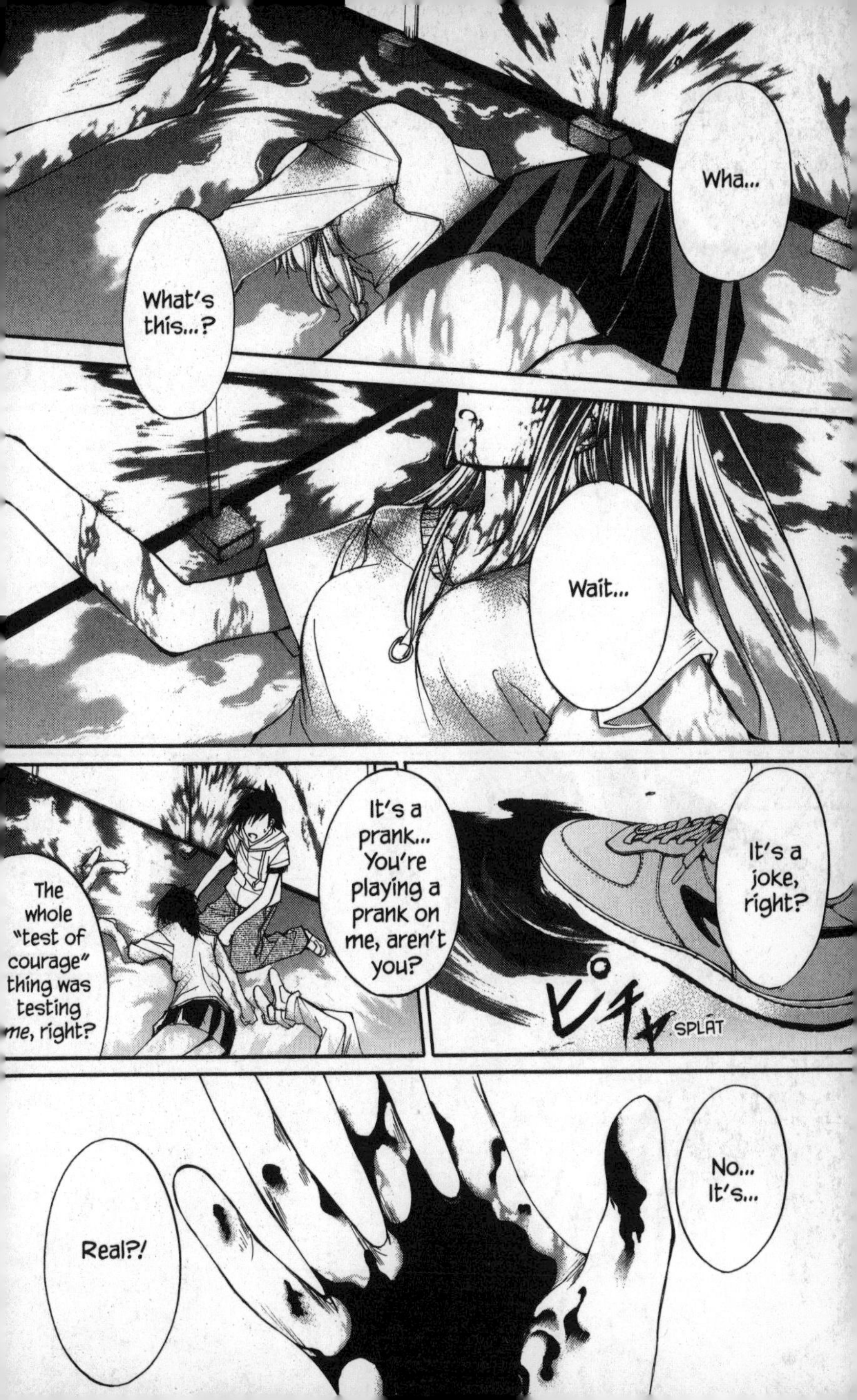
Wha...
What's this...?
Wait...
It's a joke, right?
ピチャ SPLAT
It's a prank... You're playing a prank on me, aren't you?
The whole "test of courage" thing was testing me, right?
No... It's...
Real?!

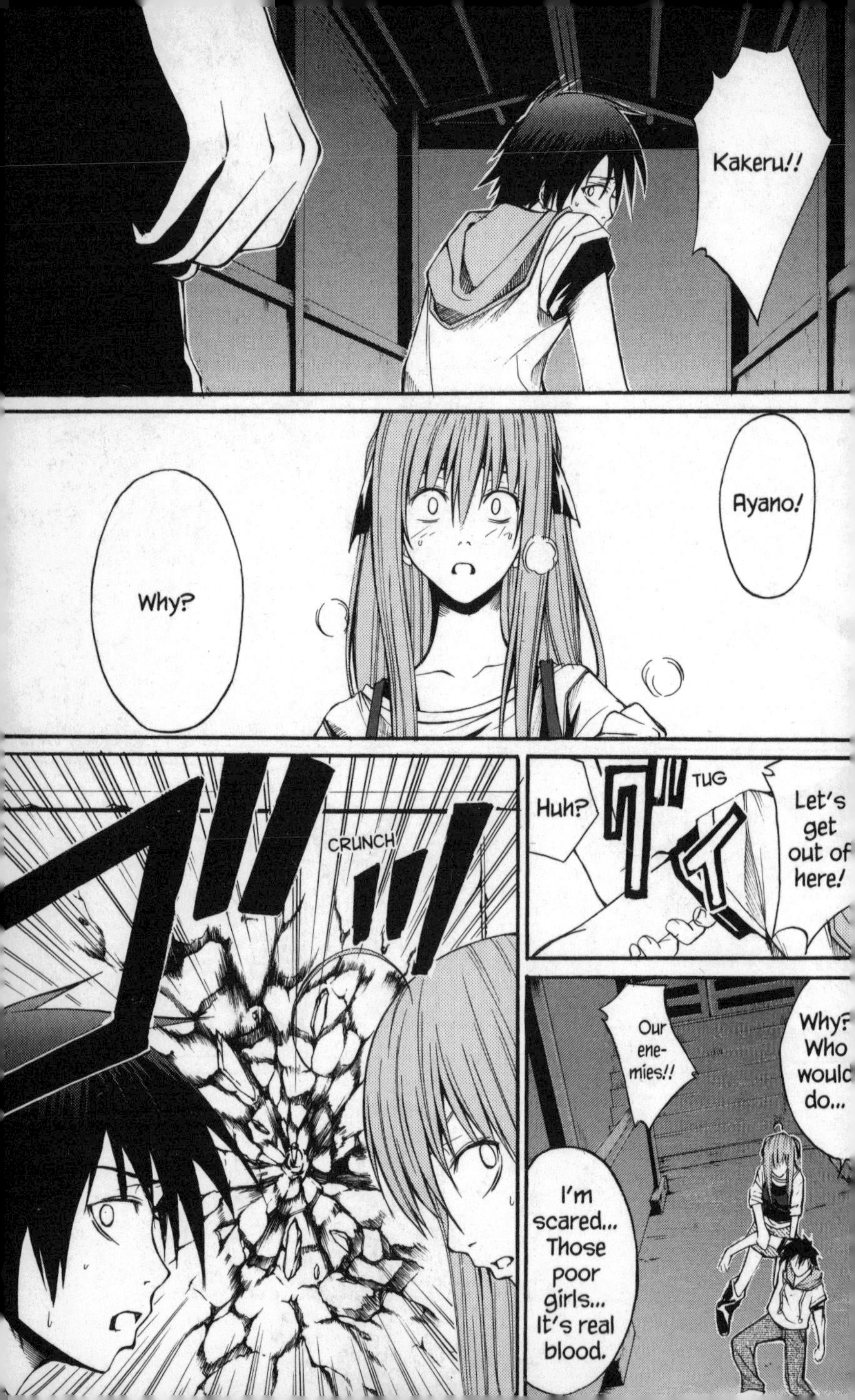
Kakeru!!
Ayano!
Why?
Let's get out of here!
TUG
Huh?
Why? Who would do...
Our ene-mies!!
I'm scared... Those poor girls... It's real blood.
CRUNCH

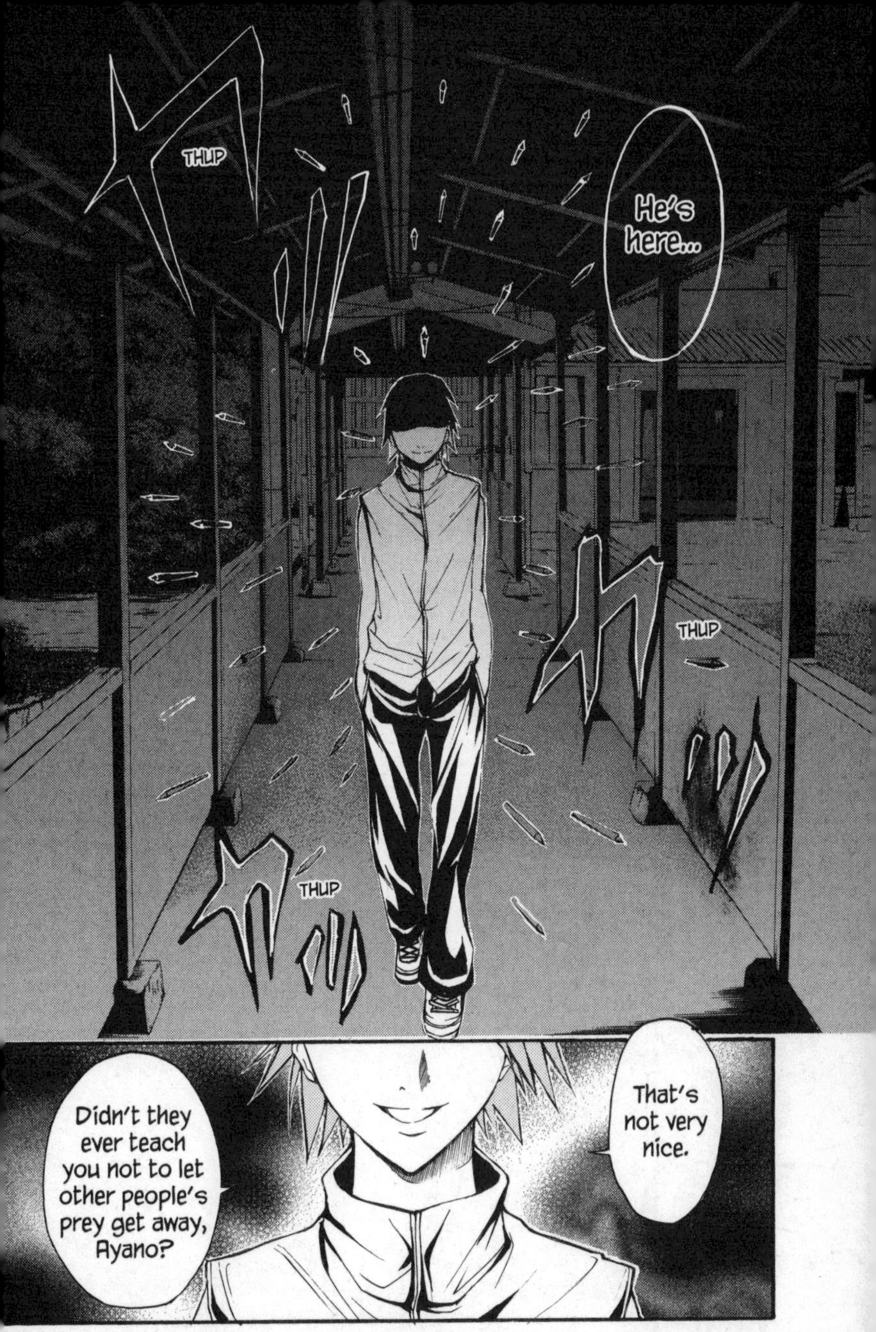
He's here...
THUP
THUP
THUP
That's not very nice.
Didn't they ever teach you not to let other people's prey get away, Ayano?

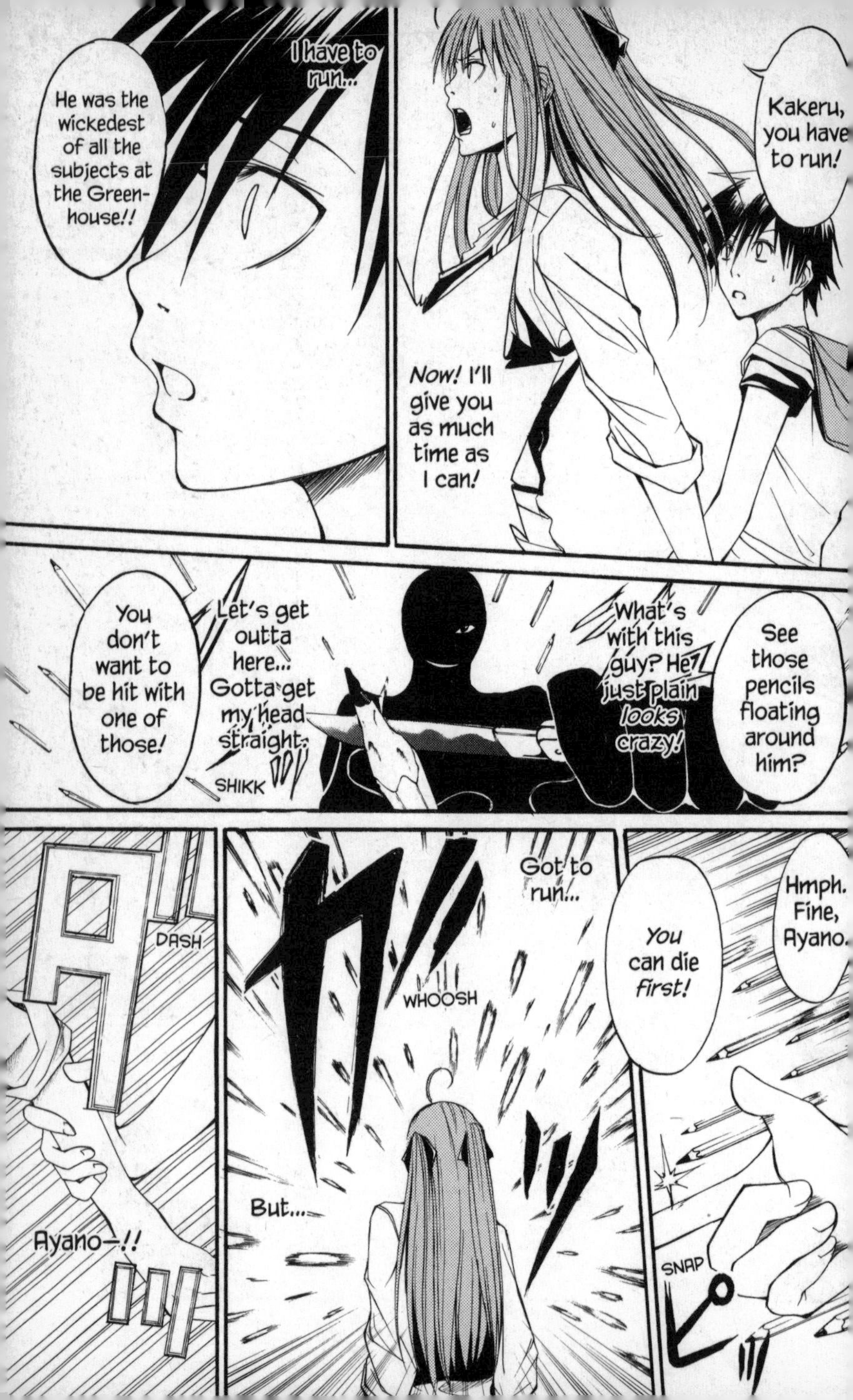
Kakeru, you have to run!
Now! I'll give you as much time as I can!
I have to run...
He was the wickedest of all the subjects at the Green-house!!
See those pencils floating around him?
What's with this guy? He just plain *looks* crazy!
Let's get outta here... Gotta get my head straight.
SHIKK
You don't want to be hit with one of those!
Hmph. Fine, Ayano.
You can die *first!*
SNAP
Got to run...
WHOOSH
But...
DASH
Ayano—!!

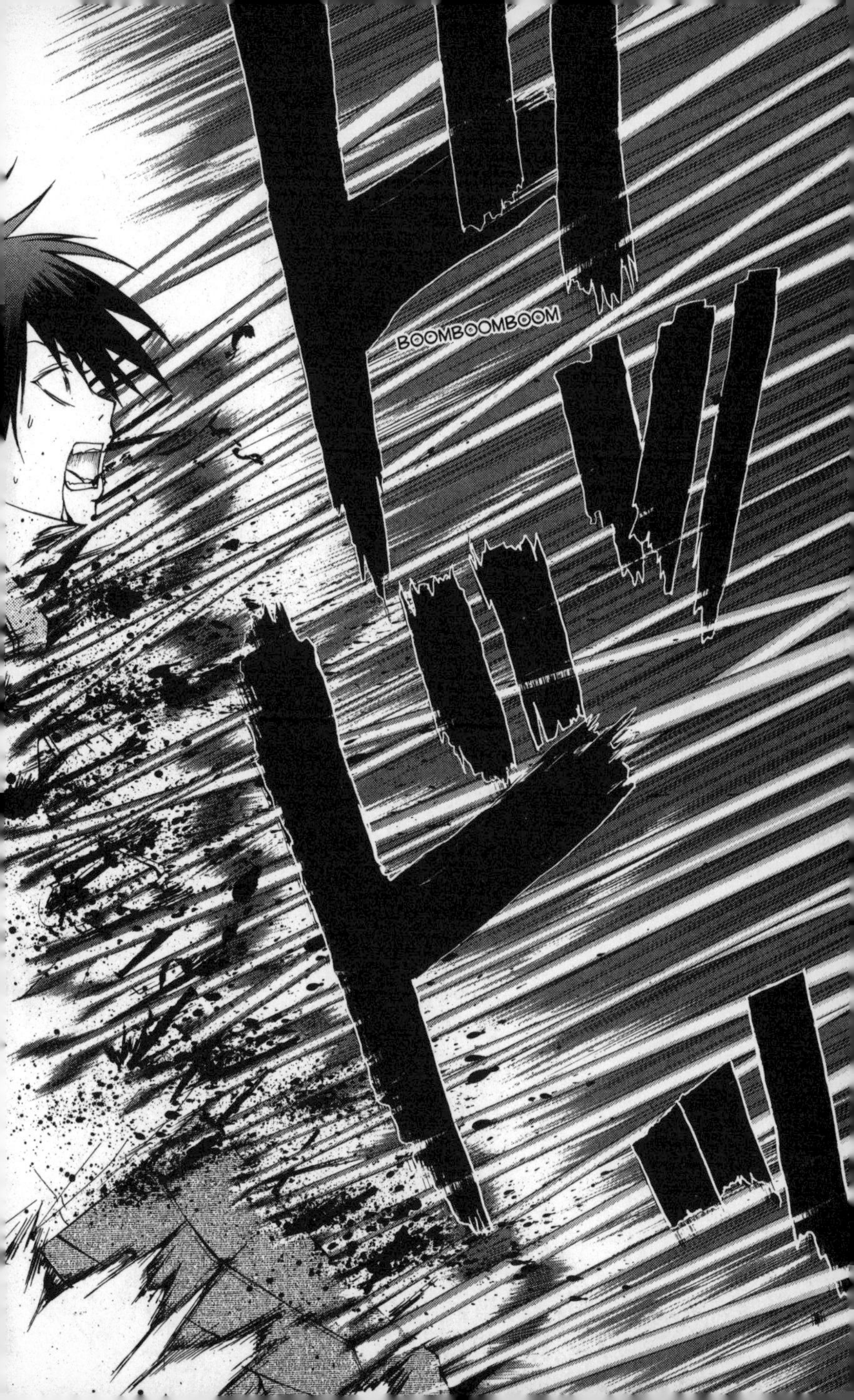
BOOMBOOMBOOM

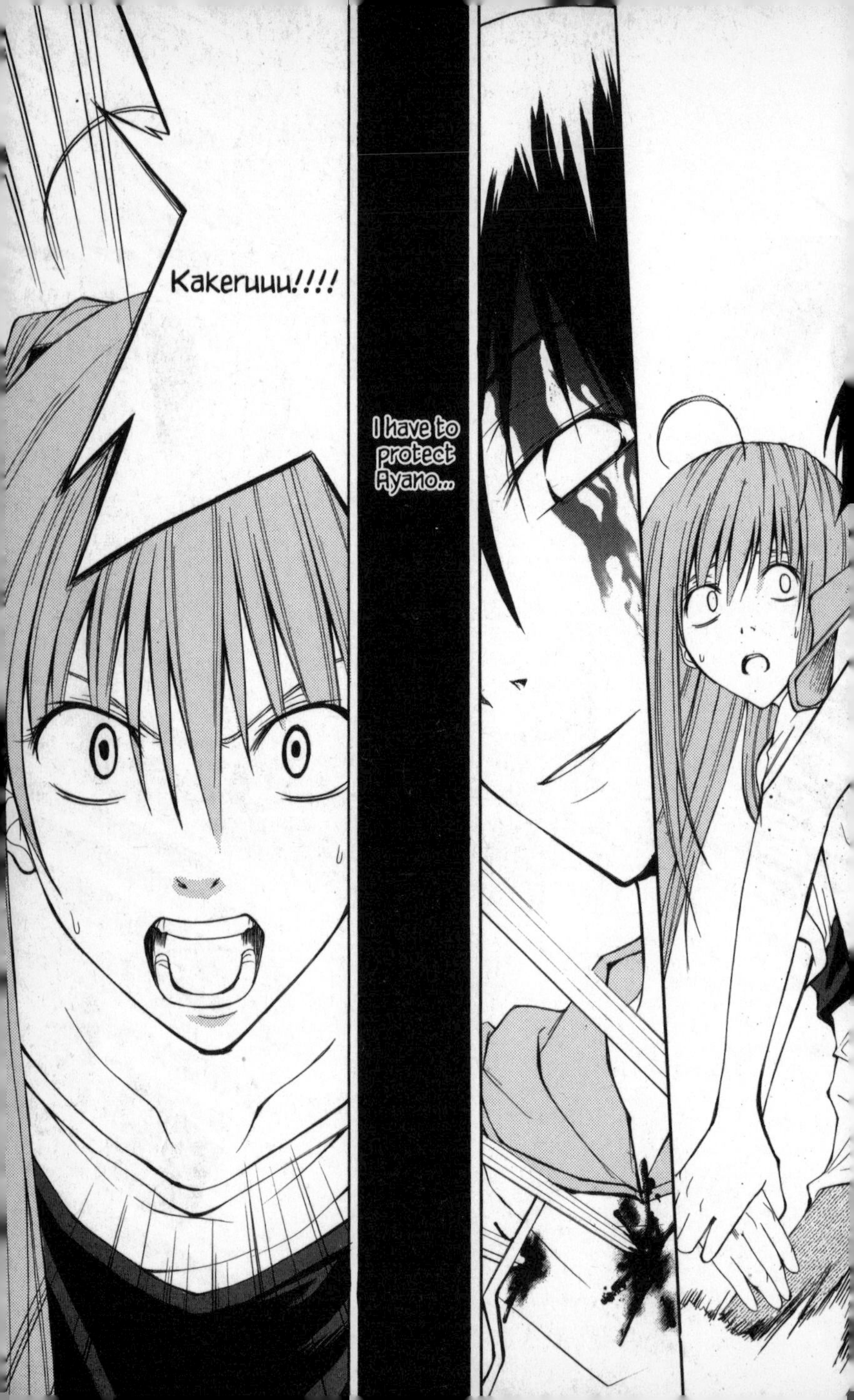
I have to protect Ayano...
Kakeruuu!!!!

Psycho Busters

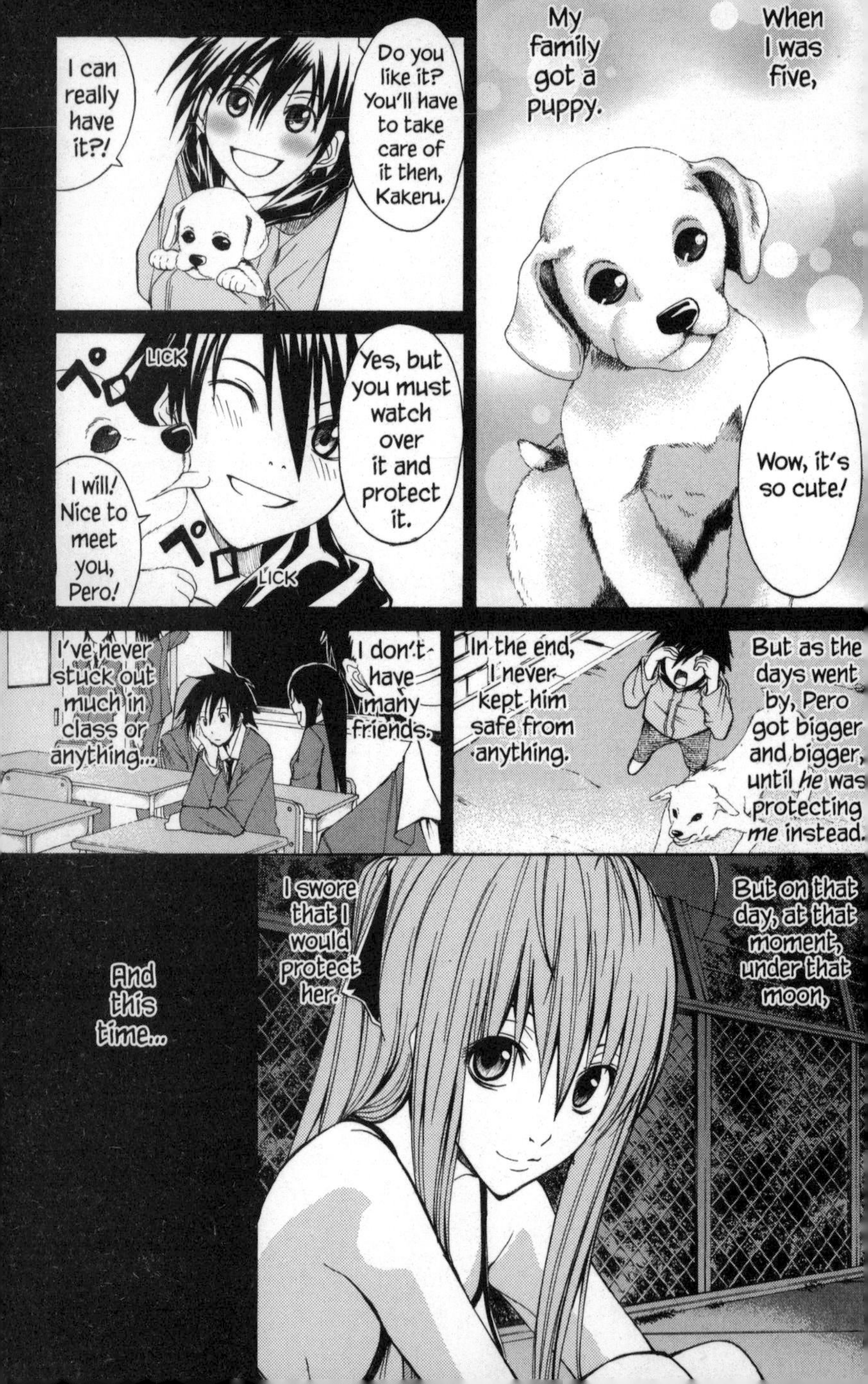

When I was five,
My family got a puppy.
Wow, it's so cute!
Do you like it? You'll have to take care of it then, Kakeru.
I can really have it?!
Yes, but you must watch over it and protect it.
ペロ
LICK
I will! Nice to meet you, Pero!
ペロ
LICK
But as the days went by, Pero got bigger and bigger, until *he* was protecting *me* instead.
In the end, I never kept him safe from anything.
I don't have many friends.
I've never stuck out much in class or anything...
But on that day, at that moment, under that moon,
I swore that I would protect her.
And this time...

CASE 7 – Awakening

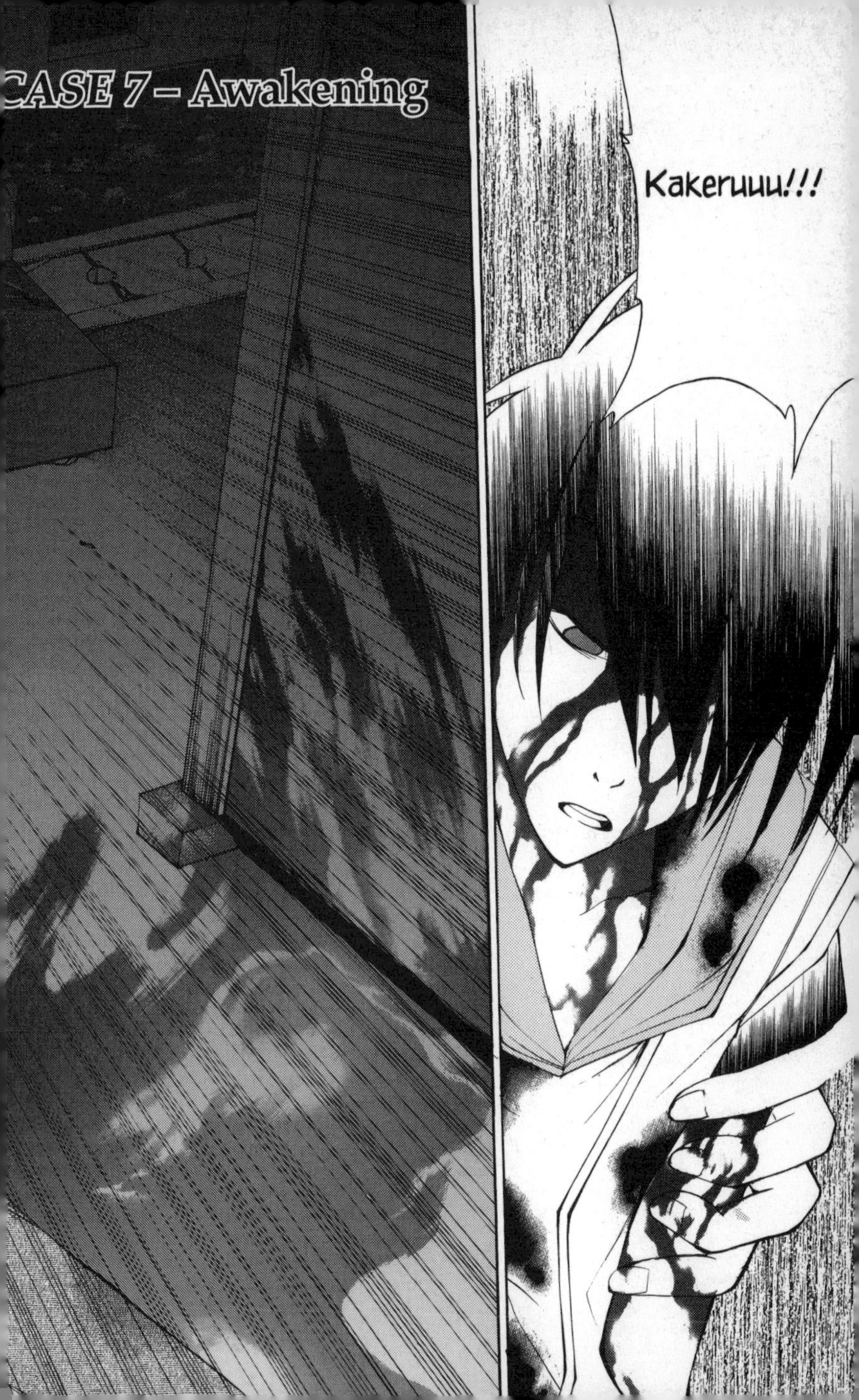
Kakeruuu!!!

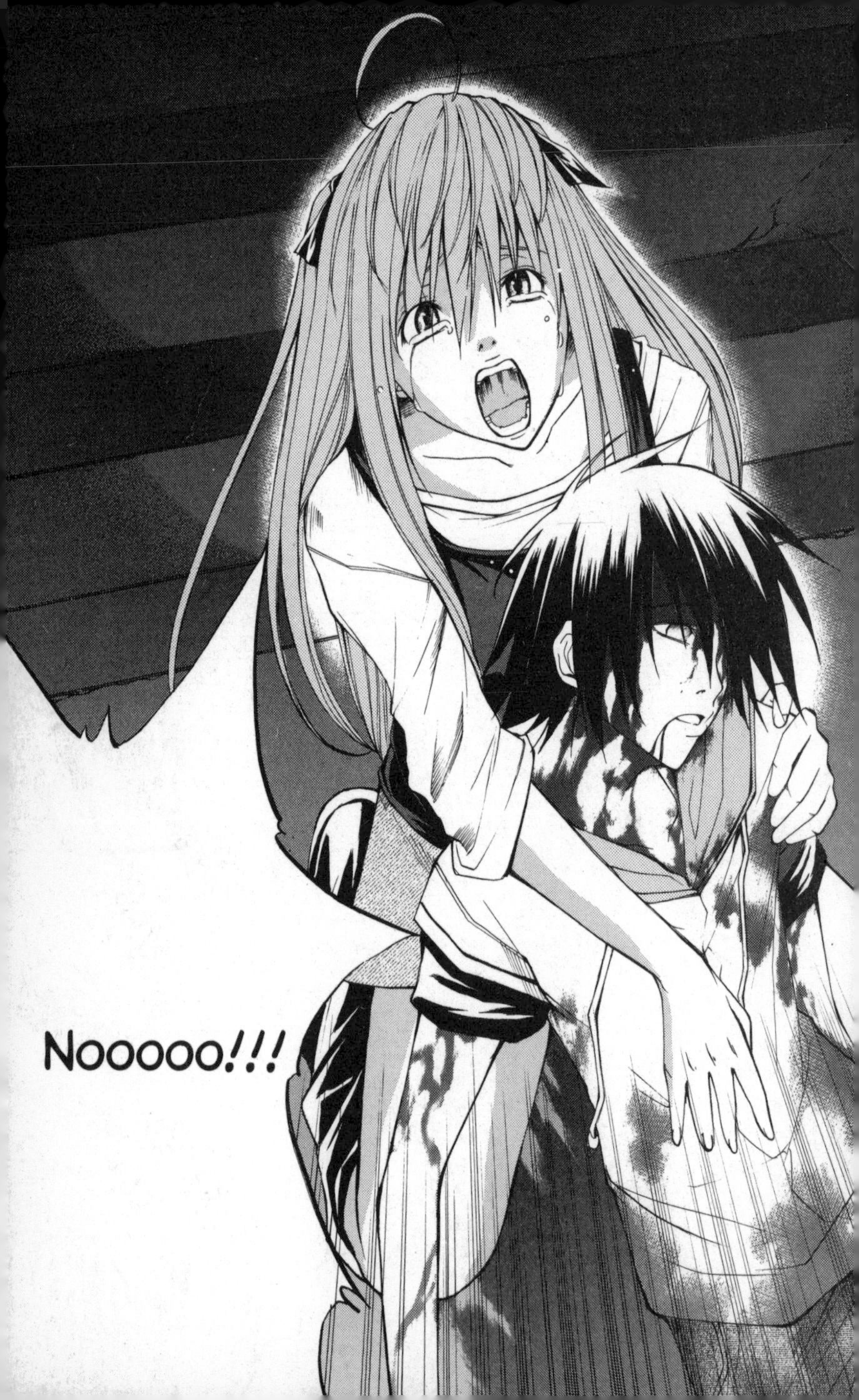
Nooooo!!!

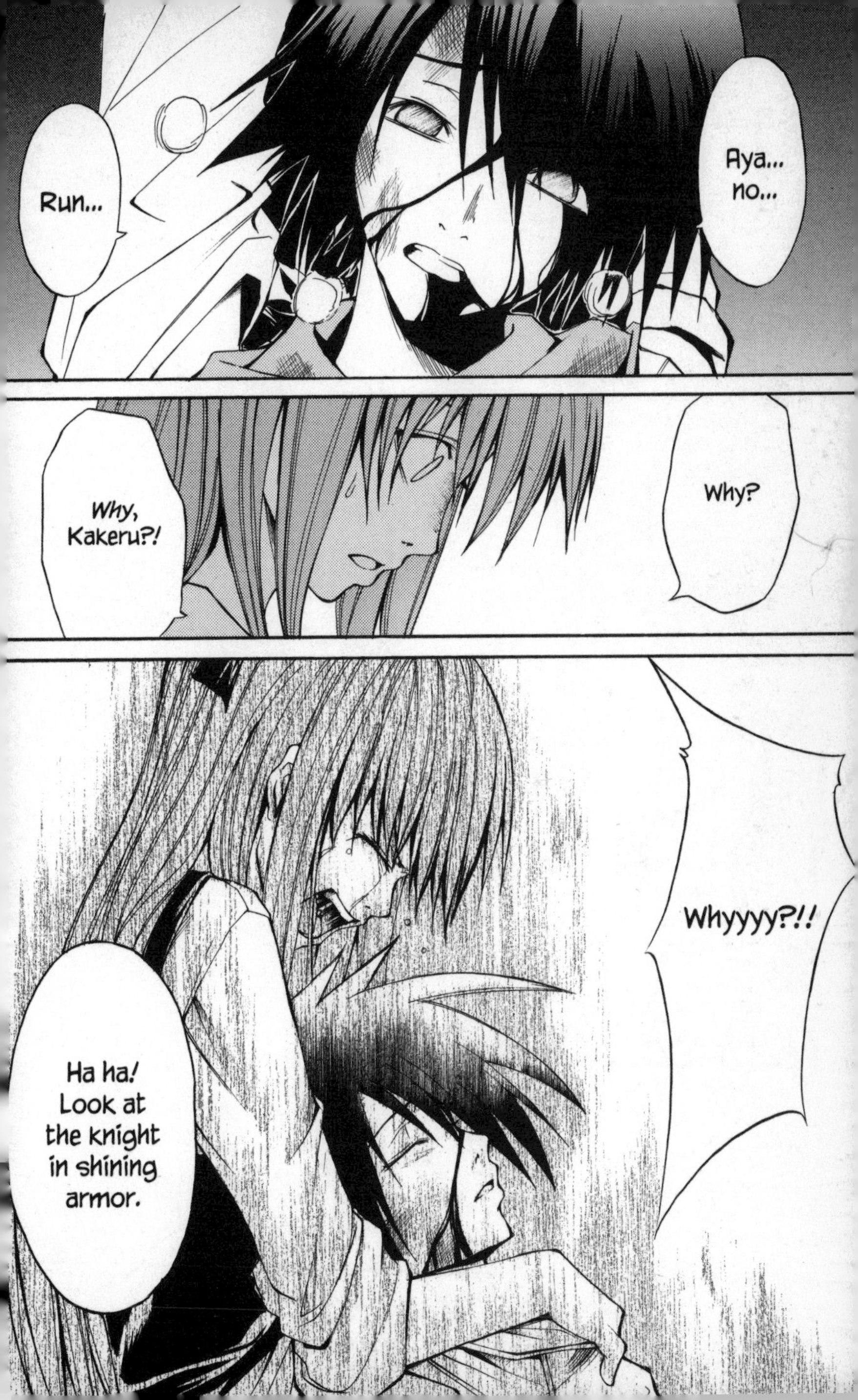
Aya... no...
Run...
Why?
Why, Kakeru?!
Whyyyy?!!
Ha ha! Look at the knight in shining armor.

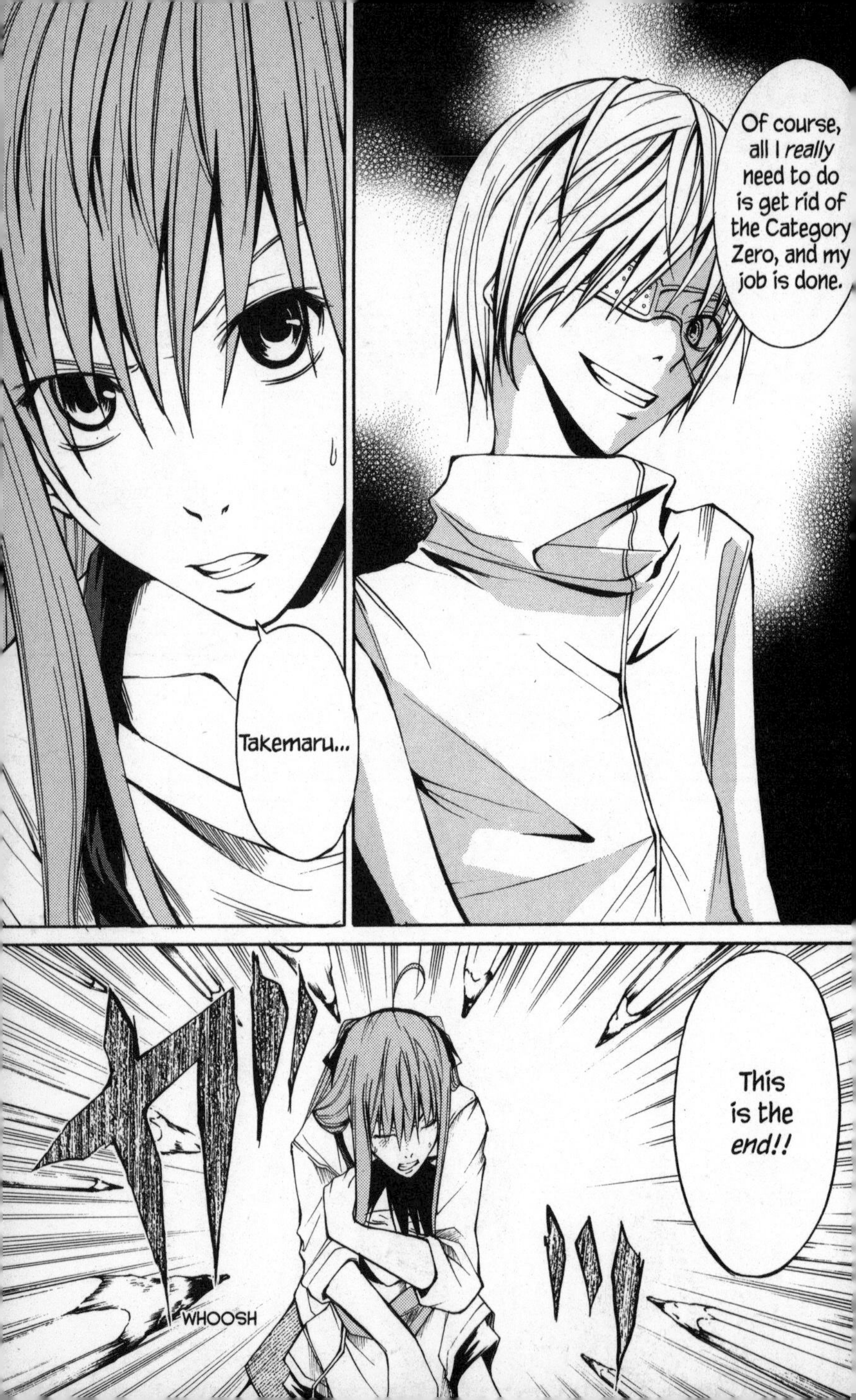
Of course, all I *really* need to do is get rid of the Category Zero, and my job is done.
Takemaru...
This is the *end!!*
WHOOSH

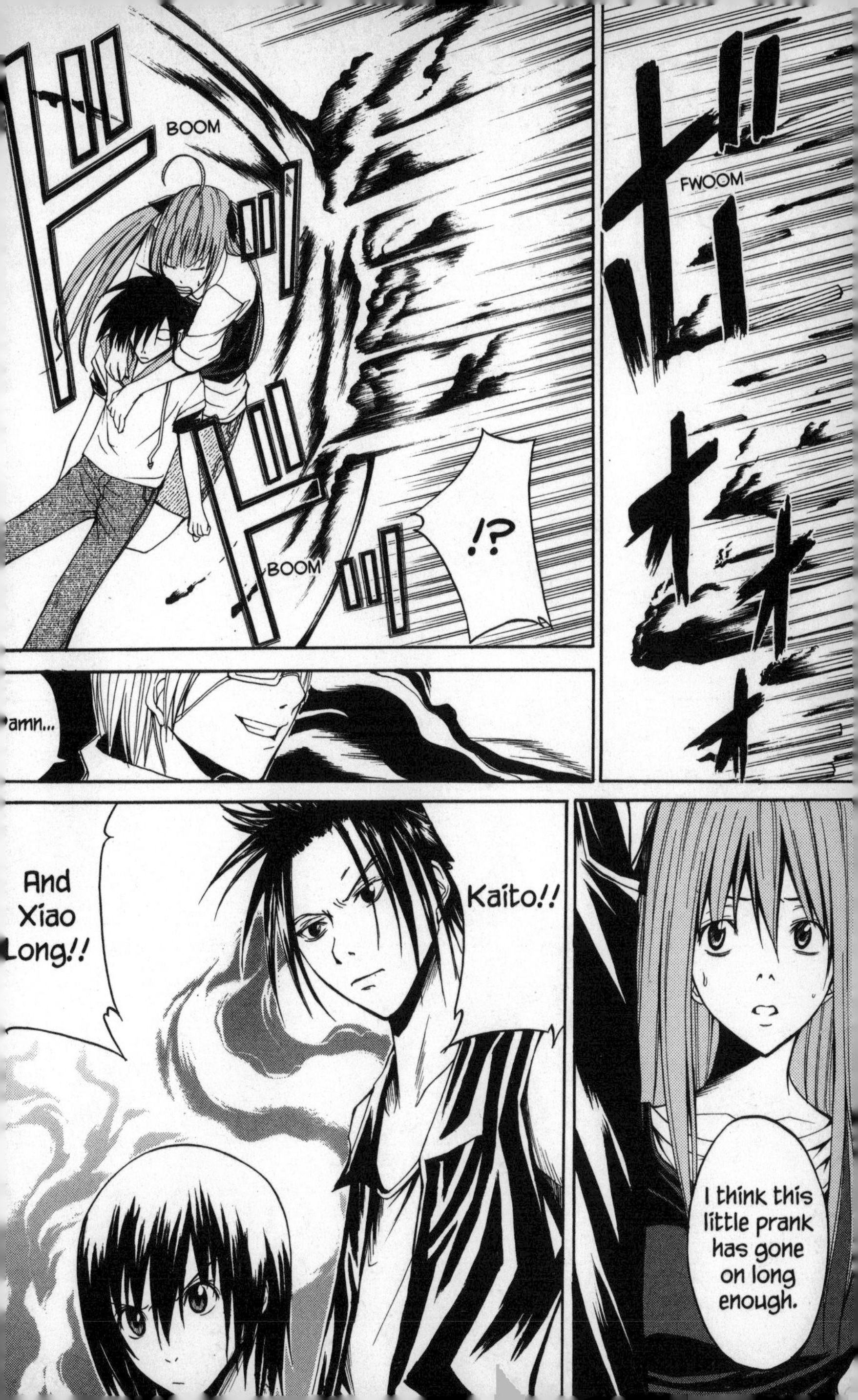
FWOOM
BOOM
!?
BOOM
amn...
I think this little prank has gone on long enough.
Kaito!!
And Xiao Long!!

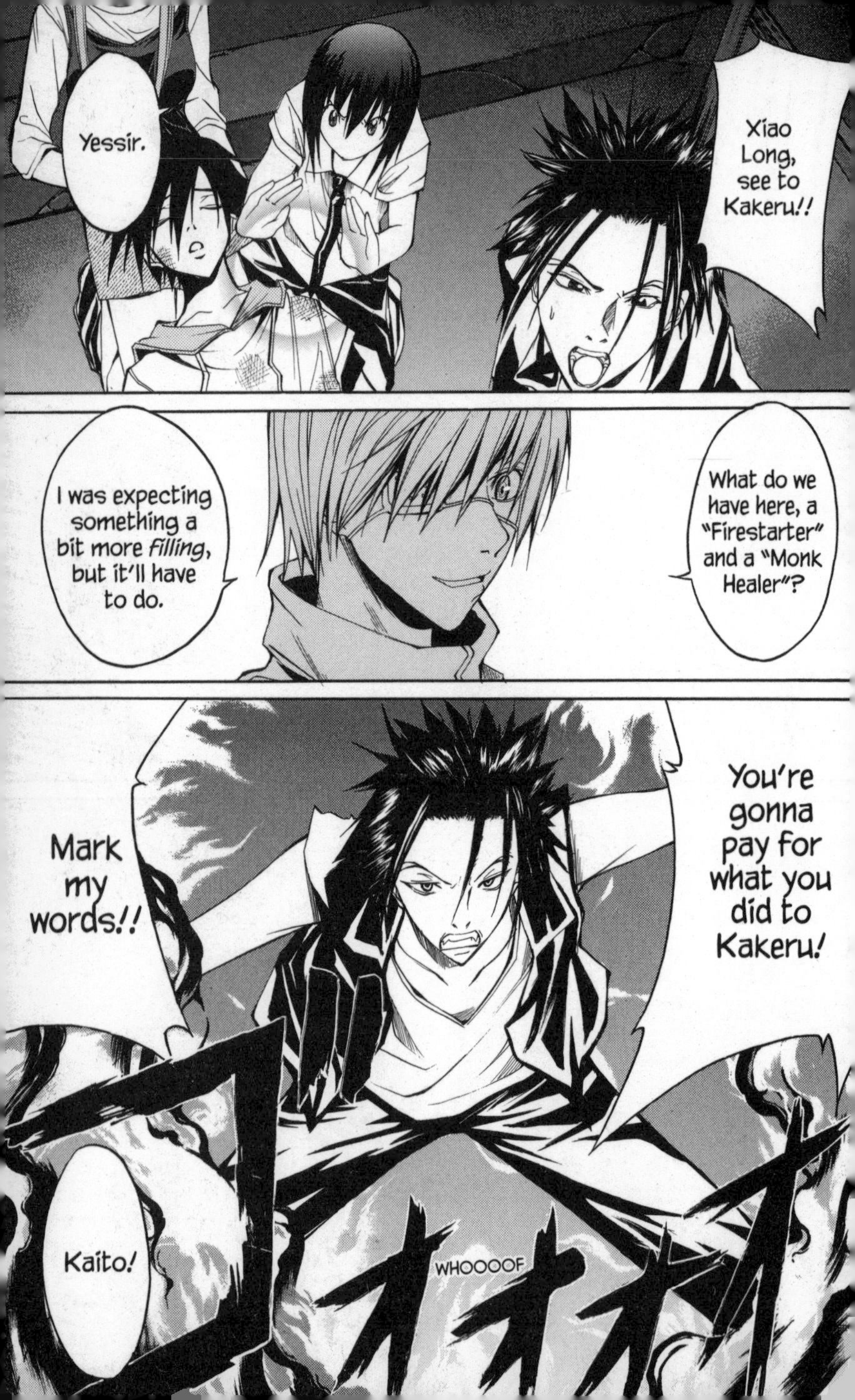
Xiao Long, see to Kakeru!!
Yessir.
What do we have here, a "Firestarter" and a "Monk Healer"?
I was expecting something a bit more *filling*, but it'll have to do.
You're gonna pay for what you did to Kakeru!
Mark my words!!
WHOOOOF
Kaito!

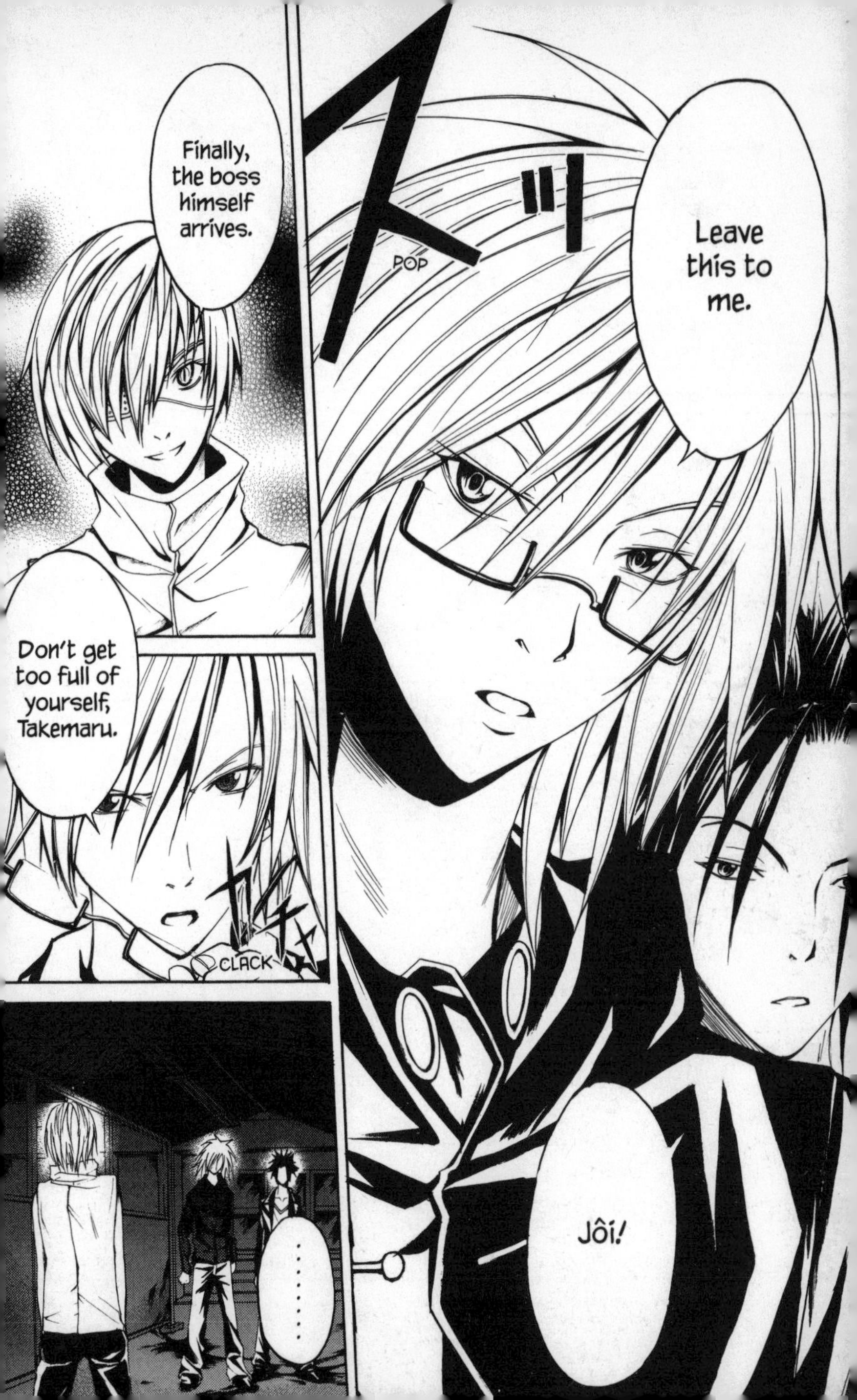
POP
Leave this to me.
Jôi!
Finally, the boss himself arrives.
Don't get too full of yourself, Takemaru.
CLACK
......

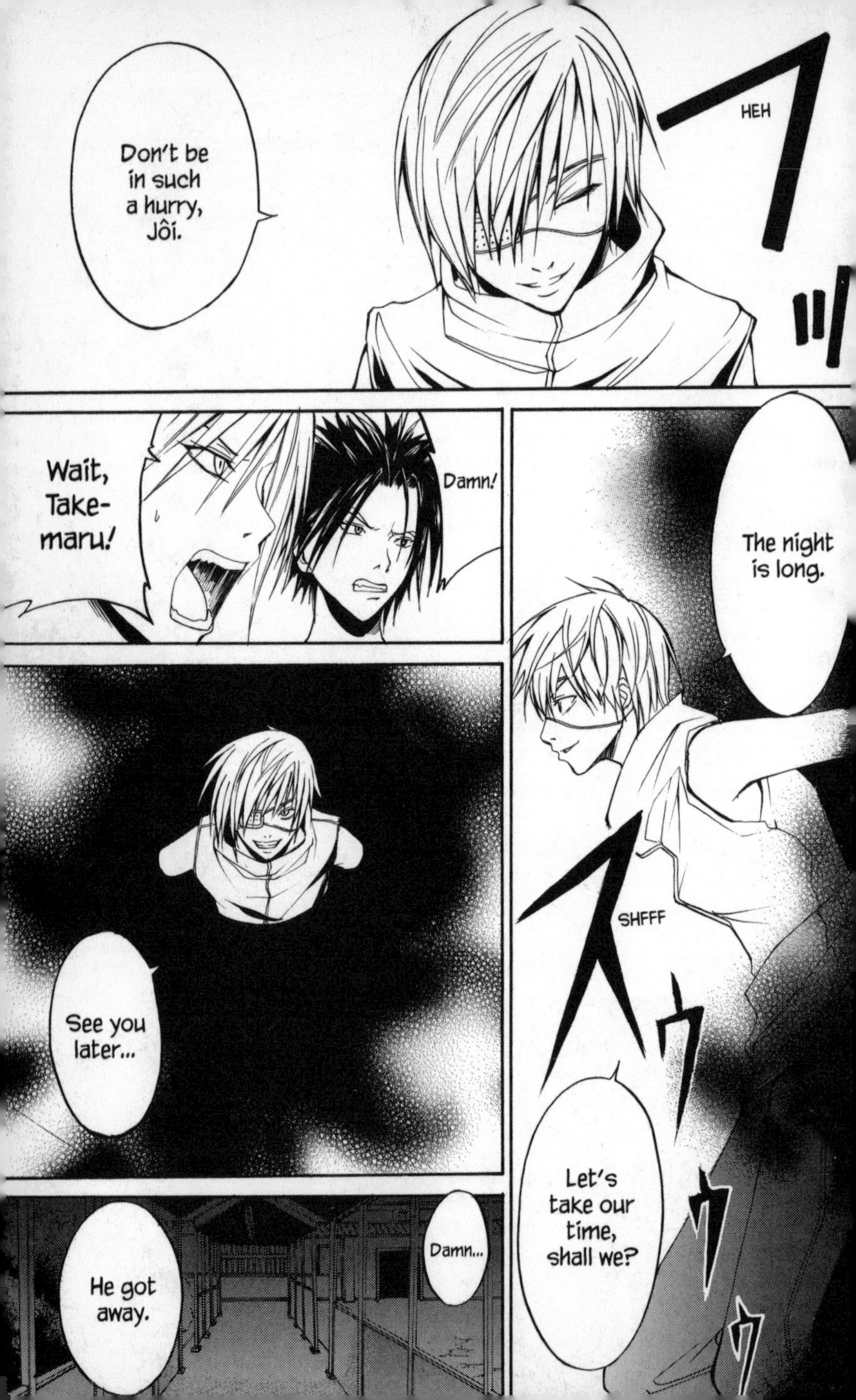
HEH
Don't be in such a hurry, Jôi.
The night is long.
SHFFF
Let's take our time, shall we?
Damn!
Wait, Take-maru!
See you later...
Damn...
He got away.

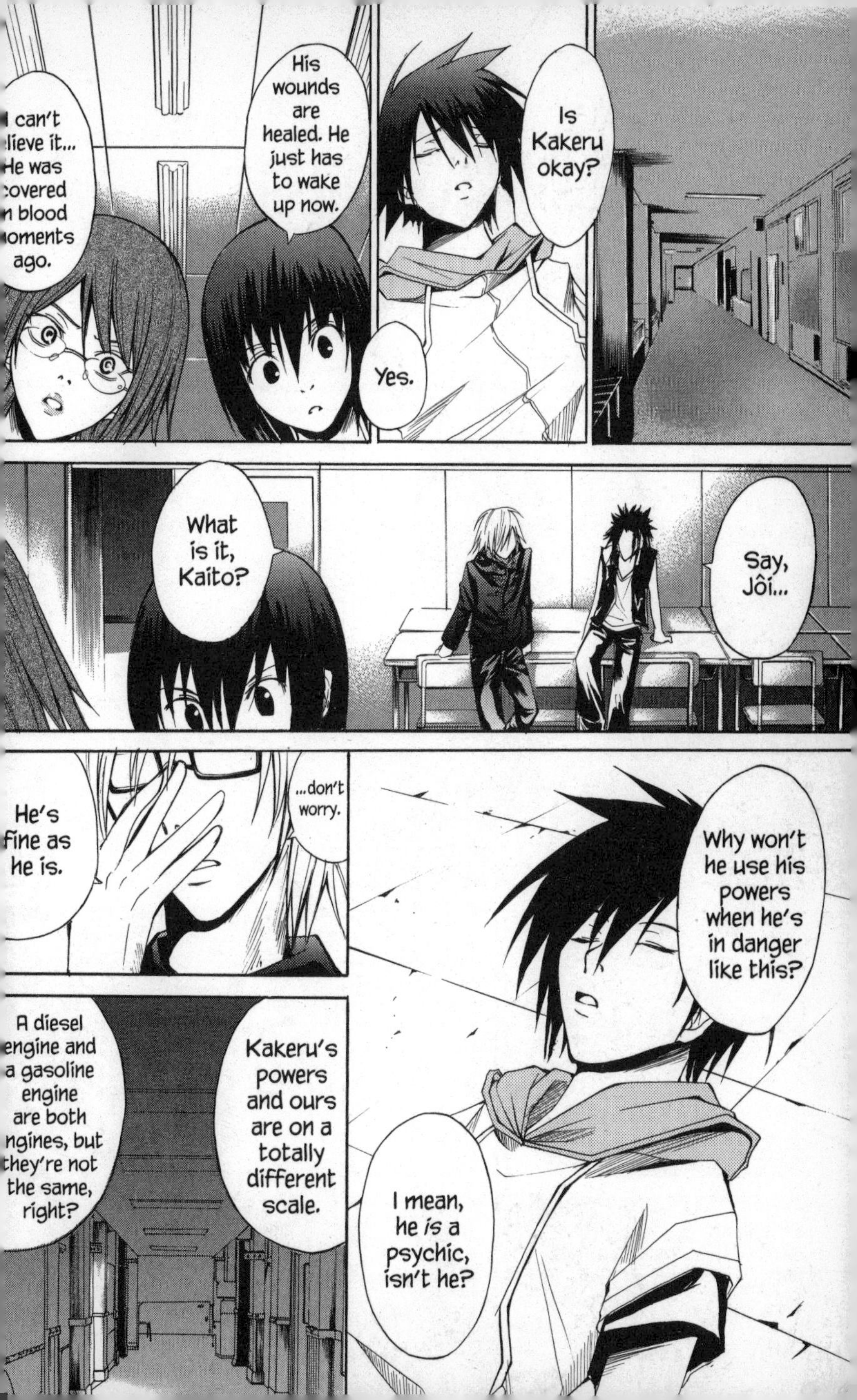
Is Kakeru okay?
Yes.
His wounds are healed. He just has to wake up now.
I can't lieve it... He was covered n blood oments ago.
Say, Jôi...
What is it, Kaito?
Why won't he use his powers when he's in danger like this?
I mean, he *is* a psychic, isn't he?
...don't worry.
He's fine as he is.
Kakeru's powers and ours are on a totally different scale.
A diesel engine and a gasoline engine are both ngines, but hey're not the same, right?

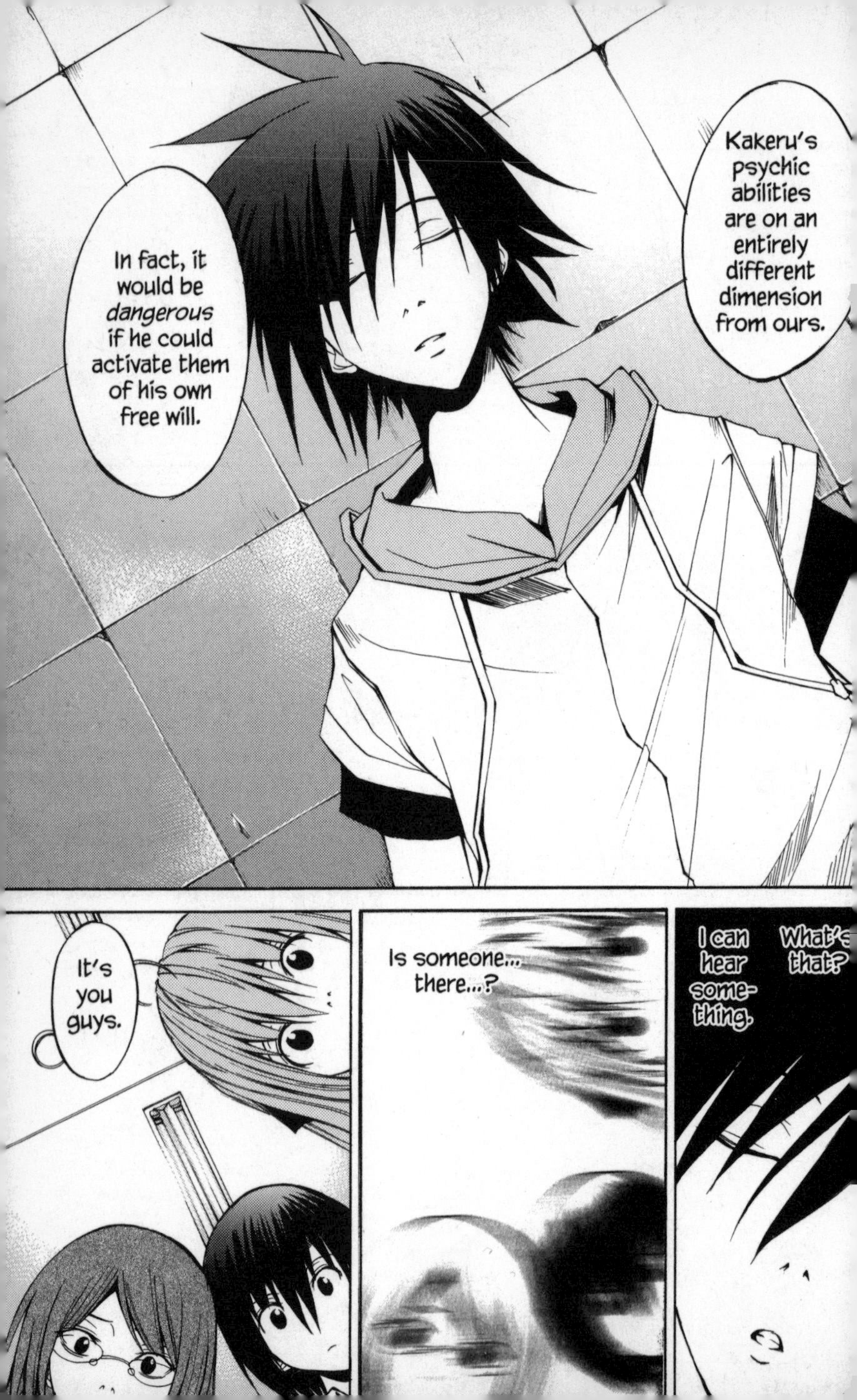
Kakeru's psychic abilities are on an entirely different dimension from ours.
In fact, it would be *dangerous* if he could activate them of his own free will.
What's that?
I can hear some-thing.
Is someone... there...?
It's you guys.

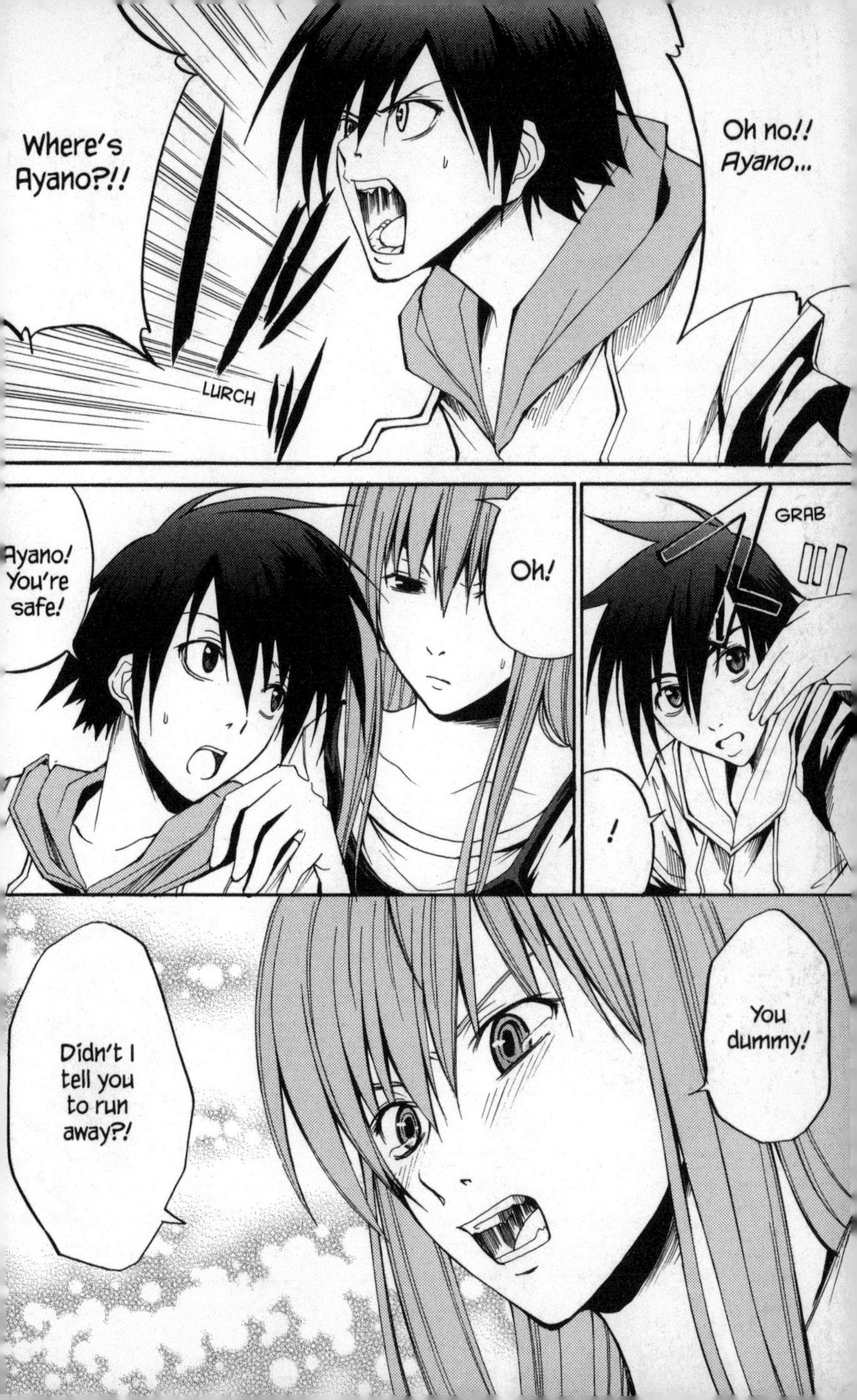
Oh no!! Ayano...
Where's Ayano?!!
LURCH
GRAB
!
Oh!
Ayano! You're safe!
You dummy!
Didn't I tell you to run away?!

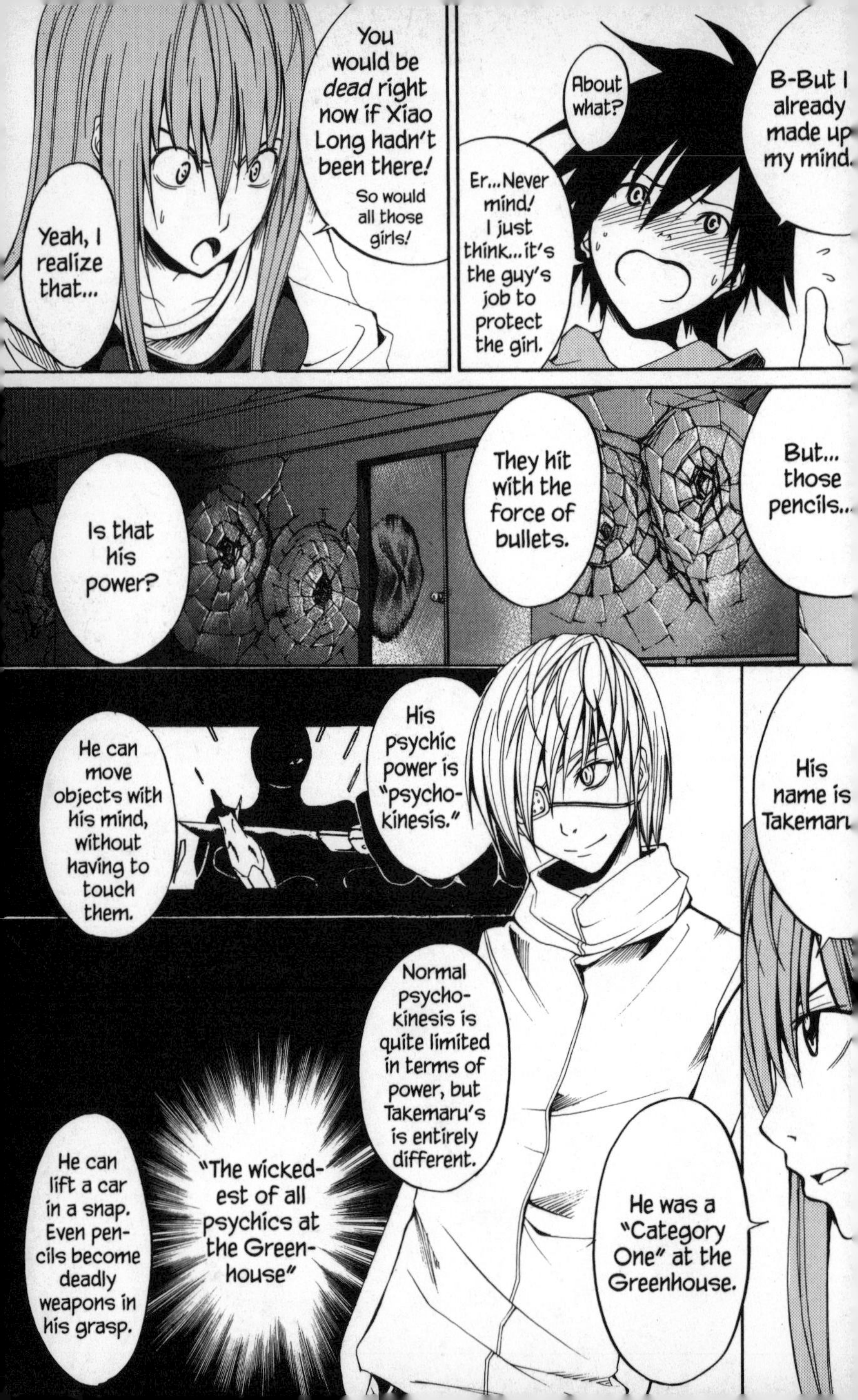
B-But I already made up my mind.
About what?
Er...Never mind! I just think...it's the guy's job to protect the girl.
You would be *dead* right now if Xiao Long hadn't been there!
So would all those girls!
Yeah, I realize that...
But... those pencils...
They hit with the force of bullets.
Is that his power?
His name is Takemaru
His psychic power is "psycho-kinesis."
He can move objects with his mind, without having to touch them.
Normal psycho-kinesis is quite limited in terms of power, but Takemaru's is entirely different.
He was a "Category One" at the Greenhouse.
"The wicked-est of all psychics at the Green-house"
He can lift a car in a snap. Even pen-cils become deadly weapons in his grasp.

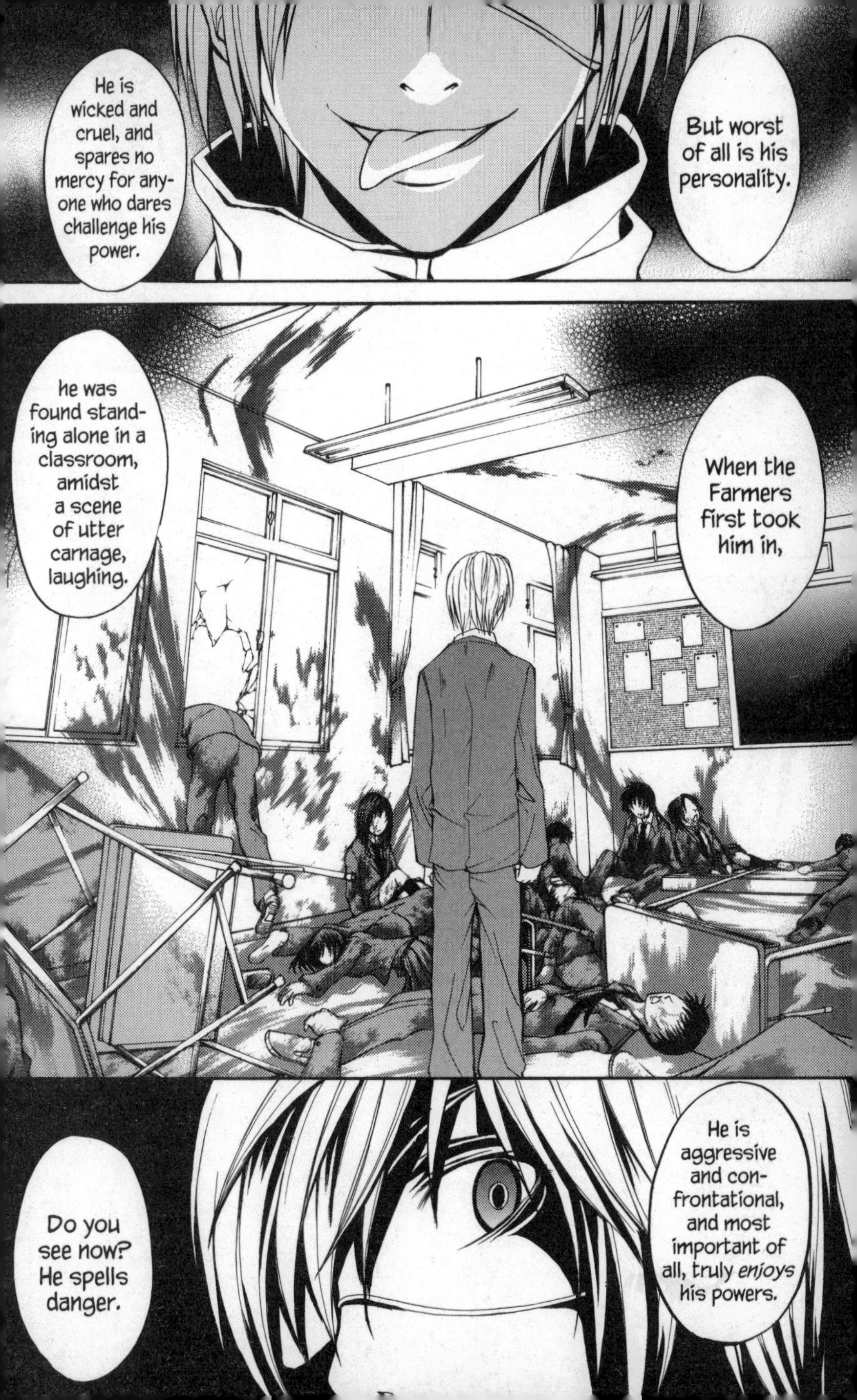
But worst of all is his personality.
He is wicked and cruel, and spares no mercy for anyone who dares challenge his power.
When the Farmers first took him in,
he was found standing alone in a classroom, amidst a scene of utter carnage, laughing.
He is aggressive and confrontational, and most important of all, truly *enjoys* his powers.
Do you see now? He spells danger.

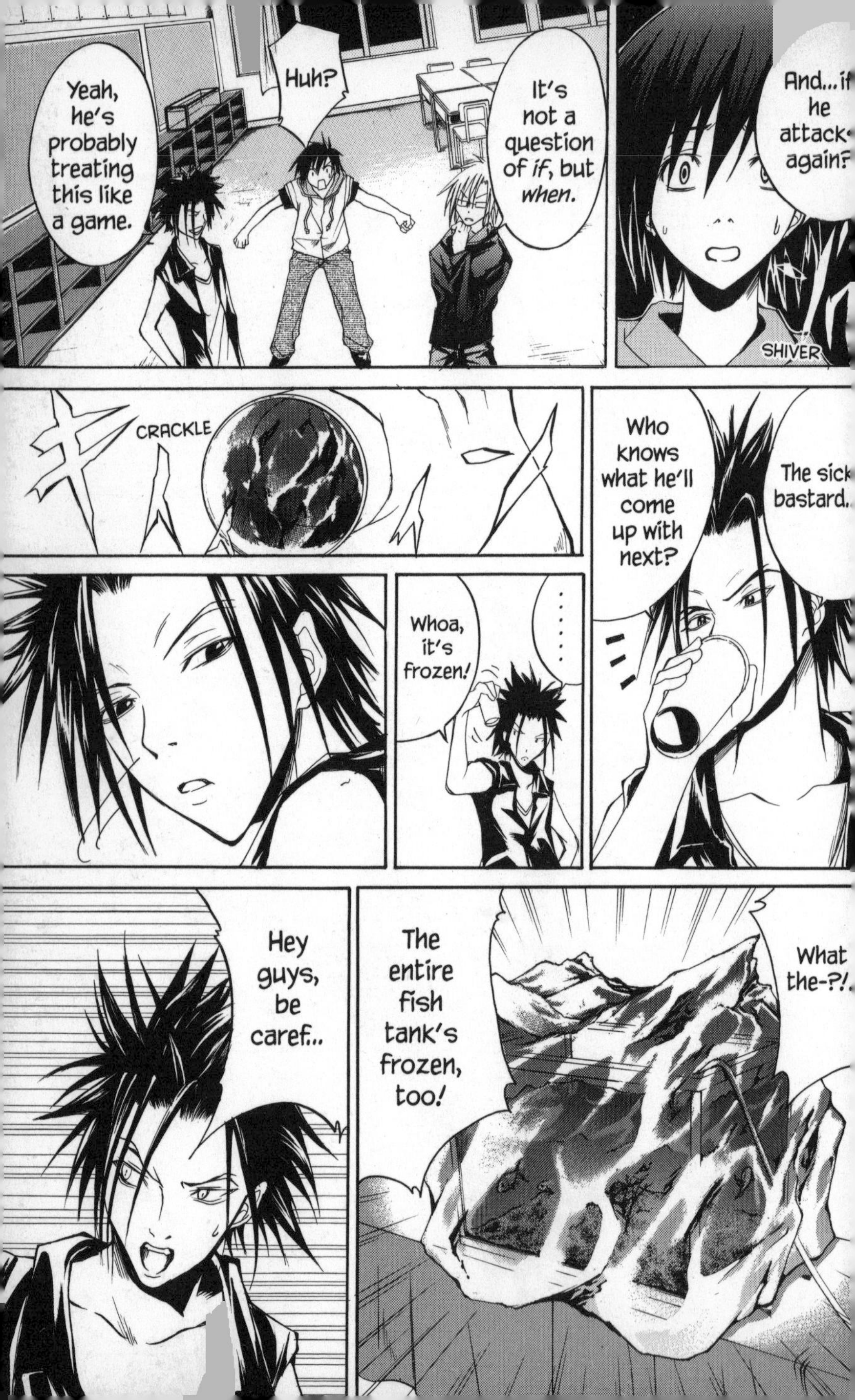
And...if he attack again?
SHIVER
It's not a question of *if*, but *when*.
Huh?
Yeah, he's probably treating this like a game.
The sick bastard...
Who knows what he'll come up with next?
CRACKLE
......
Whoa, it's frozen!
What the-?!
The entire fish tank's frozen, too!
Hey guys, be caref...

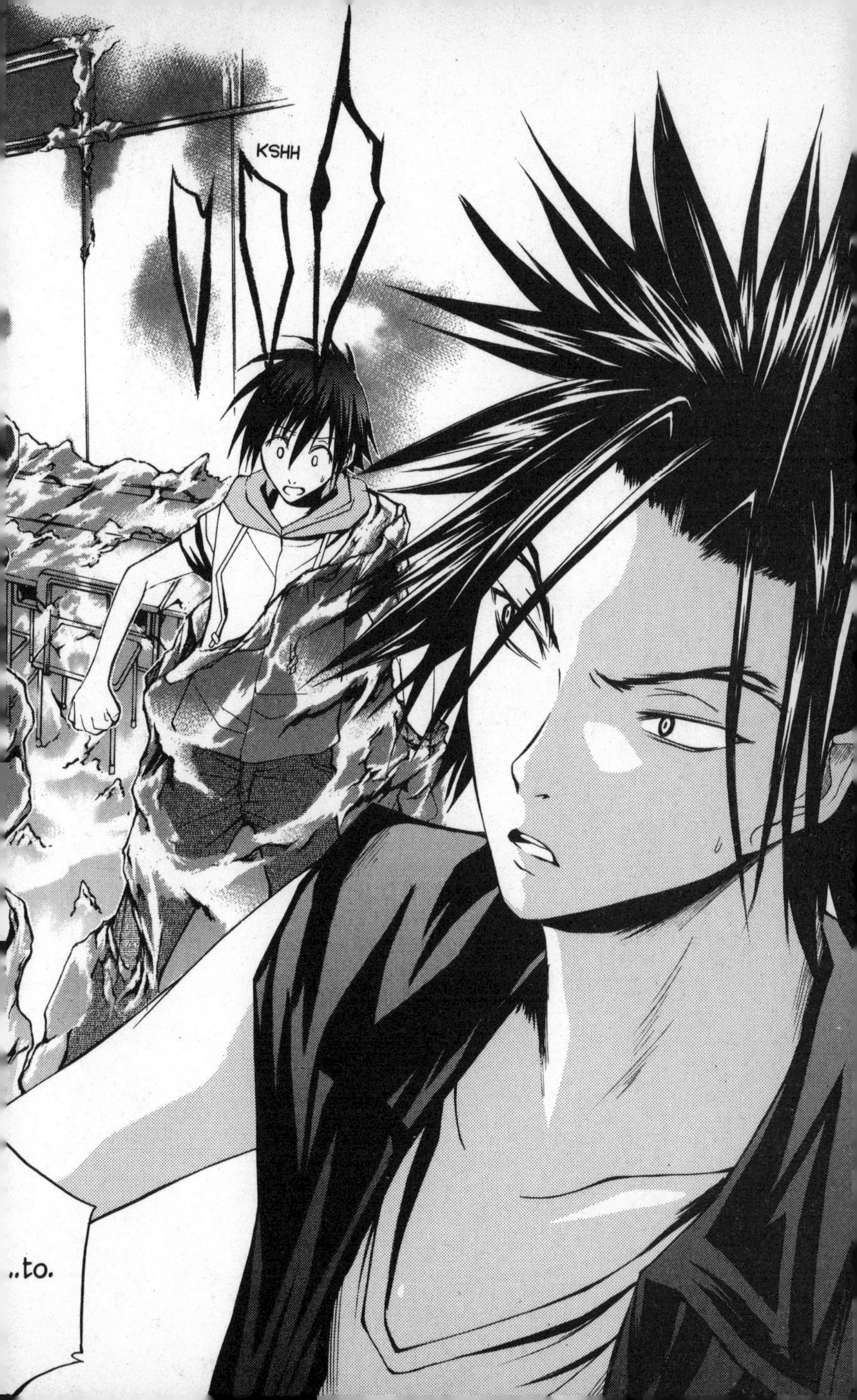
KSHH
..to.

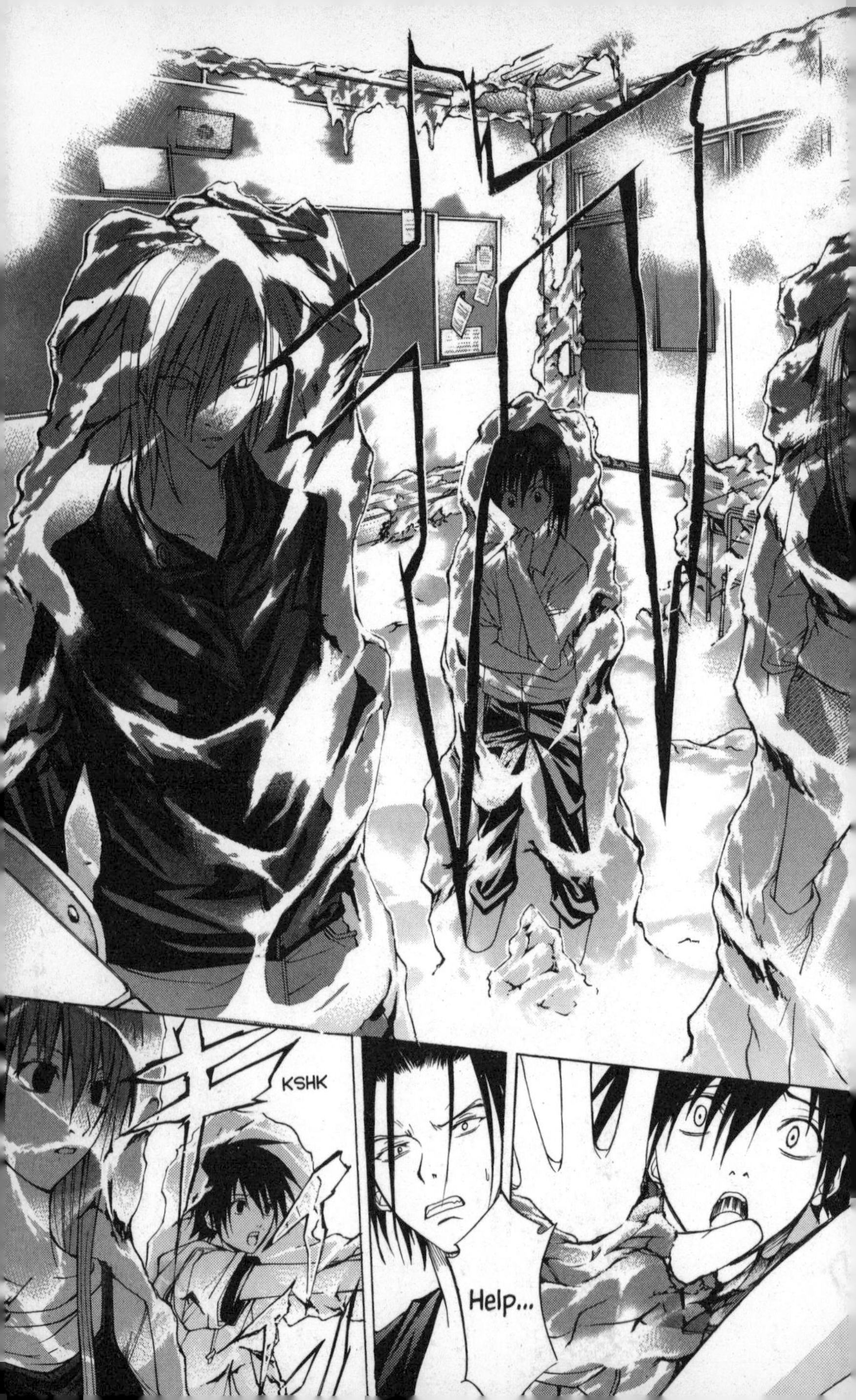
Help...
KSHK

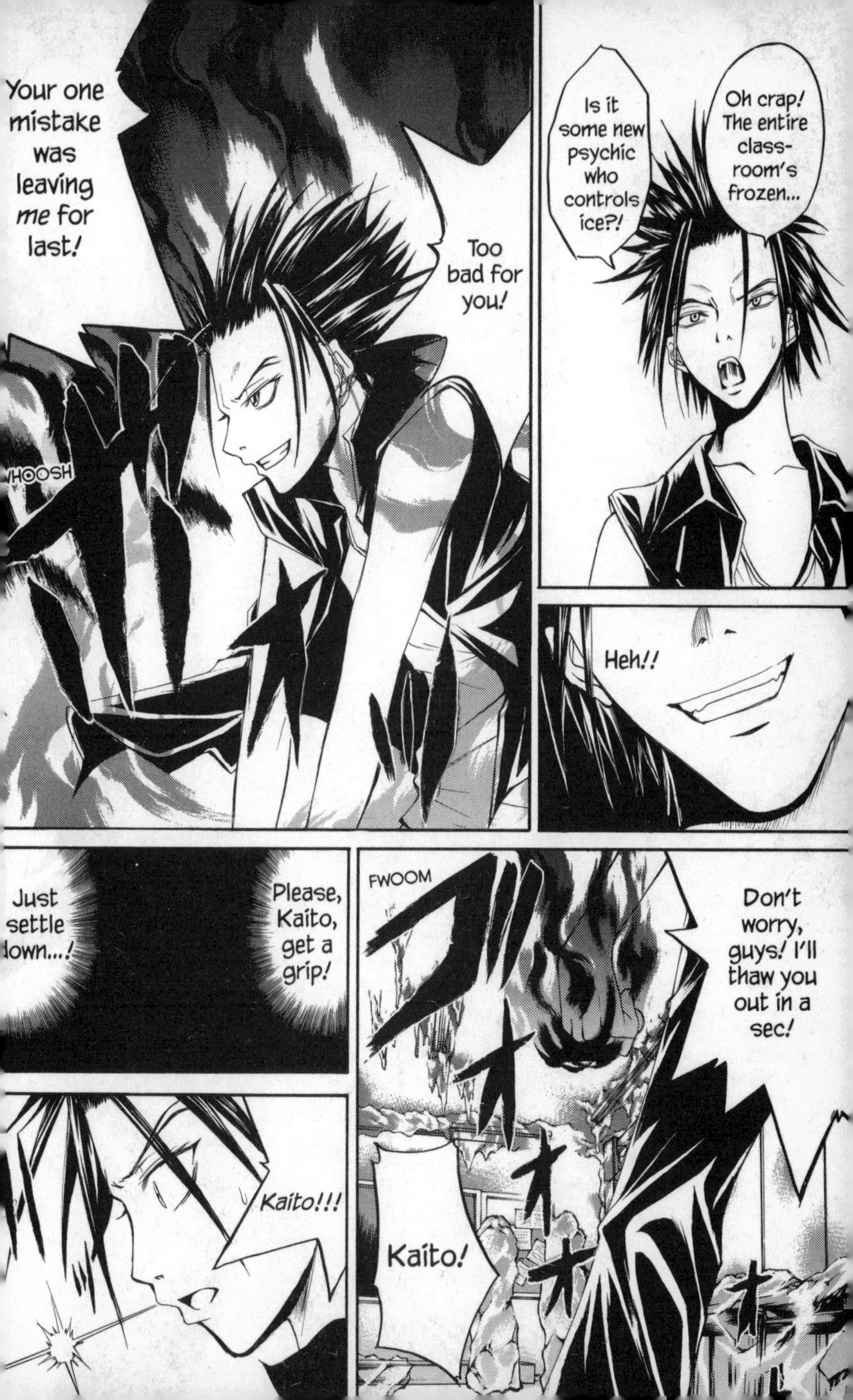

Oh crap! The entire class-room's frozen...
Is it some new psychic who controls ice?!
Heh!!
Your one mistake was leaving *me* for last!
Too bad for you!
WHOOSH
Don't worry, guys! I'll thaw you out in a sec!
FWOOM
Kaito!
Please, Kaito, get a grip!
Just settle down...!
Kaito!!!

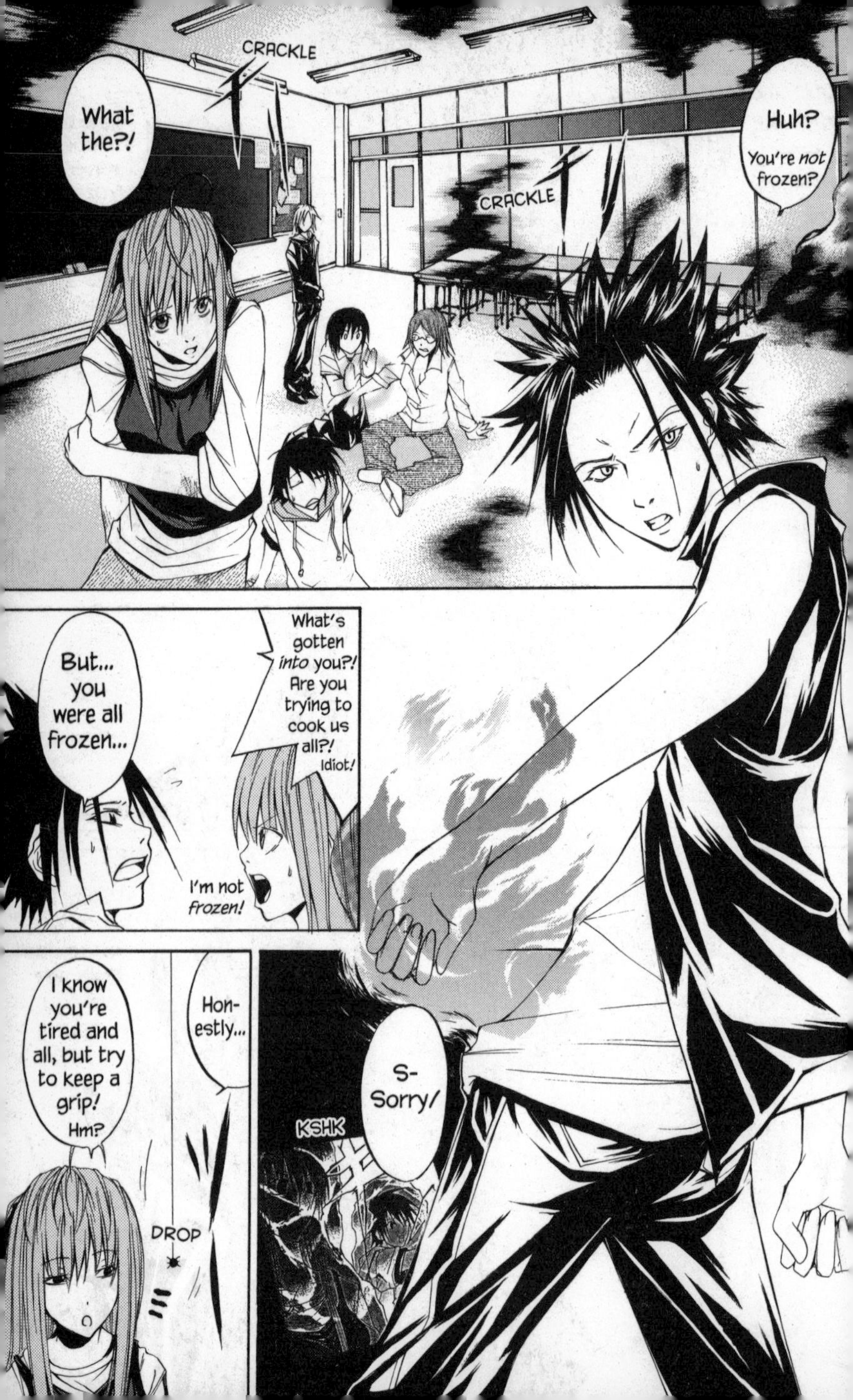

Huh?
You're *not* frozen?
CRACKLE
CRACKLE
What the?!
What's gotten *into* you?! Are you trying to cook us all?!
Idiot!
But... you were all frozen...
I'm not *frozen!*
S-Sorry!
KSHK
Hon-estly...
I know you're tired and all, but try to keep a grip!
Hm?
DROP

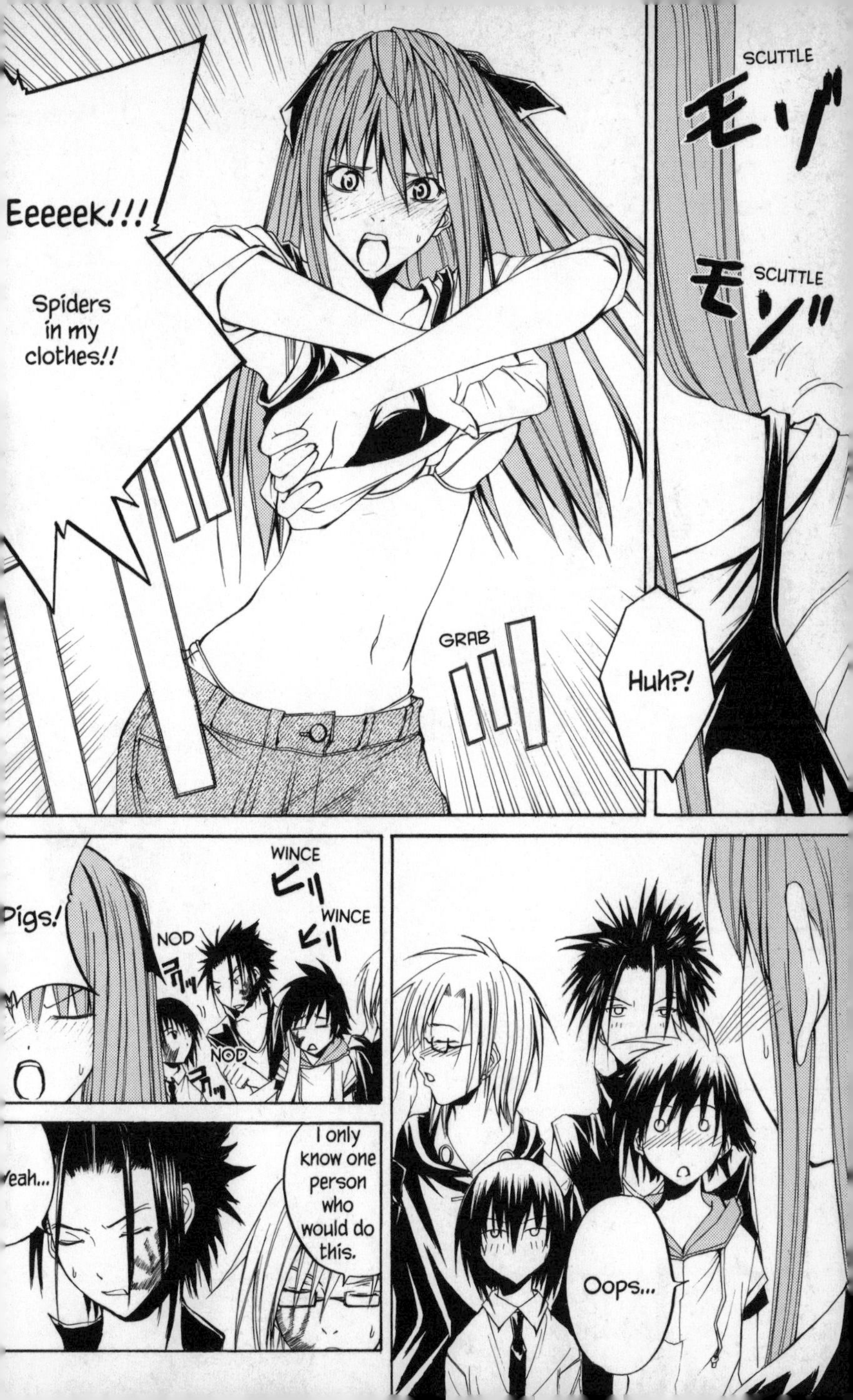
SCUTTLE
モゾ
SCUTTLE
モゾ
Huh?!
Eeeeek!!!
Spiders in my clothes!!
GRAB
Oops...
WINCE
ビリ
WINCE
ビリ
NOD
NOD
Pigs!
I only know one person who would do this.
eah...

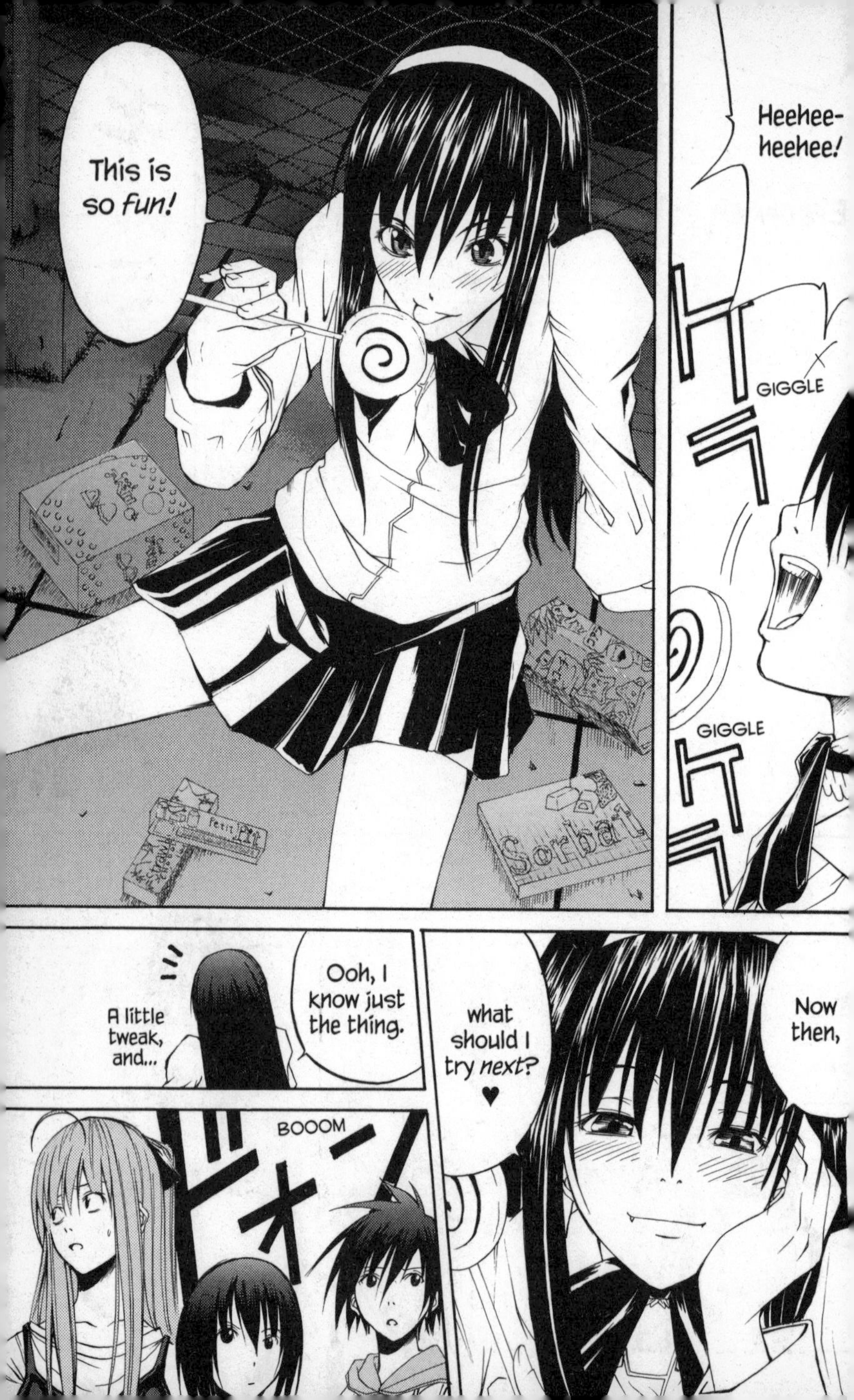
Heehee-heehee!
GIGGLE
GIGGLE
This is so *fun*!
Now then,
what should I try *next*? ♥
Ooh, I know just the thing.
A little tweak, and...
BOOOM

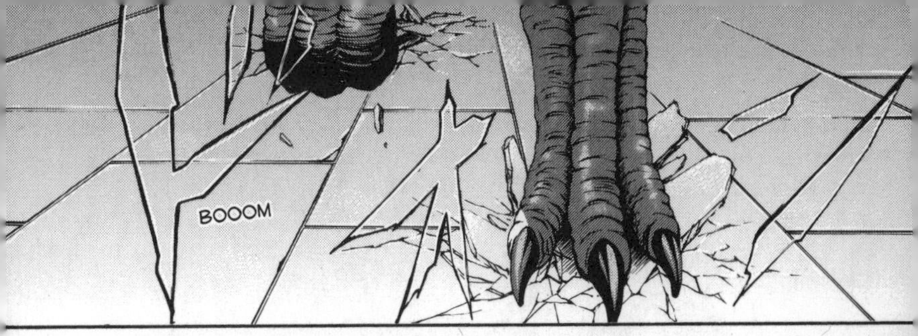
BOOOM
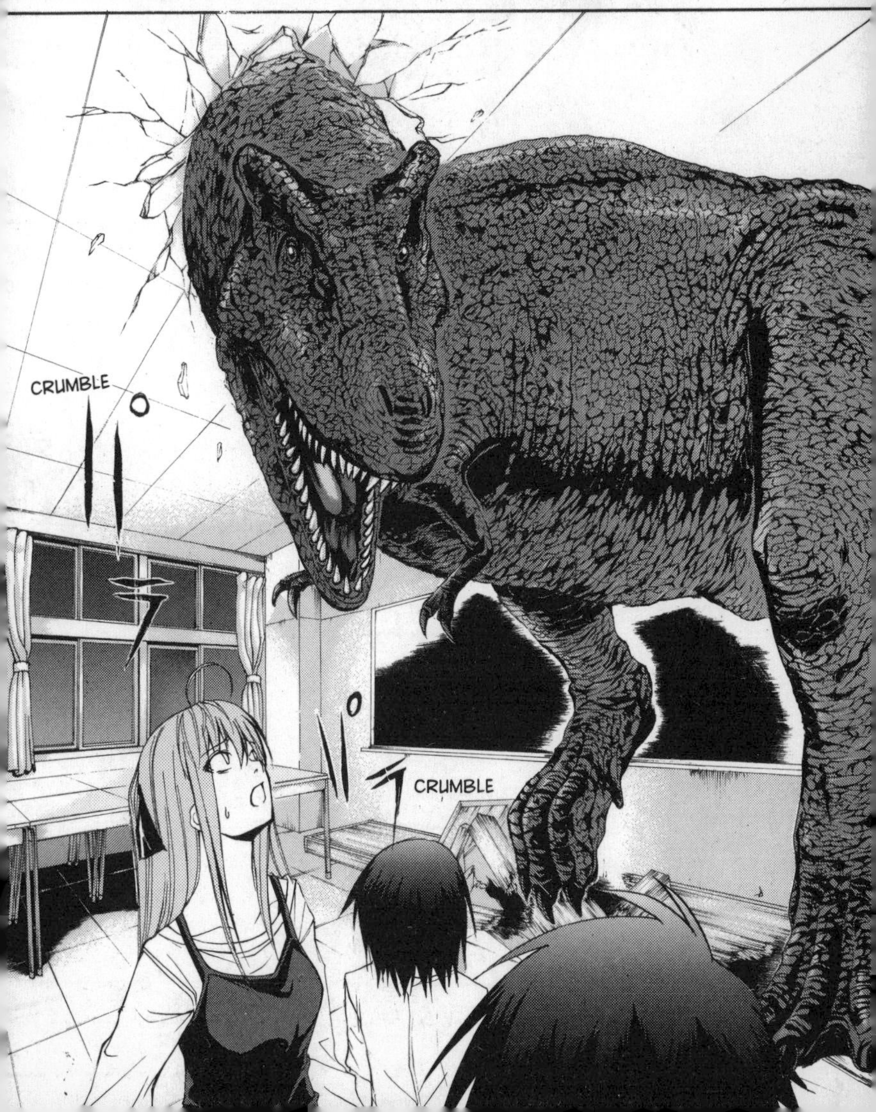
CRUMBLE
CRUMBLE

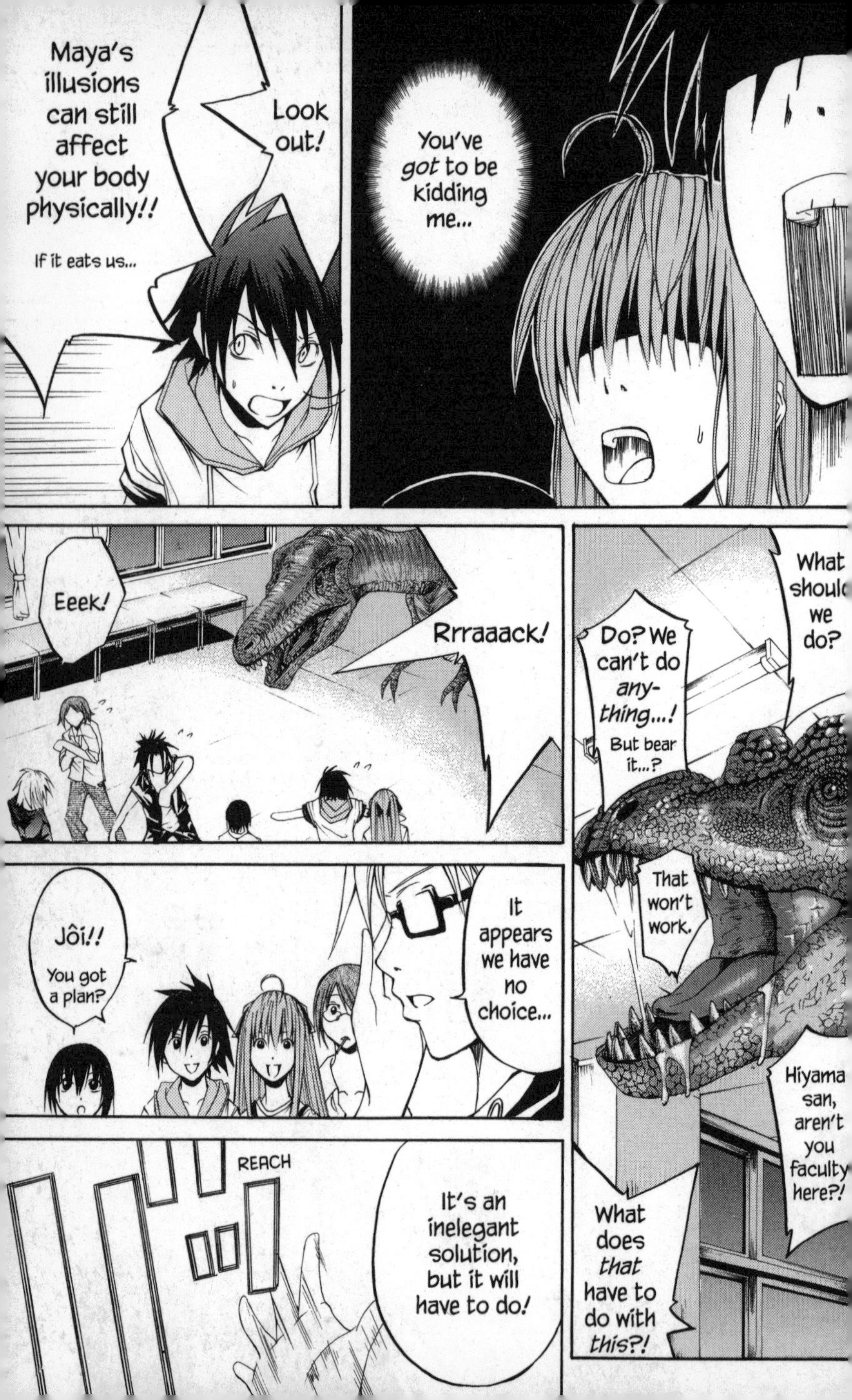
You've *got* to be kidding me...
Look out!
Maya's illusions can still affect your body physically!!
If it eats us...
What should we do?
Do? We can't do *any-thing*...!
But bear it...?
That won't work.
Hiyama san, aren't you faculty here?!
What does *that* have to do with *this*?!
Rrraaack!
Eeek!
It appears we have no choice...
Jôi!!
You got a plan?
It's an inelegant solution, but it will have to do!
REACH

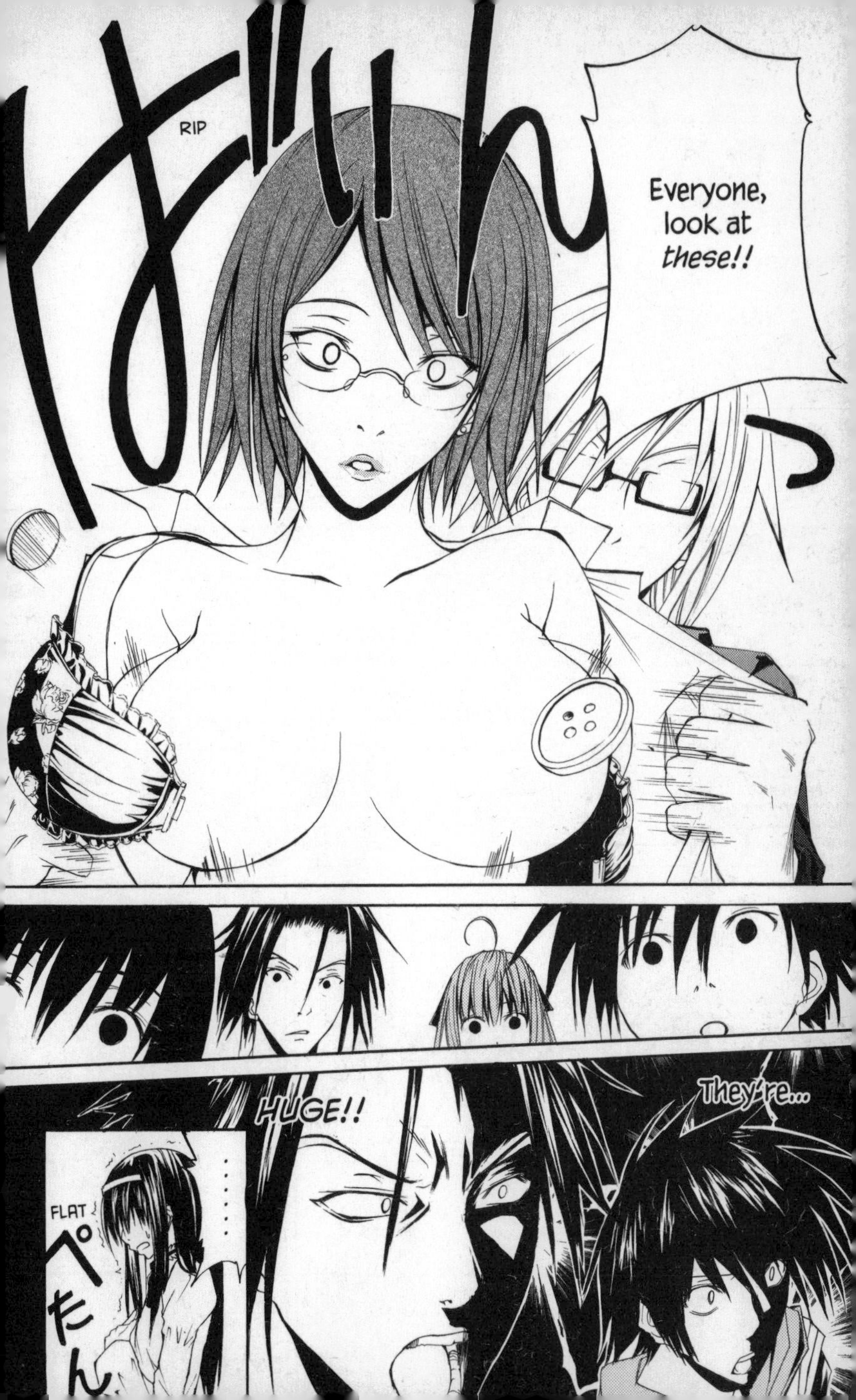
Everyone, look at these!!
RIP
They're...
HUGE!!
......
FLAT
ぺたん

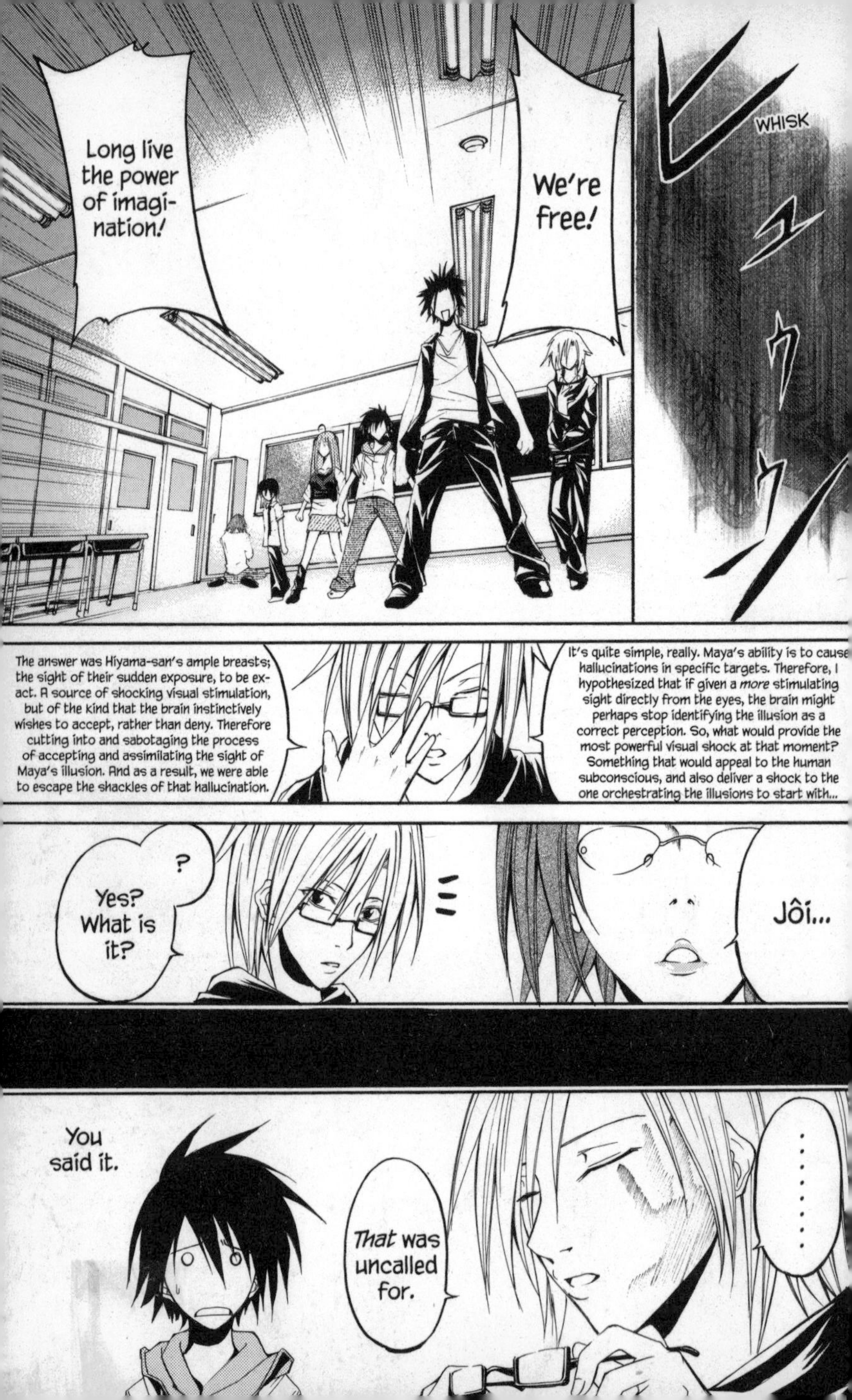
WHISK
We're free!
Long live the power of imagination!
It's quite simple, really. Maya's ability is to cause hallucinations in specific targets. Therefore, I hypothesized that if given a *more* stimulating sight directly from the eyes, the brain might perhaps stop identifying the illusion as a correct perception. So, what would provide the most powerful visual shock at that moment? Something that would appeal to the human subconscious, and also deliver a shock to the one orchestrating the illusions to start with...
The answer was Hiyama-san's ample breasts; the sight of their sudden exposure, to be exact. A source of shocking visual stimulation, but of the kind that the brain instinctively wishes to accept, rather than deny. Therefore cutting into and sabotaging the process of accepting and assimilating the sight of Maya's illusion. And as a result, we were able to escape the shackles of that hallucination.
Jôi...
?
Yes? What is it?
......
That was uncalled for.
You said it.

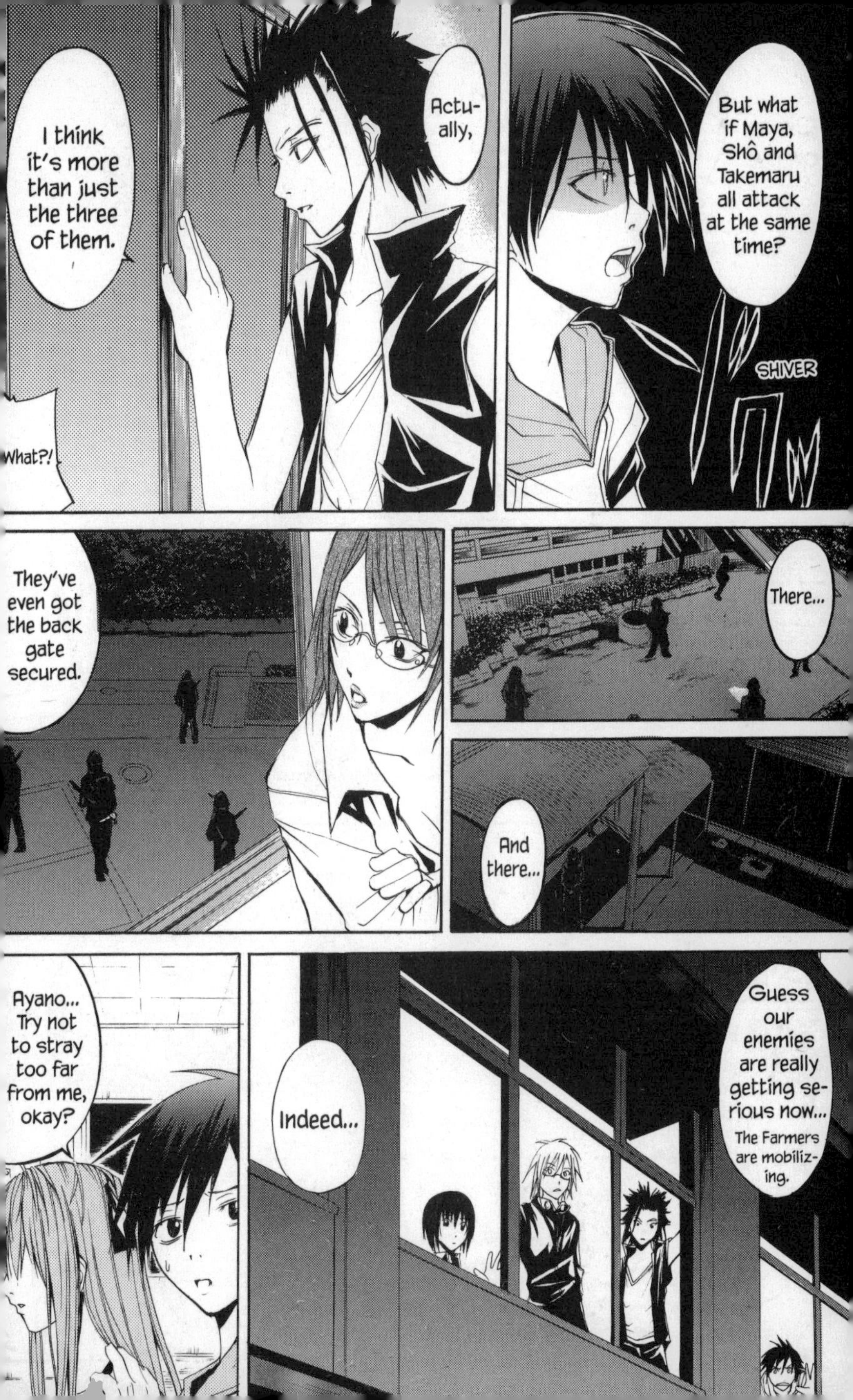
But what if Maya, Shô and Takemaru all attack at the same time?
SHIVER
Actu-ally,
I think it's more than just the three of them.
What?!
There...
And there...
They've even got the back gate secured.
Guess our enemies are really getting se-rious now...
The Farmers are mobiliz-ing.
Indeed...
Ayano... Try not to stray too far from me, okay?

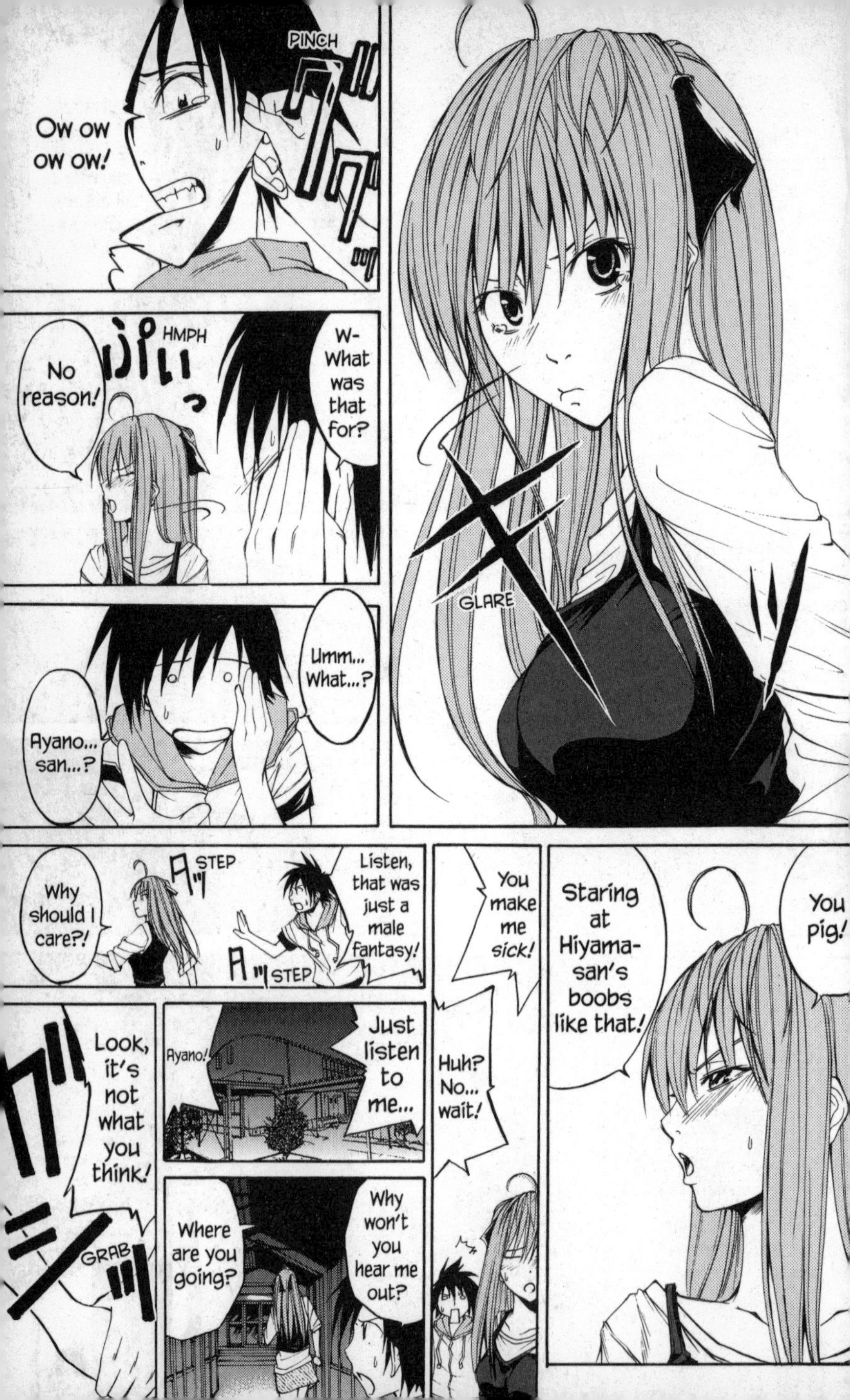
GLARE
PINCH
Ow ow ow ow!
W- What was that for?
HMPH
No reason!
Umm... What...?
Ayano... san...?
You pig!
Staring at Hiyama-san's boobs like that!
You make me sick!
Huh? No... wait!
Listen, that was just a male fantasy!
STEP
Why should I care?!
STEP
Just listen to me...
Ayano!
Why won't you hear me out?
Where are you going?
Look, it's not what you think!
GRAB

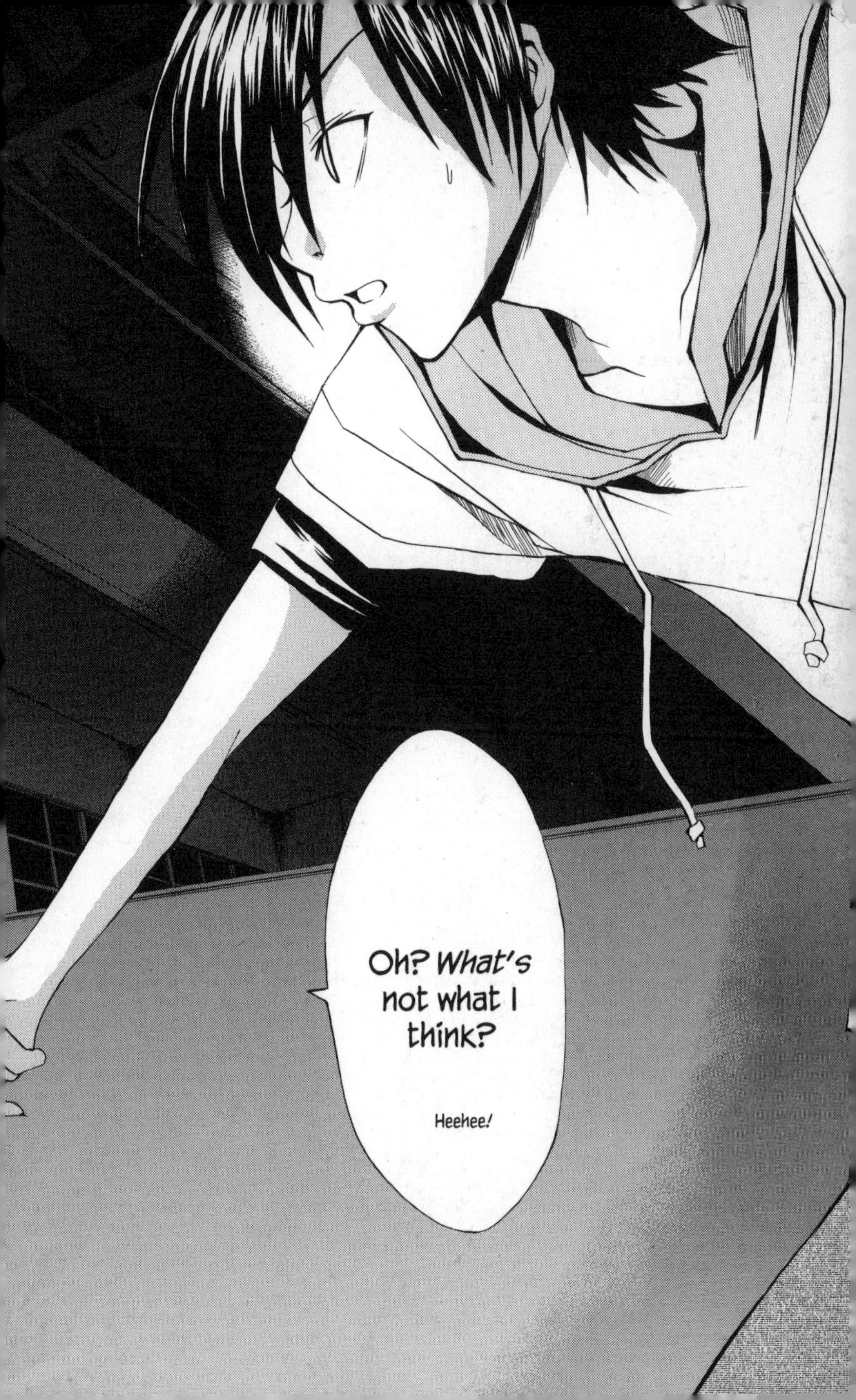
Oh? What's not what I think?
Heehee!

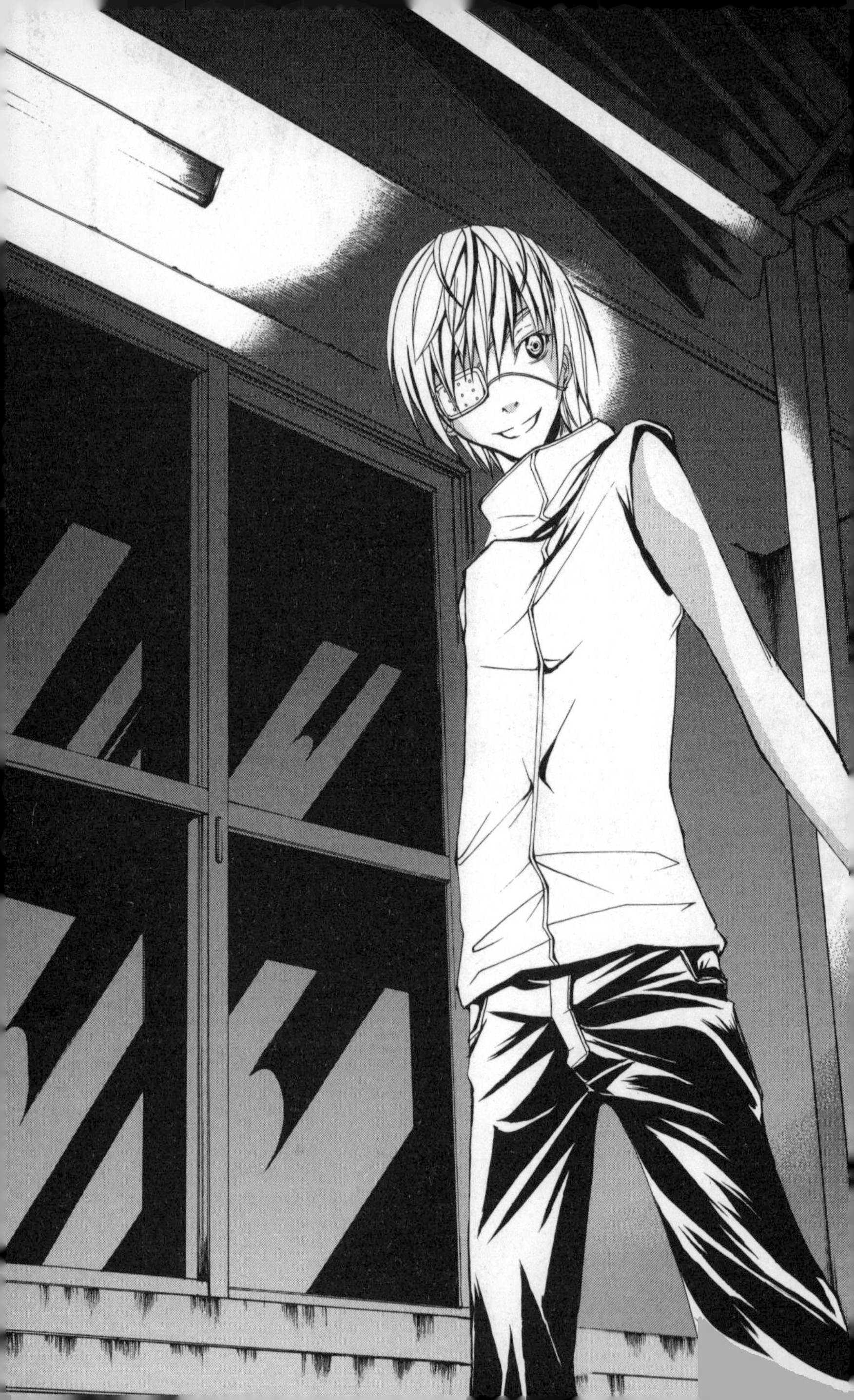

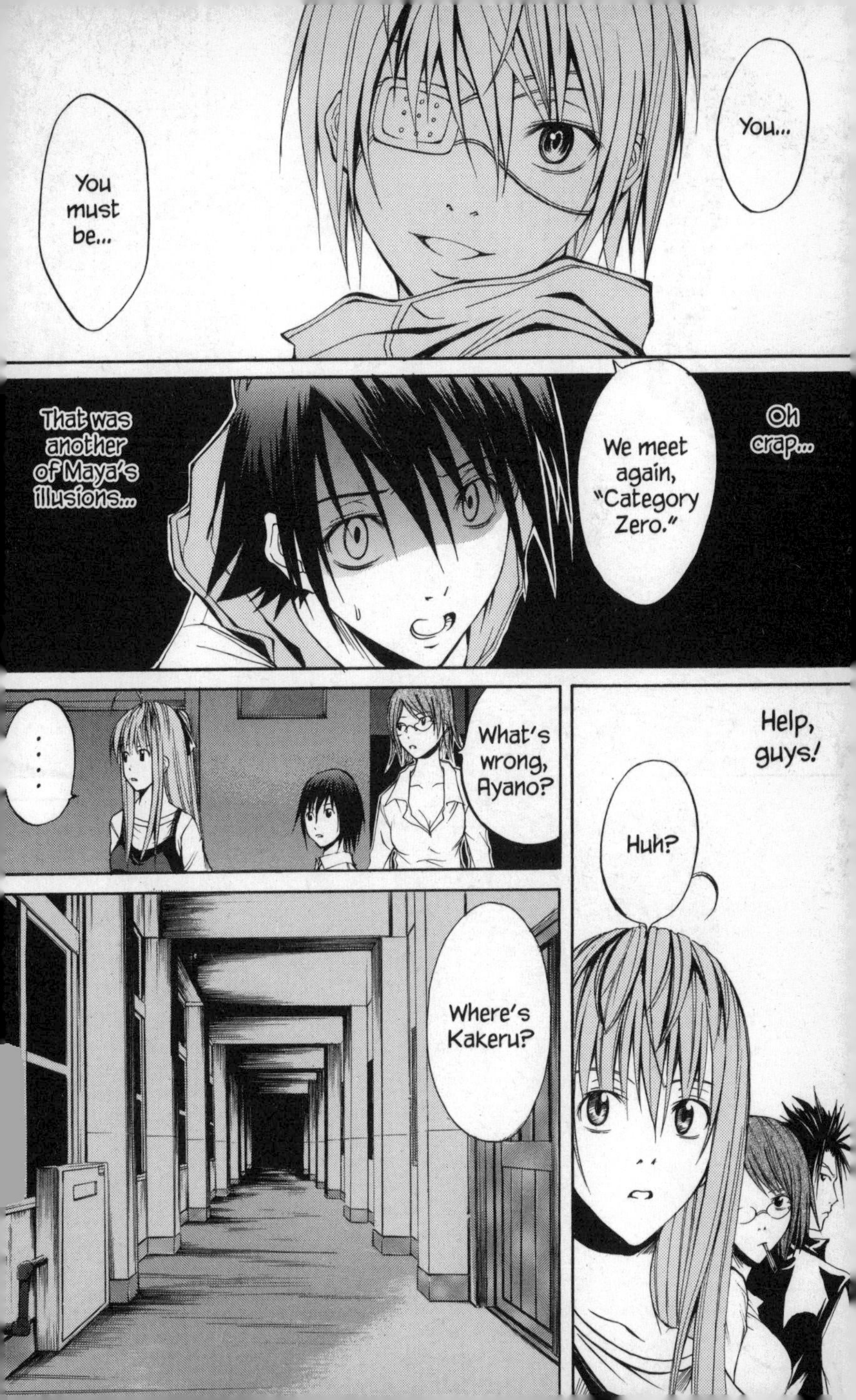

You...
You must be...
Oh crap...
We meet again, "Category Zero."
That was another of Maya's illusions...
Help, guys!
Huh?
What's wrong, Ayano?
.....
Where's Kakeru?

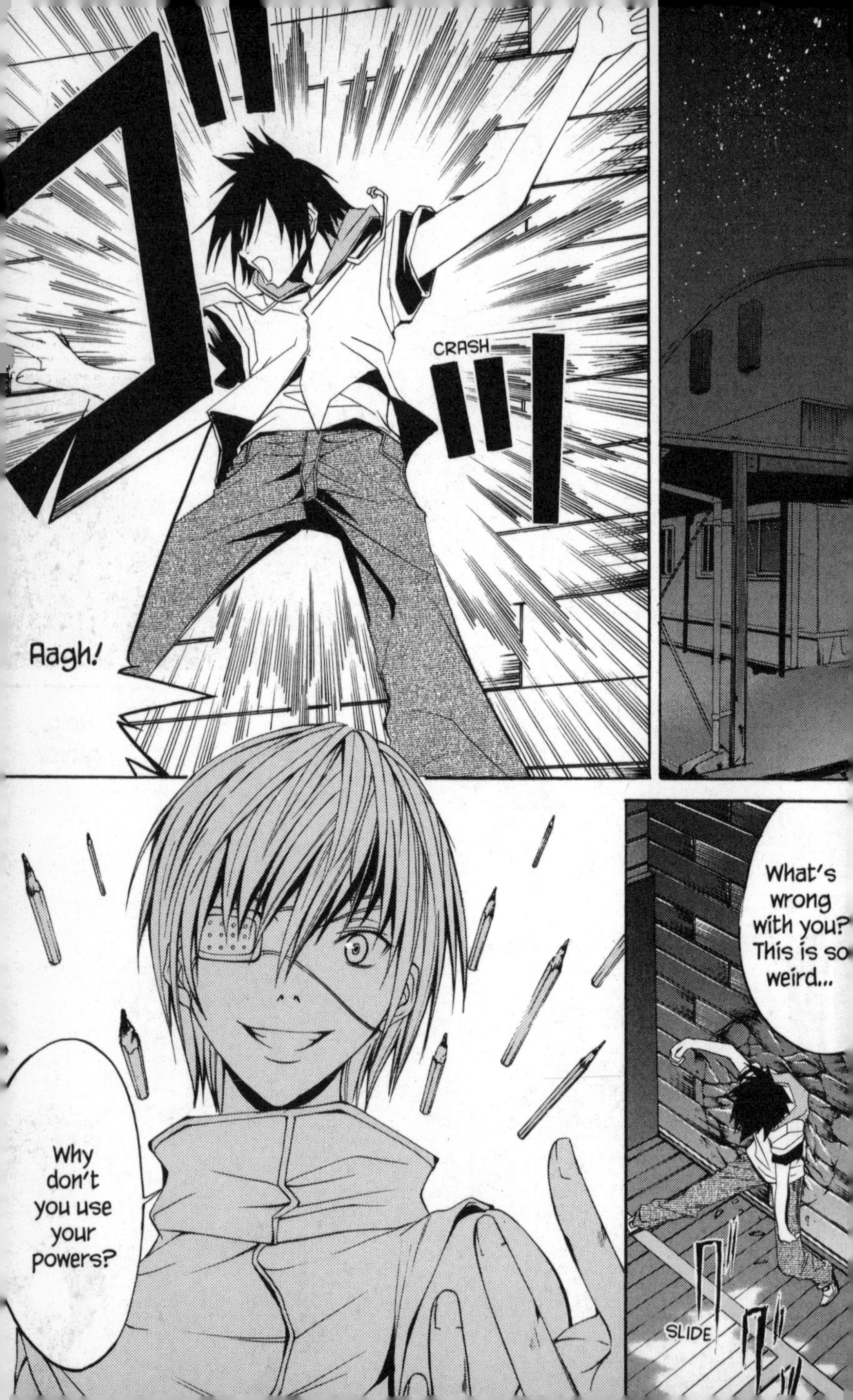
CRASH
Aagh!
What's wrong with you? This is so weird...
SLIDE
Why don't you use your powers?

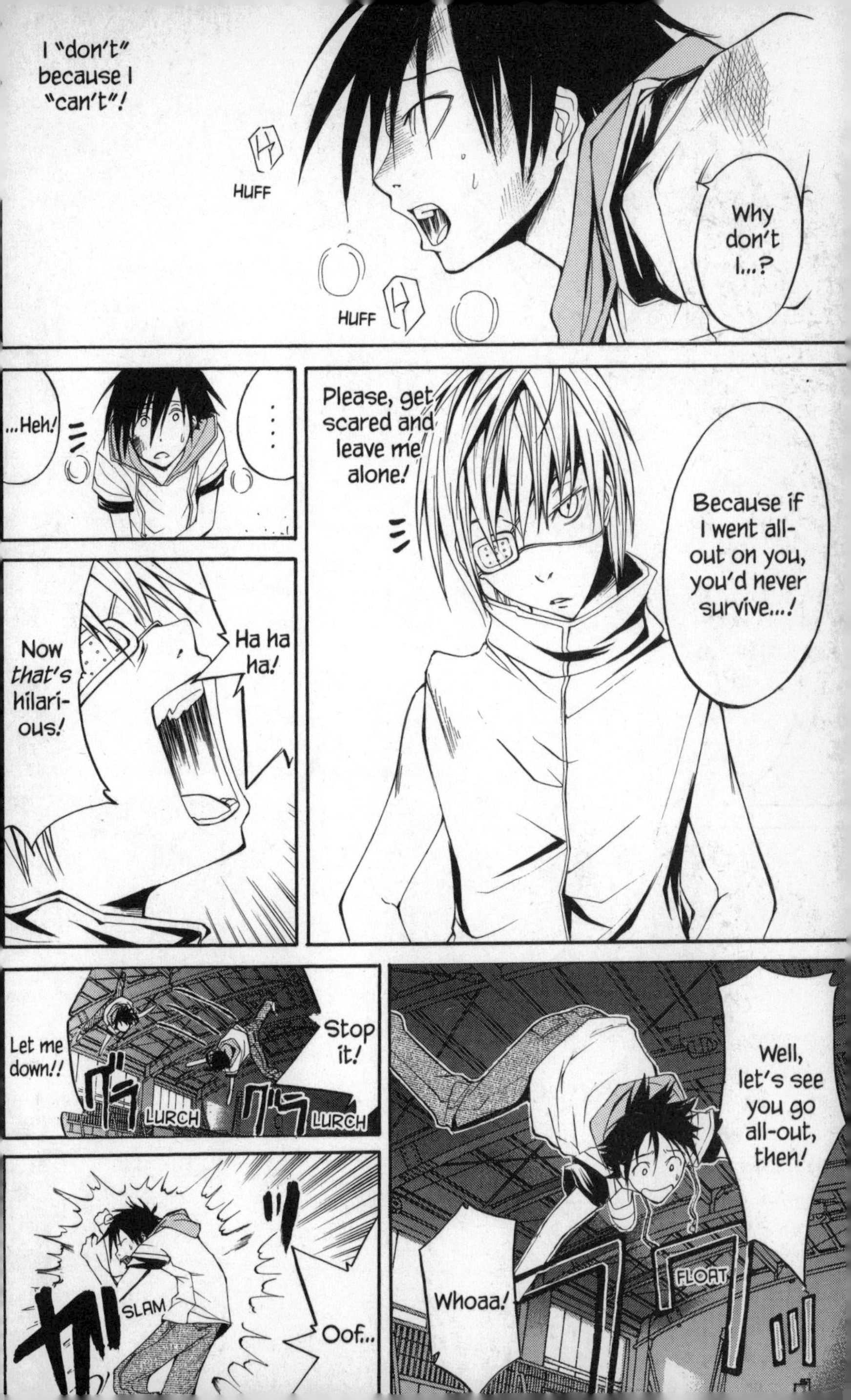
Why don't I...?
I "don't" because I "can't"!
HUFF
HUFF
Because if I went all-out on you, you'd never survive...!
Please, get scared and leave me alone!
....
...Heh!
Ha ha ha!
Now *that*'s hilarious!
Well, let's see you go all-out, then!
FLOAT
Whoaa!
Stop it!
LURCH
Let me down!!
LURCH
Oof...
SLAM

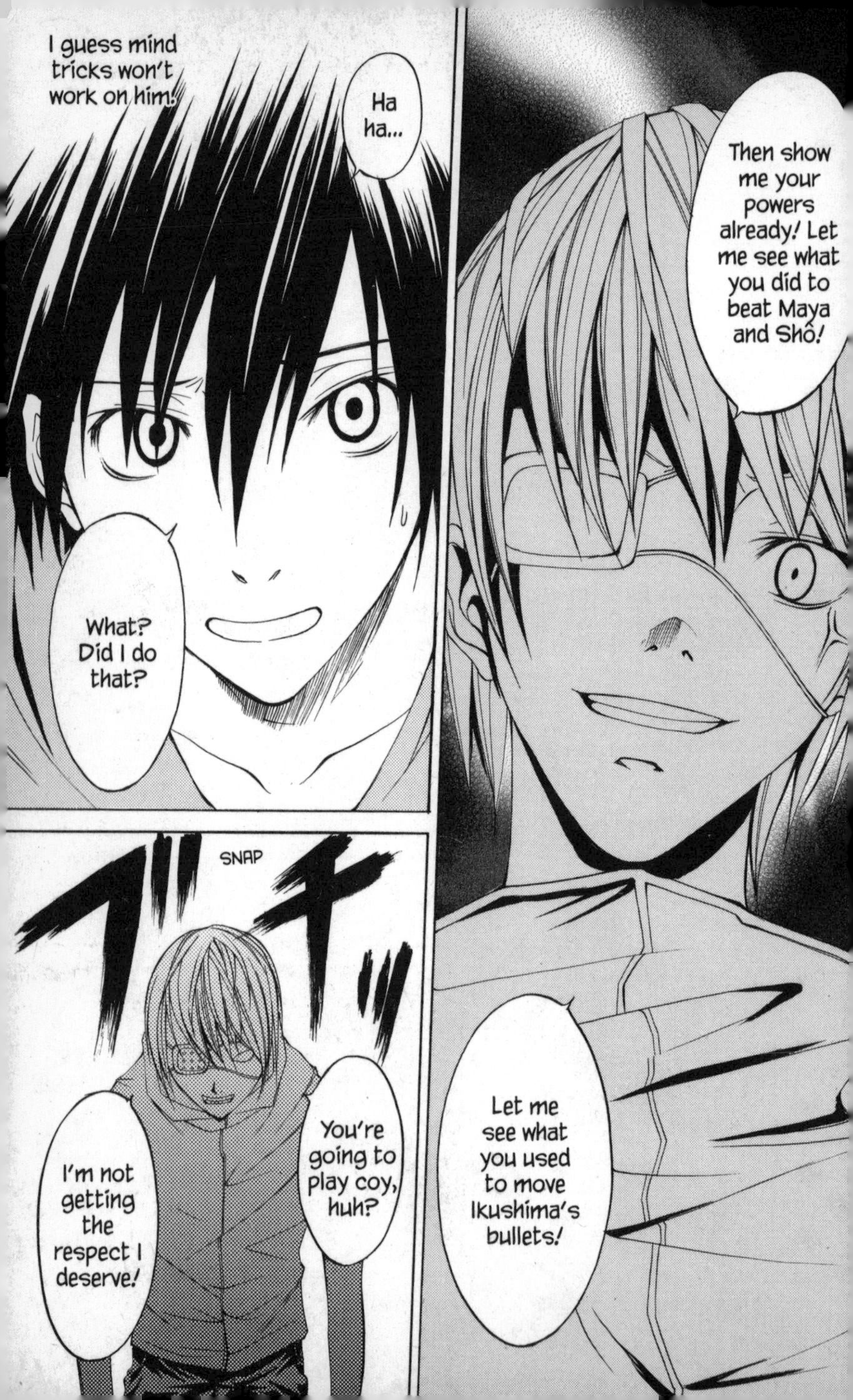
Then show me your powers already! Let me see what you did to beat Maya and Shô!
Let me see what you used to move Ikushima's bullets!
Ha ha...
I guess mind tricks won't work on him!
What? Did I do that?
SNAP
You're going to play coy, huh?
I'm not getting the respect I deserve!

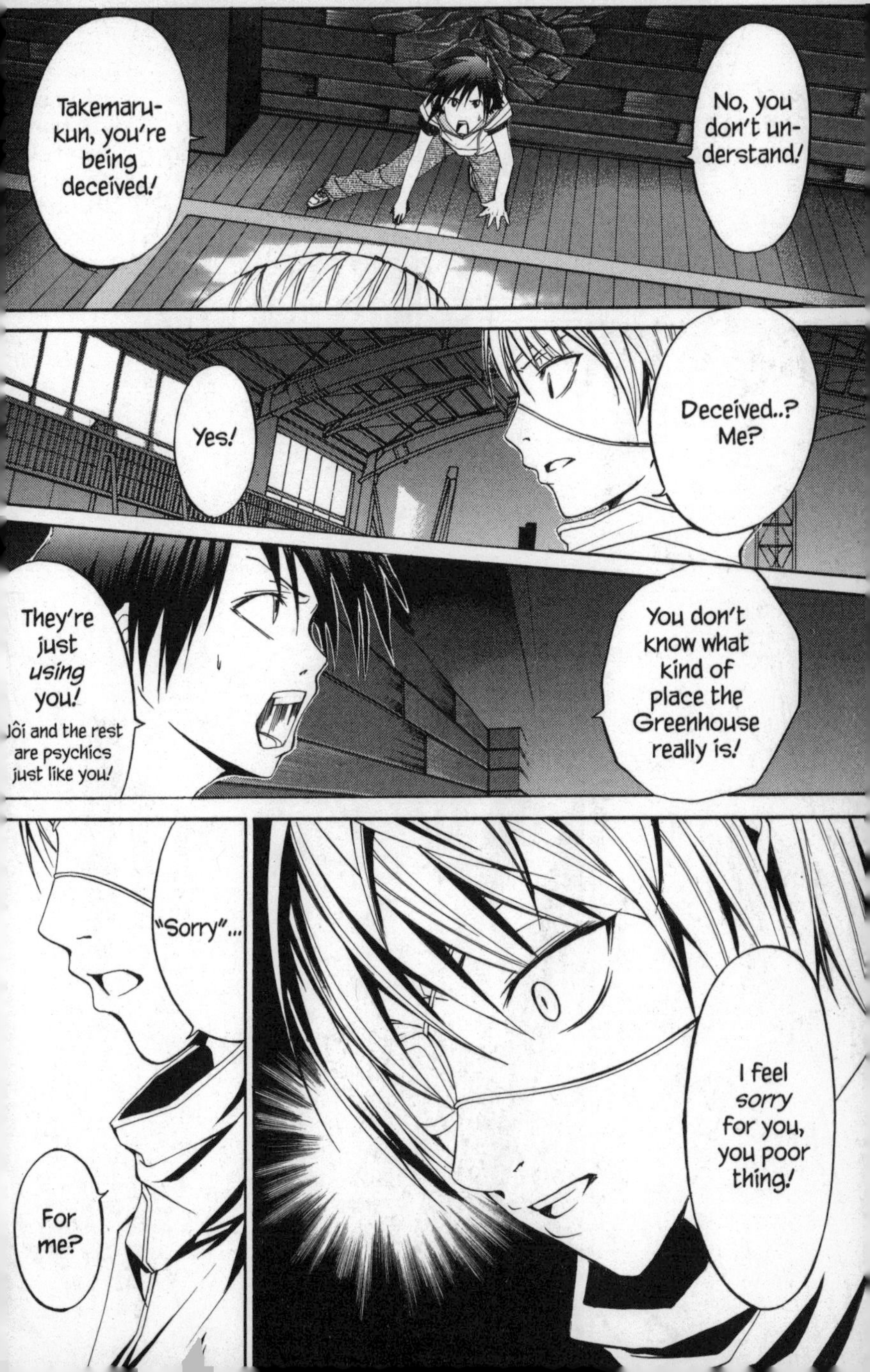
No, you don't understand!
Takemaru-kun, you're being deceived!
Deceived..? Me?
Yes!
You don't know what kind of place the Greenhouse really is!
They're just *using* you!
Jôi and the rest are psychics just like you!
I feel *sorry* for you, you poor thing!
"Sorry"...
For me?

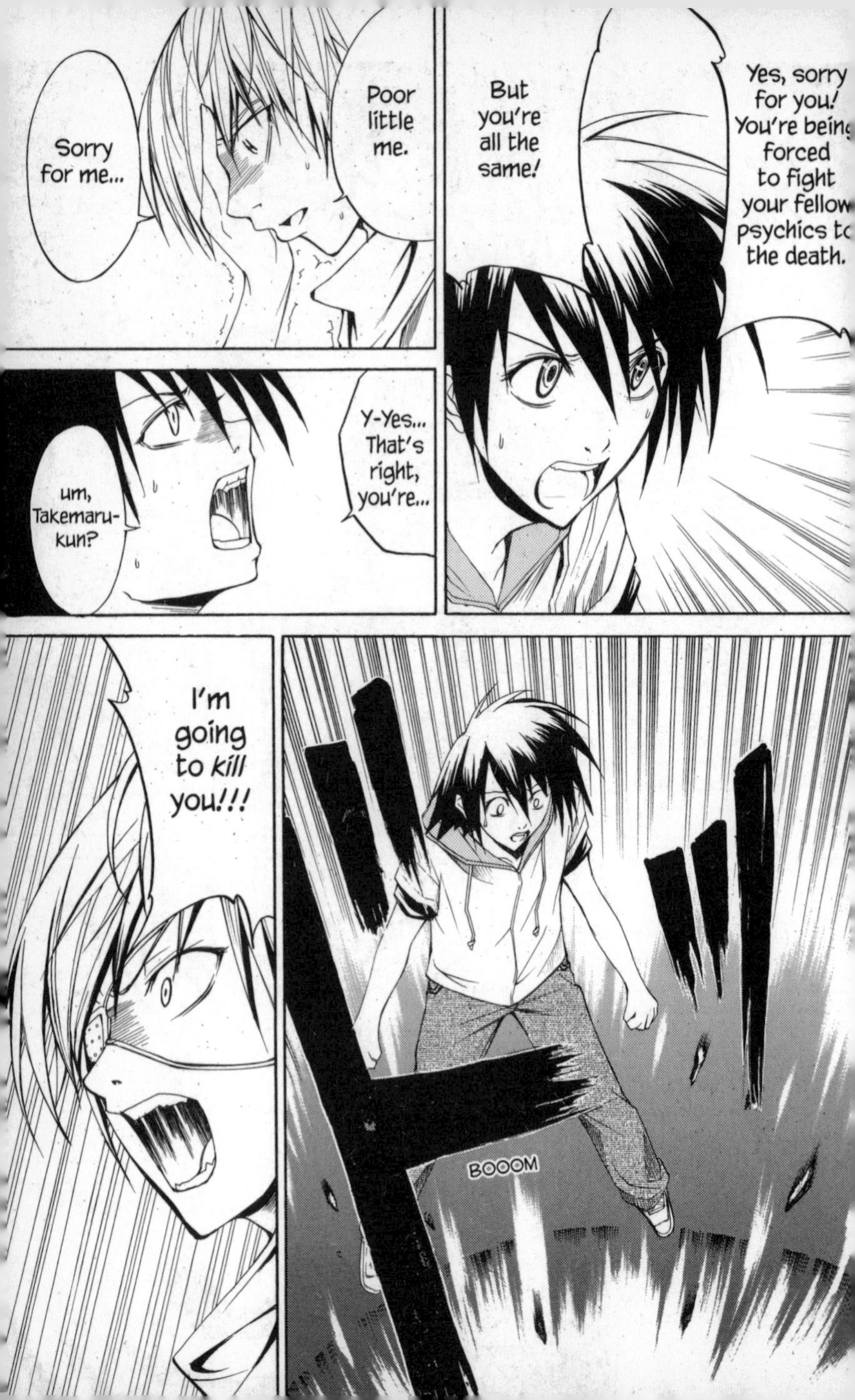
Yes, sorry for you! You're being forced to fight your fellow psychics to the death.
But you're all the same!
Poor little me.
Sorry for me...
Y-Yes... That's right, you're...
um, Takemaru-kun?
BOOOM
I'm going to *kill* you!!!

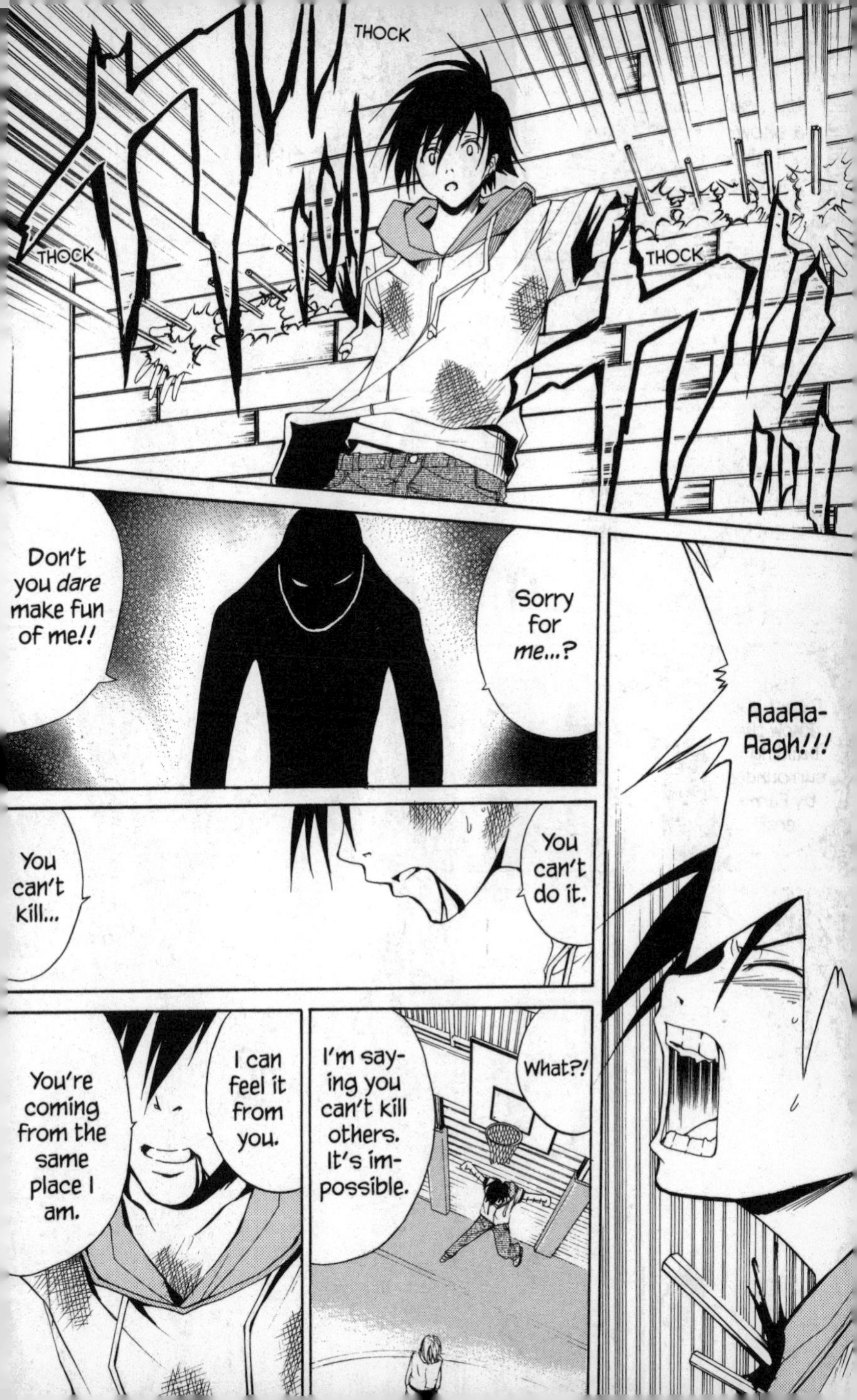
THOCK
THOCK
THOCK
AaaAa-Aagh!!!
Sorry for *me*...?
Don't you *dare* make fun of me!!
You can't do it.
You can't kill...
What?!
I'm saying you can't kill others. It's impossible.
I can feel it from you.
You're coming from the same place I am.

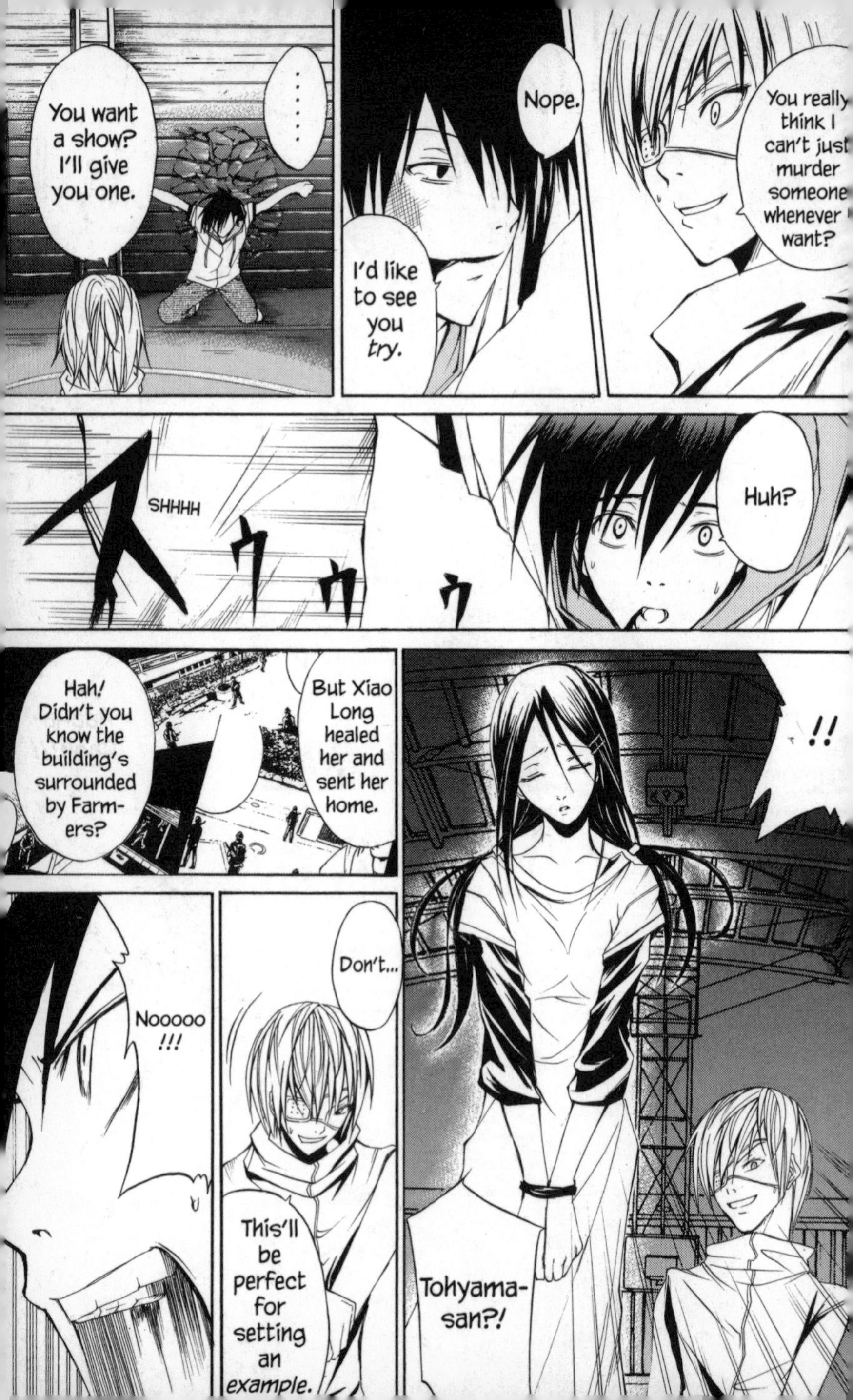
You really think I can't just murder someone whenever I want?
Nope.
I'd like to see you try.
......
You want a show? I'll give you one.
Huh?
SHHHH
!!
Tohyama-san?!
But Xiao Long healed her and sent her home.
Hah! Didn't you know the building's surrounded by Farmers?
Don't...
This'll be perfect for setting an *example.*
Nooooo!!!

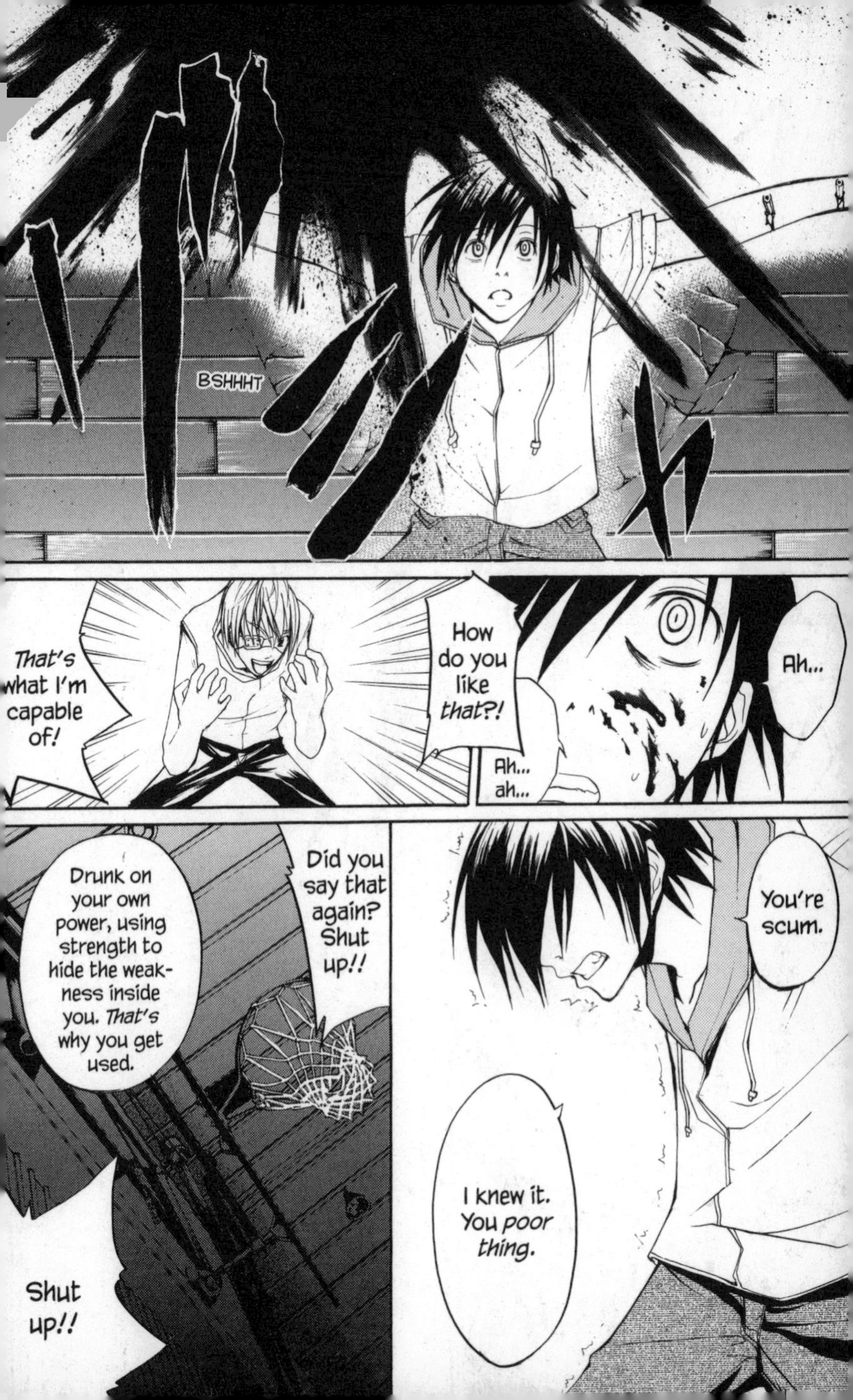
BSHHHT
Ah...
How do you like *that*?!
Ah... ah...
That's what I'm capable of!
You're scum.
I knew it. You *poor thing*.
Did you say that again? Shut up!!
Drunk on your own power, using strength to hide the weakness inside you. *That's* why you get used.
Shut up!!

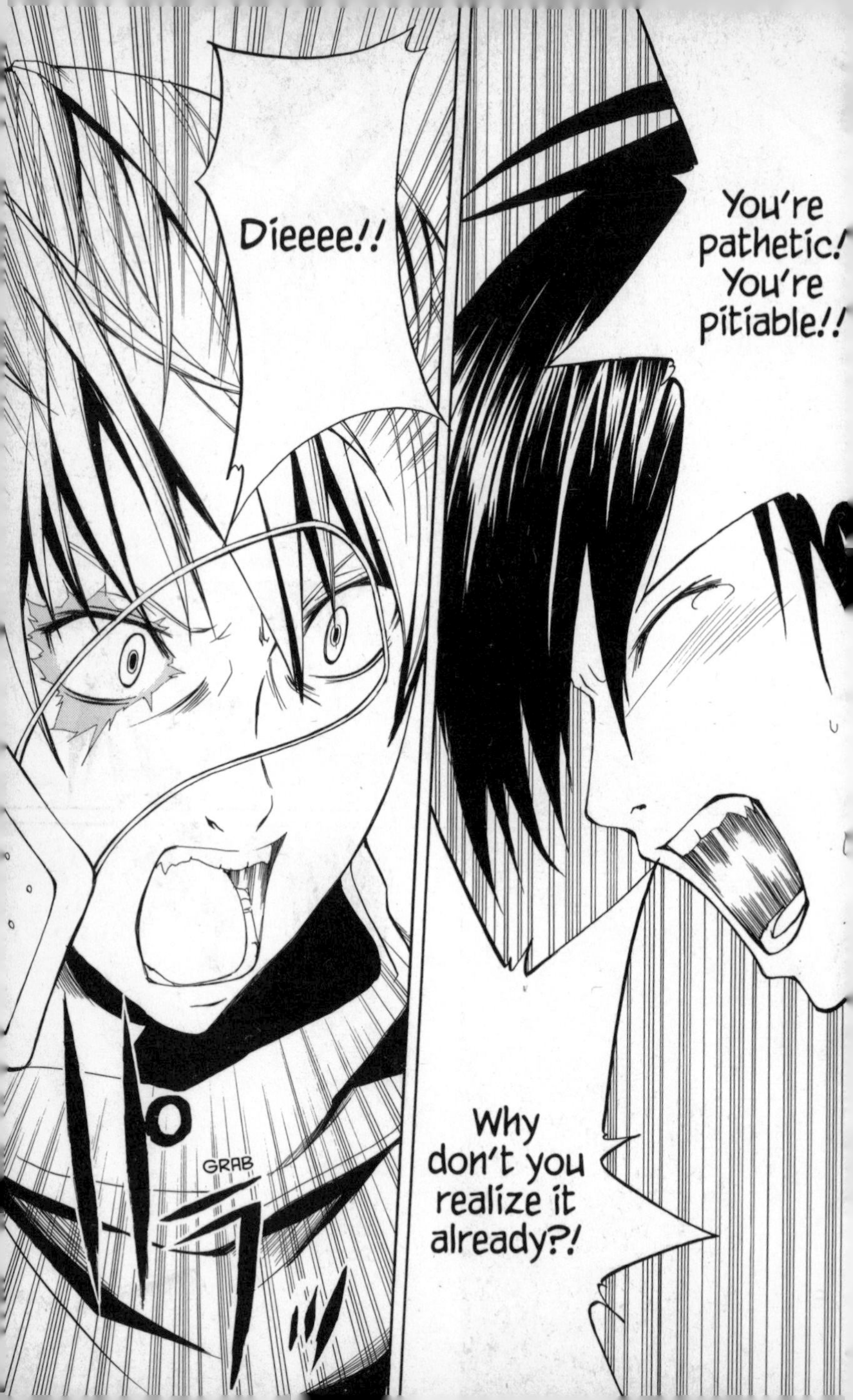
You're pathetic! You're pitiable!!
Why don't you realize it already?!
Dieeee!!
GRAB

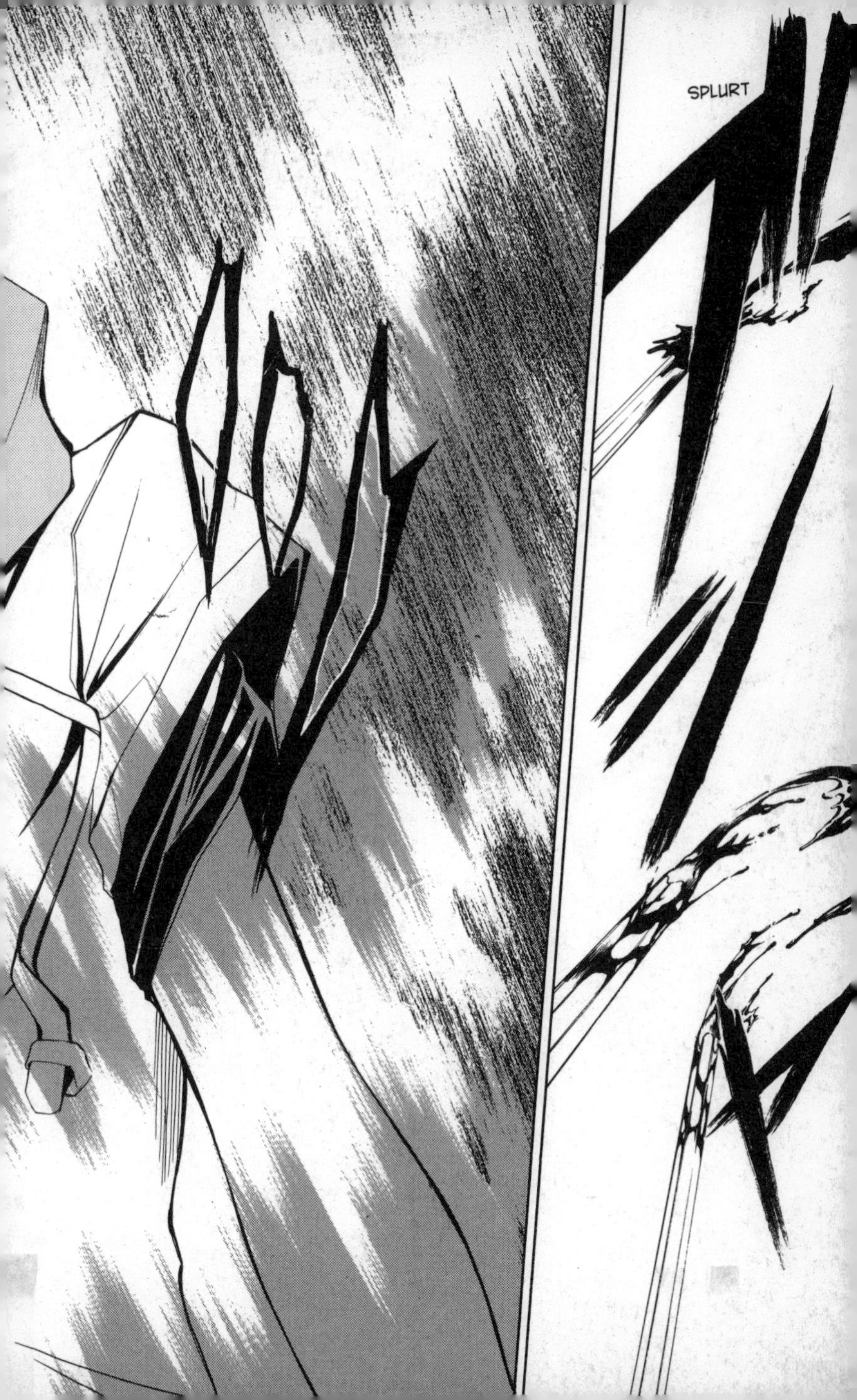
SPLURT

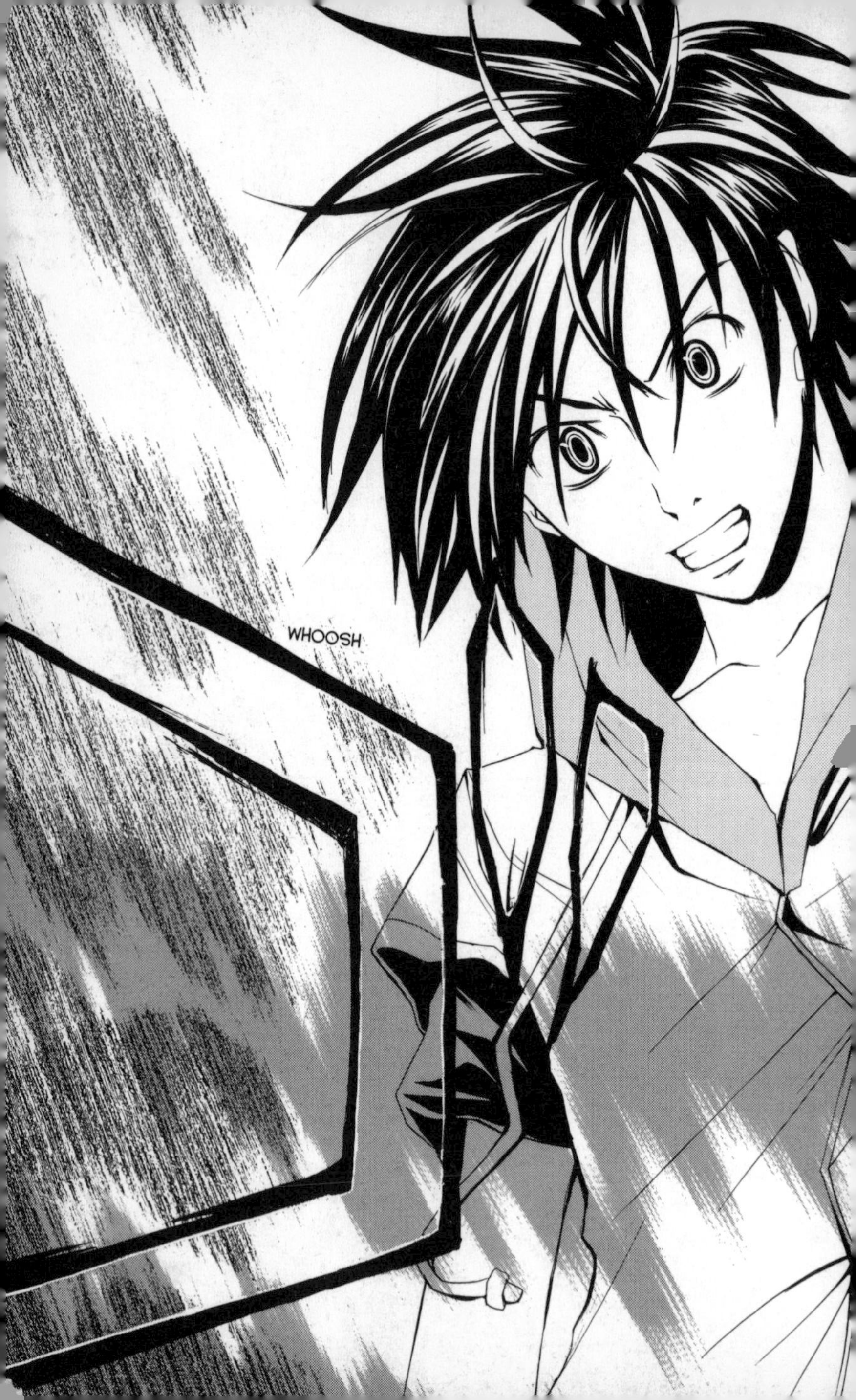
WHOOSH

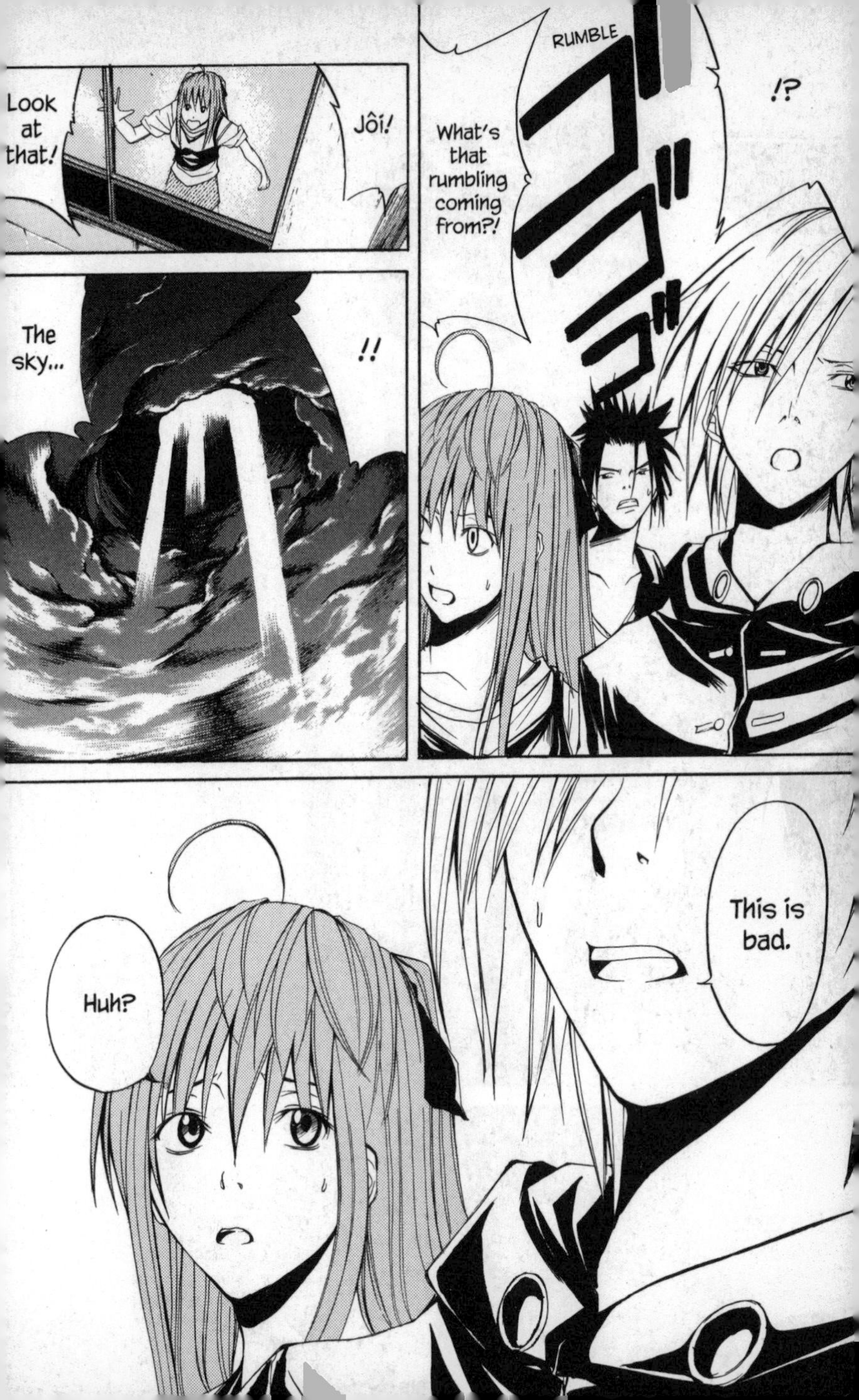
RUMBLE
!?
What's that rumbling coming from?!
Jôi!
Look at that!
!!
The sky...
This is bad.
Huh?

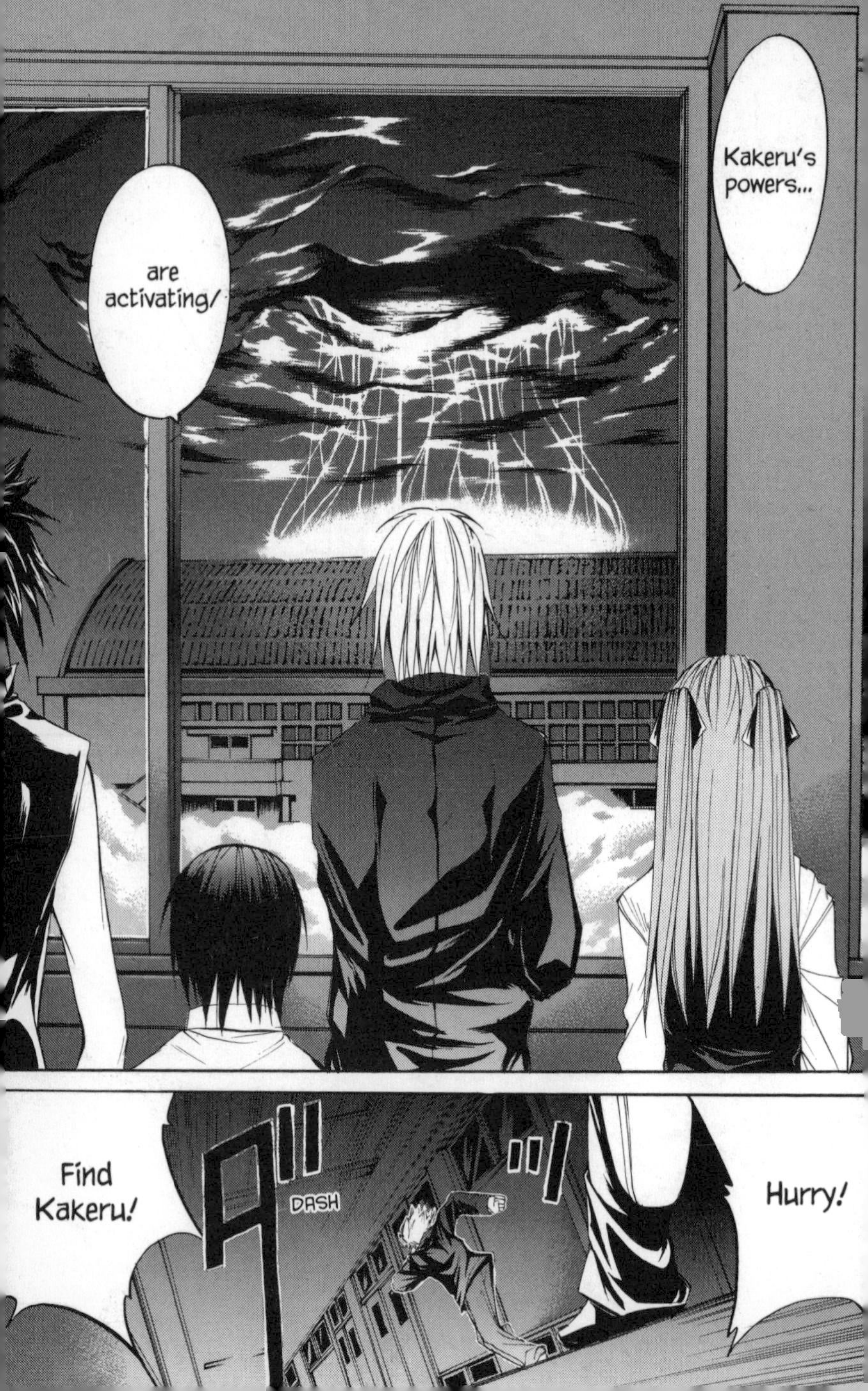
Kakeru's powers...
are activating!
Hurry!
DASH
Find Kakeru!

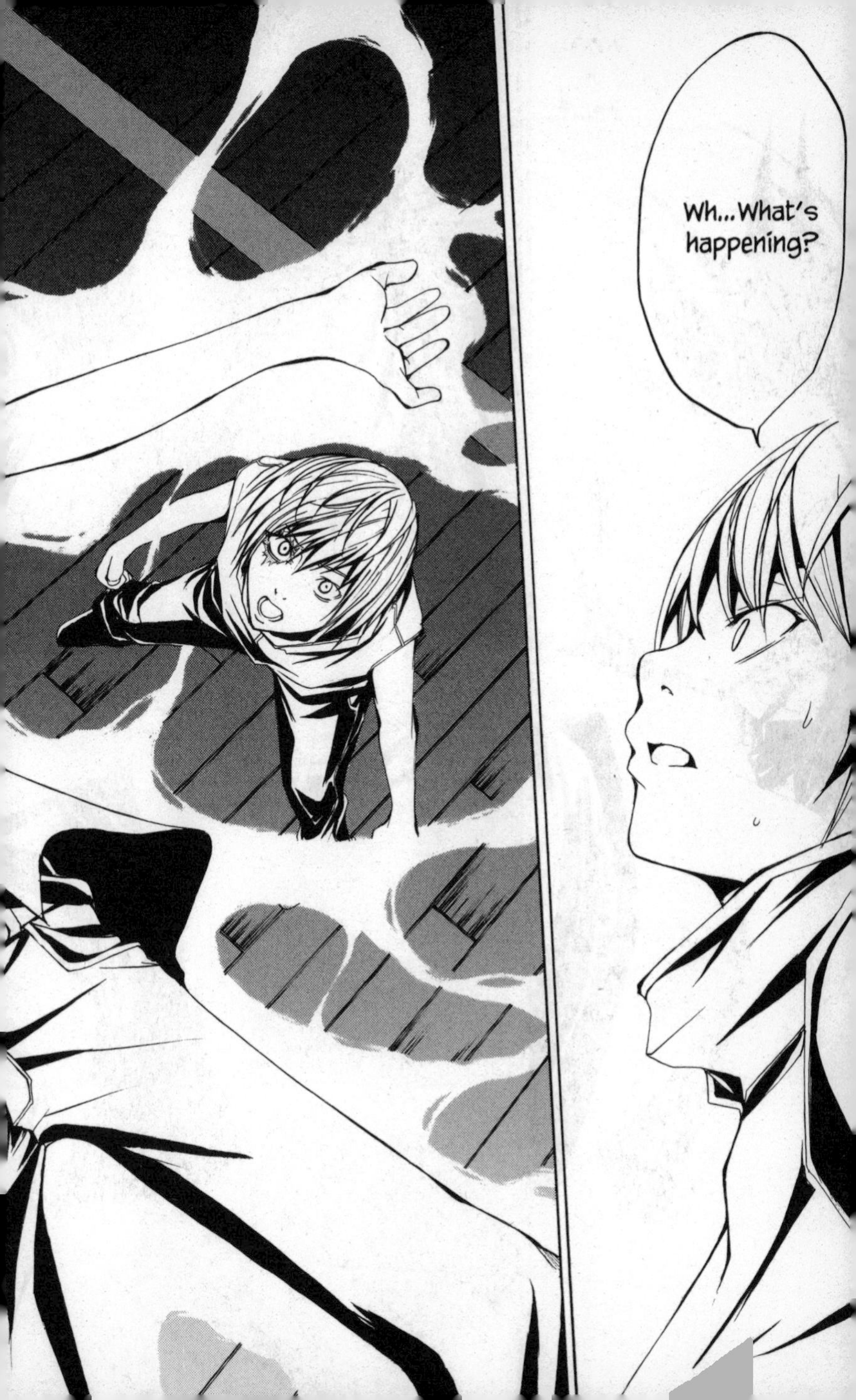
Wh...What's happening?

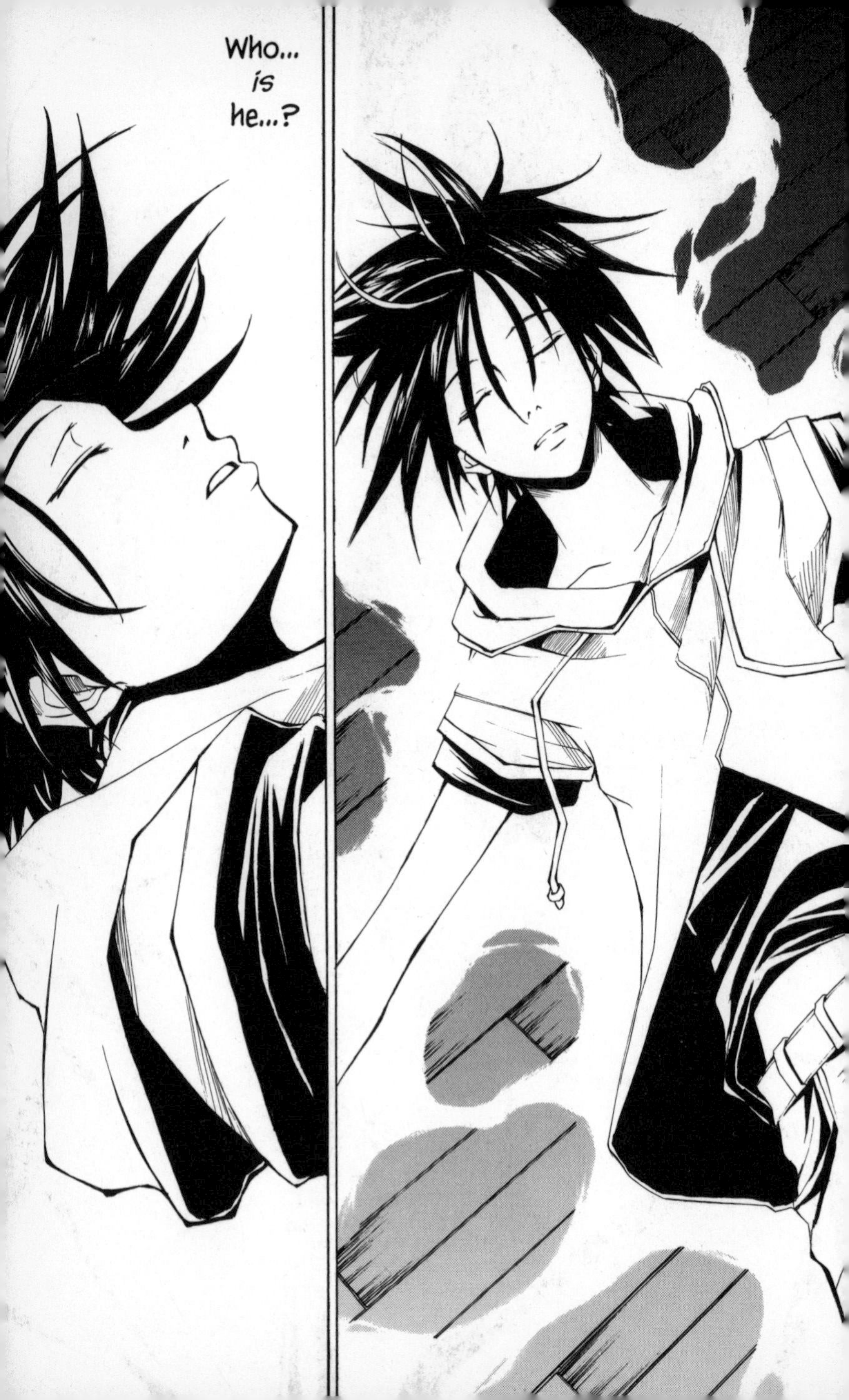
Who... is he...?

Special Thanks Illustration

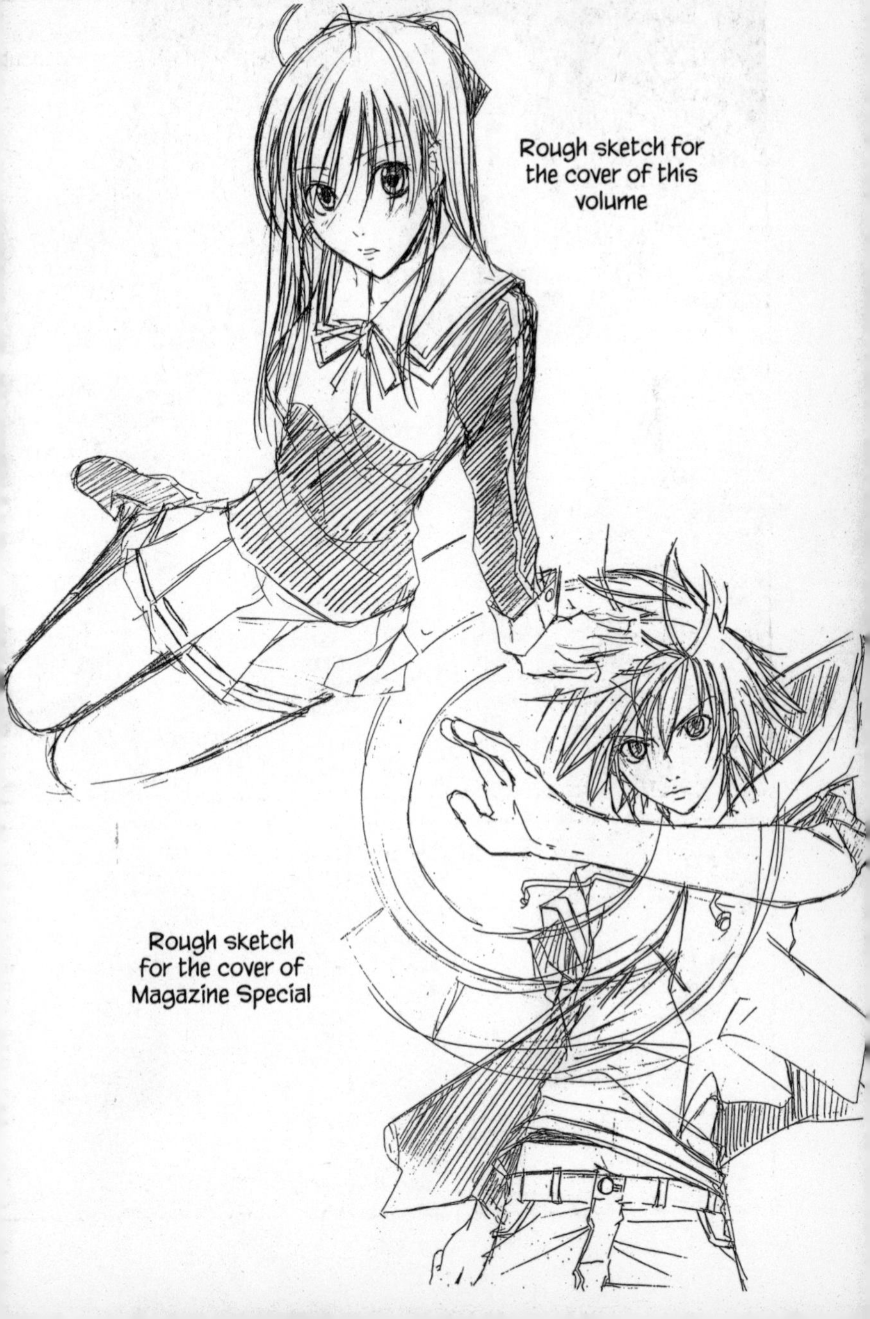

Rough sketch for the cover of this volume

Rough sketch for the cover of Magazine Special

CASE 8 – Activation

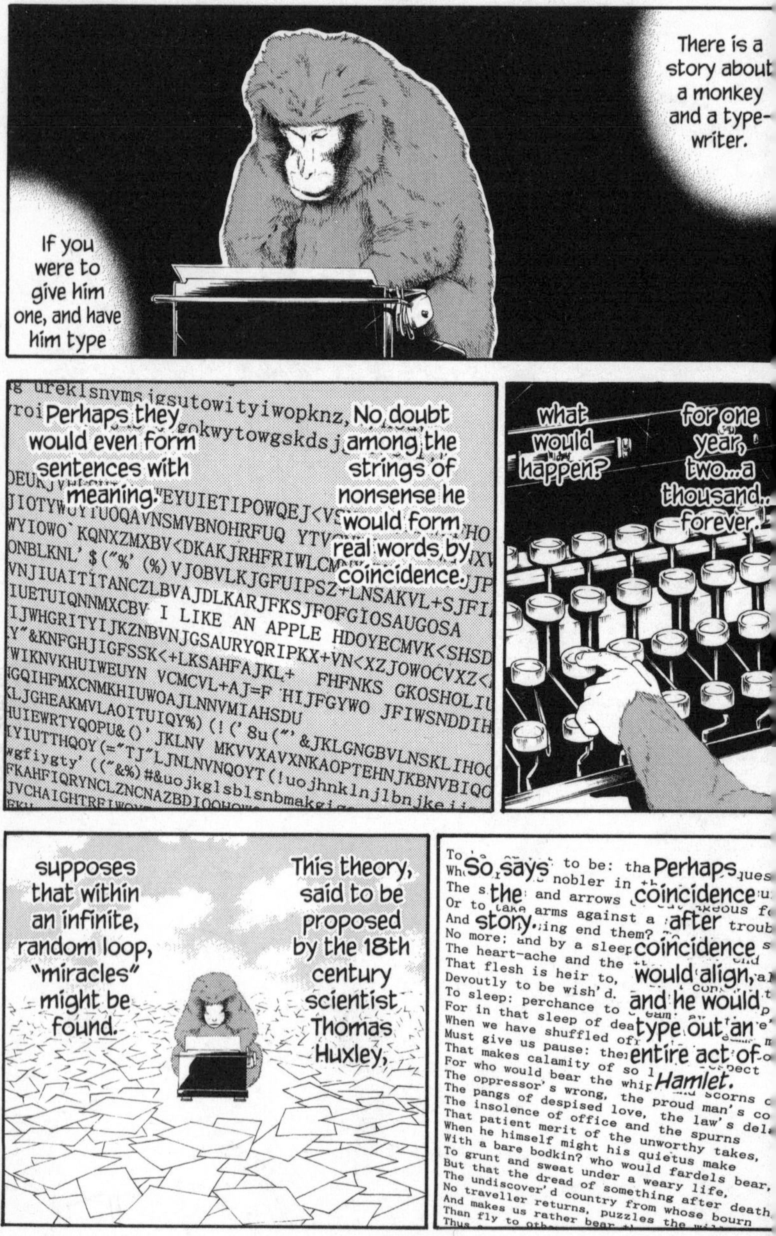
There is a story about a monkey and a type-writer.
If you were to give him one, and have him type
for one year, two...a thousand... forever.
what would happen?
No doubt among the strings of nonsense he would form real words by coincidence.
Perhaps they would even form sentences with meaning.
Perhaps coincidence after coincidence would align, and he would type out an entire act of *Hamlet*.
So says the story.
This theory, said to be proposed by the 18th century scientist Thomas Huxley,
supposes that within an infinite, random loop, "miracles" might be found.

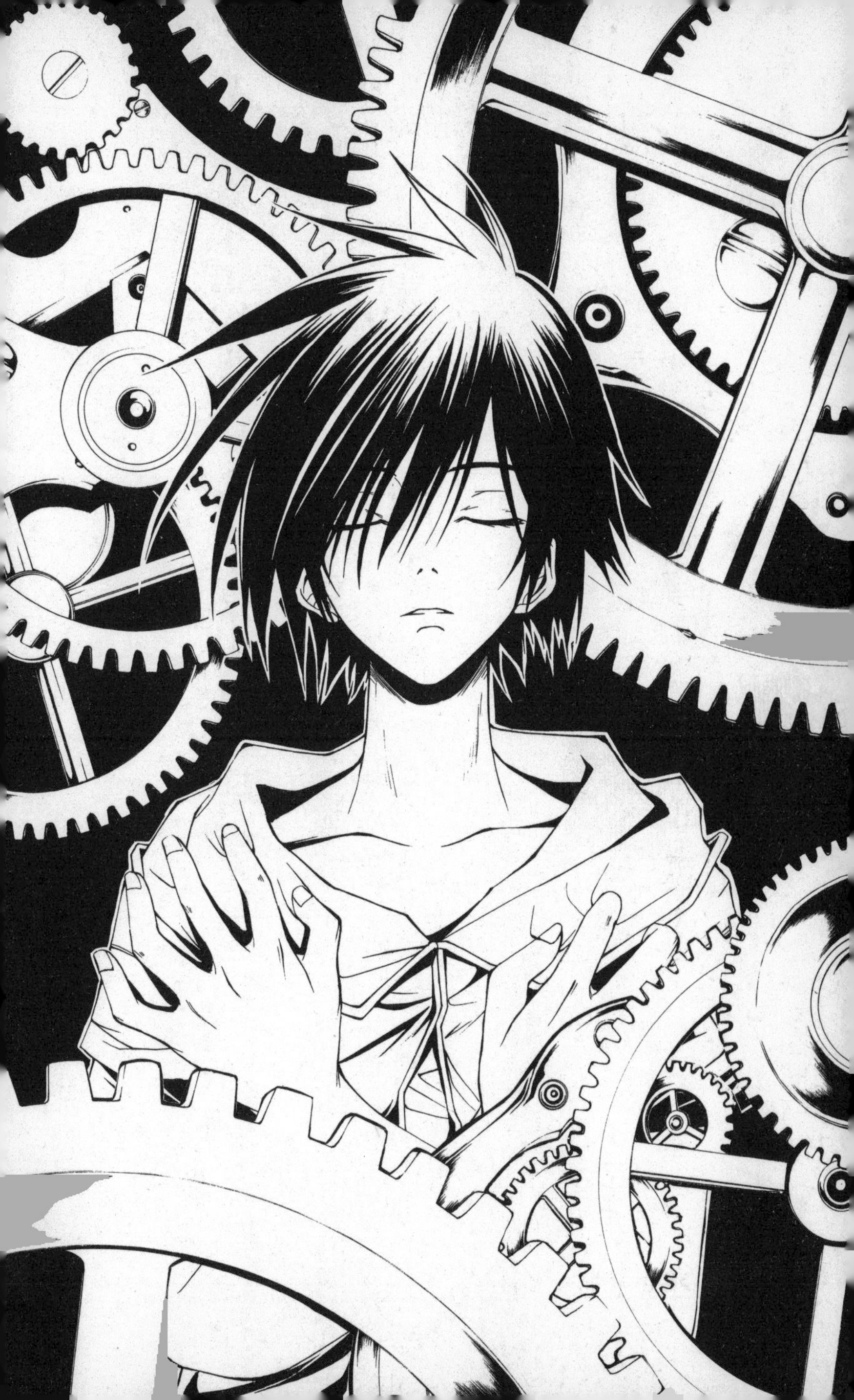

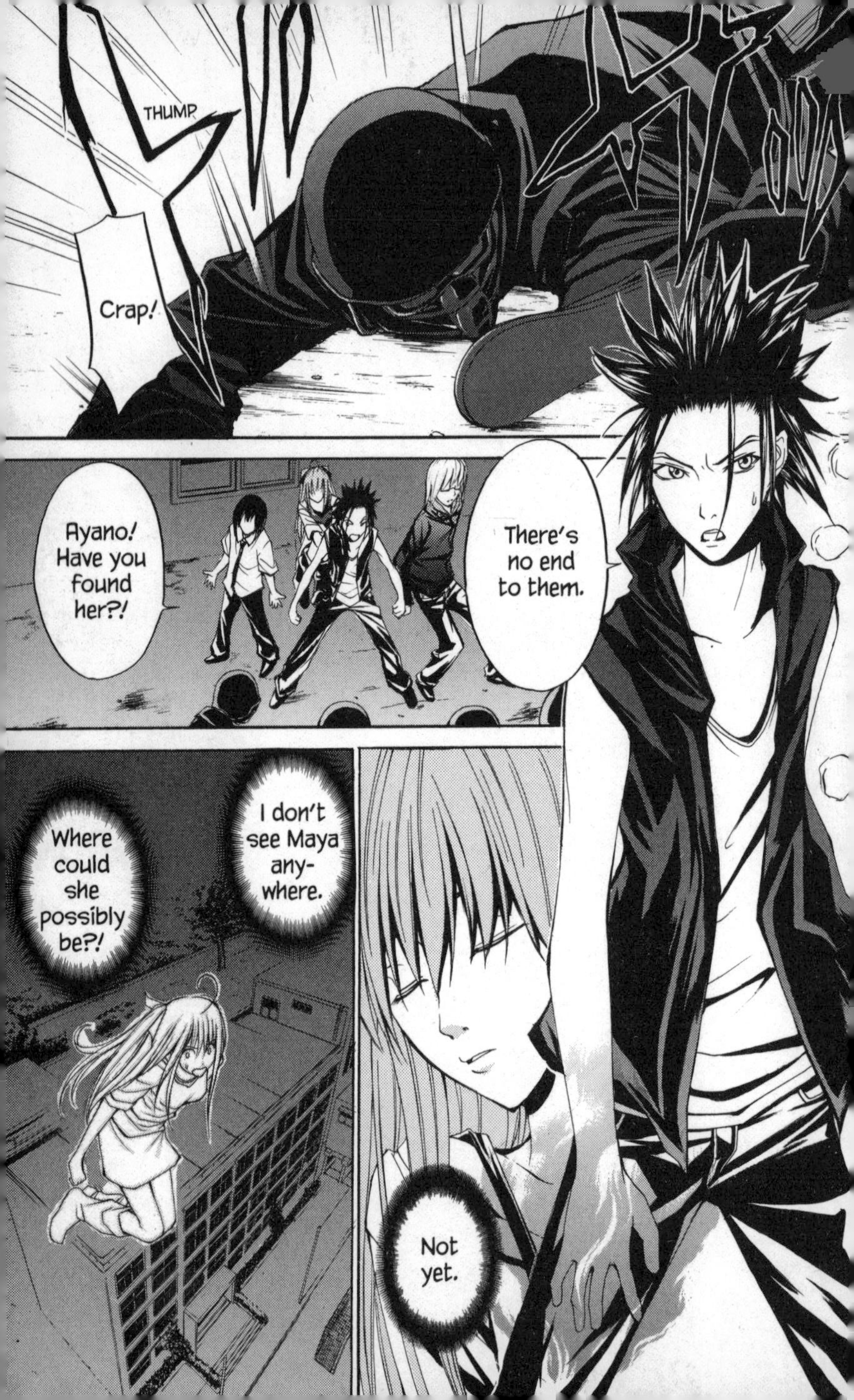
THUMP
Crap!
There's no end to them.
Ayano! Have you found her?!
I don't see Maya anywhere.
Not yet.
Where could she possibly be?!

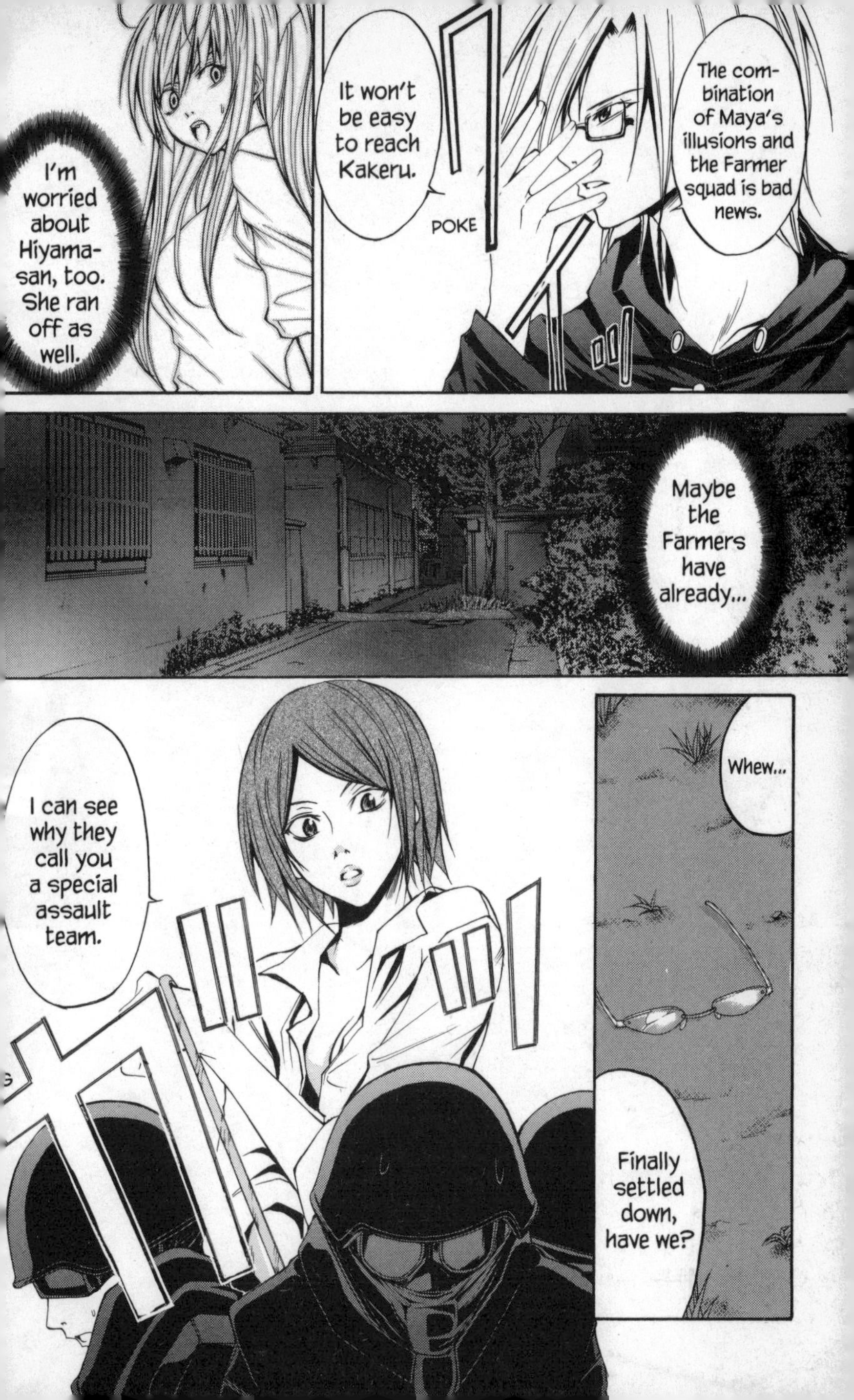
The combination of Maya's illusions and the Farmer squad is bad news.
It won't be easy to reach Kakeru.
POKE
I'm worried about Hiyama-san, too. She ran off as well.
Maybe the Farmers have already...
Whew...
Finally settled down, have we?
I can see why they call you a special assault team.

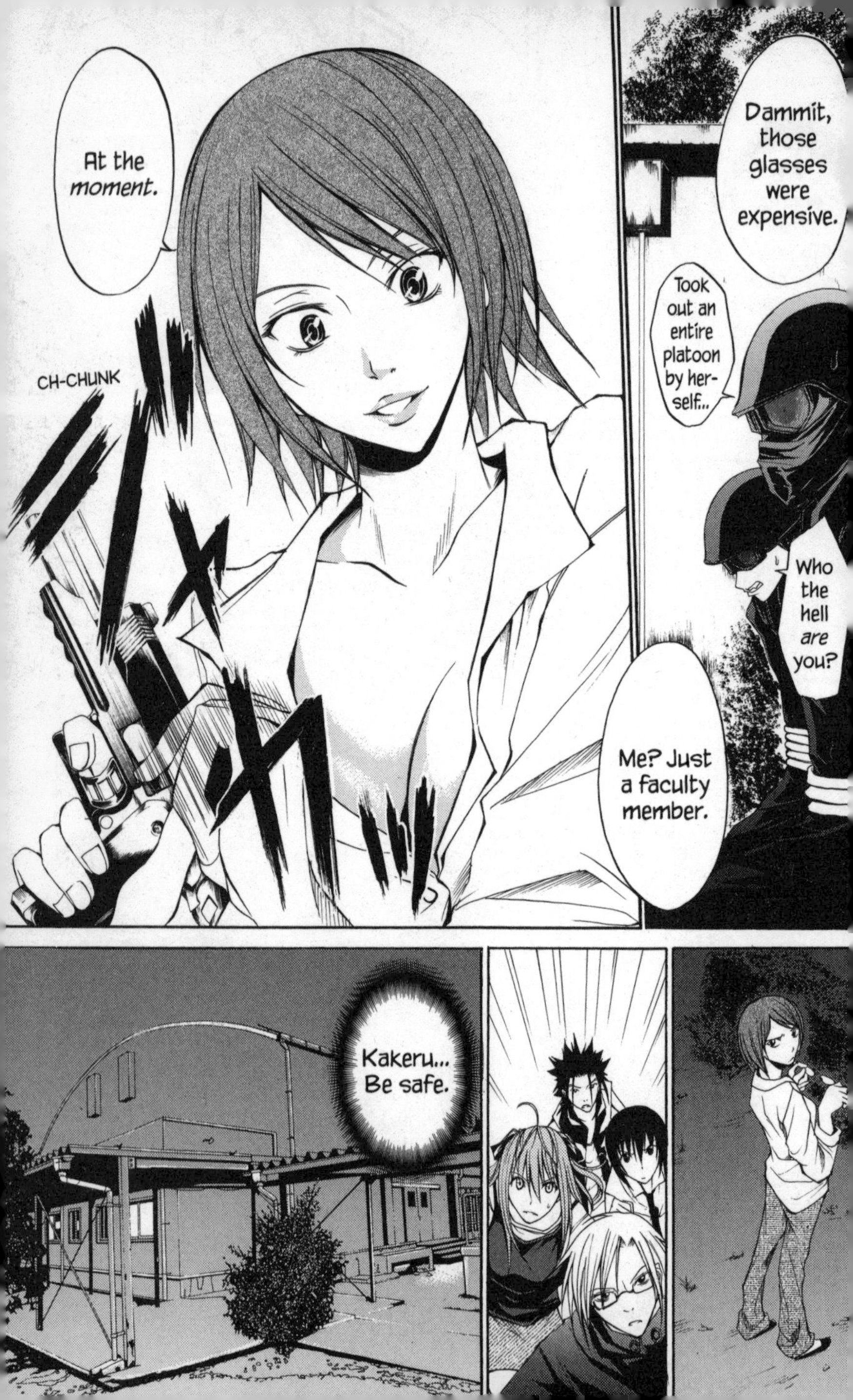
Dammit, those glasses were expensive.
Took out an entire platoon by her-self...
Who the hell are you?
Me? Just a faculty member.
At the moment.
CH-CHUNK
Kakeru... Be safe.

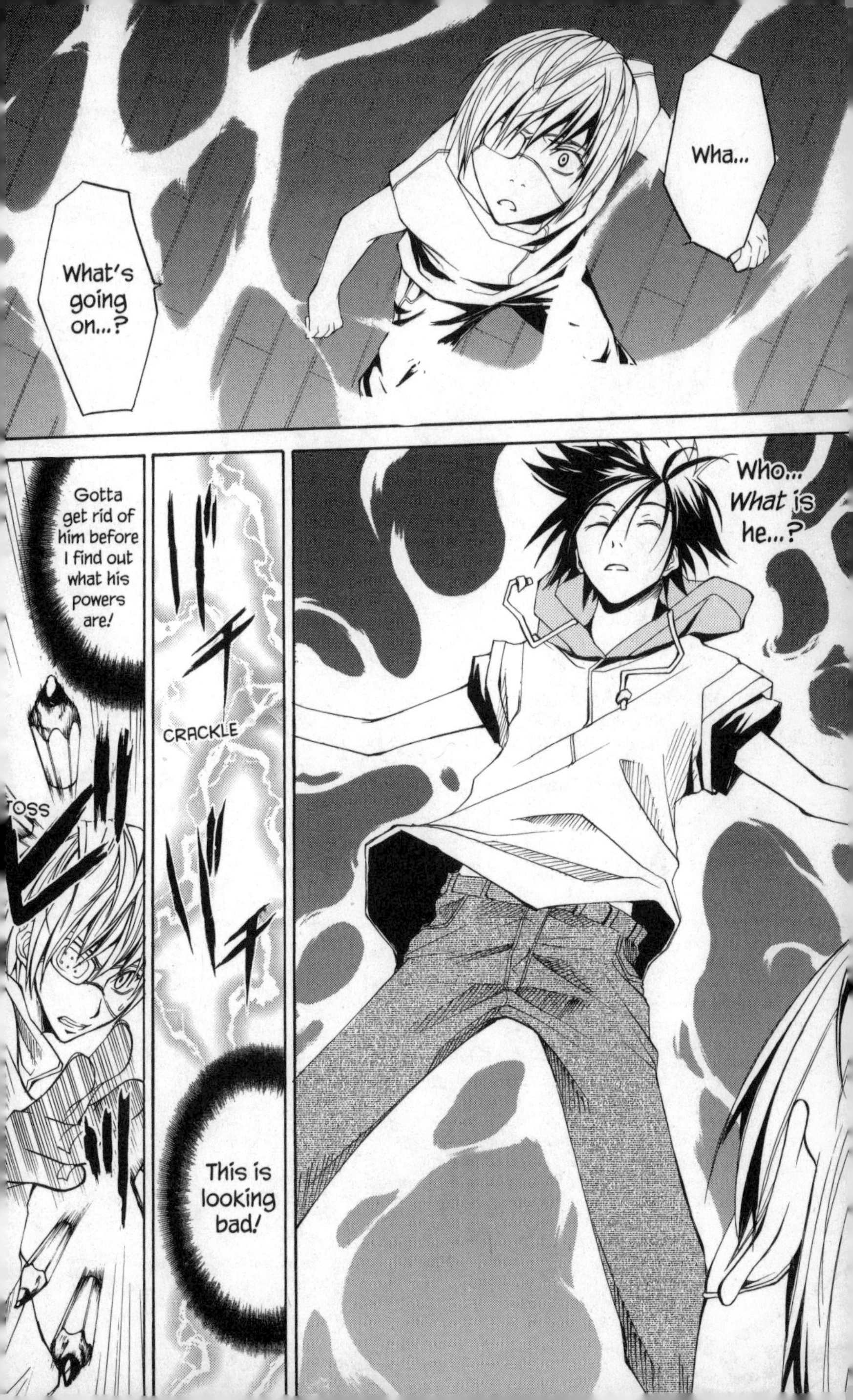
Wha...
What's going on...?
Who... What is he...?
CRACKLE
This is looking bad!
Gotta get rid of him before I find out what his powers are!
TOSS

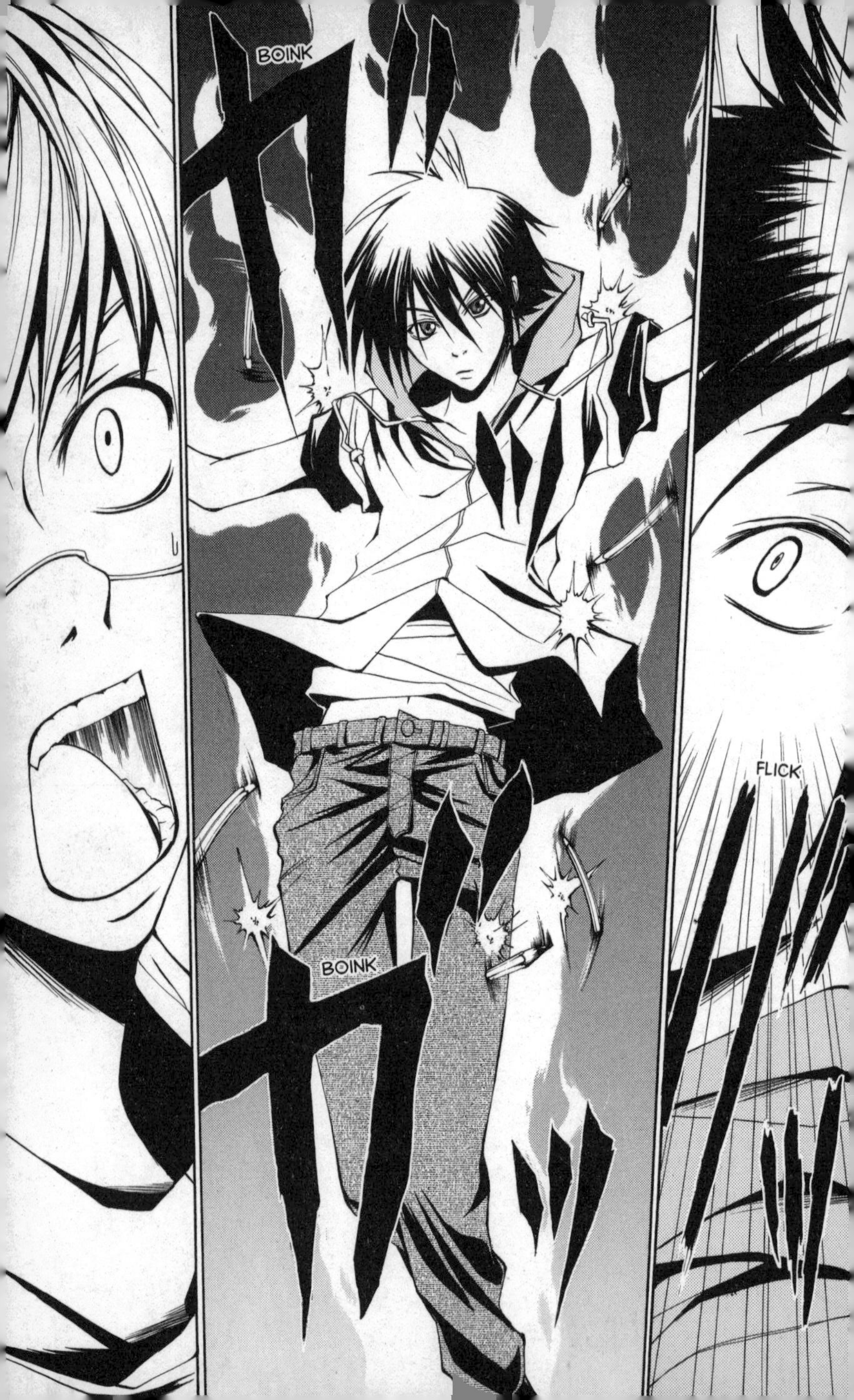
FLICK
BOINK
BOINK

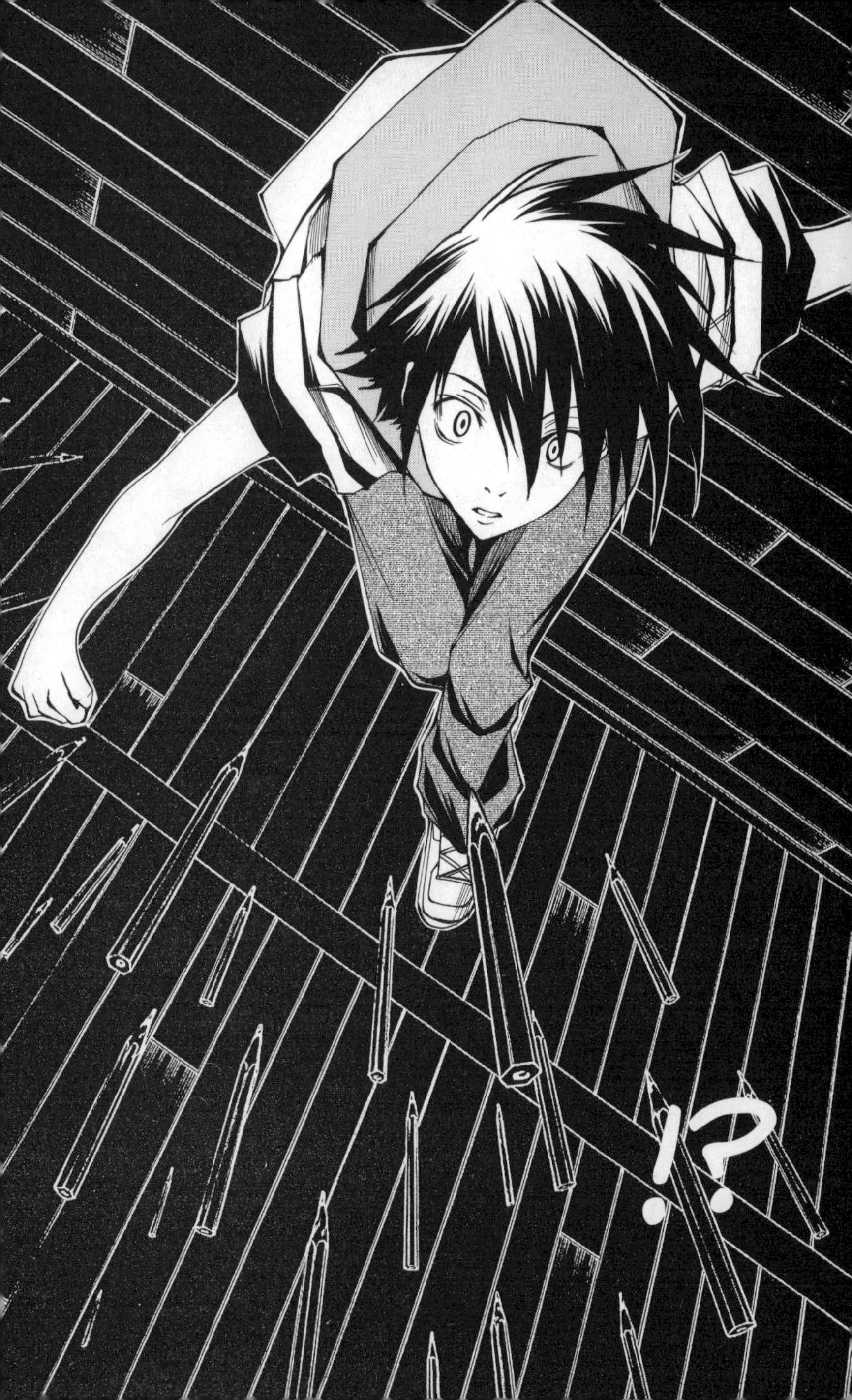
!?

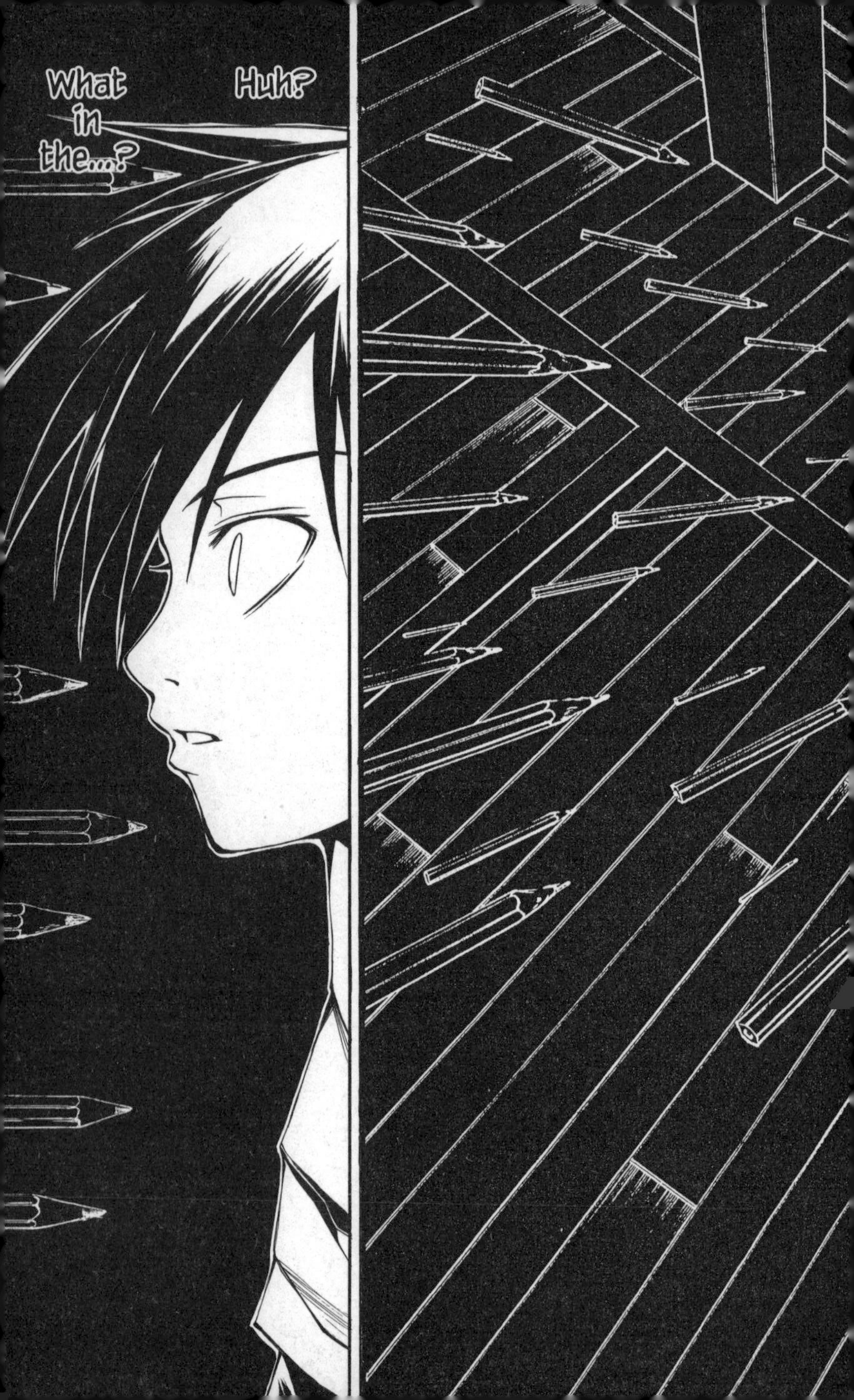
Huh?
What in the...?

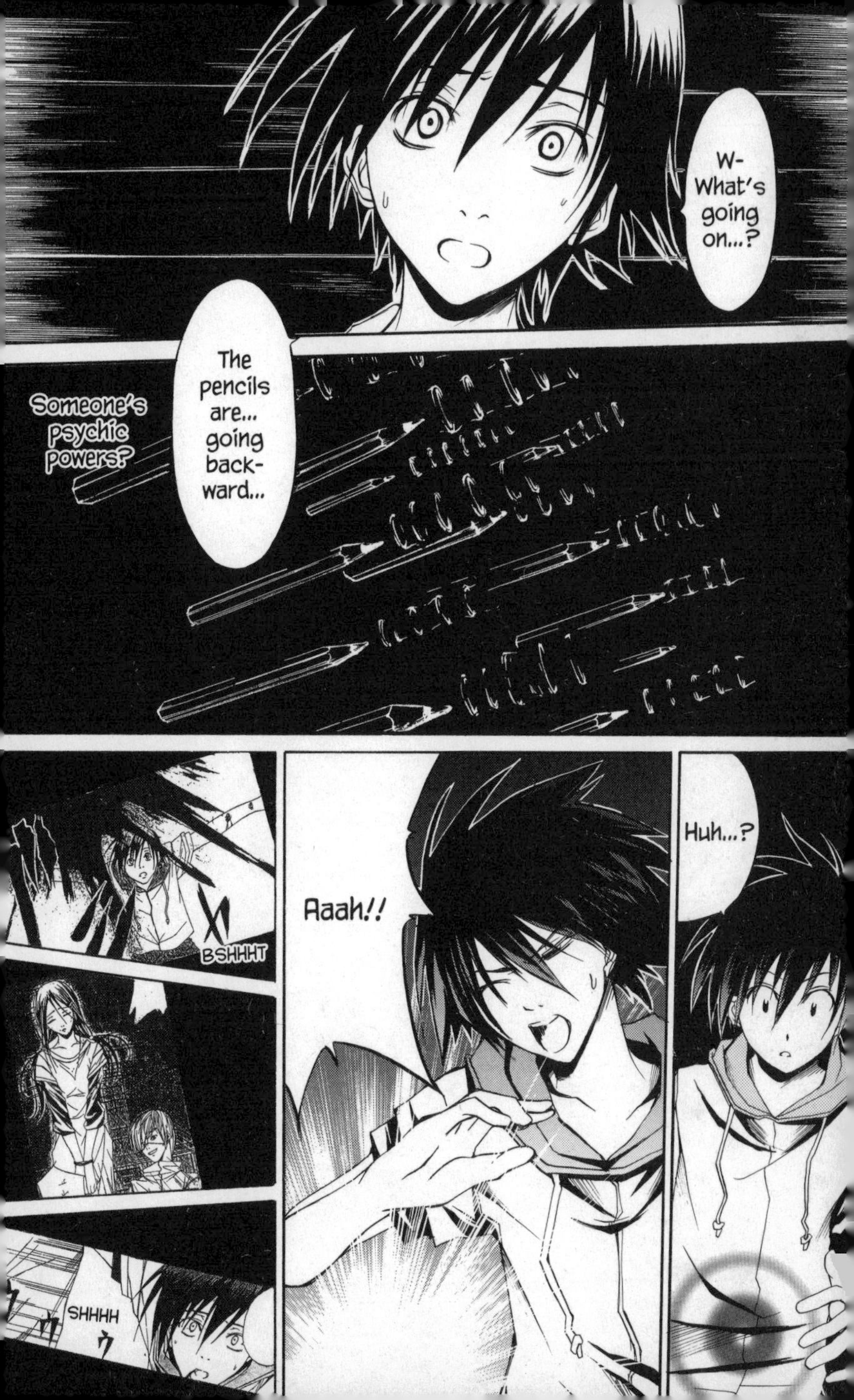
W- What's going on...?
The pencils are... going back-ward...
Someone's psychic powers?
Huh...?
Aaah!!
BSHHHT
SHHHH

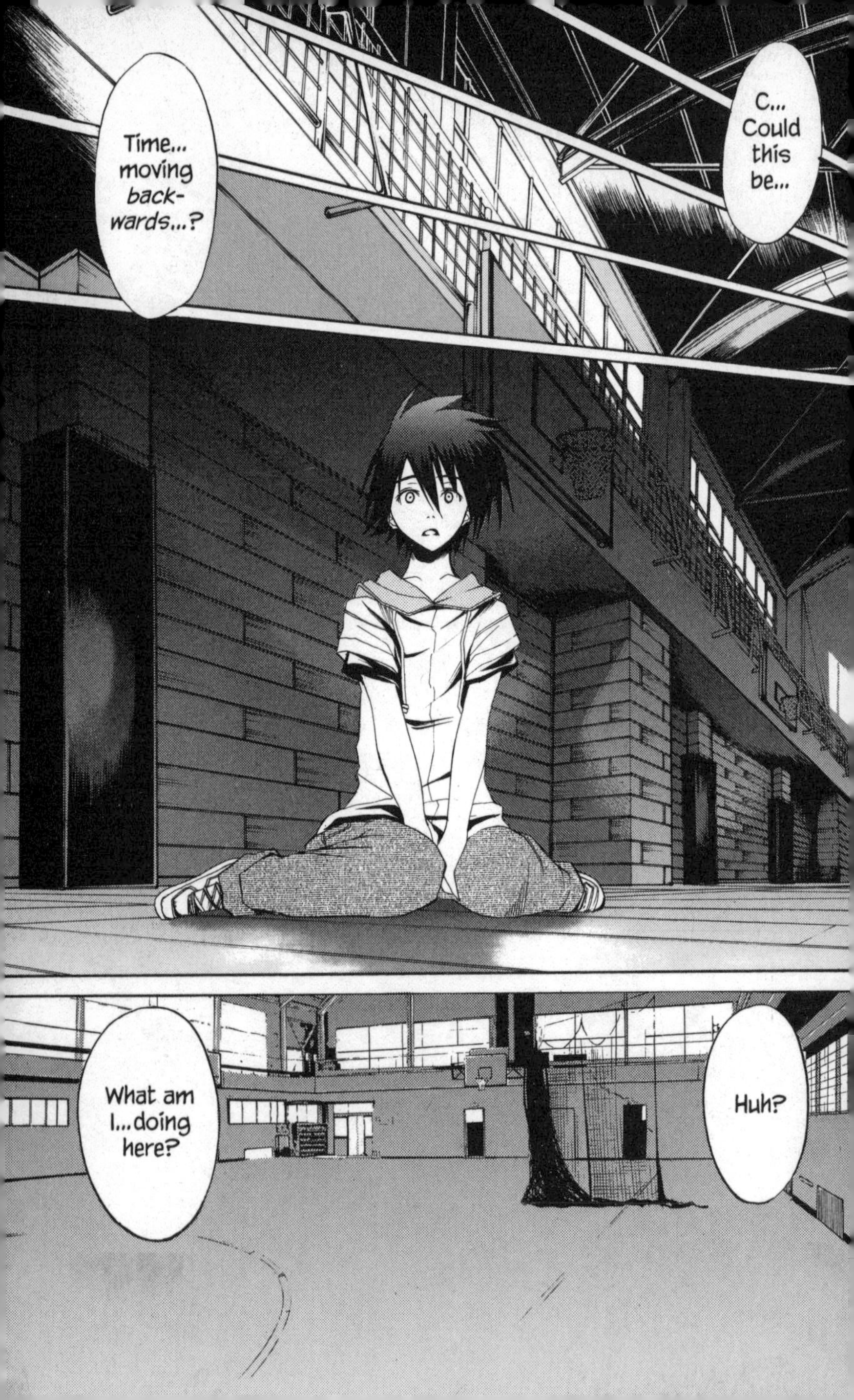
C... Could this be...
Time... moving back-wards...?
Huh?
What am I...doing here?

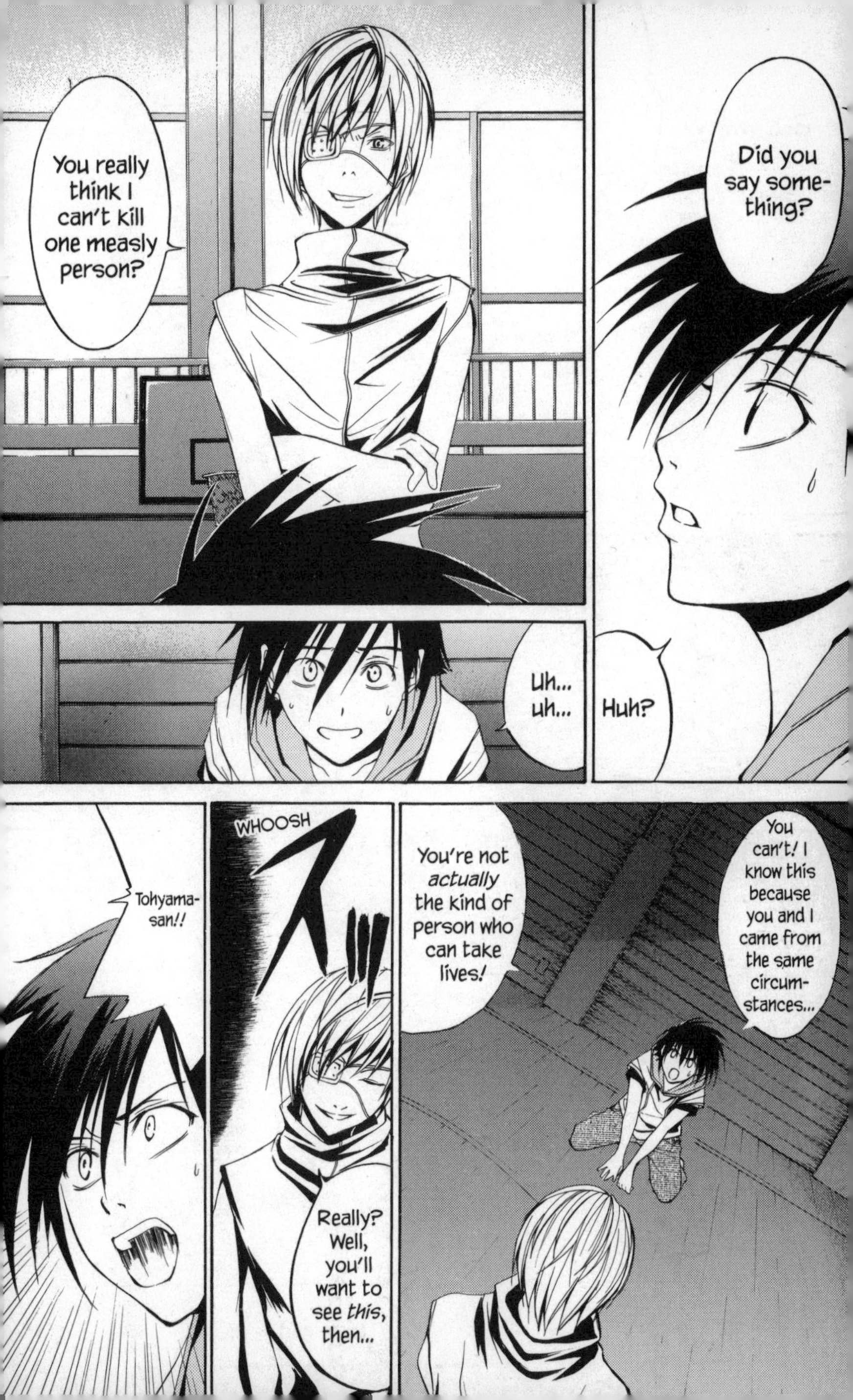
Did you say some-thing?
You really think I can't kill one measly person?
Huh?
Uh... uh...
You can't! I know this because you and I came from the same circum-stances...
You're not *actually* the kind of person who can take lives!
WHOOSH
Really? Well, you'll want to see *this*, then...
Tohyama-san!!

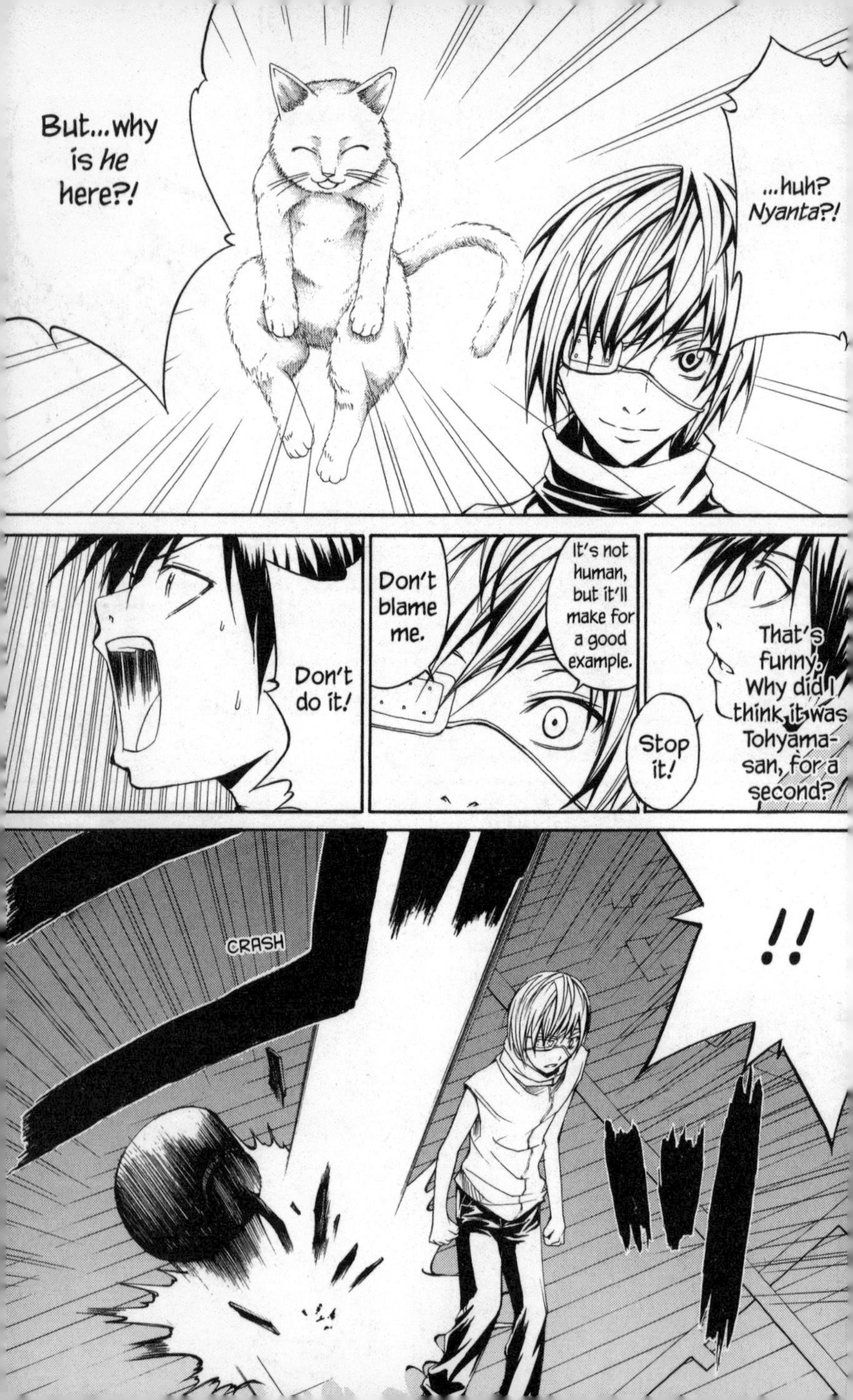
...huh? Nyanta?!
But...why is he here?!
That's funny. Why did I think it was Tohyama-san, for a second?
Stop it!
It's not human, but it'll make for a good example.
Don't blame me.
Don't do it!
!!
CRASH

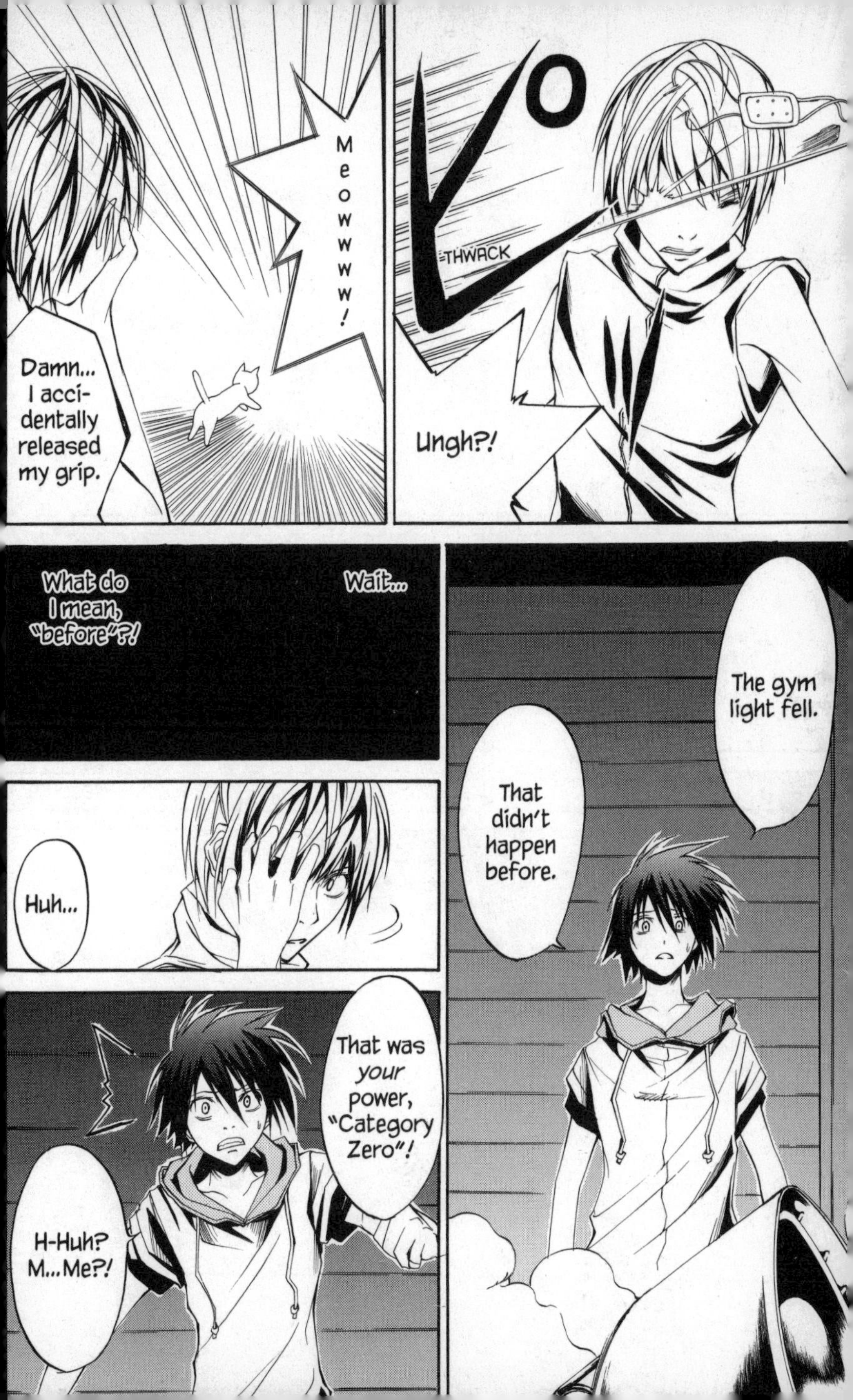

Ungh?!
THWACK
Meowwwww!
Damn... I acci-dentally released my grip.
The gym light fell.
That didn't happen before.
Wait...
What do I mean, "before"?!
Huh...
That was *your* power, "Category Zero"!
H-Huh? M...Me?!

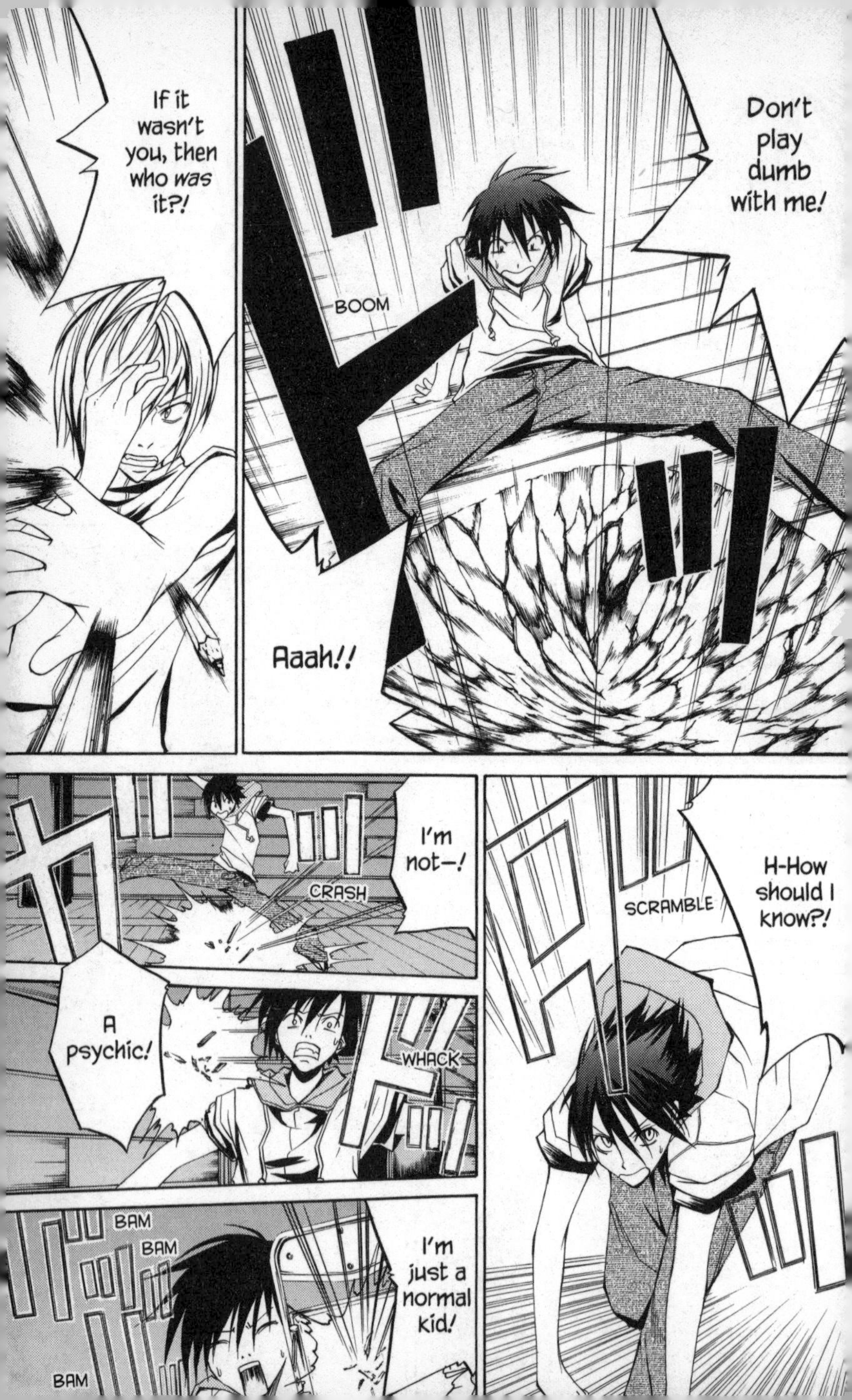
Don't play dumb with me!
BOOM
Aaah!!
If it wasn't you, then who was it?!
H-How should I know?!
SCRAMBLE
I'm not—!
CRASH
A psychic!
WHACK
I'm just a normal kid!
BAM
BAM
BAM

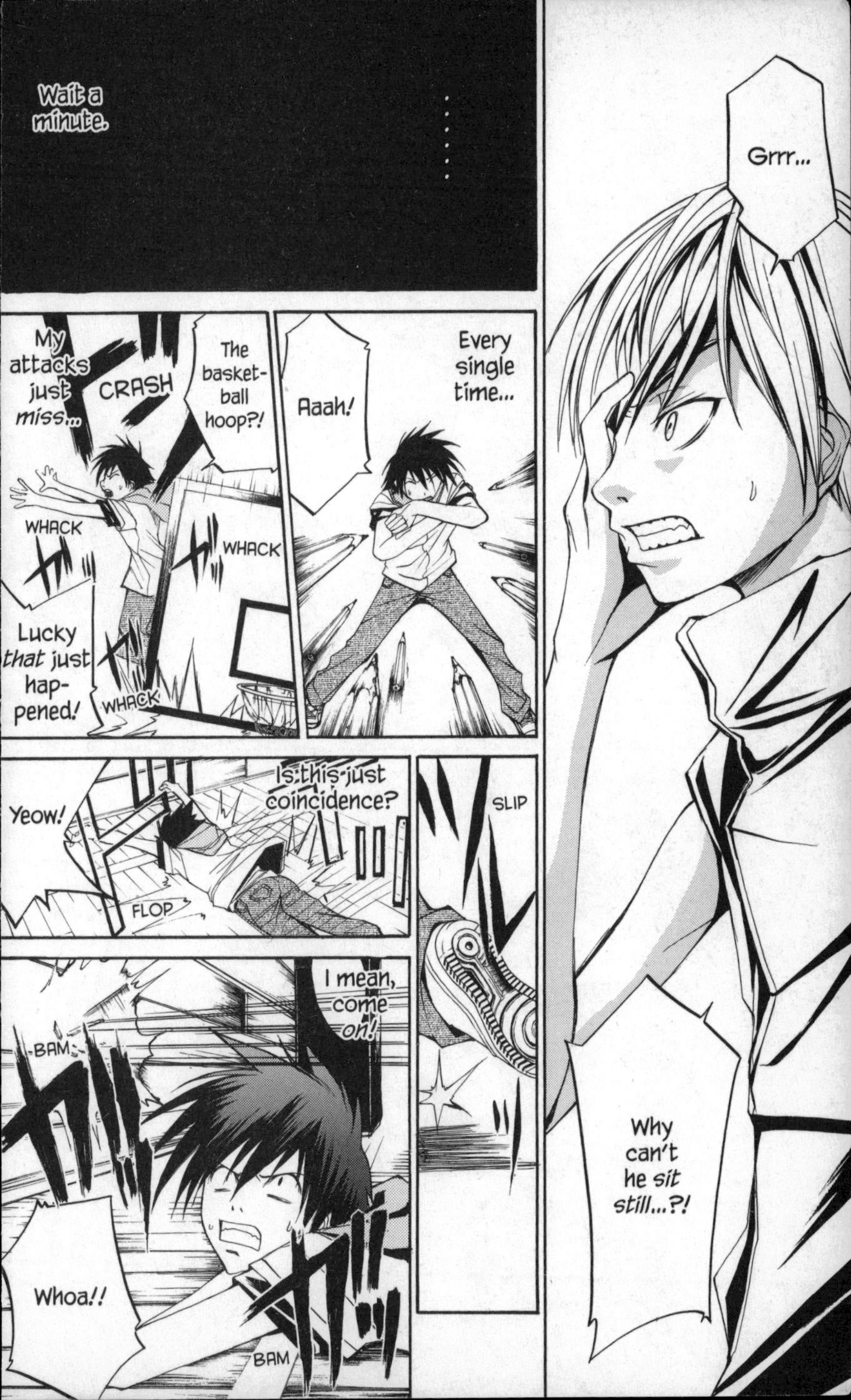
Grrr...
Why can't he sit still...?!
Wait a minute.
......
Every single time...
Aaah!
The basket-ball hoop?!
CRASH
My attacks just miss...
WHACK
WHACK
WHACK
Lucky that just hap-pened!
SLIP
Is this just coincidence?
Yeow!
FLOP
I mean, come on!
BAM
Whoa!!
BAM

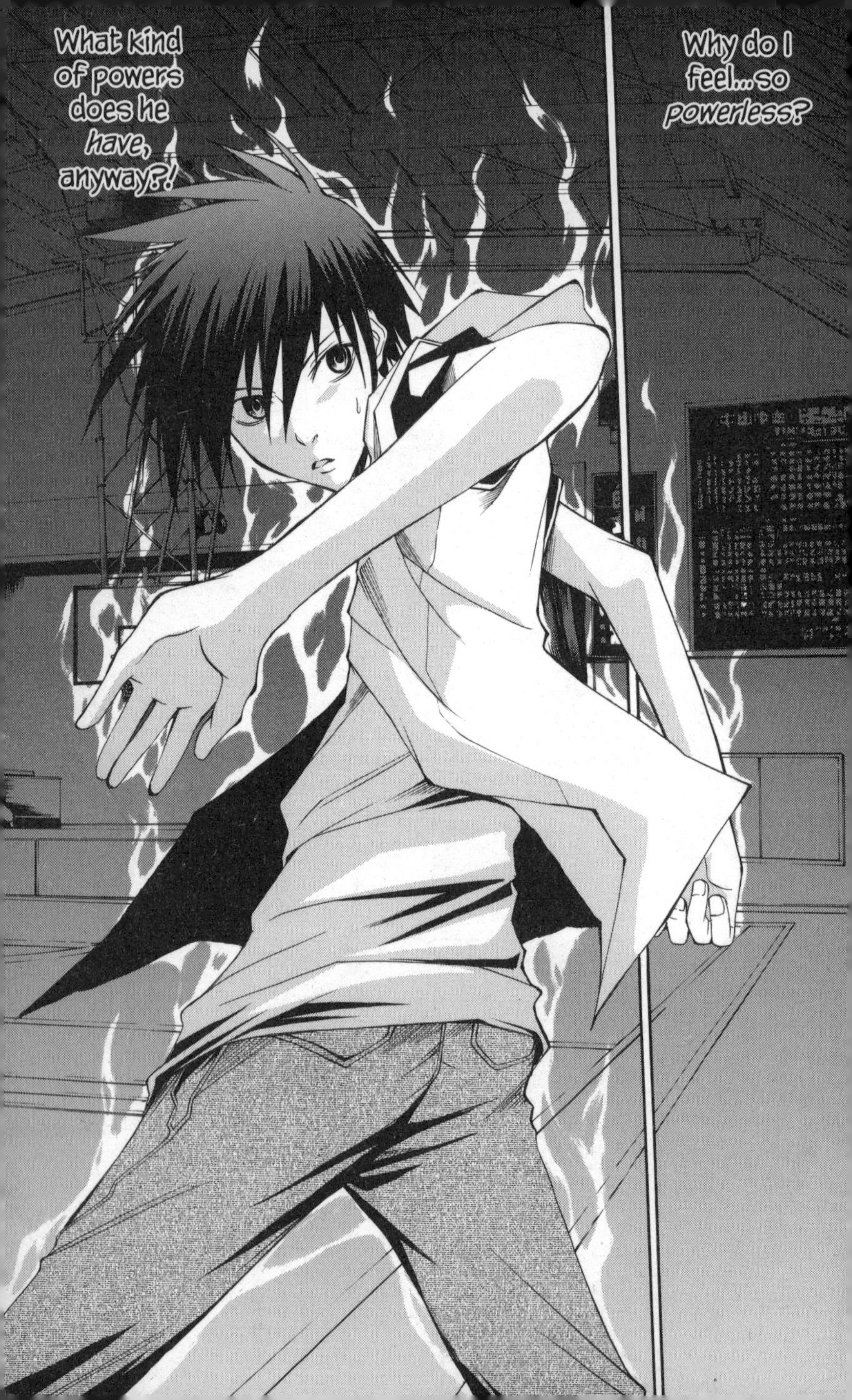
Why do I feel...so *powerless?*
What kind of powers does he *have,* anyway?!

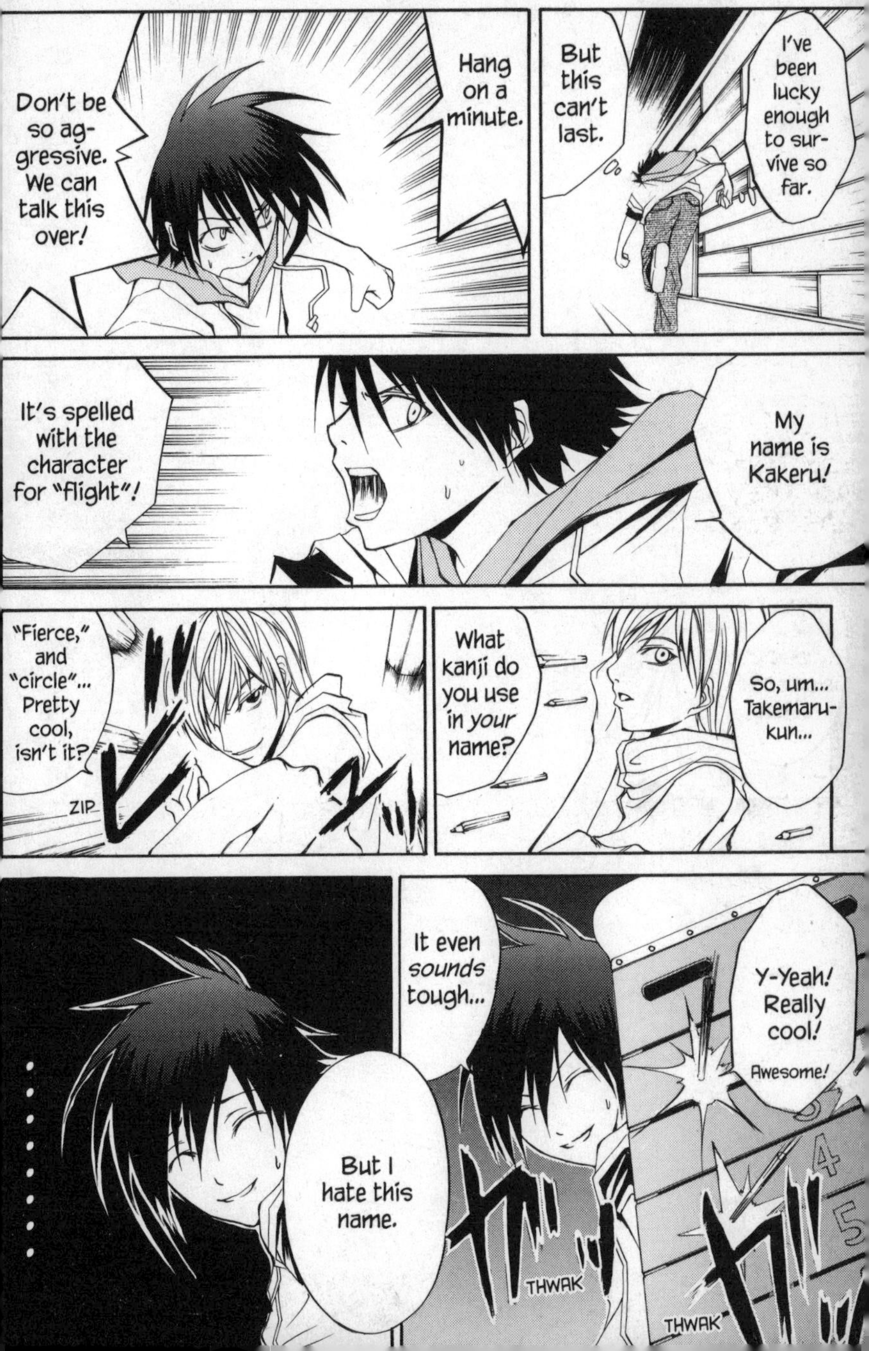
I've been lucky enough to survive so far.
But this can't last.
Hang on a minute.
Don't be so aggressive. We can talk this over!
My name is Kakeru!
It's spelled with the character for "flight"!
So, um... Takemaru-kun...
What kanji do you use in *your* name?
"Fierce," and "circle"... Pretty cool, isn't it?
ZIP
Y-Yeah! Really cool!
Awesome!
It even *sounds* tough...
THWAK
THWAK
But I hate this name.

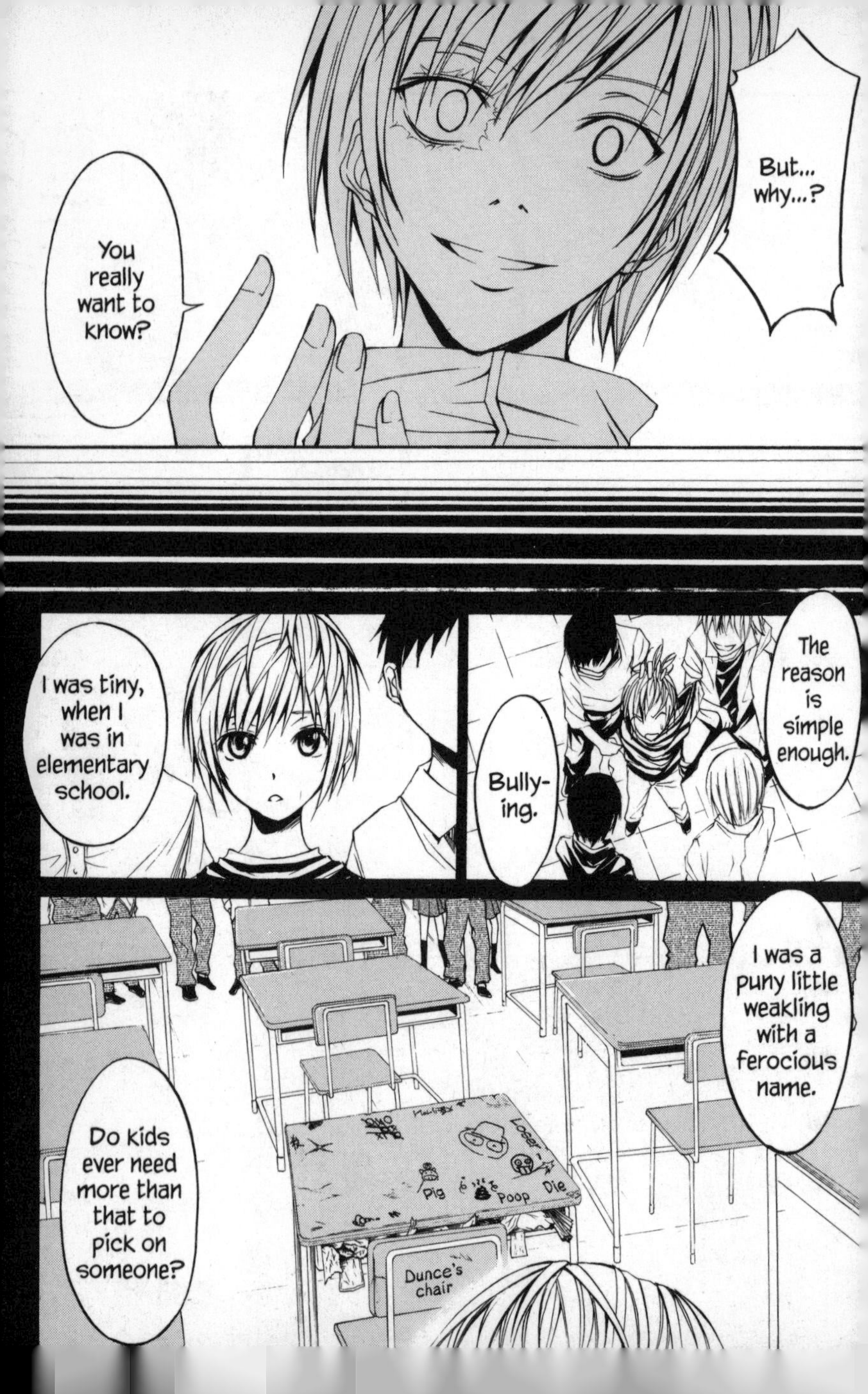
But... why...?
You really want to know?
The reason is simple enough.
Bully-ing.
I was tiny, when I was in elementary school.
I was a puny little weakling with a ferocious name.
Loser
Die
Poop
Pig
Dunce's chair
Do kids ever need more than that to pick on someone?

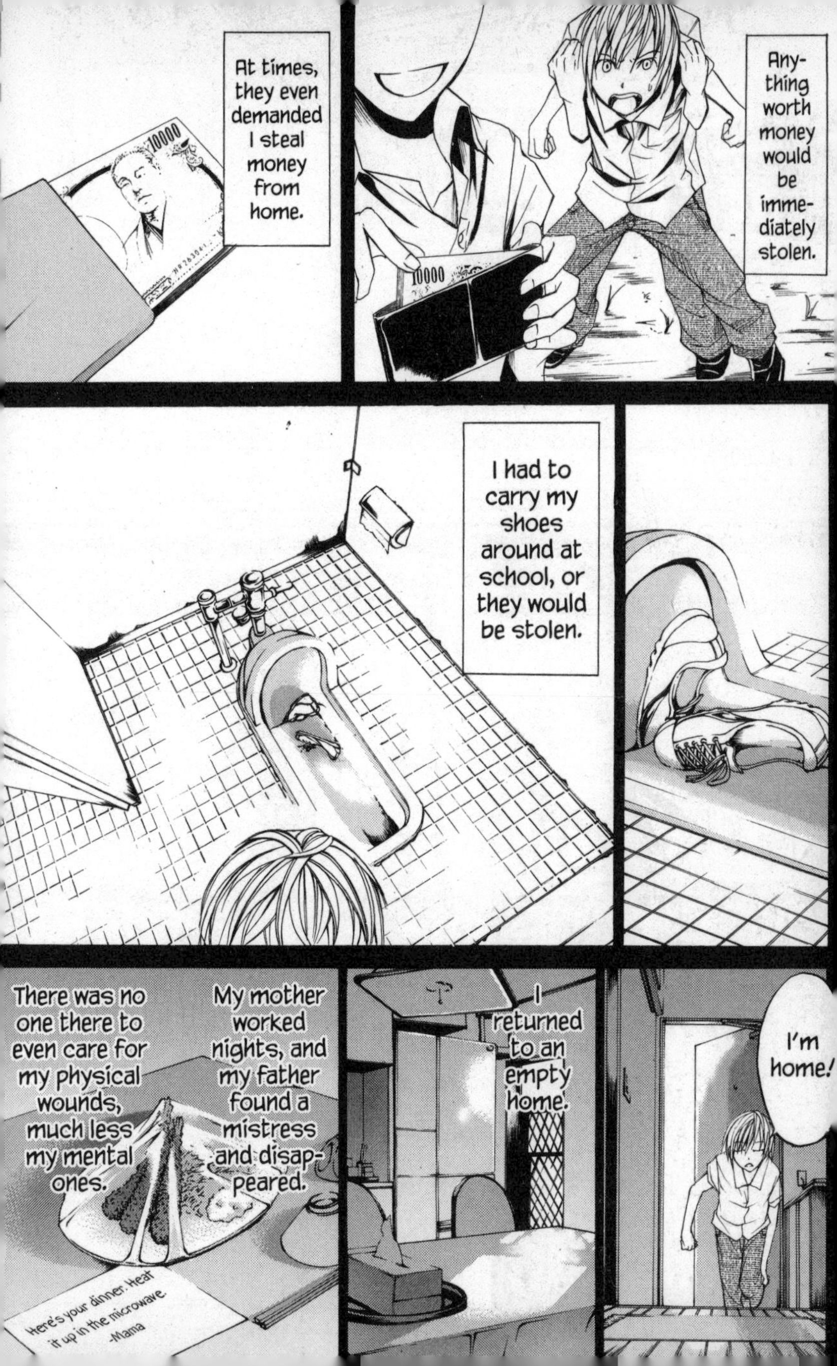

Any-thing worth money would be imme-diately stolen.
At times, they even demanded I steal money from home.
I had to carry my shoes around at school, or they would be stolen.
I'm home!
I returned to an empty home.
My mother worked nights, and my father found a mistress and disap-peared.
There was no one there to even care for my physical wounds, much less my mental ones.
Here's your dinner. Heat it up in the microwave. -Mama

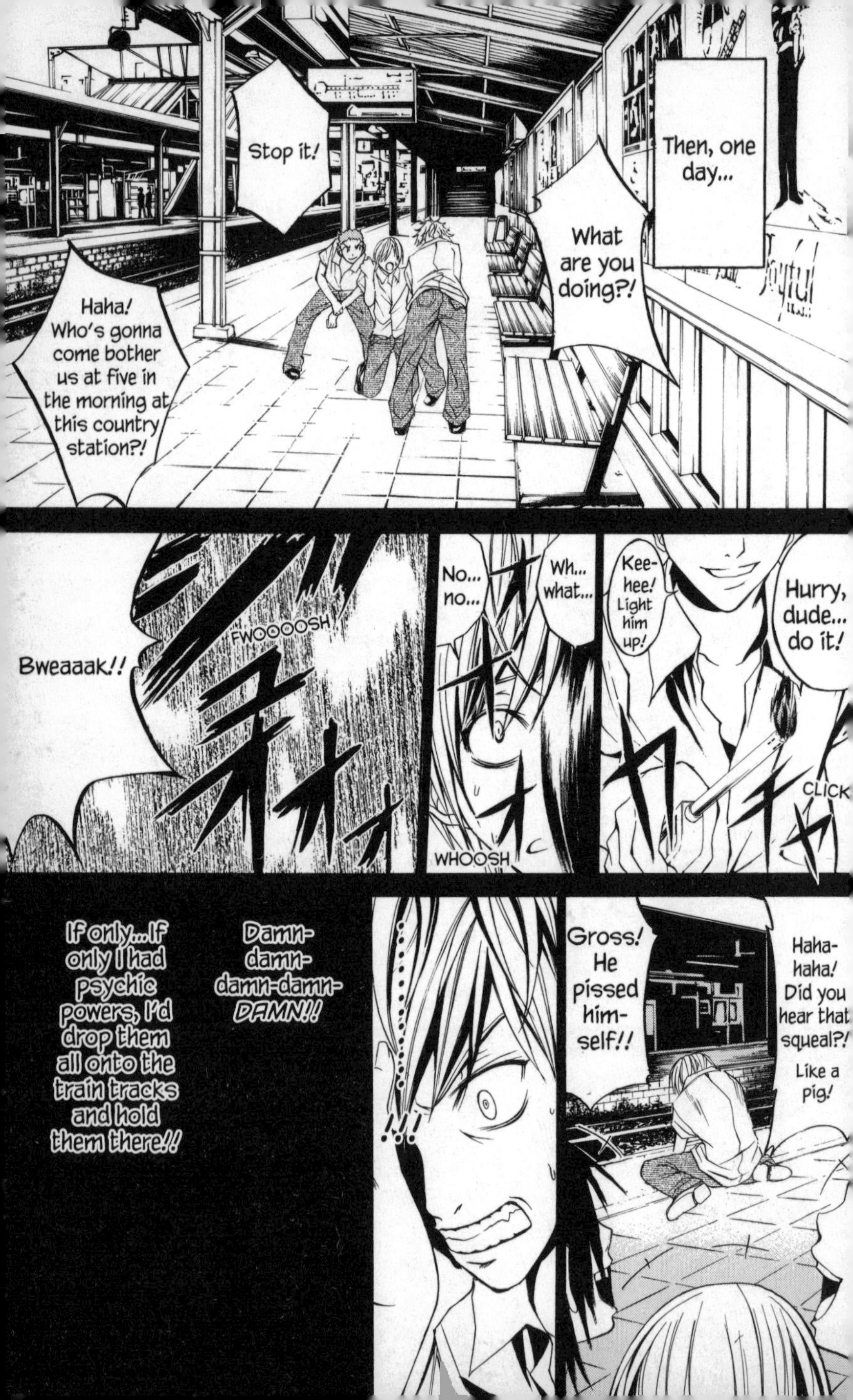
Then, one day...
What are you doing?!
Stop it!
Haha! Who's gonna come bother us at five in the morning at this country station?!
Hurry, dude... do it!
Kee-hee! Light him up!
CLICK
Wh... what...
No... no...
WHOOSH
FWOOOOSH
Bweaaak!!
Haha-haha! Did you hear that squeal?!
Like a pig!
Gross! He pissed him-self!!
!!
Damn-damn-damn-damn-DAMN!!
If only...If only I had psychic powers, I'd drop them all onto the train tracks and hold them there!!

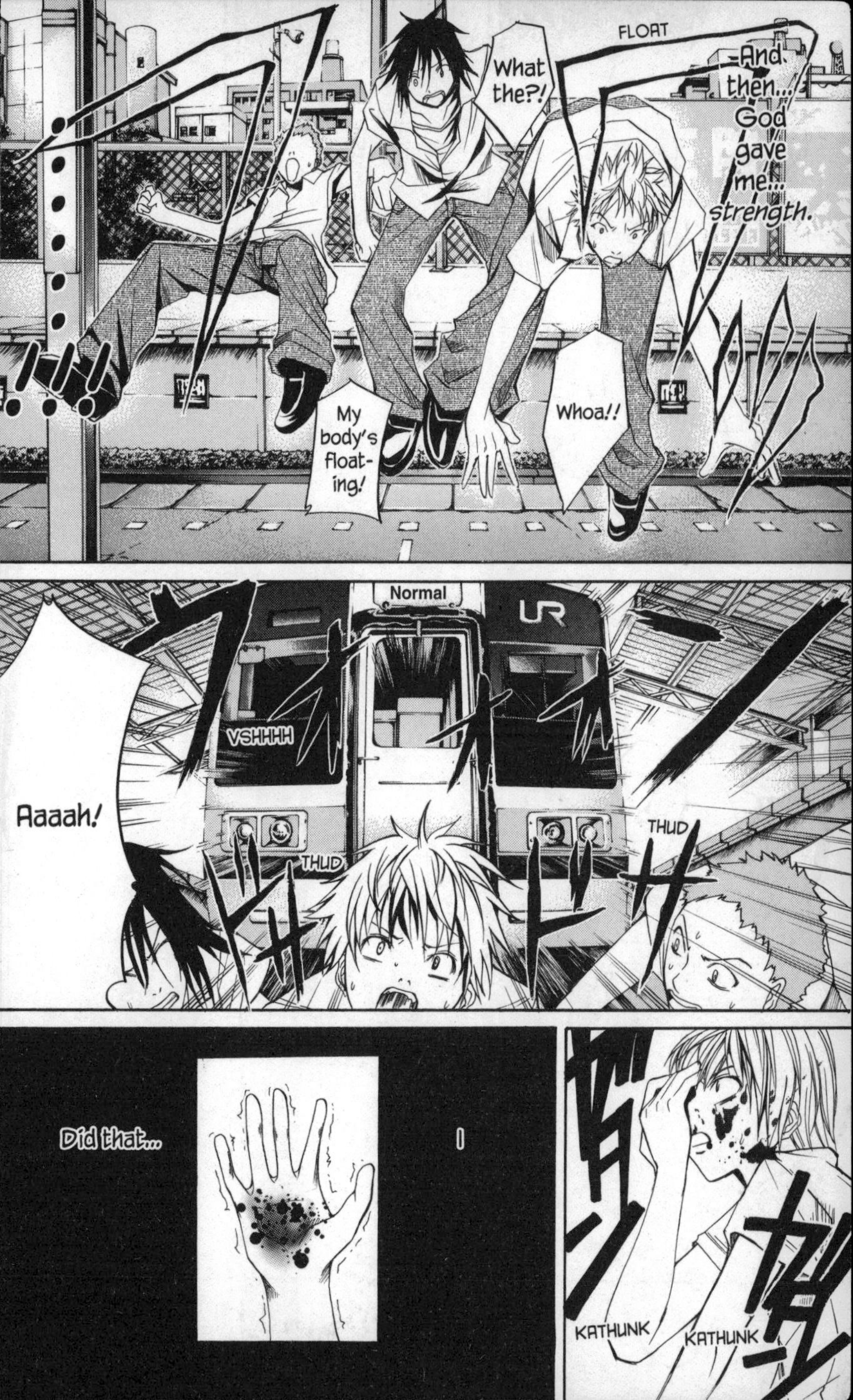
And then... God gave me... strength.
FLOAT
What the?!
Whoa!!
My body's floating!
!!!
Normal
THUD
VSHHHH
THUD
Aaaah!
KATHUNK
KATHUNK
Did that...
I

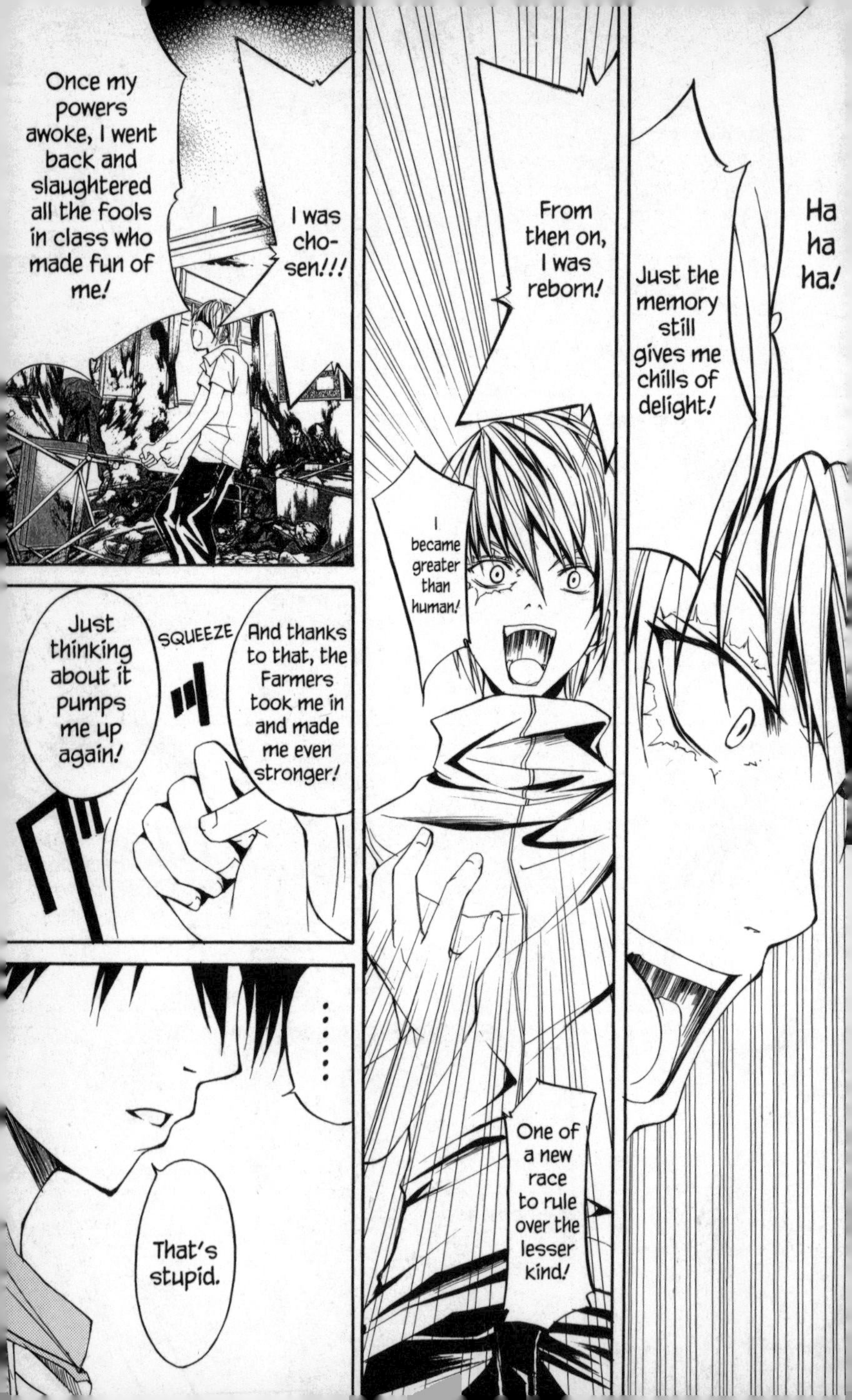
Ha ha ha!
Just the memory still gives me chills of delight!
From then on, I was reborn!
I became greater than human!
One of a new race to rule over the lesser kind!
I was cho-sen!!!
Once my powers awoke, I went back and slaughtered all the fools in class who made fun of me!
And thanks to that, the Farmers took me in and made me even stronger!
SQUEEZE
Just thinking about it pumps me up again!
......
That's stupid.

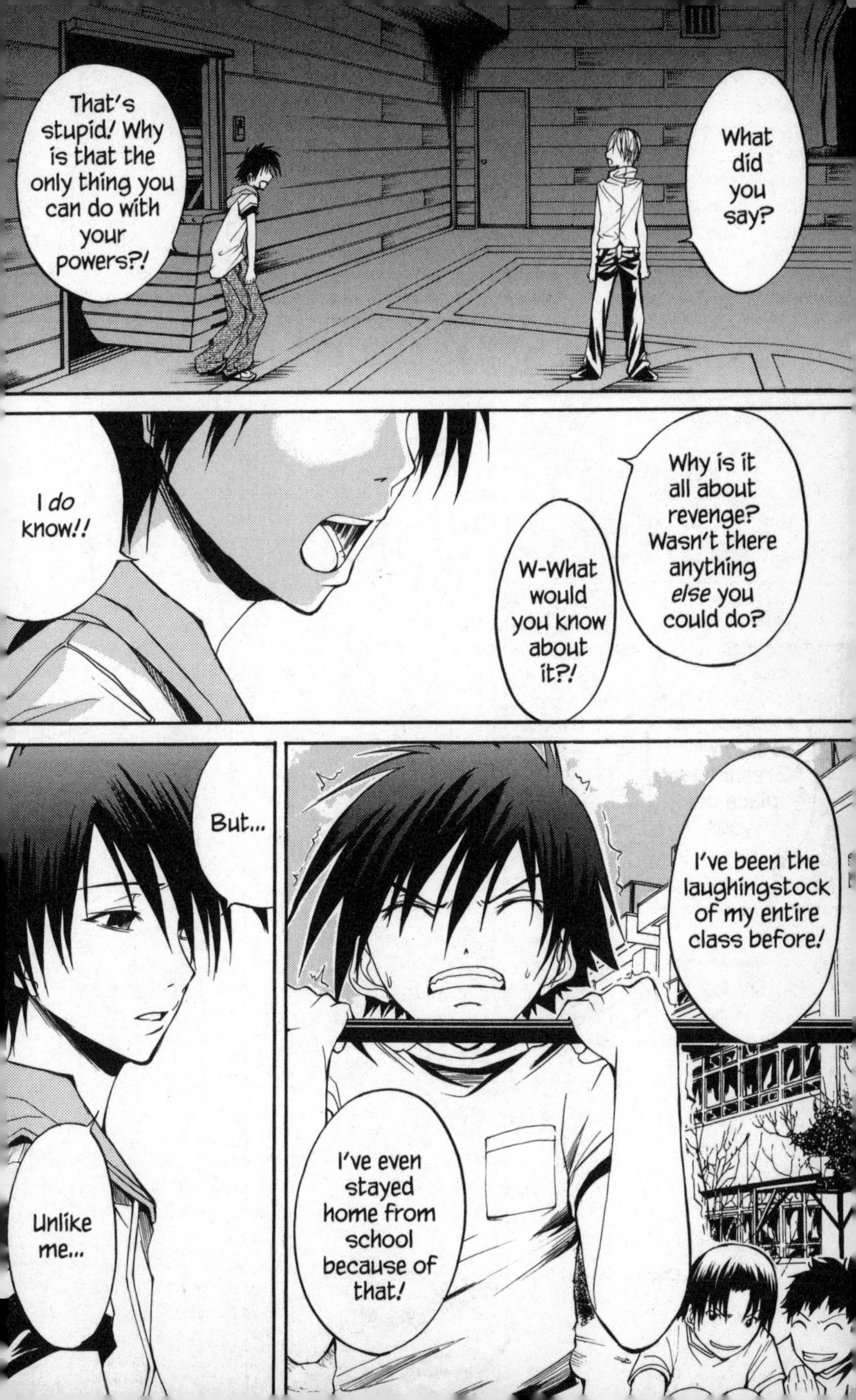
That's stupid! Why is that the only thing you can do with your powers?!
What did you say?
Why is it all about revenge? Wasn't there anything *else* you could do?
W-What would you know about it?!
I *do* know!!
I've been the laughingstock of my entire class before!
I've even stayed home from school because of that!
But...
Unlike me...

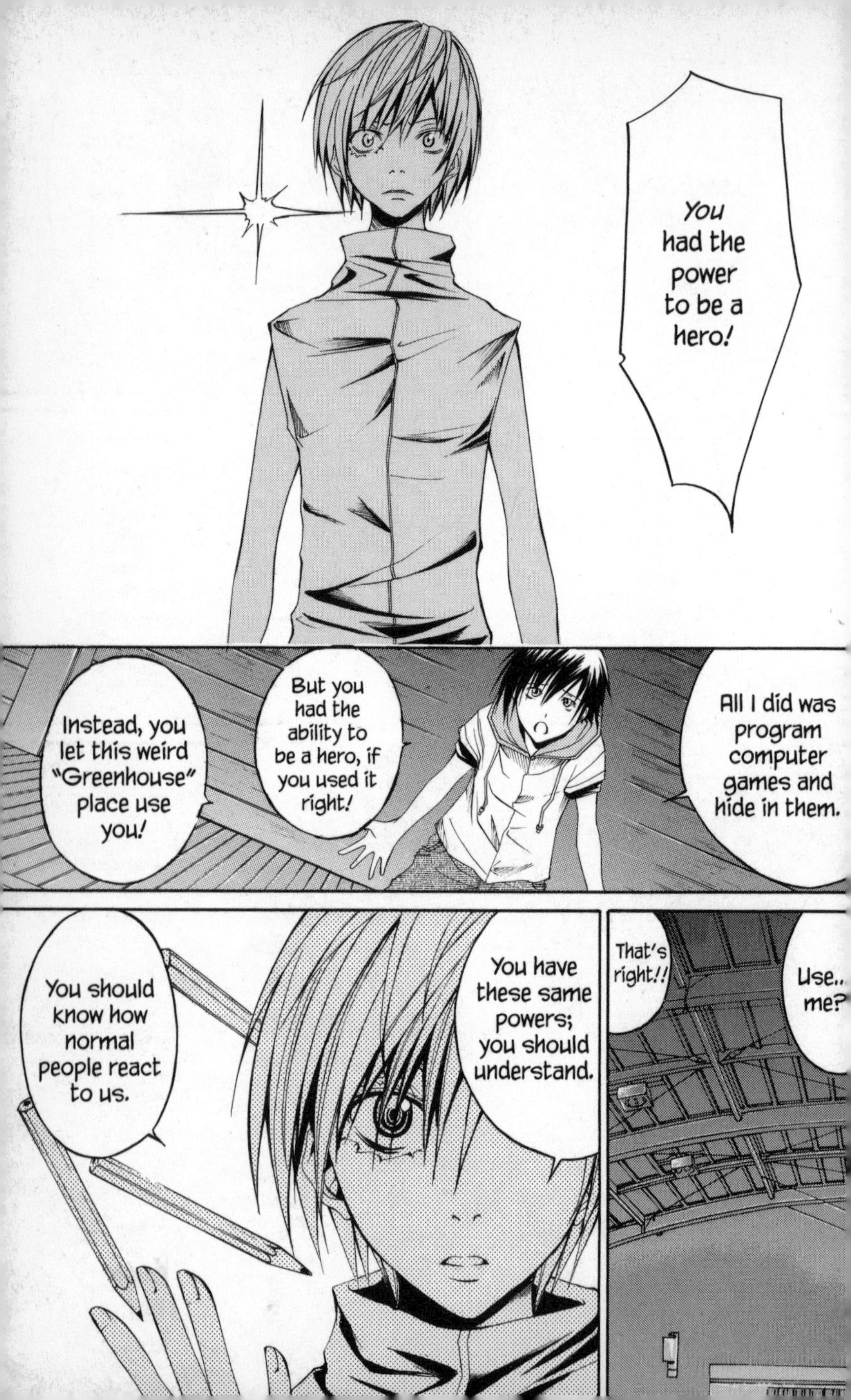
You had the power to be a hero!
All I did was program computer games and hide in them.
But you had the ability to be a hero, if you used it right!
Instead, you let this weird "Greenhouse" place use you!
Use.. me?
That's right!!
You have these same powers; you should understand.
You should know how normal people react to us.

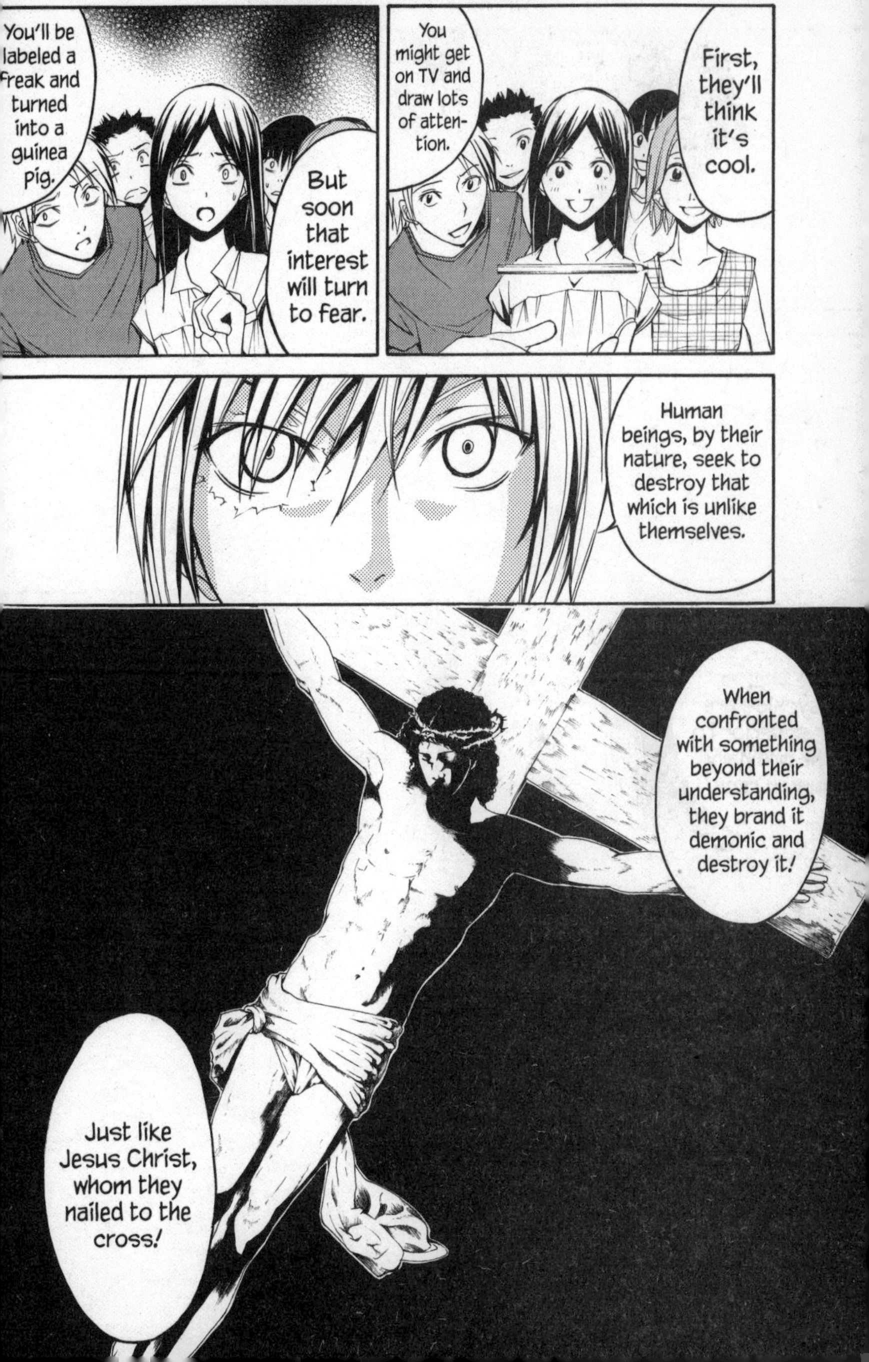
First, they'll think it's cool.
You might get on TV and draw lots of attention.
But soon that interest will turn to fear.
You'll be labeled a freak and turned into a guinea pig.
Human beings, by their nature, seek to destroy that which is unlike themselves.
When confronted with something beyond their understanding, they brand it demonic and destroy it!
Just like Jesus Christ, whom they nailed to the cross!

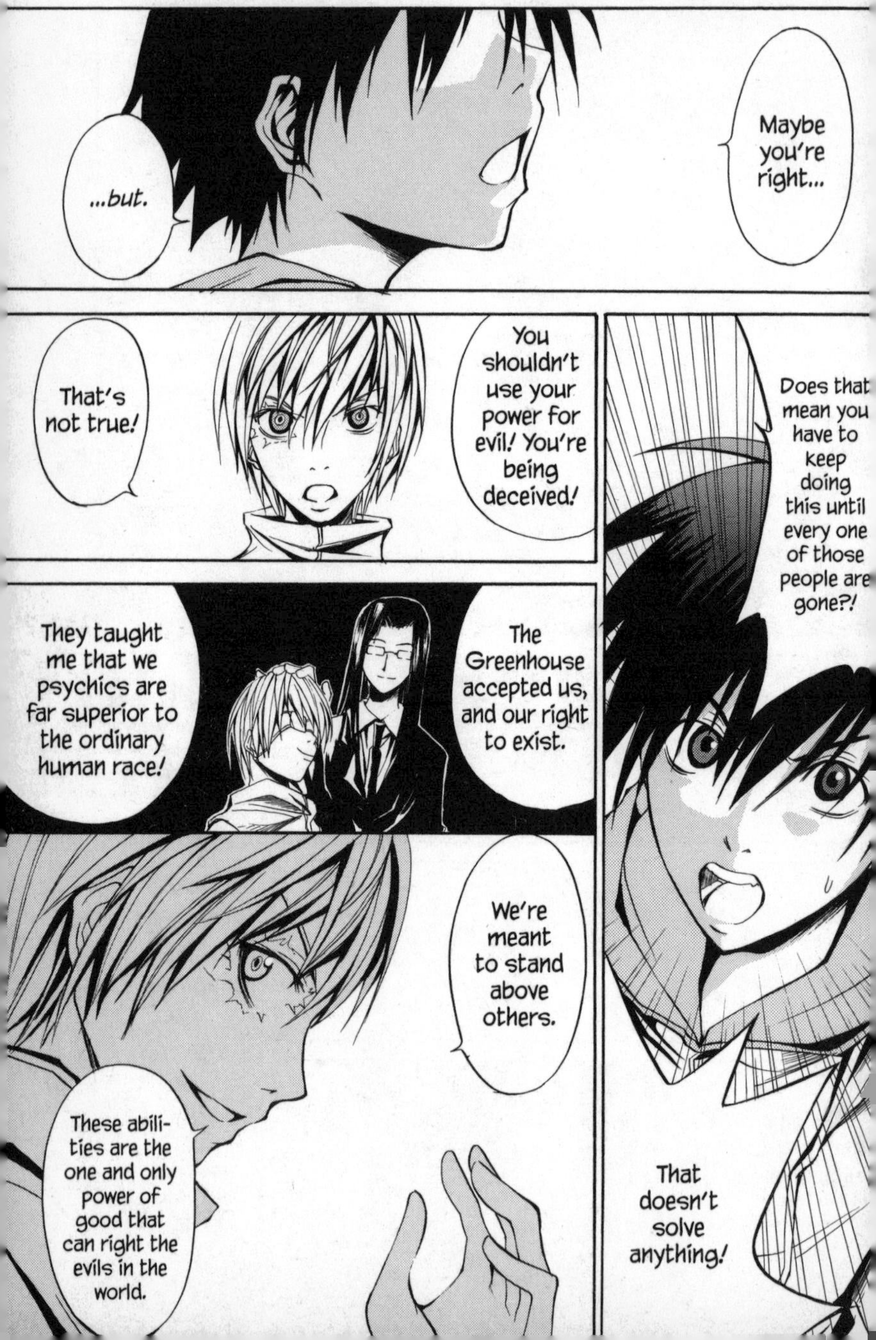
Maybe you're right...
...but.
Does that mean you have to keep doing this until every one of those people are gone?!
That doesn't solve anything!
You shouldn't use your power for evil! You're being deceived!
That's not true!
The Greenhouse accepted us, and our right to exist.
They taught me that we psychics are far superior to the ordinary human race!
We're meant to stand above others.
These abili-ties are the one and only power of good that can right the evils in the world.

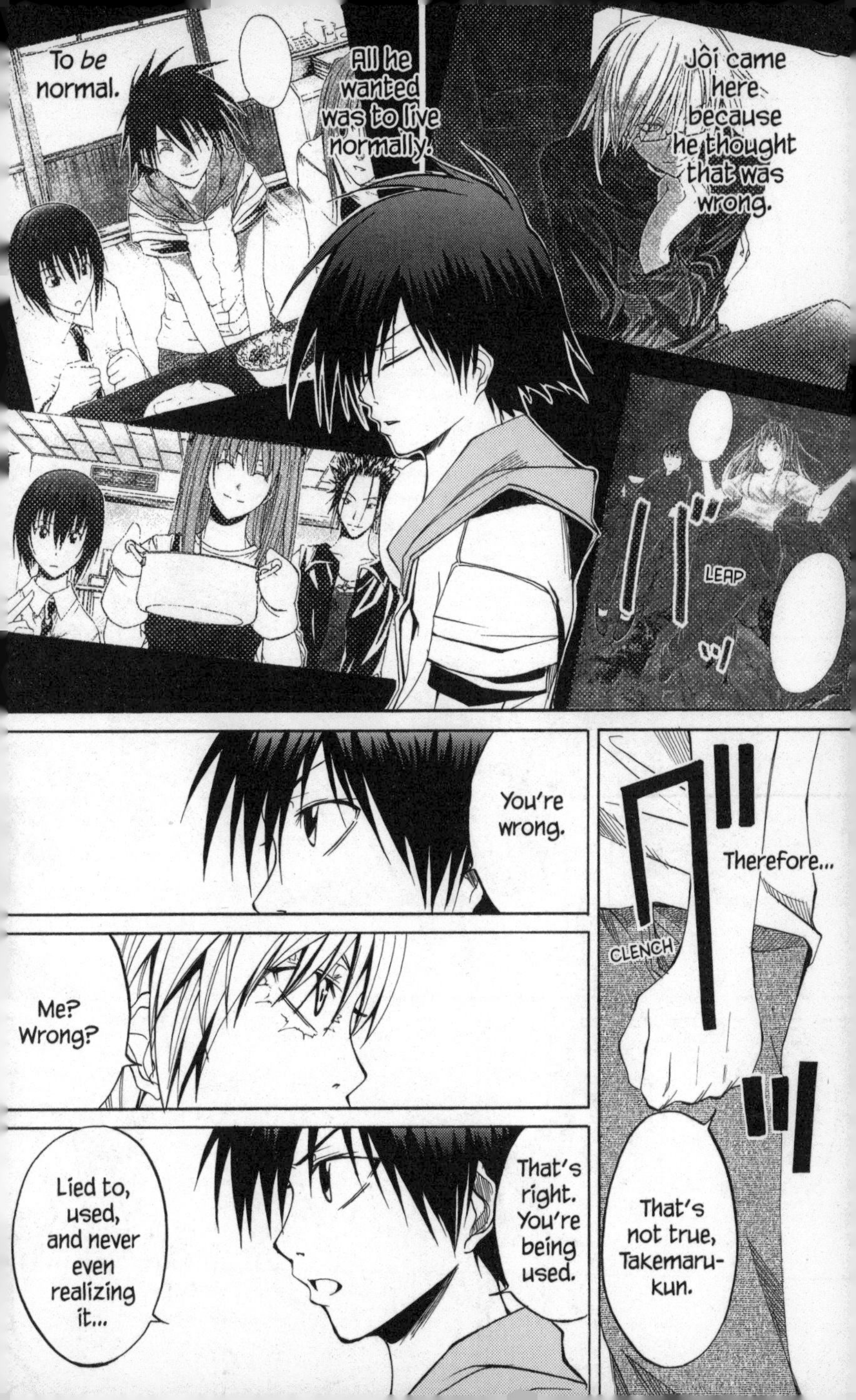
Jôi came here because he thought that was wrong.
All he wanted was to live normally.
To be normal.
LEAP
Therefore...
CLENCH
That's not true, Takemaru-kun.
You're wrong.
Me? Wrong?
That's right. You're being used.
Lied to, used, and never even realizing it...

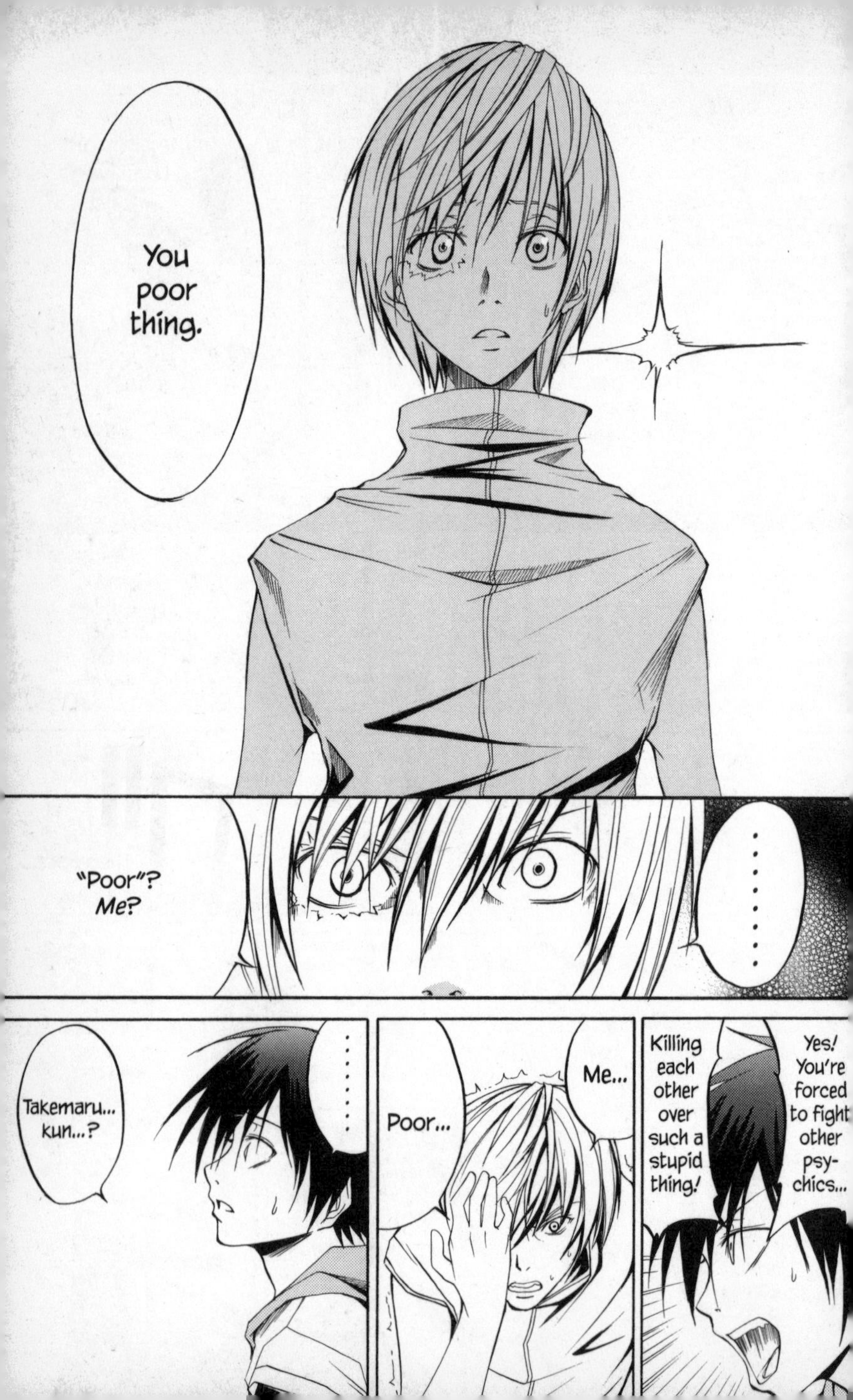
You poor thing.
......
"Poor"? Me?
Yes! You're forced to fight other psychics...
Killing each other over such a stupid thing!
Me...
Poor...
......
Takemaru... kun...?

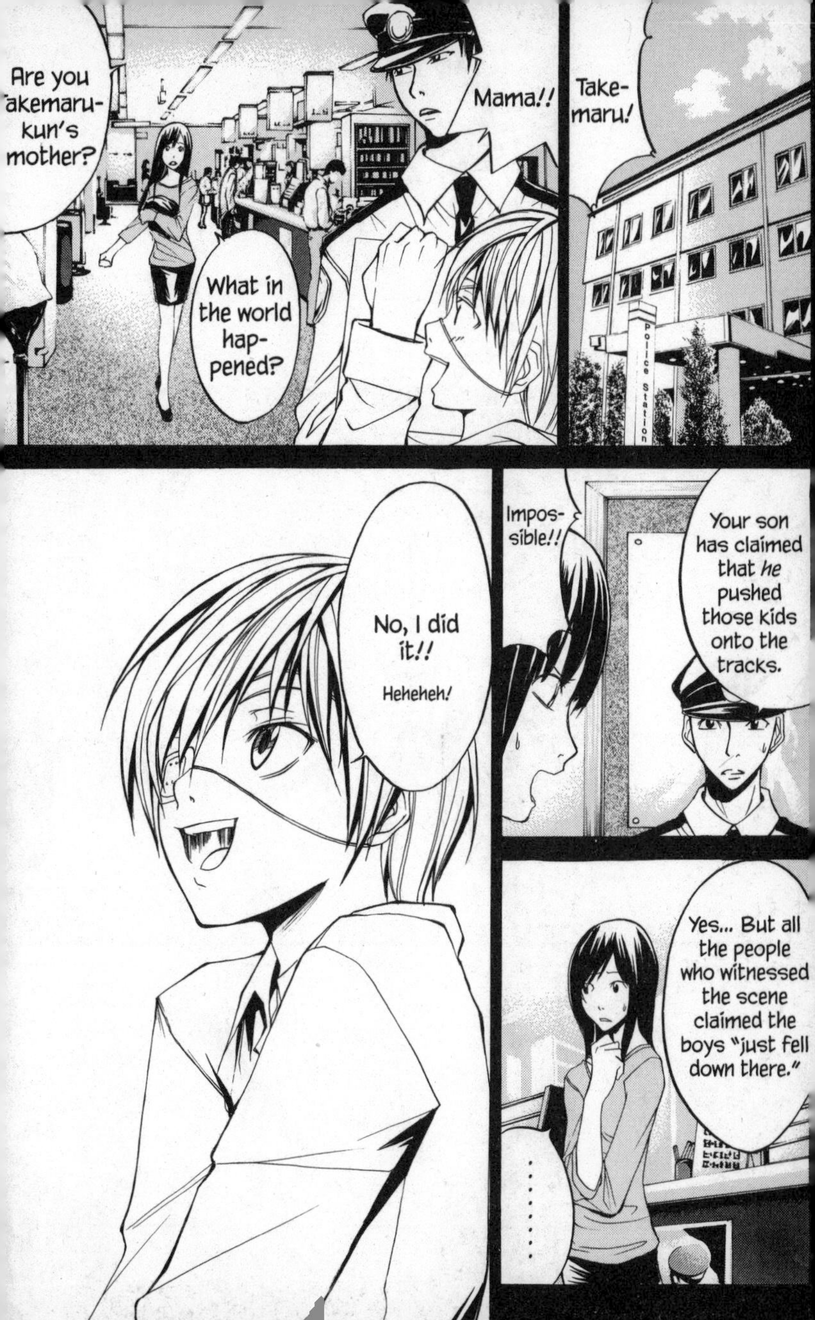
Take-maru!
Mama!!
Are you Takemaru-kun's mother?
What in the world hap-pened?
Your son has claimed that *he* pushed those kids onto the tracks.
Impos-sible!!
Yes... But all the people who witnessed the scene claimed the boys "just fell down there."
......
No, I did it!!
Heheheh!
Police Station

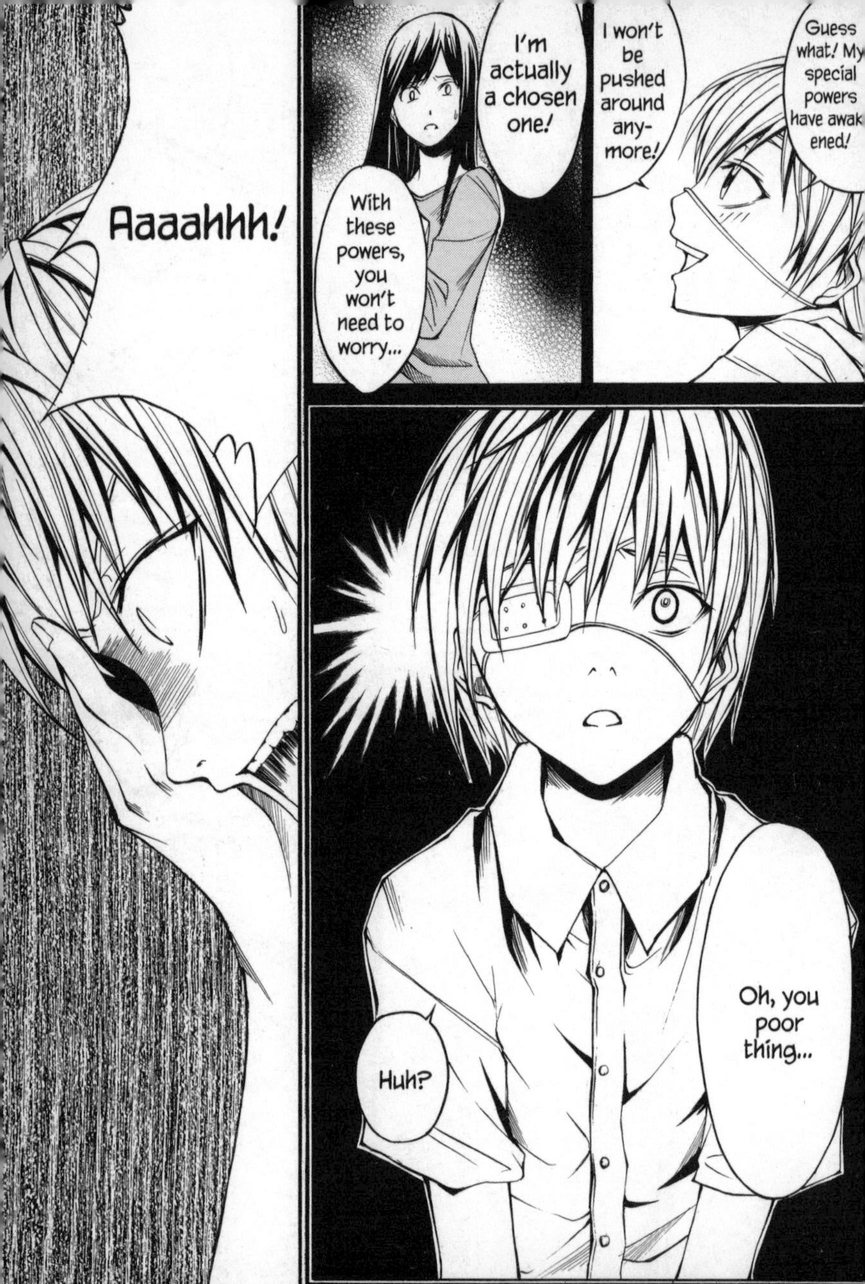
Guess what! My special powers have awakened!
I won't be pushed around anymore!
I'm actually a chosen one!
With these powers, you won't need to worry...
Oh, you poor thing...
Huh?
Aaaahhh!

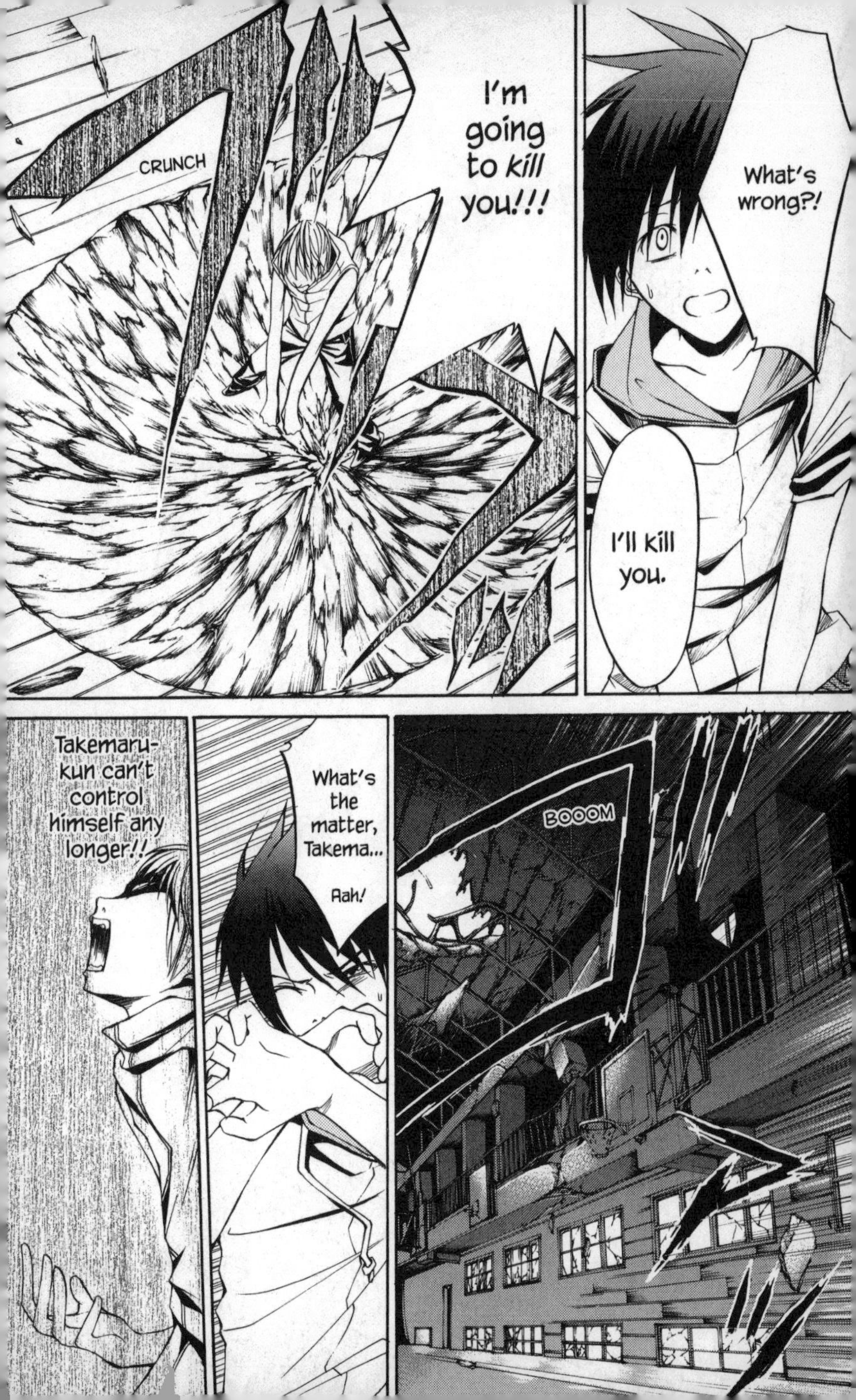
What's wrong?!
I'll kill you.
I'm going to *kill* you!!!
CRUNCH
BOOOM
What's the matter, Takema...
Aah!
Takemaru-kun can't control himself any longer!!

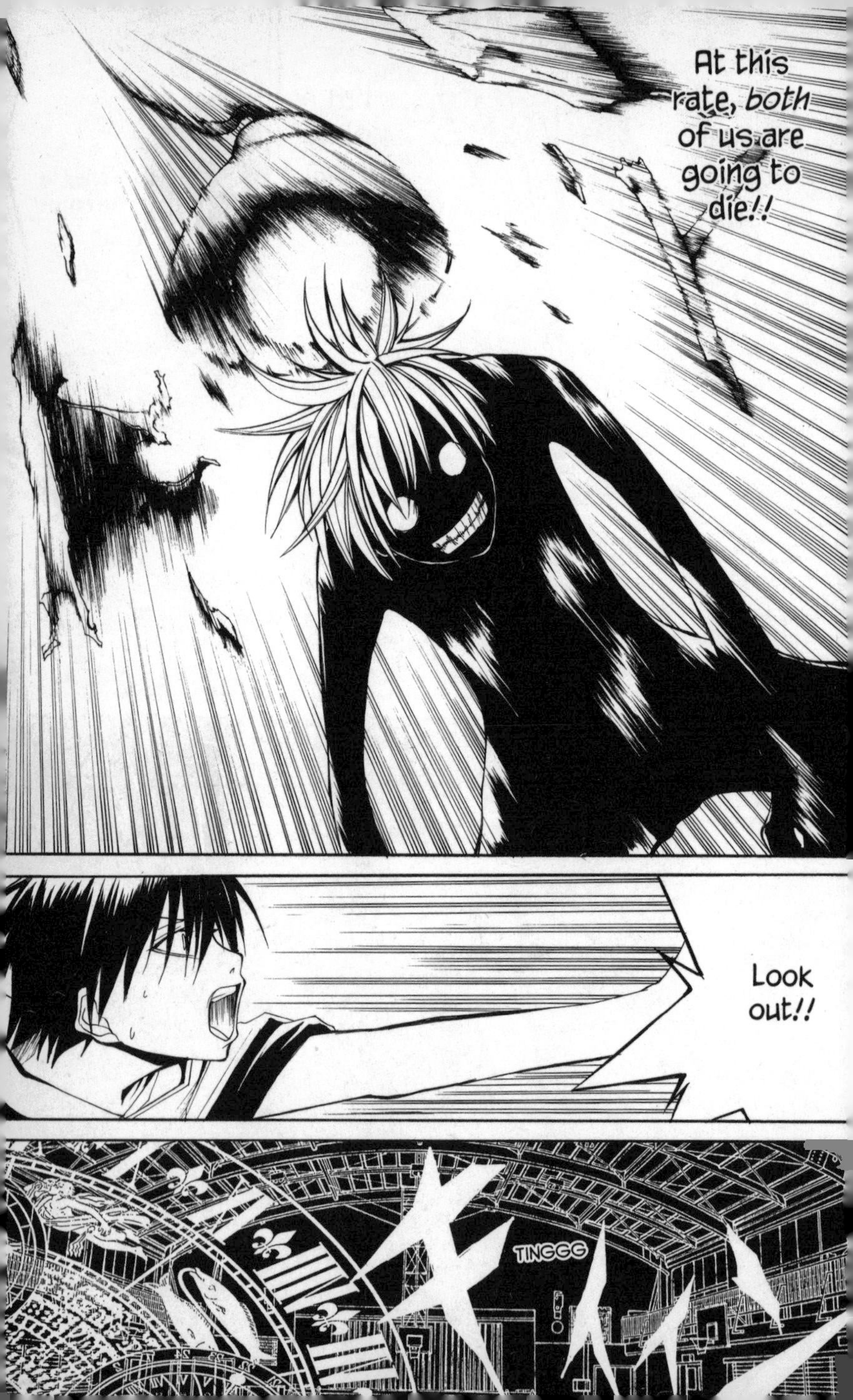
At this rate, *both* of us are going to die!!
Look out!!
TINGGG

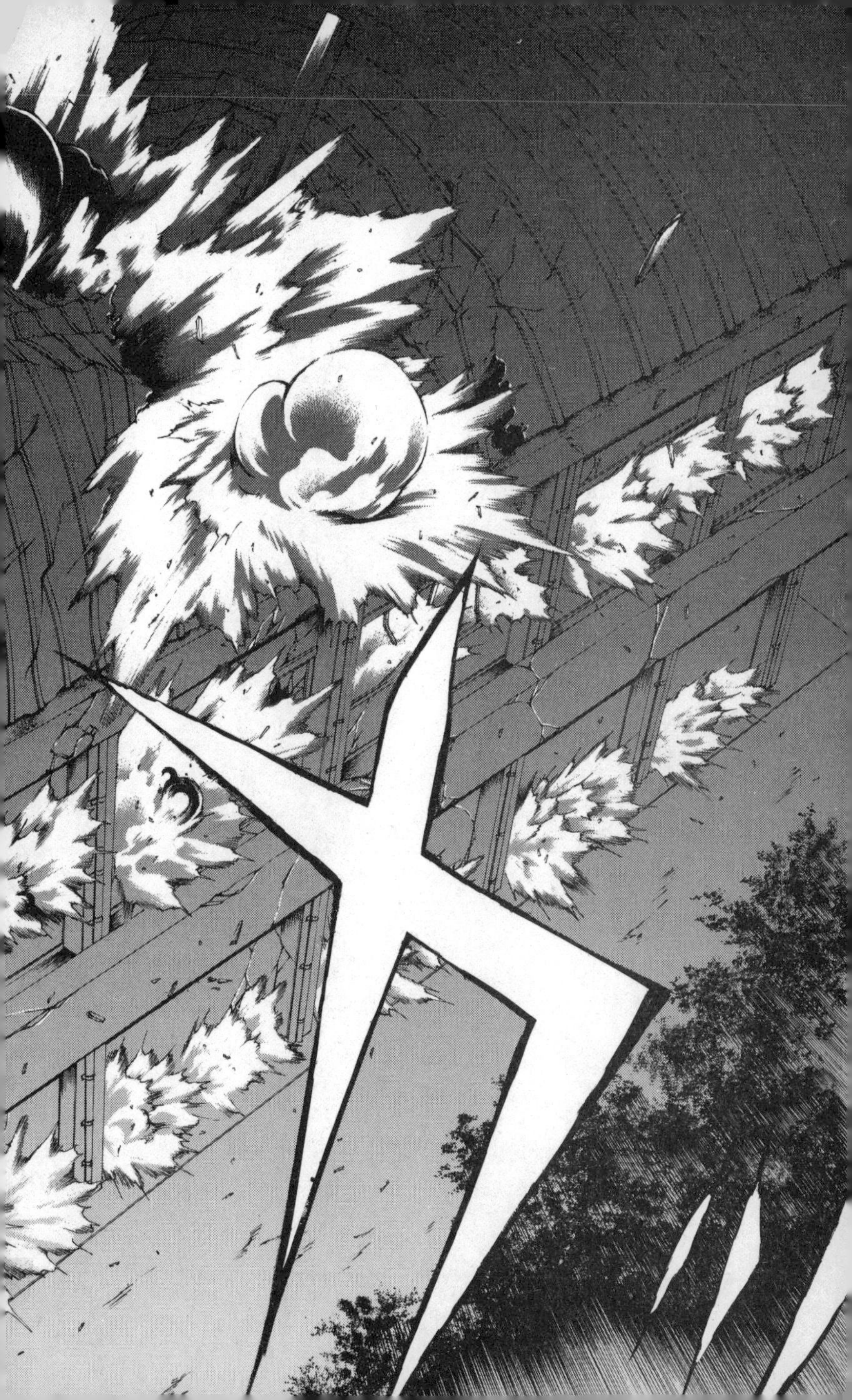

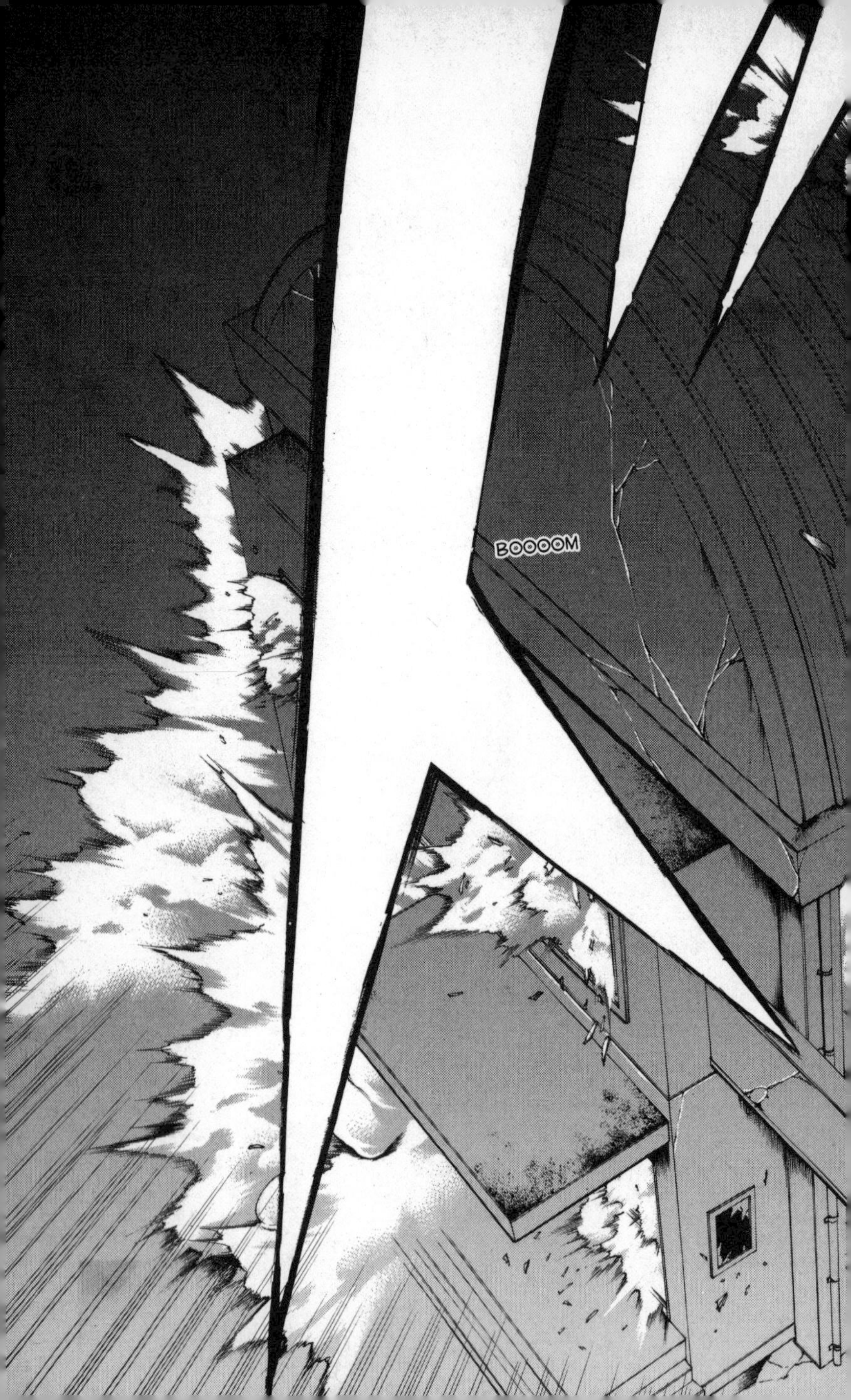
BOOOOM

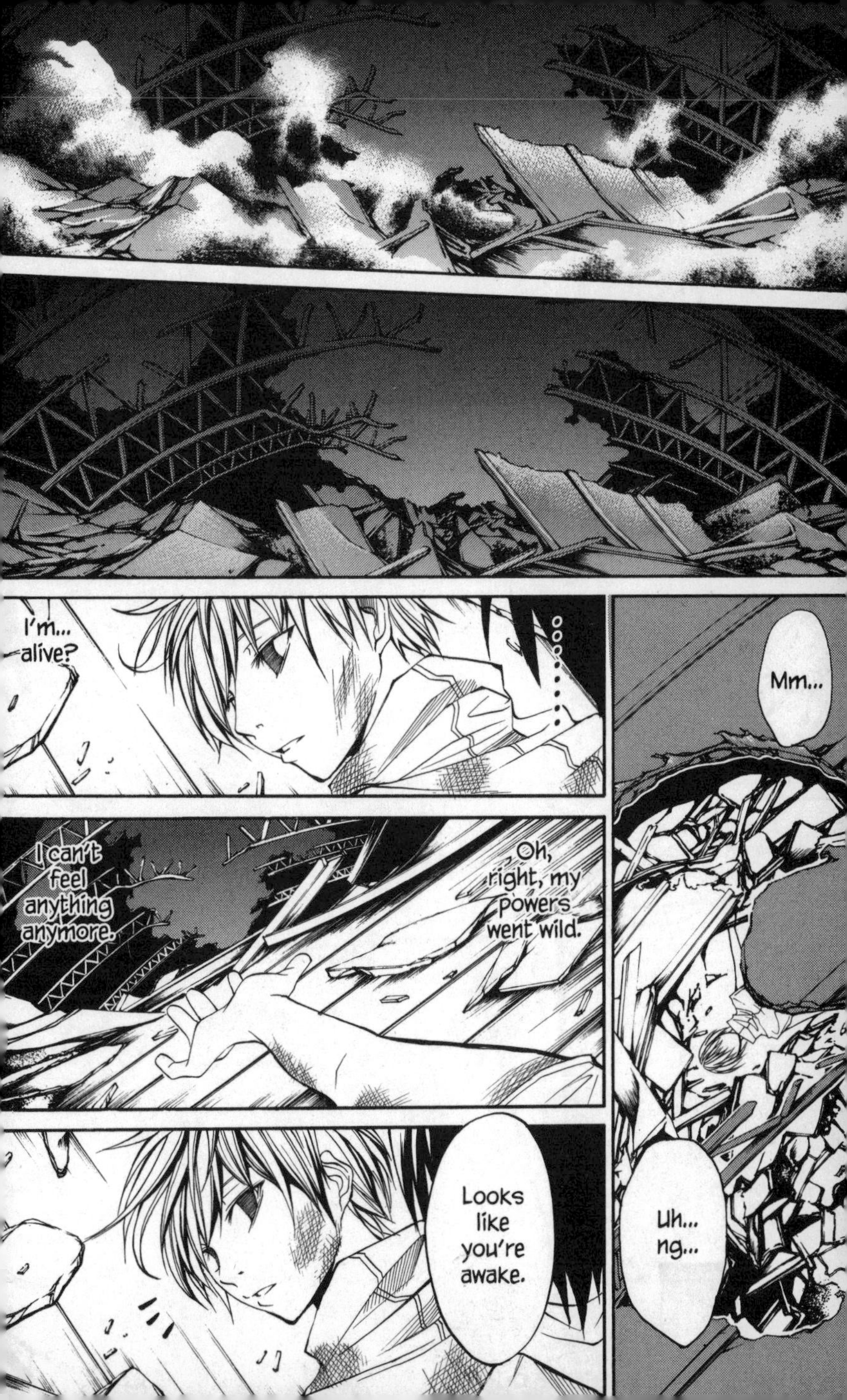

Mm...
Uh... ng...
ooo......
I'm... alive?
Oh, right, my powers went wild.
I can't feel anything anymore.
Looks like you're awake.

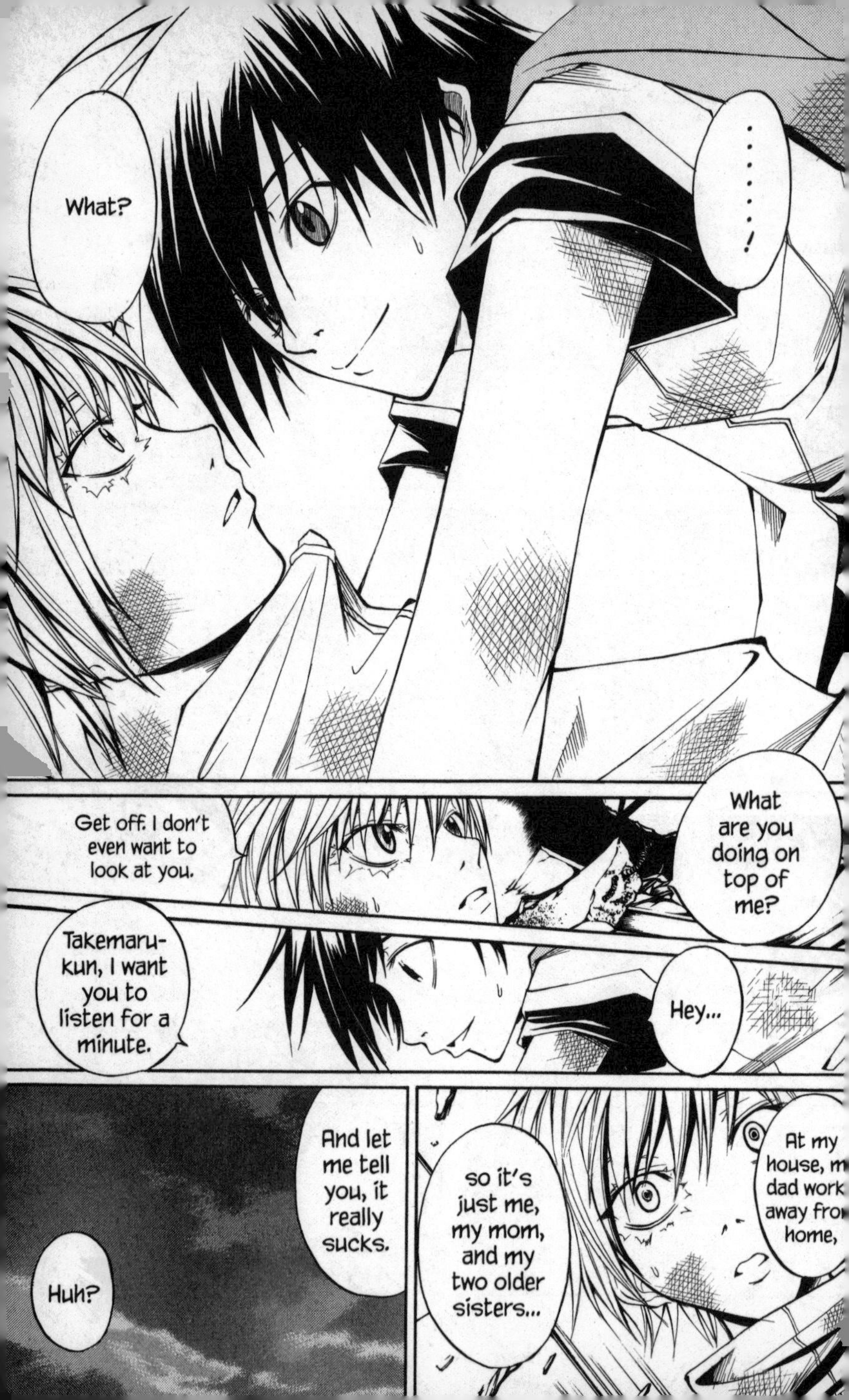
......!
What?
What are you doing on top of me?
Get off. I don't even want to look at you.
Hey...
Takemaru-kun, I want you to listen for a minute.
At my house, m dad work away fro home,
so it's just me, my mom, and my two older sisters...
And let me tell you, it really sucks.
Huh?

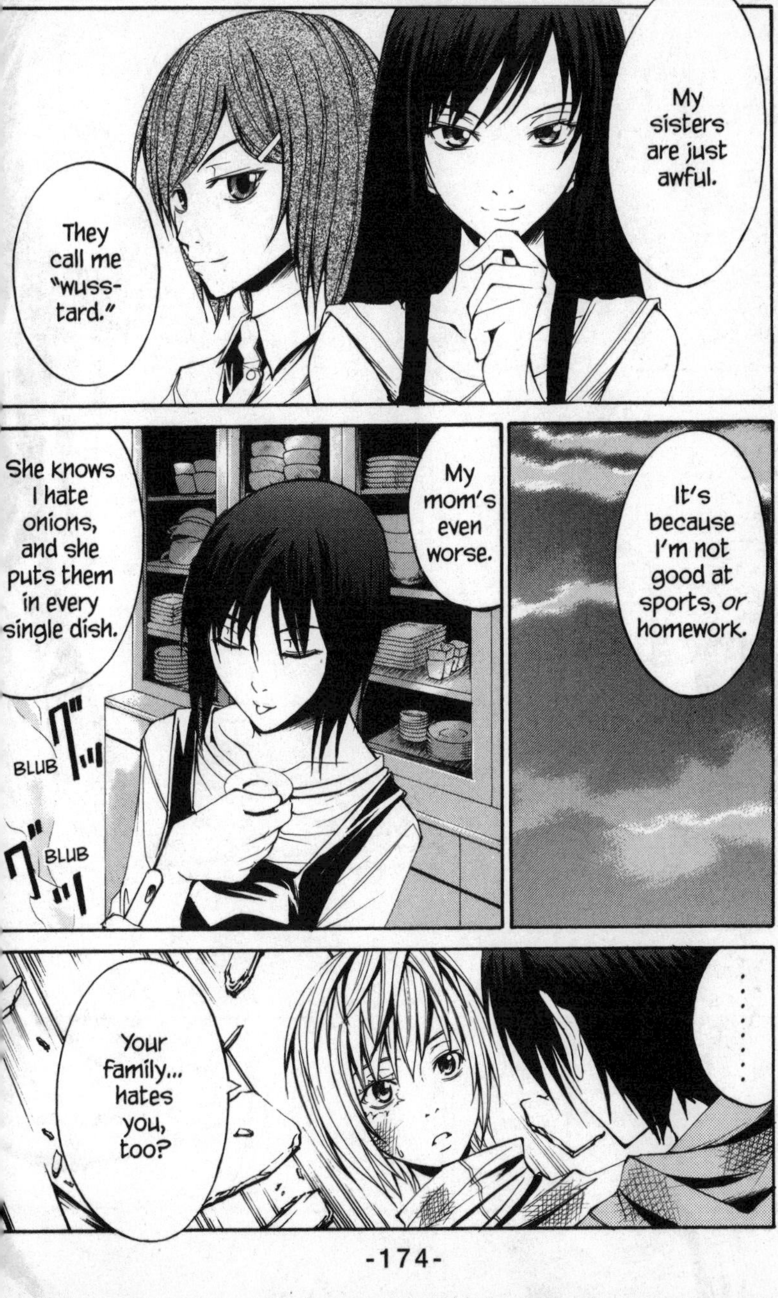
My sisters are just awful.
They call me "wusstard."
It's because I'm not good at sports, *or* homework.
My mom's even worse.
She knows I hate onions, and she puts them in every single dish.
BLUB
BLUB
......
Your family... hates you, too?

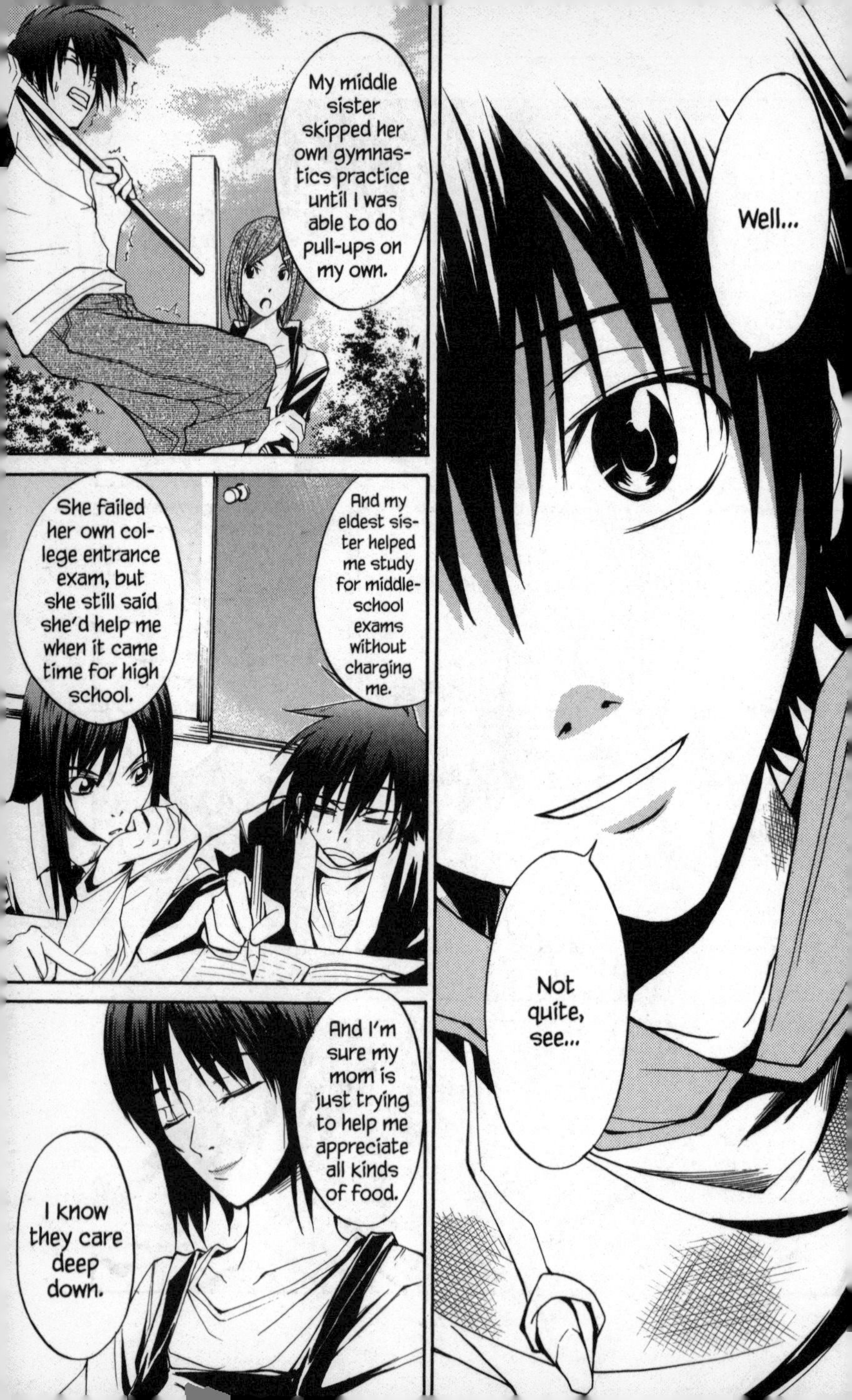
Well...
Not quite, see...
My middle sister skipped her own gymnastics practice until I was able to do pull-ups on my own.
And my eldest sister helped me study for middle-school exams without charging me.
She failed her own college entrance exam, but she still said she'd help me when it came time for high school.
And I'm sure my mom is just trying to help me appreciate all kinds of food.
I know they care deep down.

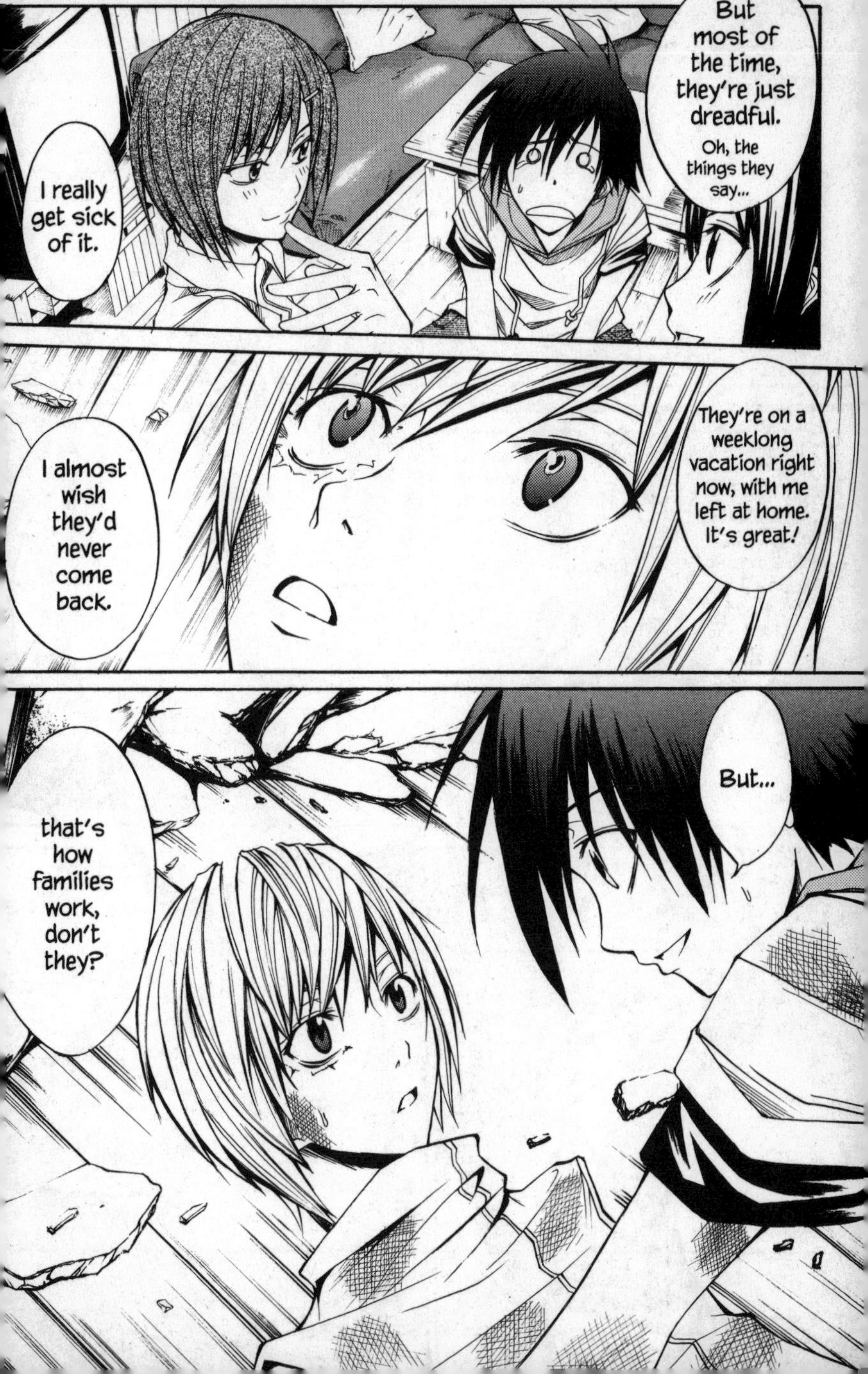
But most of the time, they're just dreadful.
Oh, the things they say...
I really get sick of it.
They're on a weeklong vacation right now, with me left at home. It's great!
I almost wish they'd never come back.
But...
that's how families work, don't they?

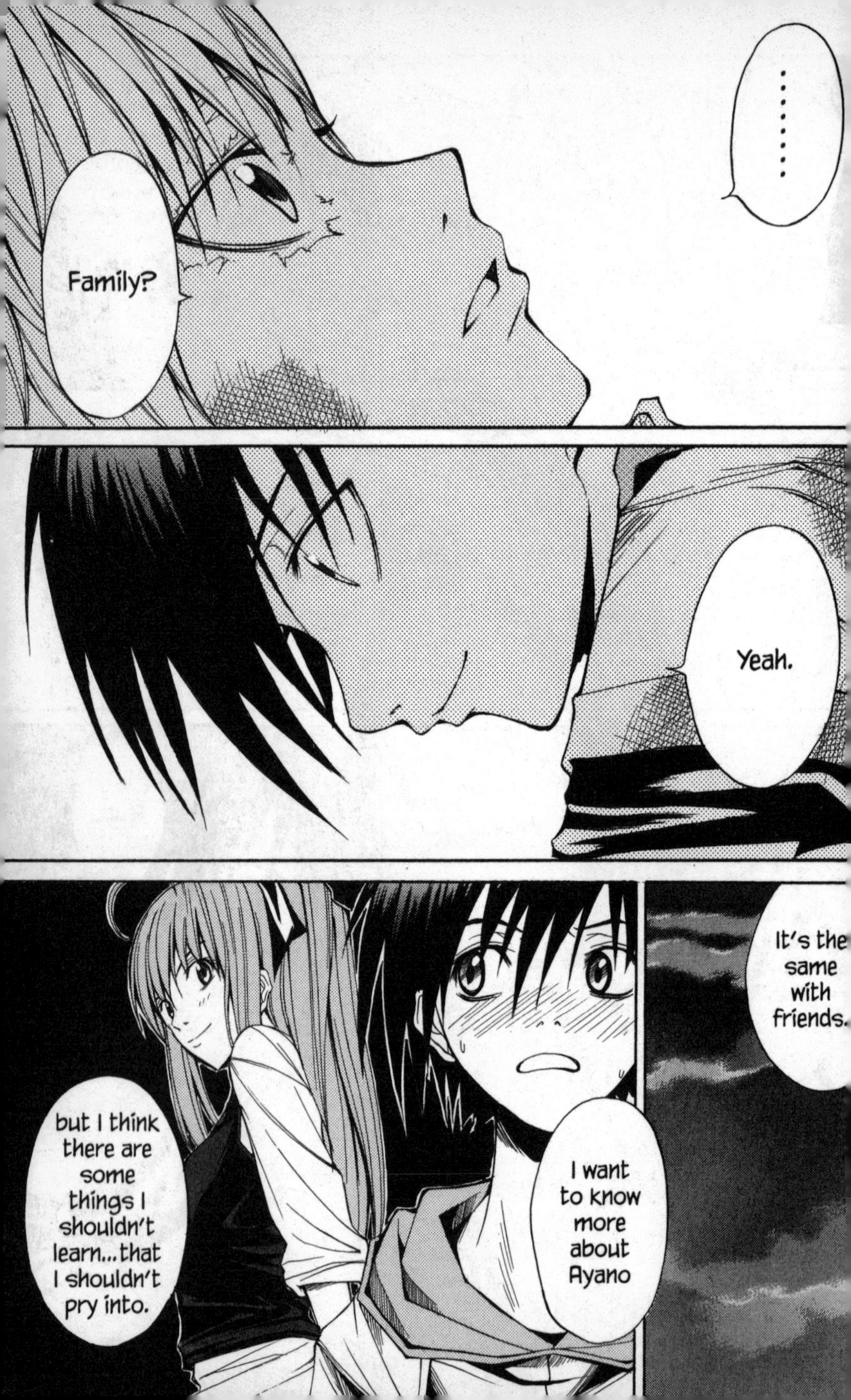
......
Family?
Yeah.
It's the same with friends.
I want to know more about Ayano
but I think there are some things I shouldn't learn...that I shouldn't pry into.

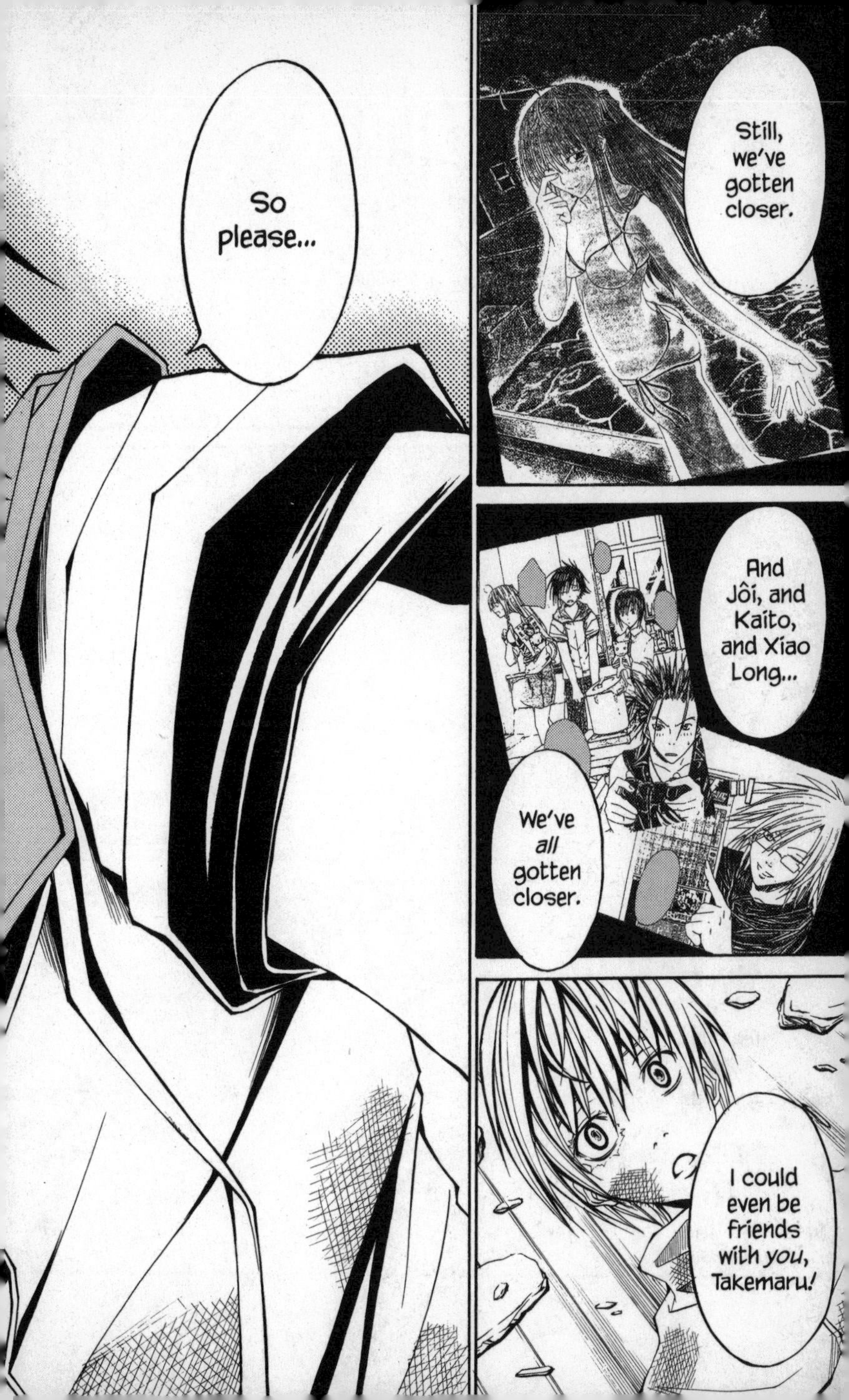
Still, we've gotten closer.
And Jôi, and Kaito, and Xiao Long...
We've *all* gotten closer.
I could even be friends with *you*, Takemaru!
So please...

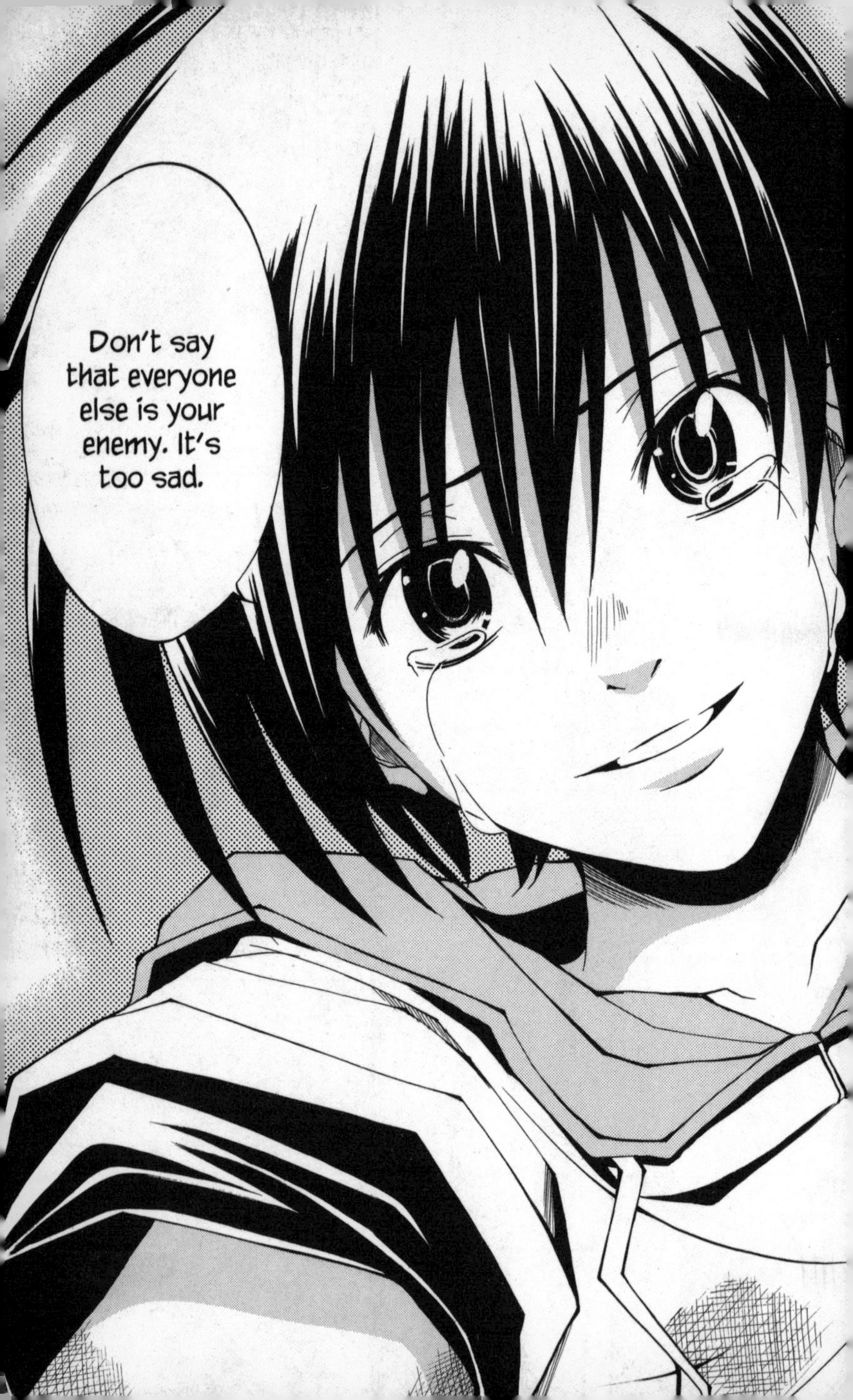
Don't say that everyone else is your enemy. It's too sad.

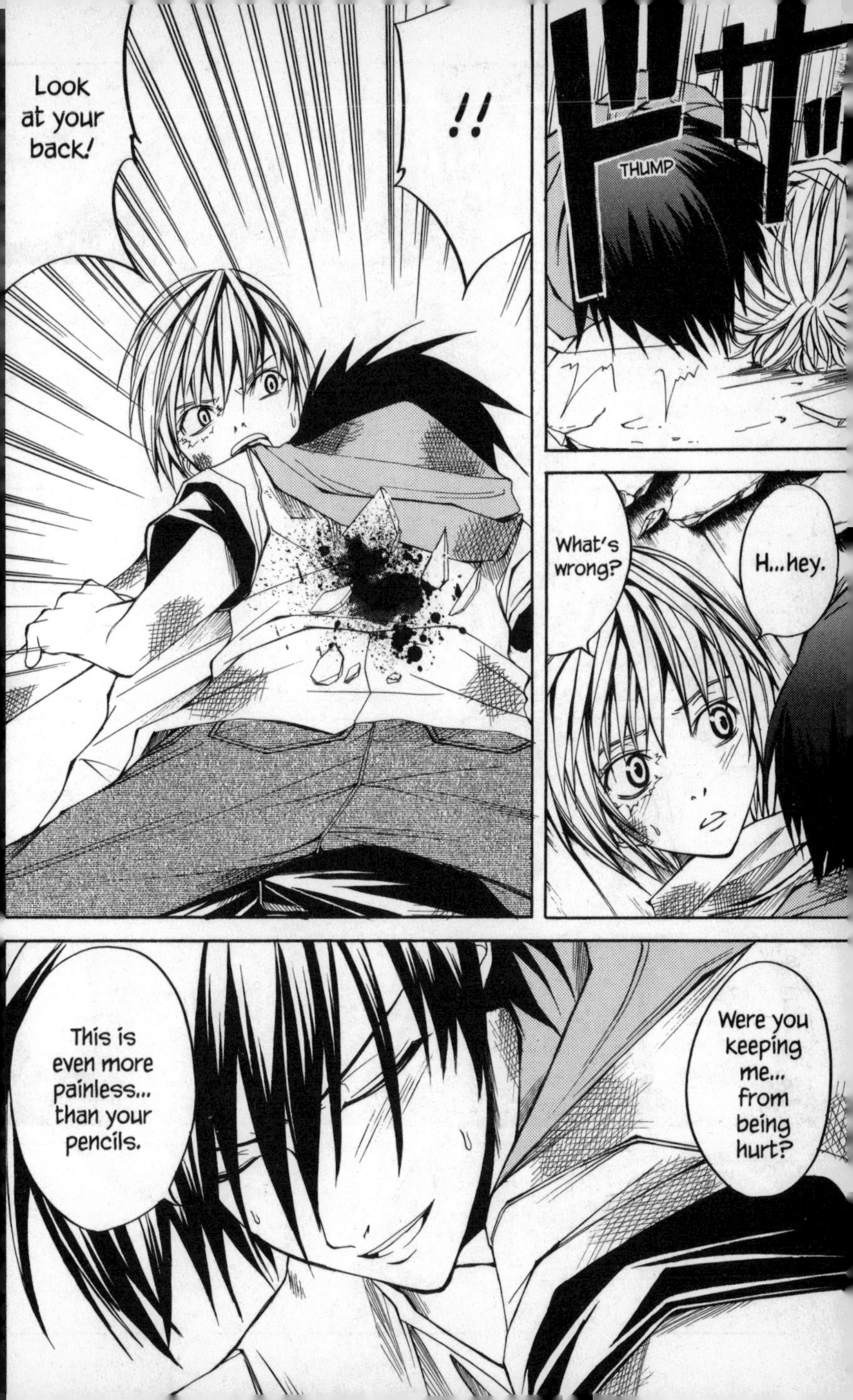
ドサッ
THUMP
H...hey.
What's wrong?
!!
Look at your back!
Were you keeping me... from being hurt?
This is even more painless... than your pencils.

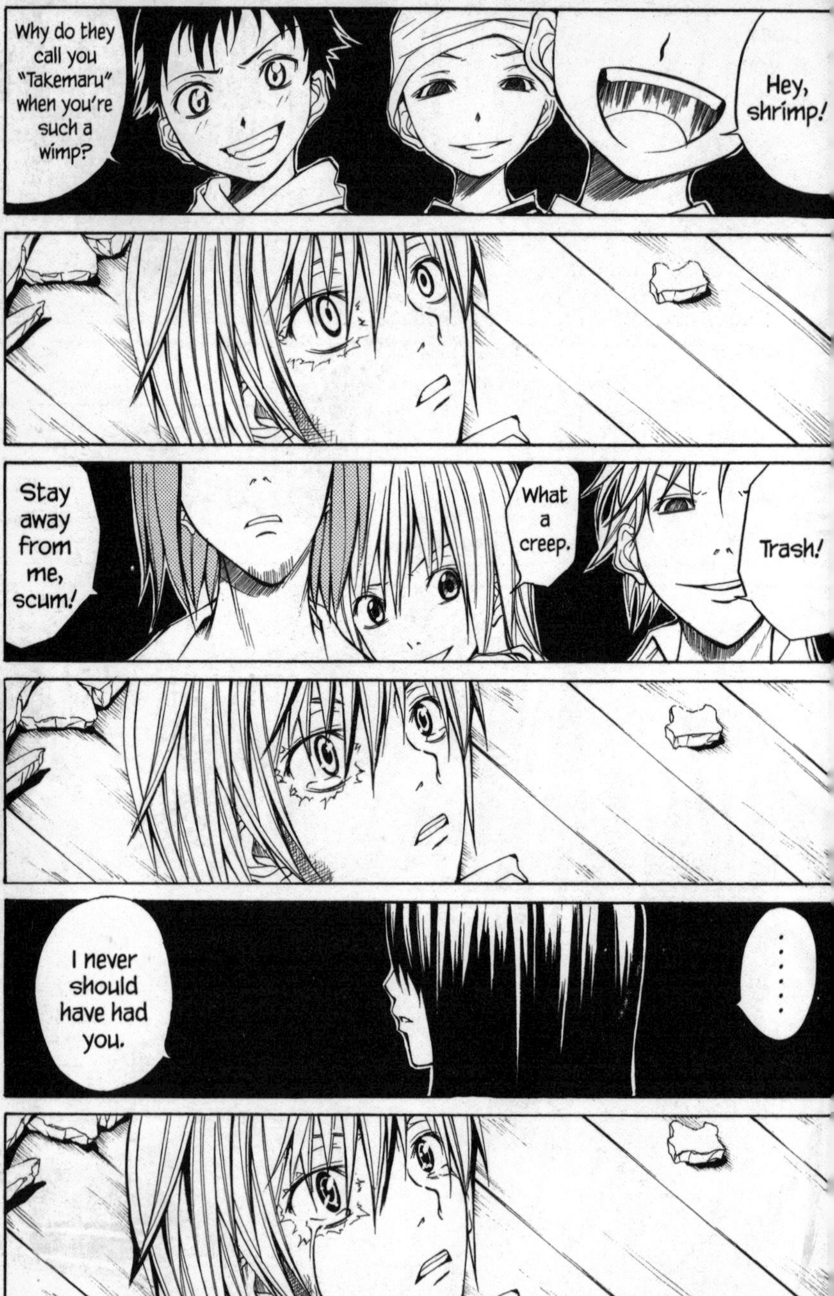
Hey, shrimp!
Why do they call you "Takemaru" when you're such a wimp?
Trash!
What a creep.
Stay away from me, scum!
......
I never should have had you.

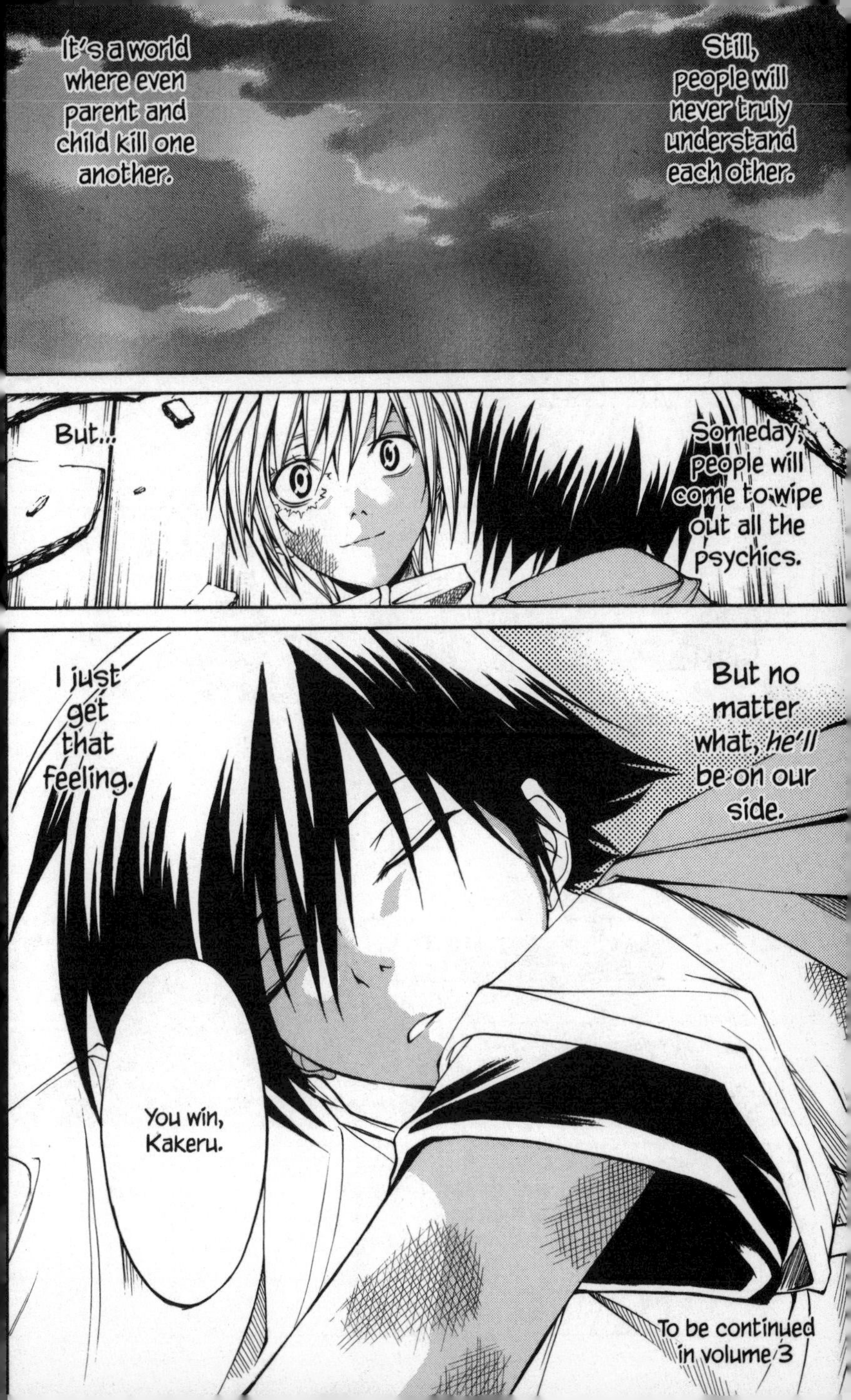
Still, people will never truly understand each other.
It's a world where even parent and child kill one another.
Someday, people will come to wipe out all the psychics.
But...
But no matter what, *he'll* be on our side.
I just get that feeling.
You win, Kakeru.
To be continued in volume 3

Omake 4-Panel Manga

Psycho Busters

Daily

Hobbies

Hobby: Computer
カタ
TAP
TAP
カタ
TAP
Hobby: Cooking
ジャアアア
FRY
Hobby: Shogi
パチッ
SNAP
Hobby?
スヤ
ZZZ
スヤ
ZZZ

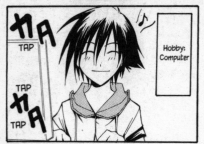

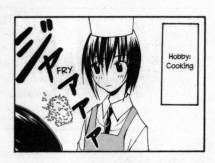

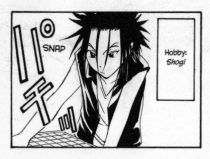

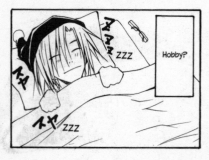

Hand-Me-Down

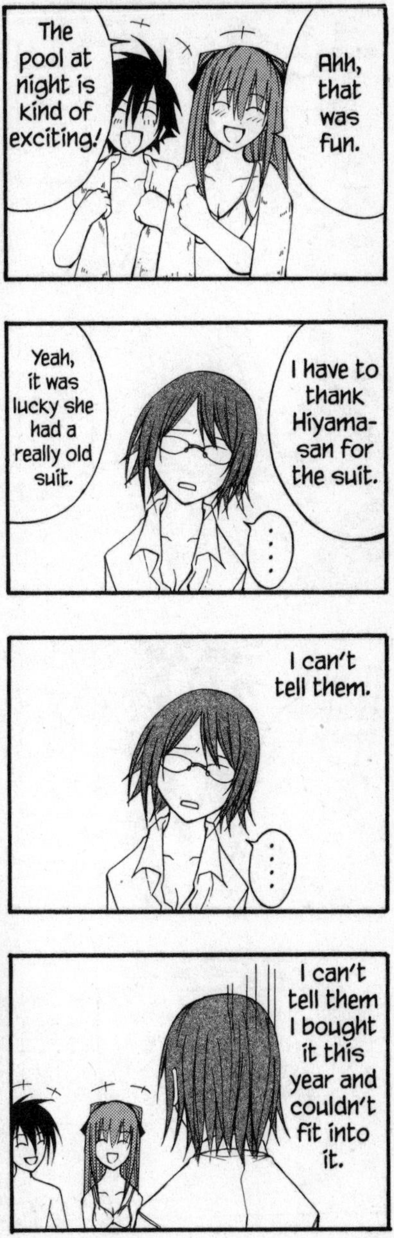
Ahh, that was fun.
The pool at night is kind of exciting!
I have to thank Hiyama-san for the suit.
Yeah, it was lucky she had a really old suit.
....
I can't tell them.
....
I can't tell them I bought it this year and couldn't fit into it.

Jôi's Powers

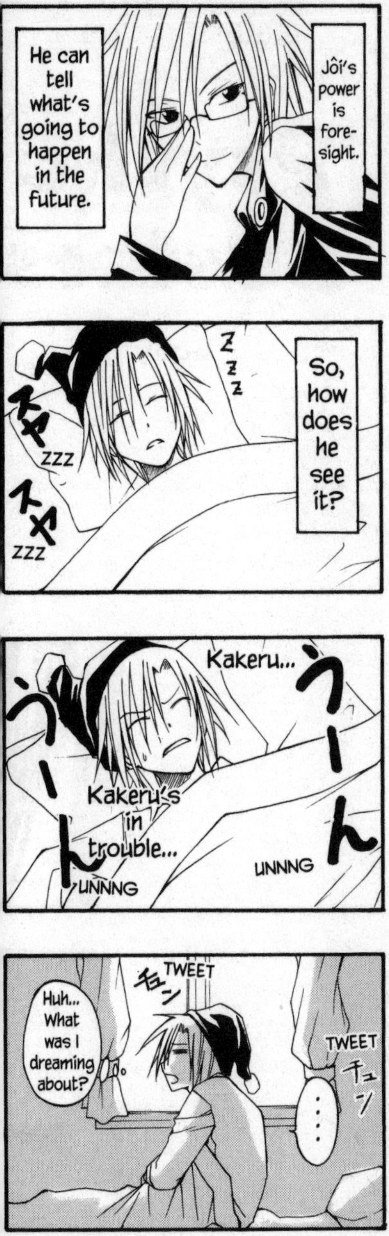
Jôi's power is fore-sight.
He can tell what's going to happen in the future.
So, how does he see it?
Z z z
スヤ zzz
スヤ zzz
うーん UNNNG
Kakeru...
Kakeru's in trouble...
うーん UNNNG
チュン TWEET
....
チュン TWEET
Huh... What was I dreaming about?

Rock Star

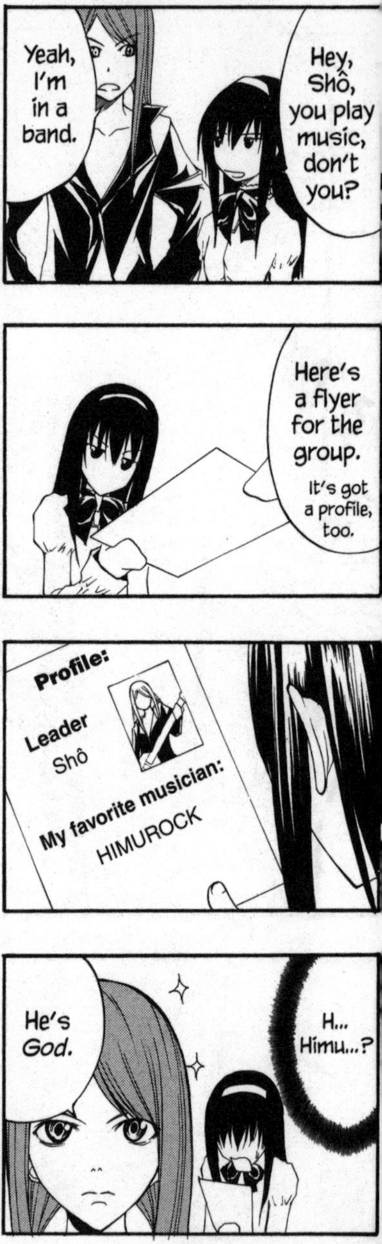
Hey, Shô, you play music, don't you?
Yeah, I'm in a band.
Here's a flyer for the group.
It's got a profile, too.
Profile:
Leader
Shô
My favorite musician:
HIMUROCK
H... Himu...?
He's *God*.

Sweet on the Inside

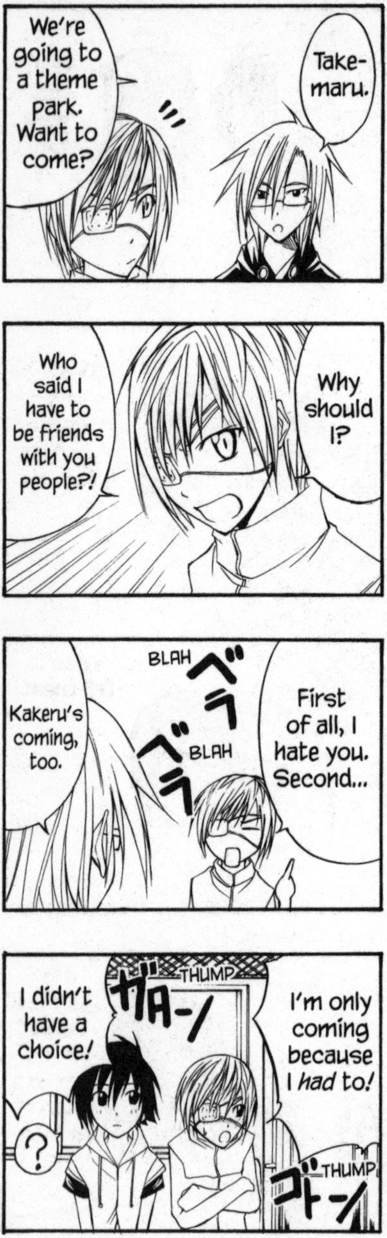
Take-maru.
We're going to a theme park. Want to come?
Why should I?
Who said I have to be friends with you people?!
First of all, I hate you. Second...
BLAH
BLAH
Kakeru's coming, too.
I'm only coming because I *had* to!
THUMP
I didn't have a choice!
THUMP
?

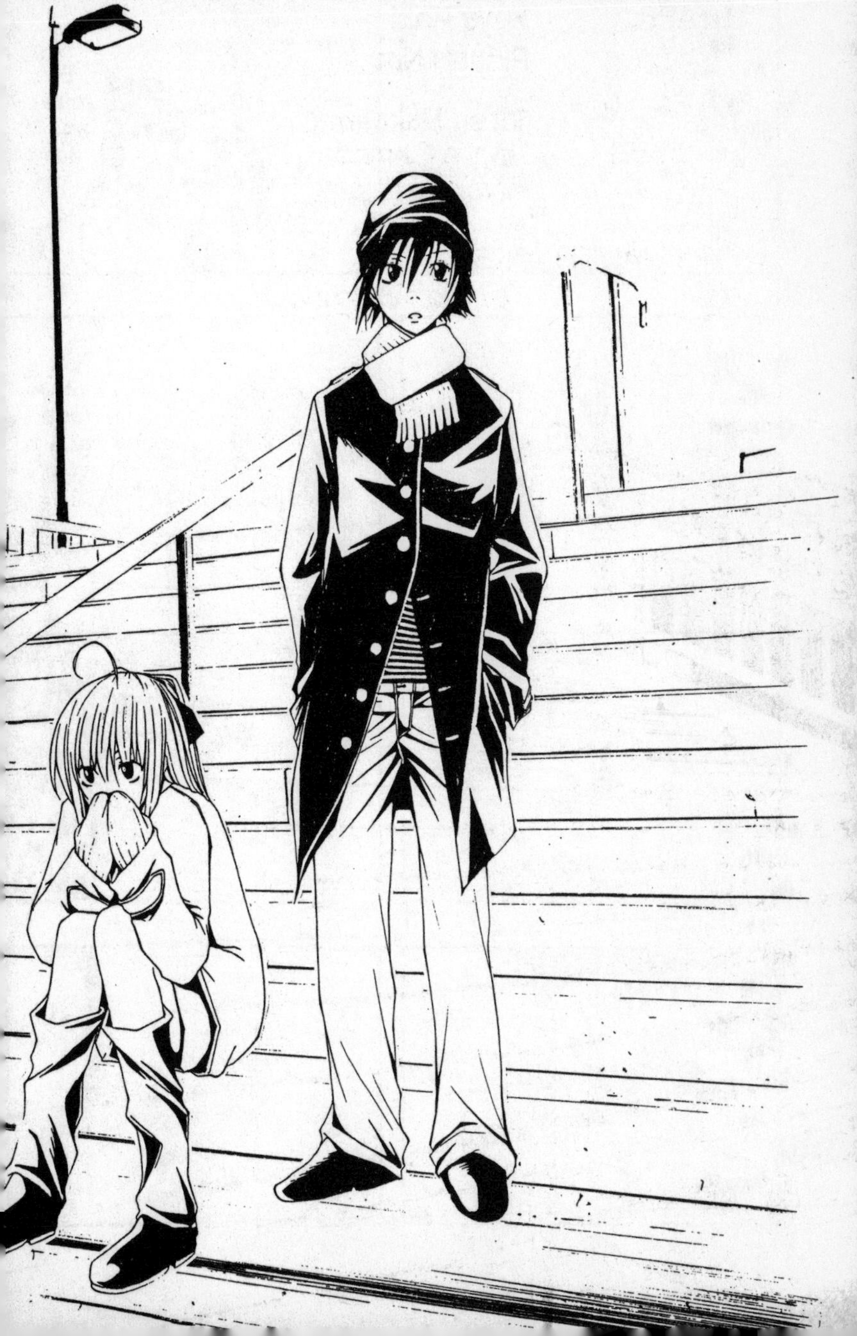

STAFF: Yûya Aoki
Akinari Nao

Tatsu Nakajima
Naoto Shinoda
Kiyomizu

SPECIAL THANKS:
Keitaro Yanagibashi

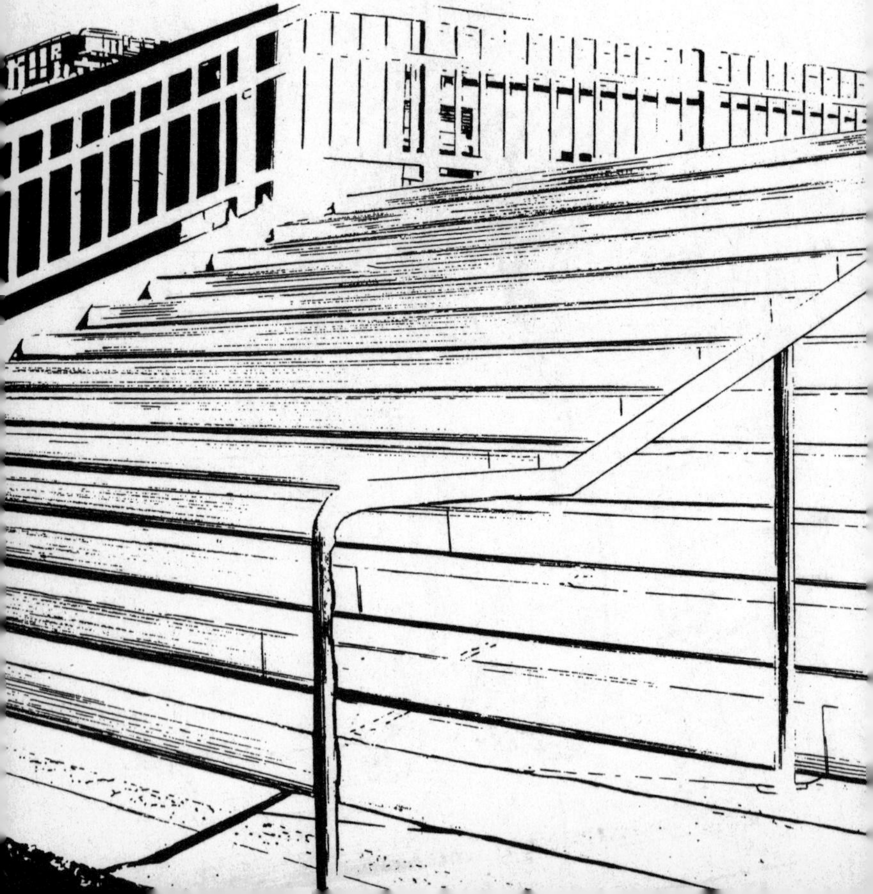

Special Thanks Illustration

Rejected Magazine Special cover sketch

At first it was going to be Kakeru and Ayano, so I tried to come up with something that would suit the magazine and settled on this design, which was rejected. They said they needed something more "battle-like," despite the fact that my editor told me to draw a romantic comedy-style picture...

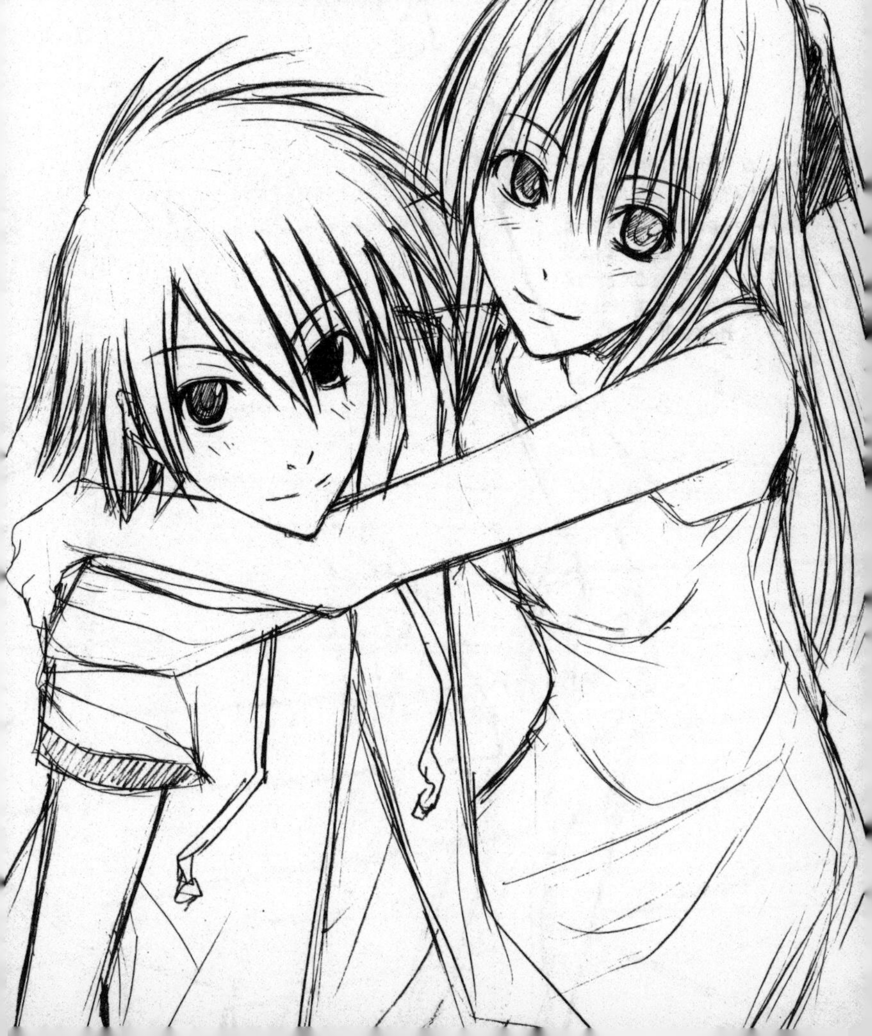

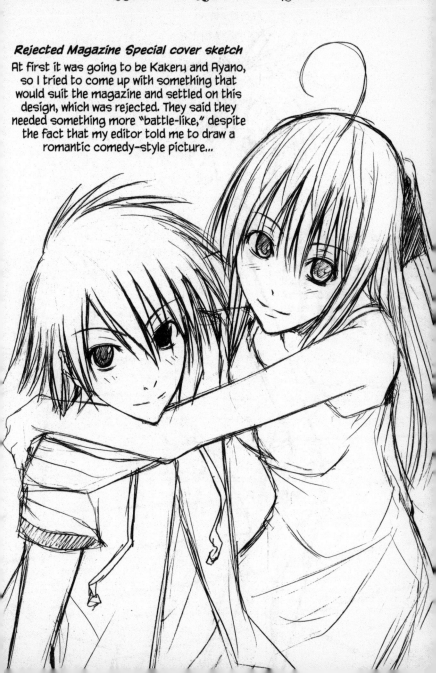

Special Thanks Illustration

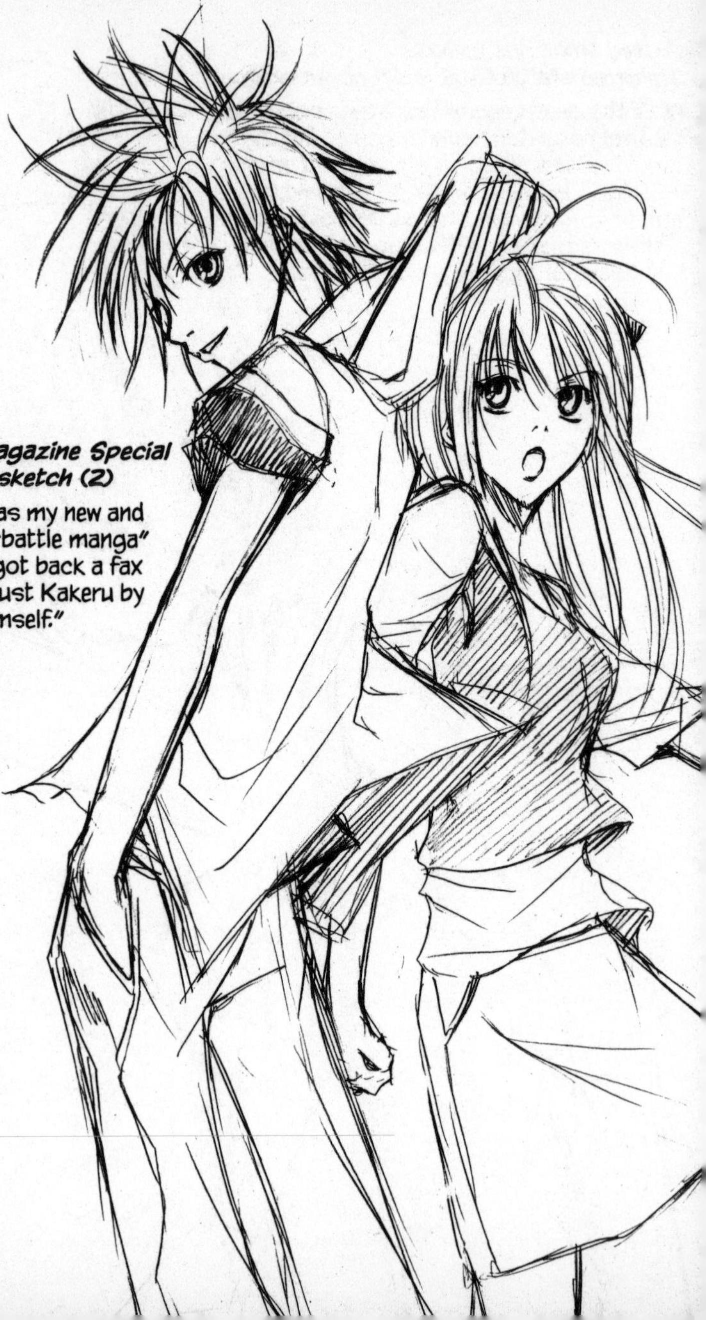

Rejected Magazine Special cover sketch (2)

So here was my new and improved "battle manga" sketch. I got back a fax saying, "Just Kakeru by himself."

Special Thanks Illustration

Rejected Magazine Special cover sketch (3)

One of the ideas I submitted after they requested "Kakeru by himself."

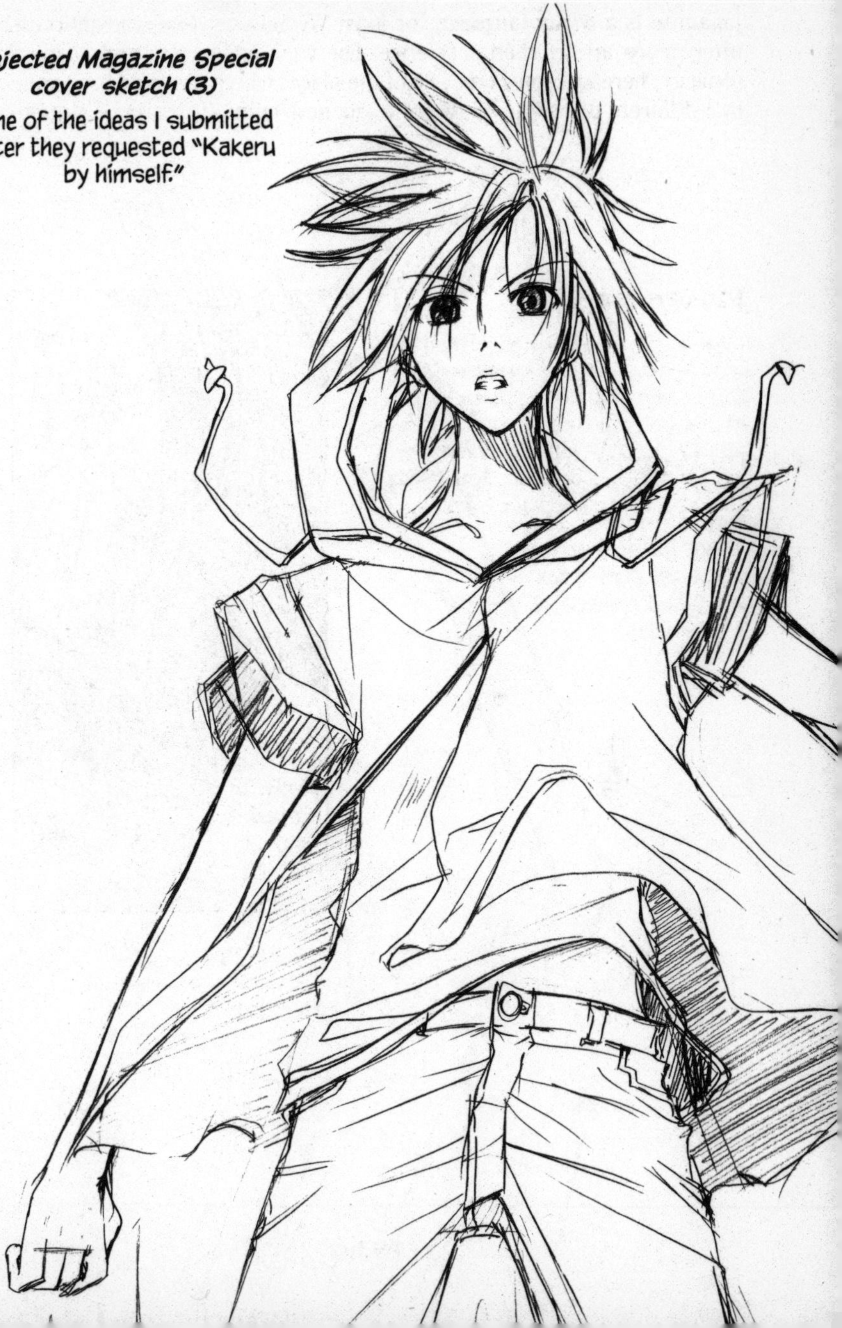

Translation Notes

Japanese is a tricky language for most Westerners, and translation is often more an art than a science. For your edification and reading pleasure, here are notes on some of the places where we could have gone in a different direction, or where a Japanese cultural reference is used.

Janken, page 21

In Japan, the time-honored method of settling minor disputes known as "Rock Paper Scissors" is called *janken*. After counting 1-2-3, before showing your move, you say "*jan-ken-pon!*" The three moves have their own names, too: Rock is *guu*, scissors is *choki*, and paper is *paa*.

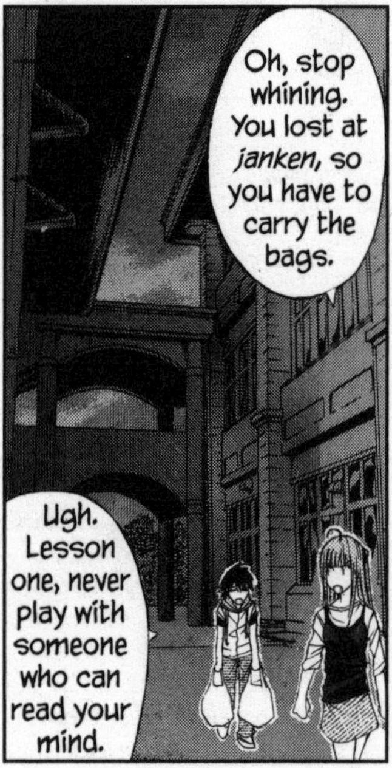
Oh, stop whining. You lost at *janken*, so you have to carry the bags.
Ugh. Lesson one, never play with someone who can read your mind.

Makazine, page 72

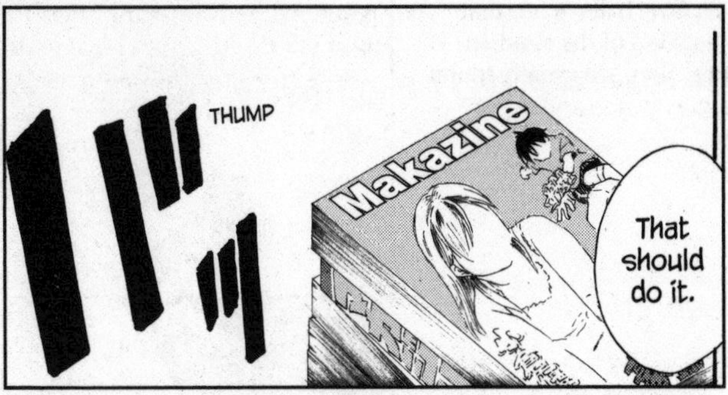
That should do it.
Makazine
THUMP

Many manga set in the present day will often use the introduction of magazines in the story to parody the publication their own work appears in. *Psycho Busters* is published in a special supplement to *Weekly Shonen Magazine* called *Magazine Special*. In this case, the author has given a little cameo to *Magazine* by altering the title just a bit.

Test of courage, page 75

The test of courage, known as *kimodameshi*, is a popular children's group activity in Japan. It carries strong connotations of summertime and often involves searching for "ghosts" in spooky buildings at night. It's a good way for kids to create fun memories, especially during summer vacation, as in this case.

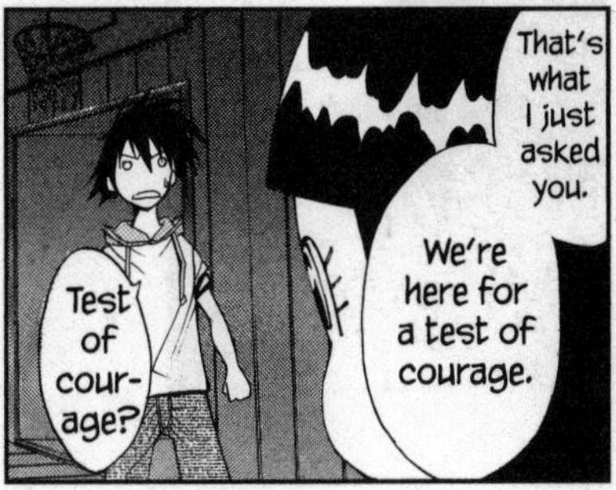
That's what I just asked you.
We're here for a test of courage.
Test of cour-age?

Hitodama, page 76

Hitodama are floating balls of fire that are said to be the souls of the dead, in Japanese folklore. They are usually found floating around graveyards and other haunted places.

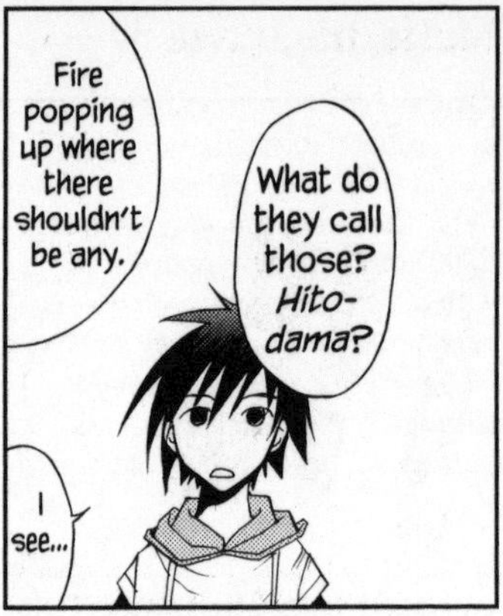

What do they call those? *Hito-dama?*
Fire popping up where there shouldn't be any.
I see...

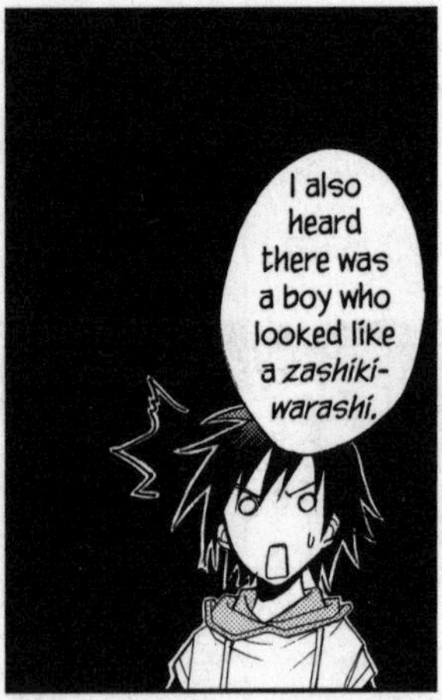

I also heard there was a boy who looked like a *zashiki-warashi.*

Zashiki-warashi, page 76

A *zashiki-warashi* is a kind of *yôkai* (traditional Japanese spirit/creature). They inhabit houses, supposedly bringing great fortune with their presence, but terrible misfortune should they leave. They are said to resemble small children with bobbed hair, so no doubt the girls have confused Xiao Long for one.

Pero, page 91

Pero is the Japanese onomatopoeia for "lick."

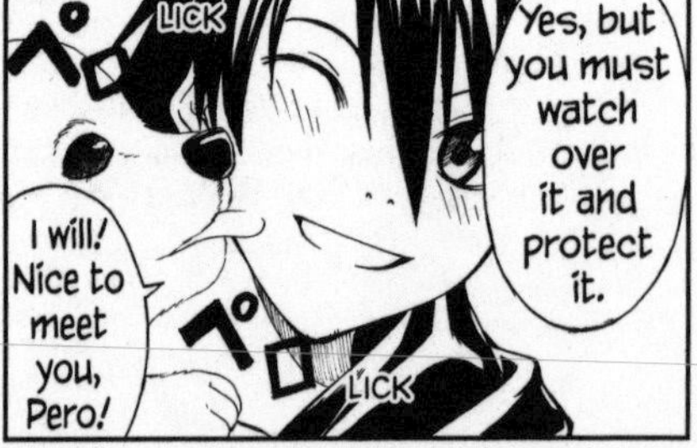

Yes, but you must watch over it and protect it.
LICK
I will! Nice to meet you, Pero!
LICK

Kanji, page 154

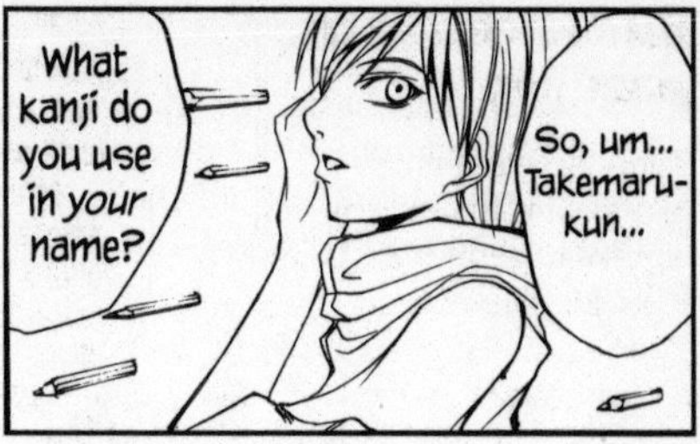
So, um... Takemaru-kun...
What kanji do you use in *your* name?

Kanji are the complex Chinese-derived characters that provide specific meanings to words in Japanese. They are especially useful for differentiating homophones, words with different meanings that are pronounced the same way. Since all Japanese names are spelled with them, it's easiest to identify a person by knowing their kanji.

School shoes, page 156

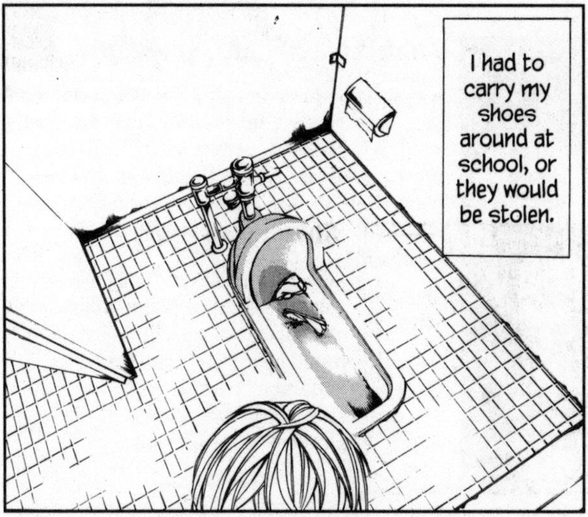
I had to carry my shoes around at school, or they would be stolen.

In addition to all Japanese schools having uniforms, they also all have school shoes. In the morning, students must remove their personal shoes, put them in their shoe locker at the front of the school, and wear their school shoes. At the end of the day, they change back into their personal shoes.

Entrance exams, page 175

There are very important exams that must be passed to get into any school in Japan, from grade school all the way to college. Because you must pass them to get into your school of choice, considerable time is spent in the final year of schooling to prepare for them.

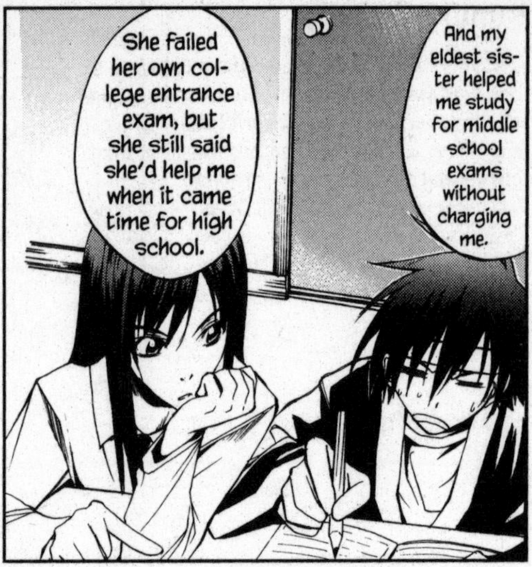
And my eldest sister helped me study for middle school exams without charging me.
She failed her own college entrance exam, but she still said she'd help me when it came time for high school.

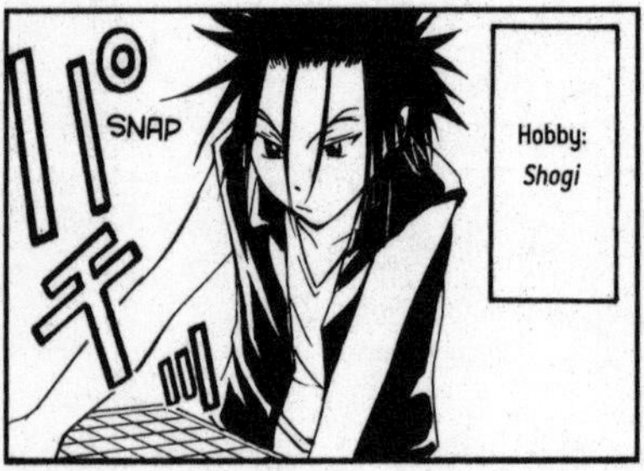
Hobby: Shogi
パチッ
SNAP

Shogi, page 183

Shogi is a traditional Japanese board game that bears a strong similarity to chess. Like *go*, it is played on a large, raised board that is hollowed out underneath so that the pieces produce a particular clicking noise when placed or moved on the board.

Himurock, page 185

Himurock is the nickname of Japanese rock star Kyosuke Himuro. Himuro is famous for being the singer of the legendary '80s J-rock band Boøwy (pronounced "Boy"). He's a little bit like the Japanese equivalent of Axl Rose.

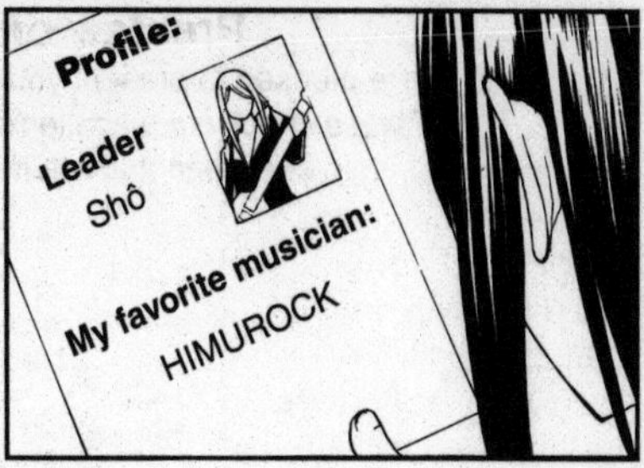
Profile:
Leader
Shô
My favorite musician:
HIMUROCK

Preview of Volume 3

We're pleased to present you with a preview of volume 3. Please check our website (www.delreymanga.com) to see when this volume will be available.

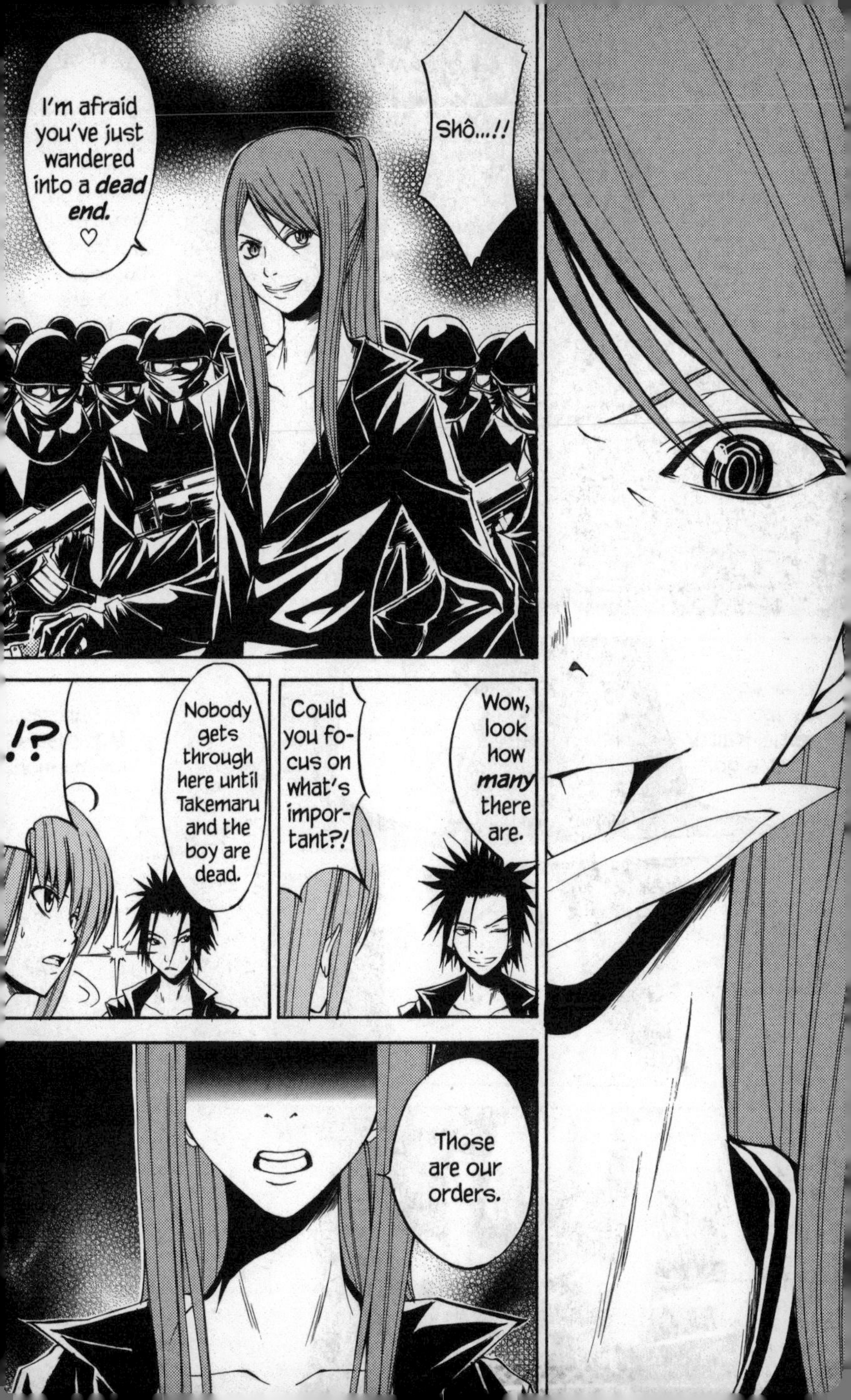
Shô...!!
I'm afraid you've just wandered into a *dead end.* ♡
Wow, look how *many* there are.
Could you fo-cus on what's impor-tant?!
Nobody gets through here until Takemaru and the boy are dead.
!?
Those are our orders.

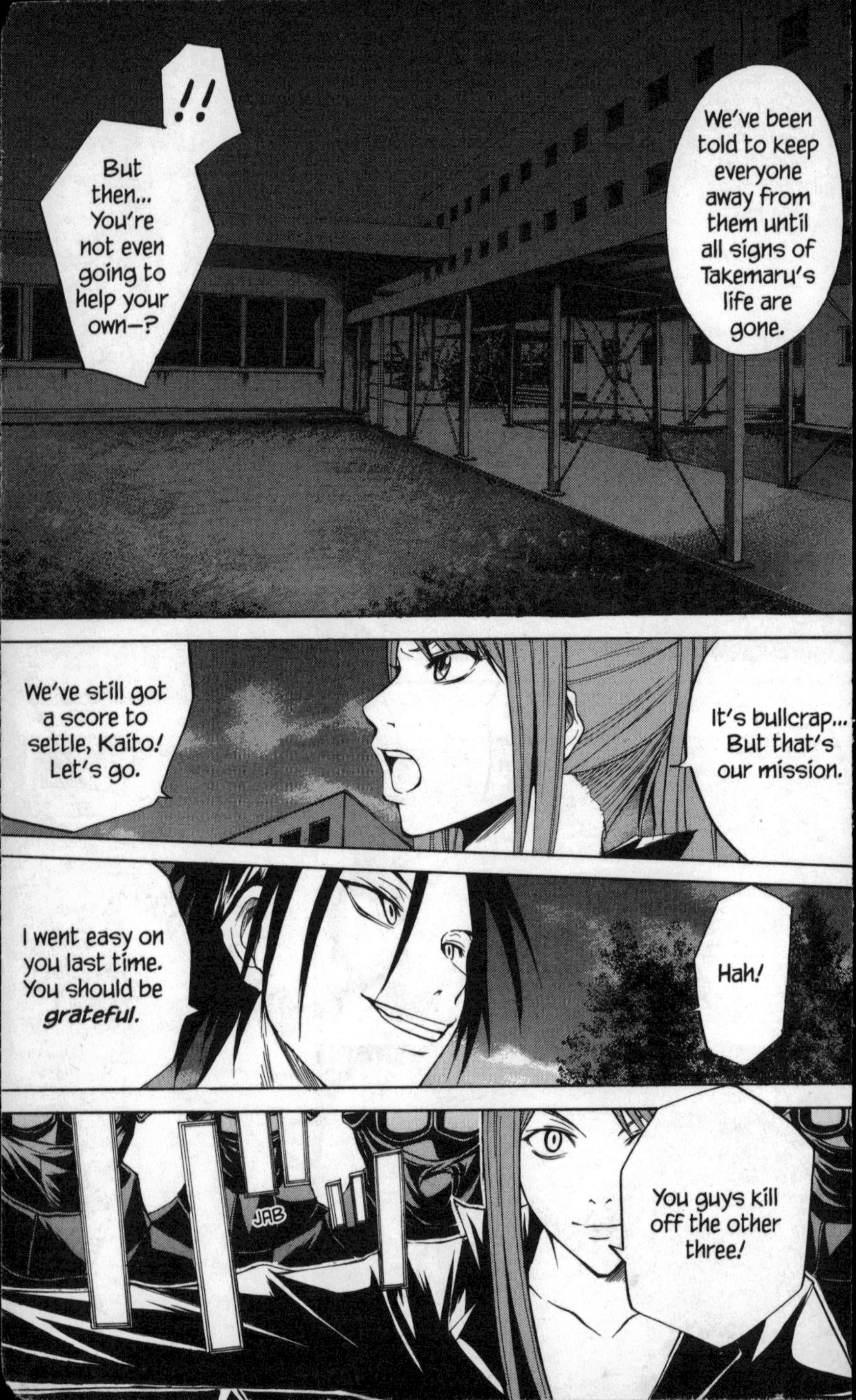
We've been told to keep everyone away from them until all signs of Takemaru's life are gone.
!!
But then... You're not even going to help your own—?
It's bullcrap... But that's our mission.
We've still got a score to settle, Kaito! Let's go.
Hah!
I went easy on you last time. You should be *grateful*.
You guys kill off the other three!
JAB

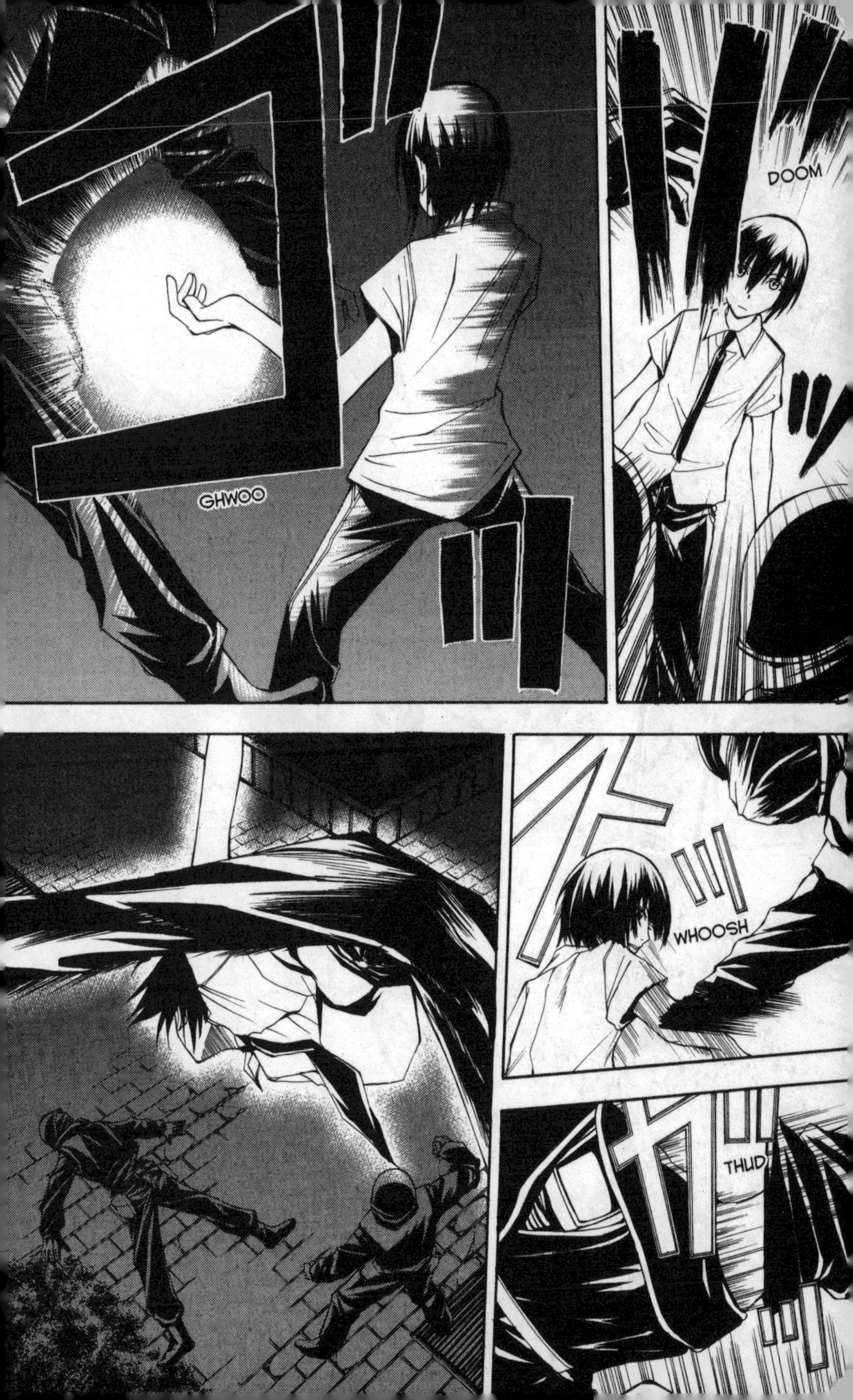
DOOM
GHWOO
WHOOSH
THUD

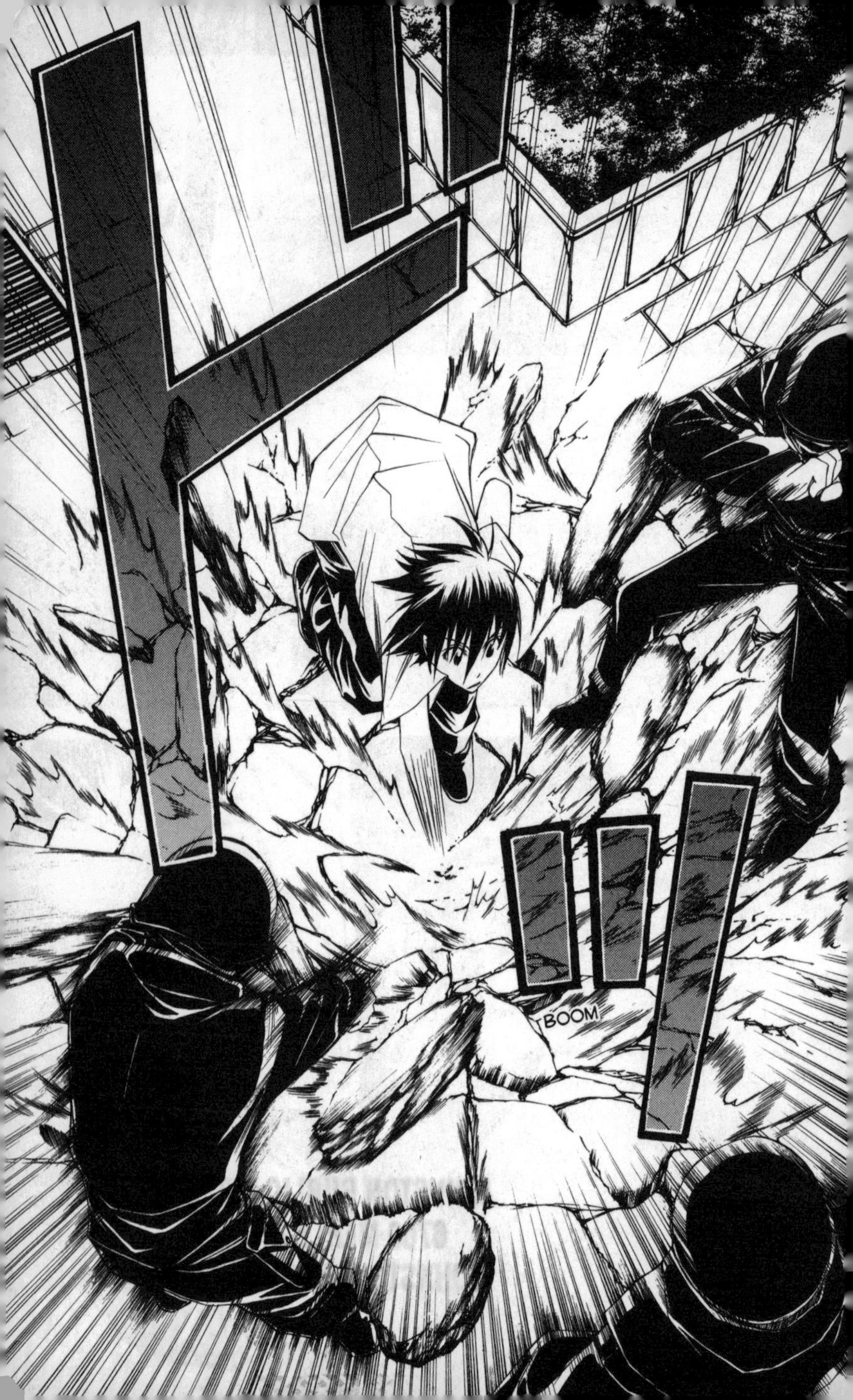
BOOM

TOMARE!

[STOP!]

You're going the wrong way!

Manga is a completely
different type of reading
experience.

To start at the *beginning,*
go to the *end!* WITHDRAWN

That's right! Authentic manga is read the traditional Japanese way—
from right to left. Exactly the opposite of how American books are read.
It's easy to follow: Just go to the other end of the book, and read each
page—and each panel—from right side to left side, starting at the top
right. Now you're experiencing manga as it was meant to be!